CW00924976

The Rise of the Trans-Atlantic Slave Trade in Western Africa, 1300–1589

The region between the Senegal River and Sierra Leone saw the onset of the first trans-Atlantic slave trade in the sixteenth century. Drawing on many new sources, Toby Green challenges current quantitative approaches to the history of the slave trade. New data on slave origins can show how and why Western African societies responded to Atlantic pressures. Green argues that answering these questions requires a cultural framework and uses the idea of creolisation – the formation of mixed cultural communities in the era of plantation societies – to argue that preceding social patterns in both Africa and Europe were crucial. Major impacts of the sixteenth-century slave trade included political fragmentation, changes in identity, and the reorganisation of ritual and social patterns. The book shows which peoples were enslaved, why they were vulnerable and the consequences in Africa and beyond.

Toby Green is currently a Leverhulme Early Career Fellow at King's College London. He has published several books, the most recent of which is *Inquisition: The Reign of Fear* (2007). His books have been translated into ten languages. He is a director of the Amilcar Cabral Institute for Economic and Political Research. His articles have appeared in *History in Africa*, the *Journal of Atlantic Studies, Journal of Mande Studies*, and *Slavery and Abolition*. Green has also written widely for the British press, including book reviews for the *Independent* and features for *Financial Times*, the *Observer*, and the *Times*. He has given lectures at various institutes, including the Universities of Cambridge, Lisbon, Oxford, and Paris-Sorbonne as well as Duke University and the School of Oriental and African Studies in London.

African Studies

The *African Studies Series*, founded in 1968, is a prestigious series of monographs, general surveys, and textbooks on Africa covering history, political science, anthropology, economics, and ecological and environmental issues. The series seeks to publish work by senior scholars as well as the best new research.

A list of books in this series will be found at the end of this volume.

The Rise of the Trans-Atlantic Slave Trade in Western Africa, 1300–1589

TOBY GREEN

King's College London

CAMBRIDGE UNIVERSITY PRESS
Cambridge, New York, Melbourne, Madrid, Cape Town,
Singapore, São Paulo, Delhi, Tokyo, Mexico City

Cambridge University Press
32 Avenue of the Americas, New York, NY 10013-2473, USA

www.cambridge.org
Information on this title: www.cambridge.org/9781107014367

First published 2012

Printed in the United States of America

A catalog record for this publication is available from the British Library.

Library of Congress Cataloging in Publication data
Green, Toby, 1974–
The rise of the trans-Atlantic slave trade in western
Africa, 1300–1589 / Toby Green.
p. cm.
Includes bibliographical references and index.
ISBN 978-1-107-01436-7
1. Slave trade – Africa, West – History. 2. Slave trade – America – History.
3. Creoles – Africa, West – History. I. Title.
HT1331.G74 2012
306.3′620966–dc22   2011015312

ISBN 978-1-107-01436-7 Hardback

For Emily, Flora and Lily, whose love and support made this book possible, and for Paulo, without whose generosity of spirit it would not exist.

In memory of those whose suffering is the subject of this book

Since God created this world,
wherever prosperity is found,
people will follow it,
and in turn they will have relations.

Sayo Mane[1]

[1] NCAC/OHAD, Cassette 550A: an elder from Kolda, Casamance; interview and translation by Bakary Sidibe.

Contents

Maps

Acknowledgements

This book would not have been possible without the consistent support of many institutions and people. Over the years I have been overwhelmed by the generosity of intellect and belief, which so many friends have shown in this work as it has evolved. It is my hope simply that I may in the future be able to respond in kind.

I would never have written this book if I had not first researched and written a travel book called *Meeting the Invisible Man*, which was published in 2001. My thanks to Ion Trewin for commissioning that book and giving me the chance to think properly for the first time about West African peoples and histories; to Ian Rakoff, who helped me greatly on that book, and whose own decades-long engagement and work on precolonial Africa certainly influenced me; and, as always, to my friend in Guinea-Bissau, El Hadji Mamadou Kabir Ndiaye.

Many years later, initial drafts of this book were diligently read in their entirety by Paulo Farias and Walter Hawthorne; Bruce Hall, José Nafafé and Konstantin Richter also read substantial sections, and the advice of all of them has been extremely valuable in helping to shape the final version. To all of them, my utmost thanks. Eric Crahan has been a wonderfully supportive and insightful editor at Cambridge University Press, and this book has benefited immeasurably from his shrewd guidance; it has been a great experience to work together with him, Abigail Zorbaugh and the team at Newgen Publishing and Data Services to see this book through to publication.

I was also extremely fortunate to be able to receive important feedback at seminars given at the African Studies Association Conference in San Francisco of November 2010, at Duke University, at the German

Historical Institute in London, at King's College London, at the School of Oriental and African Studies, and at the Centre des Études des Mondes Africaines at Paris-Sorbonne Panthéon. To Walter Hawthorne – whose support throughout this project has been immense – David Wheat, Bruce Hall, Silke Strickrodt, Catherine Boyle, Rhiannon Stephens, and Hervé Pennec and Thomas Vernet, who arranged these events, I owe a great debt of thanks. The three anonymous readers of this book for Cambridge University Press and the series editor, Richard Roberts, all gave me extremely valuable reports which have immeasurably improved the final text. All in all, the process of finishing this book has reminded me of what a collaborative enterprise the production of academic scholarship is and how lucky I am to work in such an environment; at a time when everyone is supposed to look out for themselves, these collaborations are reminders of how much we always owe to others.

My research first took shape during my PhD at the Centre of West African Studies (CWAS), University of Birmingham. It would never have begun had it not been for my doctoral supervisor, Paulo Farias. I well remember our first meeting, one autumn's afternoon in 2001, in Birmingham; we spoke for over two hours, and it was I who had to leave in order to catch my train. This was just a foretaste of the immense generosity of spirit and intellect which it has been my lasting privilege to receive from Paulo. Subsequently, it was Paulo who also provided the key recommendation that I focus this manuscript on the formative sixteenth century and leave the seventeenth for a subsequent work. In every way, this book could not and would not now exist without his input: I can only hope that it in some way measures up to the extraordinary confidence and belief which he has always shown in me.

The Centre of West African Studies at Birmingham University was a wonderful place in which to base myself for eight years. The sense of interdisciplinary comradeship there helped to mould an exciting sense of the possibilities of research. I thank Shola Adenekan, Noel and Ayaanakai Amherd, Karin Barber, Sue Bowen, Stewart Brown, Lynne Brydon, Christian Campbell, Reg Cline-Cole, Maggie Egginton, Conrad James, Webster Kameme, Dave Kerr, Juliana Mafwil, Tom McCaskie, Insa Nolte, Tolu Ogunlesi, Katrien Pype, Farouk Seesay, Keith Shear, Ange Slater, and Kate Skinner for helping to build this remarkable and unique atmosphere. Also at Birmingham, I was very lucky to have the comradeship, camaraderie and intellectual support offered by José Lingna Nafafé. Specialists in pre-colonial Upper Guinea are very few in the world, let alone the UK, and to be with such a wonderful specialist at such close quarters has indeed been a privilege and has helped me greatly in formulating the ideas presented here.

The bulk of the research and writing for this book took place while I was at Birmingham, but in the final stage I was welcomed by the Departments of History and of Spanish, Portuguese and Latin American Studies at King's College London. I am very grateful to Marie Berry, Federico Bonaddio, Frank Bongiorno, Catherine Boyle, Amber Burrow-Goldhahn, Patrick Chabal, Richard Drayton, Anne Goldgar, Ludmilla Jordanova, Rachel Lawlor, Chris Machut, Linda Newson, Adrian Pearce, Paul Readman, Alice Rio, David Rojinsky, Sarah Stockwell, Adam Sutcliffe, David Todd and AbdoolKarim Vakil for helping me to feel at home so swiftly. In particular, I owe a great debt to Francisco Bethencourt, who has supported me in all manner of ways for many years, and from whose boundless intellectual curiosity and breadth I have learned enormously.

In terms of actually conducting the research, this would have been utterly impossible without the financial support of the now-defunct Historical School at Birmingham University, the Arts and Humanities' Research Board, and the British Academy and the Leverhulme Trust, who have all supported me most generously with grants and fellowships over the years. Friends and colleagues in countries all around the world have been immensely generous with their time and help. I would like to make a special mention of Antonio de Almeida Mendes, Konstantin Richter, Filipa Ribeiro da Silva and Maria Manuel Ferraz Torrão: all four demonstrated the sort of generosity which should be the foundation of all academic research, sharing with me their path-finding unpublished work on closely related fields and thereby helping me to track down crucial sources. I would also particularly like to thank the following, for replying to my inquiries, supporting me with my work and putting me onto all sorts of exciting pieces of material: Ralph Austen, Jean Boulègue, George Brooks, Vince Brown, René Millar Carvacho, Carol Castiel, David Cohen, Wayne Dooling, Alma Gottlieb, Nick Griffiths, José da Silva Horta, Bart Jacobs, Yosef Kaplan, Moshé Liba, Richard Lobban, Anthony Macfarlane, Peter Karibe Mendy, Malyn Newitt, Linda Newson, Hilary Pomeroy, Jonathan Schorsch, Armin Schwegler, Ibrahima Seck, Maria João Soares, Silke Strickrodt, Ruth Watson, and David Wheat.

In Lisbon, I owe great debts to several colleagues. In 2008 José da Silva Horta generously chaired a seminar for me at the Instituto de Investigação Científica Tropical, and has subsequently become a dear friend: over the subsequent years, José, his colleague Peter Mark and myself have had good-natured and supportive exchanges of ideas and information which have been of great intellectual and personal benefit to me. Gerhard Seibert arranged that seminar, and has over the years been a great friend in many ways; this project has undoubtedly benefited much from his knowledge and generosity. I was also very fortunate to meet Philip Havik at an early stage in this project; he has always shown great enthusiasm for my research, and his peerless knowledge of the period and region and hospitality in Lisbon have been very supportive. I was most fortunate to spend several delightful periods in Cabo Verde. Here I would like to thank the staff of the Arquivo Historico Nacional de Cabo Verde and of the Biblioteca Nacional. I must also thank Anildo Cruz for putting me into contact with the journalist and writer José Vicente Lopes. Vicente and his wife Marilene were immensely welcoming and helpful on several occasions in Praia, as were Antonio Correia e Silva and Zelinda Cohen. All of them made my visits to Cabo Verde so rewarding, and helped me to learn a lot. In Praia, I would also like to thank Januário Nascimento, president of the Cabo Verde Israel friendship society, for showing me some of the Hebrew tombstones in Praia's cemetery. On Fogo, Monique Widmer was most helpful and willingly shared local knowledge, and E. Akintola Hubbard put me onto many interesting factors.

As this is a book which draws heavily upon archival material, one of the greatest debts which I have incurred has been to archivists. In Colombia, Doris Donado and her daughter Manuela offered me wonderful and undeserved hospitality and help in many ways, and Tim Dowling, many insights. Mauricio Tovar and all the staff of the Archivo General de la Nación in Bogotá were most helpful and provided the necessary documents with extreme speed and professionalism. Additionally, I would like to thank all the staff at the following institutions: in Portugal, the Instituto dos Arquivos Nacionais da Torre do Tombo, the Arquivo Historico Ultramarino, the Biblioteca da Ajuda, the Sociedade de Geografia; in Spain, the Archivo General de las Indias; in the Vatican State, the staff at the Archivio Secreto Vaticano. I have also been helped greatly by the professionalism and assistance of staff at the British Library, Cambridge University Library, and the Main Library at the University of Birmingham. The job of being an archivist and librarian is a painstaking and an exacting one; I was always impressed by the vast erudition and care which these remarkable people brought to the priceless collections and documents in their care.

Shortly before this book went to press, I was fortunate enough to be able to make a last-minute research visit to Gambia, Casamance and

Guinea-Bissau, where in addition to the pleasure of reacquainting myself with many old friends, I came upon new sources which have been vital in piecing together the final draft of this book. This visit would never have been as successful as it was without the prompting of Walter Hawthorne. Bala Saho, Director of the National Centre for Arts and Culture in Banjul, Gambia, was extremely helpful in offering hospitality, making connections and putting me in touch with his brother, Buba, who was a priceless help. Assan Sarr of the College of Charleston, South Carolina, also gave me much useful advice prior to my journey to Gambia. Once there, Baba Ceesay, Director of Cultural Heritage, put himself out greatly on my arrival, as did the historian Hassoum Ceesay, and my research at the Oral History Archive in Fajara would have been thankless without the sustained input and support of Bakary Sanyang and his staff. Here indeed I must also acknowledge the extraordinary work carried out by Bakary Sidibe, whose innumerable recordings of interviews conducted in the 1960s, 1970s and 1980s, now stored at the Oral History Archive, are a priceless asset for researchers. In Casamance and Guinea-Bissau, El Hadji Mamadou Kabir Ndiaye and his brother El Hadji Omar Ndiaye were wonderful hosts and guides, arranging countless interviews which materially improved the evidence I am able to offer here. Ibrahima Mansaly, Headteacher of Goudomp-3 Primary School in Goudomp, Senegal, encouraged me to photocopy a special issue of the journal *Éthiopiques* on Kaabu which for years I had been trying to track down without success. This research visit was also greatly assisted by Seydhou Fall, Ami Jatta and her daughters, Mamadu Jao, director of the Instituto Nacional de Estudos e Pesquisa in Bissau, Ismaili Lam, Ansumane Manga, Antonio da Silva Mango, Carmen Neto, Célia Neto, Peter Thompson and João Vieira. To them all, my deepest thanks for their conviviality, generosity, and humanity.

My most enduring debt is to my family. My parents, Charlotte and Chris, educated me in the value of humanistic knowledge – to them, a million thanks. My sister, Abigail, has offered me much support over the years, as I embarked on this project and as it evolved. My wife Emily's parents, Robert Fowke and Caroline Glanville, have also encouraged me often and offered great help to our family during my research absences. And none of this work would have been possible to the slightest degree without the love and joy of Emily, Lily and Flora. They have always been there for me, and I hope this project has not been too burdensome for them. Their support has indeed lightened my own burden of researching a saddening process in the history of the world. They have always reminded me of the essential humanity which I try to bring to my work, and which I hope manages to emerge along with the many emotions which surround, and have surrounded, the subject of this book.

Cambridge, May 2011

Abbreviations

AG	As Gavetas da Torre do Tombo (1960–1975)
AGI	Archivo General de las Indias
AGN	Archivo General de la Nación, Bogotá
AHNCV	Arquivo Histórico Nacional de Cabo Verde
AHP	Arquivo Histórico Portuguez (Freire, Anselmo Braancamp et al. (eds.))
AHU	Arquivo Histórico Ultramarino
ANS/NP	Archivo Notarial de Santander, Notaria Primera de Pamplona (documentary resource in the AGN)
ASV	Archivio Segretto Vaticano
BA	Biblioteca da Ajuda
CEA	*Corpus of Early Arabic Sources for West African History* (Hopkins/Levtzion eds.)
CGSO	Conselho Geral do Santo Oficio (documentary resource in IAN/TT)
CN	*Colecção de Noticias para a Historia e Geografia das Nações Ultramarinas, que Vivem nos Dominios Portuguezes, ou lhes são Visinhas.*
CRP	*Crónicas de Rui de Pina* (Almeida ed.)
HGCV: CD	História Geral de Cabo Verde: Corpo Documental
IAN/TT	Instituto dos Arquivos Nacionais da Torre do Tombo
MMAI	*Monumenta Misonária Africana: Primeira Série.* (Brásio, António ed.)
MMAII	*Monumenta Misonária Africana: Segunda Série.* (Brásio, António ed.)

NCAC/OHAD	National Council for Arts and Culture, Oral History and Antiquities Division, Banjul
NE	Negros y Esclavos (documentary resource in the AGN)
NGC	*A New General Collection of Voyages and Travels: Consisting of The Most Esteemed Relations, Which Have Hitherto Been Published in any Language: Comprehending Every Thing Remarkable in its Kind, in Europe, Asia, Africa, and America.*
NPB	Notaría Primera de Bogotá (documentary resource in the AGN)
NT	Archivo Histórico de Boyacá, Notaría Primera de Tunja (documentary resource in the AGN)
PV	*Primeira Visitação do Santo Officio Ás Partes do Brasil: Denunciações da Bahia, 1591–1593.*
RD	*Raccolta di Documenti e Studi Publiccati Dalla R. Commissione Colombiana del Quarto Centenario della Scoperta dell'America*
SG	Sociedade da Geografía

(Note: AHU documents are usually without folio numbers, so it is only possible to refer to the document in the reference).

Glossary

Alcalde	Mayor (in Portuguese: *alcaide*).
Alforria	Act by which masters freed slaves in their wills.
Almadía	Word of Arabic origin used by Portuguese to refer to canoes in West Africa in the fifteenth century and by Columbus when he first reached the New World.
Almoravids	North African warriors, many of them Berbers, who swept into Spain in the late eleventh century and took over control of the affairs of the land, which had formerly been controlled by the Caliphate of Córdoba.
Almoxarifado	The institution handling state finances in a particular locale (in Spanish: *Almojarifado*).
Almoxarife	Administrator of royal domains.
Arrobas	Measure of weight equivalent to approximately fifteen kilogrammes.
Asiento/Asentistas	Contract/Holders of the contract (in this book, related to the slave trade).
Auto da Fe	Inquisitorial procession culminating in the reading of sentences and the punishment of the condemned.
Barafula	Measure of cloth made in Cabo Verde used as a measure of exchange in Guiné and known as far away as Cartagena.
Buur	Jolof kings.

Câmara	Council, Assembly
Capitanias	Captaincies; used to refer to administrative units of the *Ultramar* apportioned to the supervision of a captain.
Carrerra de Índias	Spanish system developed in the 1560s of exporting looted goods back from the New World to Europe in convoys of ships rendezvousing in key ports in America and the Caribbean.
Cimarrones	Escaped slaves in the New World.
Consejo	Council (of state).
Conselho Ultramarino	Arm of Portuguese government charged with supervising affairs in Portuguese overseas possessions in this period.
Contratadores	Holders of the contract to ship slaves to Spanish America.
Conversos	Converted Jews; the term is associated with Spanish converts to Christianity, especially in the fifteenth century.
Convivencia	The period of life in the Iberian peninsula when the faiths of Christianity, Islam and Judaism co-existed; the phrase is generally taken to refer to those territories under Christian control.
Corregedor	Local governor.
Creole	Language of mixed African and European roots developing as a vernacular in Western Africa during the sixteenth century.
Creolisation	The cultural and linguistic processes through which Creole developed.
Cristãos Novos	The Portuguese term for Jews who had converted to Christianity (in Spanish: *cristianos nuevos*).
Cristãos Velhos	The Portuguese term for Christians who had no Jewish or Moorish ancestry (in Spanish: *cristianos viejos*).
Cruzados	Portuguese currency: a gold coin.
Crypto-Jew	Someone who keeps secretly to the Jewish faith while professing to be a Christian.

Diaspora	A group of people forming a community in spite of extensive geographical dispersion.
Dyula	Diaspora of Mandinka traders in West Africa.
Encomienda	Parcel of land given to colonists in the New World under Spanish administration.
Escrivão	Scribe or registrar.
Escrivão do Almoxarifado	Registrar of the royal exchequer.
Escrivão da Correição	Registrar of the local governor.
Ethnonym	Literally, "ethnic name": ethnic designation used for a group in Upper Guinea.
Feitor	Factor.
Feitoria	Depot for the organising of exports (principally slaves) from the African coast.
Fidalgos	Nobles, often minor and in straitened circumstances; also used by Caboverdean authors to describe lineage heads in Upper Guinea.
Fueros	Local charters of rights in towns in Aragón and Castilla.
Griot	Praisesinger in Senegambian and Upper Guinean communities. Thought by some to derive from *criado*, Portuguese for "retainer".
Grumetes	Term for servants/shipmates commonly used by Caboverdeans and *lançados* of African retainers/servants in Upper Guinea.
Ingenio	Sugarcane plantation (Portuguese: *Engenho*).
Judiaria	Jewry.
Juiz dos Orfãos	Judge responsible for assigning homes to orphans.
Kriolu	Creole language of Cabo Verde and Upper Guinea.

Ladino	Non-Iberians (e.g. Jews, slaves) who speak Spanish.
Lançados	People of Portuguese origin living in Guiné in the sixteenth and seventeenth centuries. These people were also known as *tangomãos*.
Limpeça de Sangue	Purity of blood, i.e., absence of Jewish or Moorish antecedents (in Spanish: *limpieza de sangre*).
Lusophone	Portuguese-speaking.
Mandinguisation	Process by which decentralised communities on the Upper Guinea coast absorbed elements of Mandinka culture from the thirteenth century onwards.
Manuelline	The adjective referring to King Manoel I of Portugal (1495–1521).
Maravedí	Spanish coin, derived from Arabic; its value declined progressively from the medieval through to the early modern periods.
Matrilinear	Society where inheritance passes through the maternal line, e.g., societies from Upper Guinea, Jewish societies.
Meirinho Mor	Chief bailiff.
Mestiçagem	The process of the mixing of races (in Spanish: *mestizaje*).
Mestiços	People of mixed racial background.
Moradores	Residents; in this period used to signify residents with certain rights.
Ouvidor	Special Magistrate.
Ouvidor Geral	Chief Magistrate.
Panos di Terra	Cloths woven on Cabo Verde and used for exchange in Upper Guinea.
Panyarring	Common phrases used across Guinea Coast for "man-stealing" in the eighteenth century.
Parecer	Opinion, often legal.
Patrilinear	Society where inheritance passes through the paternal line, e.g., Senegambian societies and Iberian societies.
Pidgin	Bartering language, a prototype for Creole, used as a means of trade and communication in early Atlantic Western Africa.

Pieza de Esclavo	Literally, a "piece of slave"; slaves were not accounted as individuals but against the benchmark of the *pieza*, which was equivalent to one able-bodied healthy male slave (in Portuguese: *peça de escravo*).
Procurador	Prosecutor.
Provedor	Supplier, Purveyor.
Provedor da Fazenda	Supplier to crown property.
Real/Reais	Unit of currency in Portugal.
Reconciled	A term for a penitent of the Inquisition who has been punished in a variety of ways but readmitted to the church.
Reconquista	Reconquest of Iberia from Moslem rule.
Relajado	Someone condemned by the Inquisition to be burnt or, if they repented and died as a Christian, garrotted by the secular authorities (in Portuguese: *relaxado*).
Rendeiros	Tax collectors.
Resgate	Originally meaning "ransom", comes to refer to the process of trading goods in exchange for slaves in Upper Guinea.
Reyes Católicos	King Ferdinand of Aragón and Queen Isabela of Castile, who united the kingdoms of Aragón and Castile at the end of the fifteenth century.
Rua Nova/Vila Nova	Areas where converted Jews lived in Portuguese towns and cities.
Sanbenito	Penitential cloak worn by those who had been penanced by the Inquisition.
Sargento Maior	Sergeant-Major.
Senhores	Portuguese for "[slave]masters"
Sistema de Castas	System developed in the New World in the late sixteenth and seventeenth centuries which categorised people according to the proportion of their European ancestry.
Tabanka	Term used for fortified village in Upper Guinea by end of the sixteenth century.
Tangoma	Creolised Upper Guinean woman associated/ married to *lançados*.

"Tierra Firme"	Literally "firm land": phrased used by Spanish to distinguish the American continent from the Caribbean islands in the sixteenth century.
Ultramar	Overseas Portuguese possessions.
Vadios	Escaped slaves in the highlands of Santiago, Cabo Verde, who forged the nucleus of Caboverdean society in the seventeenth century: the Caboverdean equivalent of *cimarrones*.
Vintena	Tax owed to the Portuguese crown in the early years of the Caboverdean colony, equivalent to one-twentieth of takings.

Introduction

Rethinking the Trans-Atlantic Slave Trade from a Cultural Perspective

In 1725 the English Captain George Roberts wrote a description of the Cabo Verde islands off the coast of West Africa (hereafter, Cabo Verde). He offered a glimpse of the former "glories" of this archipelago, which had been at the heart of the Atlantic world when that world was in the process of its tortured formation. In the late sixteenth century, Roberts wrote, there was "great Trade at St. Jago [the largest and most populous island, today called Santiago], Fuego [Fogo], Mayo, Bona Vista [Boavista], Sal and Brava ... especially in Negros. They had Store of Sugar, Salt, Rice, Cotton, Wool, Ambergrease, Civet, Elephants' Teeth, Brimstone, Pumice-Stone, Spunge, and some Gold".[1] A close reading of Roberts's text reveals the source of such riches, for, he wrote, "Saint Jago formerly was the great Market for Negro Slaves, which were sent from thence immediately to the West Indies".[2]

Just four years before Roberts's book was published, an English surgeon, John Atkins, travelled between the peninsula of Cape Verde (where present-day Dakar is located; hereafter, the Cape Verde peninsula) and Whydah (present-day Benin). He described how "*panyarring* is a Term for Man-stealing along the whole Coast".[3] The headmen he met in the region of present-day Côte d'Ivoire and Liberia were called *caboceers*.[4] The term *panyarring* derived from the Portuguese *apanhar*, meaning to "catch" or "seize", and may also have been related to the term *penhorar*,

---

[1] NGC, Vol. 1, Book 2, 630.
[2] Ibid., 654.
[3] Atkins (1970: 53).
[4] Ibid., 58.

to "pledge".[5] Its use, along with *caboceer* – derived from the Portuguese *cabeça*, meaning "head" – showed how important the Portuguese role had been in procuring slaves and negotiating with African authorities. Research has indeed shown how slaves in Atlantic West Africa were usually either seized in warfare, offered for ransom after a raid, or pledged as security for credit and then sold into the Atlantic trade if the credit was not repaid.[6] Atkins's definition of *panyarring* suggests that by the eighteenth century the emphasis was increasingly on violence. As Atkins's compatriot Roberts implied, this process had begun on the African coast adjacent to Cabo Verde.

That this was a focal zone of the early trans-Atlantic slave trade is not a new discovery. Using James Lockhart's estimates for Peru, Philip Curtin suggested that between 1526 and 1550 almost 80 per cent of the slaves in the New World came from the region.[7] J. Ballong-wen-Menuda, Ivana Elbl and John Vogt showed that the early slave trade from Benin, Kongo and the Angola region fed the gold trade at Elmina, the sugar plantations of São Tomé and the trade in domestic slaves to Portugal.[8] This facilitated the prominence of Cabo Verde in the first slave trade to America; it would sit at the heart of early trans-Atlantic movements and ideas.

Yet like most parts of the African Atlantic, the region remains understudied in the early period. It was still possible for one of the key figures in the study of Atlantic slavery, David Eltis, to write not so long ago that the region "did not have strong trade connections with the Atlantic before 1700".[9] The reasons for this lack of emphasis are varied. Anglo-American schools of history have concentrated on the eighteenth and nineteenth centuries.[10] Research on the earlier period is sparse and has concentrated on the lives of slaves in Spanish America.[11] There is therefore

---

[5] I am grateful for this definition to Everts (forthcoming, 2012: n15).

[6] Baum (1999); Thornton (1999: 3).

[7] Curtin (1975: 13); Lockhart (1968: 173).

[8] Ballong-wen-Menuda (1993) shows that Elmina procured slaves from Benin and São Tomé (Vol. 1, 160), with 800 slaves taken annually from São Tomé to Elmina in the early sixteenth century, (ibid., Vol. 1, 344–57). Elbl (1997)'s work shows that by 1520 most slaves in the Atlantic came from the Gulf of Guinea, bought by the settlers of São Tomé. Vogt (1979: 57–8, 70) describes the inter-regional trade between Benin, Elmina and São Tomé.

[9] Eltis (2000: 167).

[10] On this eighteenth/nineteenth century historiographical emphasis, see Newson/Minchin (2007: 1).

[11] Most recently Carroll (2001); Bennett (2003); Navarrete (2005); Maya Restrepo (2005). Such work builds on Bowser (1974). A recent break with this tradition is Newson/Minchin (2007). Mendes's (2007) doctoral thesis presents important findings on the early Atlantic trade, especially between Senegambia and Iberia. The early trans-Atlantic trade remains without a proper study.

a curious – and important – void. Surprisingly, this book offers the first full analysis of the rise of the trans-Atlantic slave trade from the area I term Western Africa, following George Brooks.[12]

This is a subject whose implications are large. In the fifteenth century, when European ships first arrived on the West African coast to procure slaves, the economic difference between Africa and Europe was not vast; yet by the nineteenth century, there was no denying the gulf.[13] Atlantic slavery had a powerful connection to this nineteenth-century economic discrepancy which had such influence on the colonial and post-colonial histories of Africa, being a necessary though not a sufficient cause of it. In those intervening four centuries, the militarism of large predatory states affected wider productive processes in the West African agricultural sector.[14] The proliferation of wars between states and micro-level conflicts between villages to extract labourers whose productive work benefited the economies of different societies and continents could only be negative. By the colonial era, the impact on the output, economic diversification and political stability of African societies had become apparent. There is therefore no doubting the importance of this subject, and by looking at the rise of Atlantic slavery in Western Africa we may see how it helped to change political economies and social institutions from the beginning, and how trans-Atlantic cultural and economic influences developed very early.

Many readers will feel that this focus raises concerns as much moral as historical. In present-day Guinea-Bissau, for instance, people are as well aware as any scholar of the significance of this subject. Not far from the modern town of Gabú, named after the powerful pre-colonial state of the same name, a friend once remarked to me: "The slave trade is over. You are not a slaver and I am not enslaved. It was our ancestors who did that, and so we must forget history." When I suggested that forgetting history condemned people to repeat the errors of their ancestors, he replied: "But if I remember, I'm going to get angry."

I hope that my friend will like this book and that it may even help to change his mind. Moral dimensions, as Ralph Austen wrote, "are a

[12] In a path-finding work, Brooks (1993b) uses the term "Western Africa" to include Senegambia (the area between the Senegal and Gambia Rivers), Upper Guinea (the area between the Gambia and Sierra Leone) and Cabo Verde, as I do here. Rodney (1970) dealt with the early Atlantic slave trade in part but omitted the first century of African-European exchanges which was when the trade originated.

[13] Inikori (1982b: 15).

[14] On Upper Guinea, see Baum (1999: 121–3), Hawthorne (2003) and Fields-Black (2009: Chapter 6).

concern behind any production of slave trade history".[15] Slavery has been a universal human institution and remains widespread, but Atlantic slavery holds an unusual importance for thinking about modernity, foreshadowing as it did racial consciousness and the industrialisation of global economies. Ultimately, any study of this process stands or falls on the integrity of its text, and a moral context should not lead to a moralising approach.[16] What we need to grasp is that ours is a world deeply connected to and shaped by the history discussed here, and yet it is irreparably distant from it.

PROBLEMS WITH A QUANTITATIVE APPROACH
TO ATLANTIC SLAVERY

This book supports a growing body of work which argues for a shift in the focus of historical studies and the consequent memorialisation of Atlantic slavery. Whereas such studies have often concentrated on the quantitative issue of the numbers of slaves involved in the trade, a tendency which has been enhanced by the online publication of a revised version of the Trans-Atlantic Slave Trade Database (www.slavevoyages.org), work by scholars such as Judith Carney, Edda Fields-Black, Walter Hawthorne, Linda Heywood and John Thornton, and Gwendolyn Midlo Hall have shown the significance of a culturally centred approach.[17] Although their work remains controversial and has provoked dispute, it has shown the importance of understanding the histories of West Africa during the Atlantic era from the perspective of changing productive practices and social institutions; it has also emphasised the need to see human transfers from West Africa to the Americas not only through the prism of the labour needs of the plantation economy, but also in terms of identity, production and the built environment.[18] This book is supportive of such work; it argues that a quantitative emphasis distracts attention from seeing how the advent of Atlantic slavery affected African societies, and from

[15] Austen (2001: 236, 239).
[16] As Mendes (2007: 15) notes, discussions of Atlantic slavery tend to be moralising and omit the reality that most large-scale civilisations rely on forced labour. Austen (2001: 243) notes how, in Europe, discussion of the slave trade is approached through the lens of abolition. As the 2007 bicentenary of abolition of the slave trade by the British parliament confirmed, this permits an inauthentic and self-congratulatory moral narrative.
[17] Carney (2001); Fields-Black (2009); Hawthorne (2003; 2010); Heywood/Thornton (2007); G. Hall (2005).
[18] For some of the disputes which have arisen, see the discussion on "Black Rice" in the *American Historical Review* (115/1), January 2010.

thinking through what the cultural, political and social consequences of this phenomenon were.[19]

To make this point, I concentrate primarily on events in Western Africa itself. This requires engagement with cultural histories. Slaves sold into the Atlantic system via Cabo Verde in the sixteenth and seventeenth centuries came from present-day Sierra Leone, Guinea-Bissau and the Casamance region of what today is southern Senegal. In the late fifteenth and first half of the sixteenth centuries, they also came from the Jolof and Sereer peoples who lived between the Senegal and Gambia Rivers in Senegambia.[20] The deep interconnections between these sub-regions of Western Africa emerge in accounts of the late sixteenth and early seventeenth centuries. The Caboverdean trader André Alvares d'Almada described in the 1590s how dyes were procured in the Nunes River (present-day Guinea-Conakry) and shipped north to the São Domingos River (present-day Guinea-Bissau), where they were exchanged for slaves and provisions.[21] The Dutch sailor Dirck Ruiters wrote in 1623 how salt was taken from the Caboverdean islands of Maio and Sal to Sierra Leone and traded there for gold, ivory and kola nuts. The goods obtained in Sierra Leone were then taken north of the Gambia to Joal and Portudal, where kola was traded for cotton cloths. The Caboverdean traders then went south to Cacheu on the São Domingos River, where the rest of the goods from Sierra Leone were exchanged for slaves. From Cacheu, the traders returned to the archipelago.[22]

This rich network of trade could not have developed without some pre-existing frameworks of both commercial and cultural exchange. It turns out that the former great wealth of Cabo Verde, alluded to by the Englishman George Roberts in the eighteenth century, depended not only on the commercial realities of slavery but also on those cultural exchanges which allowed the slave trade to develop in the first place.

---

[19] Though some scholars have criticised "culturalist" paradigms as static and homogenising of the complexity of human societies, I share the view of Ulf Hannerz (1996: 31–63) that the idea of "culture", though imperfect, is ultimately one of the best explanatory ideas we have to understand how human societies operate in both material and ritual terms. Hannerz powerfully argues that culture is acquired in social life; thus its acquisition varies according to social contexts which themselves reflect shifting material and ritual patterns of given times and places; this shifting context allows cultures to change along with that context, so that the idea of "culture" does not enforce a static view.

[20] For a fuller description of these sub-regions of Western Africa, see below, Chapter 1, Introductory Section.

[21] MMAII: Vol. 3, 342.

[22] Cit. Brooks (1993b: 157).

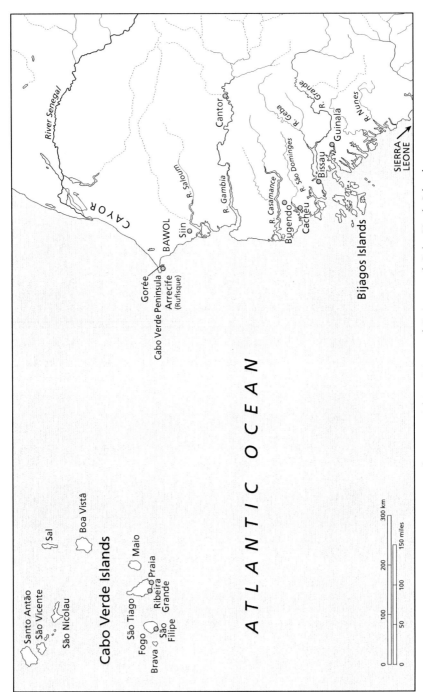

MAP 1. Map of Western Africa: Rivers of Guinea and Cabo Verde Islands.

6

Here we glimpse why studies of Atlantic slavery in an African context must focus on cultural questions as well as on quantitative data.

The quantitative focus derives from Philip Curtin's famous "census" of Atlantic slavery.[23] Yet although Curtin made many important contributions to the study of African societies, his estimates of slave exports for the sixteenth century were far too low. His figures proposed an average of 1,098 slaves a year leaving Senegambia and Upper Guinea (cf. note 12 for definitions of both these geographical zones) for America and Europe between 1526 and 1550.[24] They suggested an annual average of only 421 slaves exported from all of Upper Guinea in the period 1551–1595.[25] However these figures are unsustainable. They take no account of the vast contraband trade, in which evidence shows that slave exports were four and even five times the officially registered cargo.[26] They also ignore the evidence implying social change in Upper Guinea which does not tally with these low numbers. Moreover, it is impossible to square these figures with the labour needs of the New World following the demographic collapse of the Native Americans in the sixteenth century, a need which could not have been met by such a small influx of African labour.

Rightly, these figures have been derided as indicative of a "great level of underestimate".[27] Historians have attempted to recalibrate them. Eltis suggests doubling Curtin's estimate of 75,000 slave exports for the sixteenth century to 150,000.[28] The new Trans-Atlantic Slave Trade Database proposes a revised estimate of 196,940 slaves shipped to the Americas between 1501 and 1590 at an annual average of 2,188, of which 143,316 came from the part of Africa examined by this book, producing an annual average of 1,592.[29] Yet even this does not do justice to

---

[23] Curtin (1969).

[24] Ibid., 101.

[25] Ibid., 108–10; Bühnen (1993: 83).

[26] For evidence on this, see Green (2007b: 246); and also Wheat (2009) for the seventeenth century. Cf. also below, Chapters 6 and 7. Mark and Horta's analysis of the contraband trade in the second decade of the seventeenth century also suggests the need to substantially increase estimates for exported slaves from Upper Guinea (Mark/Horta 2011: 165–71).

[27] Inikori (1982b: 20); see also Barry (1998: 39–40).

[28] Eltis (2001: 23–4); see also Mellafe (1975: 72–3), who suggests doubling the ratio of slaves/tonnage of shipping allowed for by Curtin to account for the contraband trade. Curtin criticises this because it is double the ratio permitted by the contracts (Curtin 1969: 24 n.13). However, Mellafe's strategy brings us much nearer the reality than Curtin's approach.

[29] www.slavevoyages.org, data accessed May 15, 2011. Much of this important new research was carried out by António Mendes. See Mendes (2007: 451–73) and Mendes (2008).

the need to rethink this early trade. It is still possible for scholars to imply that Western Africa was not a region where enslavement for the Atlantic trade was commonplace.[30] Moreover, these figures themselves still represent significant underestimates. They only allow a 10 per cent surplus for contraband and nothing at all for undocumented illegal voyages.[31] Yet several important scholars of the sixteenth-century Atlantic trade are broadly agreed of both the importance of the contraband trade and the difficulties of using official figures as a benchmark to estimate them.[32]

This book shows that this approach is unsatisfactory. Important new documentary records which I discuss here reveal that even to raise these annual average estimates from Western Africa to approximately 2,500 slaves per year from 1525–50 and 5,000 per year from 1550–1590 represents a conservative approach (cf. Chapters 6 and 7). Yet these are not the sort of records which can readily be accommodated by the requirements of existing tools of quantitative analysis, such as those on which the Trans-Atlantic Slave Trade Database are founded. It may indeed be that the records used in this book indicate the methodological problems inherent in trying to produce a database, broadly using the same techniques, when that database covers a vast temporal period in which the institutional context of metropolitan power lying behind the production of records varied enormously.

So in spite of the significance of the quantitative findings in this book, I do not take a quantitative approach. The problem is that the quantitative approach "remains locked into the same questions that scholars have asked since the publication of Philip Curtin's *The Atlantic Slave Trade*".[33] In general, a reliance on quantitative methods depends on the comprehensiveness of imperfect European bureaucracies, as Hall and Hawthorne have argued.[34] It may well be that, as Joseph Miller once suggested, gross export figures "have no meaning either in human terms or in perceiving the operational complexity and diversity of the [trans-Atlantic slave] trade".[35] As António Mendes has written, the responses of societies to this trade are a great deal more complex than the mechanical

---

[30] Heywood/Thornton (2007: 48) – "West Central Africa ... was the one region in Africa ... where enslavement for the Atlantic trade was commonplace".

[31] Mendes (2007: 470) and (2008: 80) allows 10 per cent surplus for contraband.

[32] Amaral (1996: 68) argues that the contraband from Angola to Brazil was very large from 1575 onwards; and Torrão (2010: 8) notes the difficulties of the separation of official figures from the contraband trade.

[33] G. Hall (2010: 139).

[34] G. Hall (2010); Hawthorne (2010a).

[35] Miller (1976b: 76).

compilation of the statistics of the trade can allow.[36] The database is of course important, and it is proving extremely useful to historians trying to match up origins of slaves in Africa and destinations in America, which can show how African skills were employed in the Americas. And of course, David Eltis and David Richardson are right to suggest that there are connections between quantitative discoveries and cultural patterns and influences. Indeed, this is exemplified by this book's argument for an increased volume of trade in the sixteenth century, which is of course connected to the increased patterns of violent disorder in Western Africa and the consequent socio-political corollaries emphasised here.[37] Other approaches, however, need to be considered. Indeed, as Eltis himself has perceptively written elsewhere, "in the end any economic interpretation of history risks insufficient probing of the behaviour of people. At the very least, it will run the risk of missing the cultural parameters within which economic decisions are made".[38]

This book thus looks primarily at cultural, political and ritual changes in Western Africa, dealing step by step with the early trans-Atlantic trade. It does not discuss the details of European individuals holding licences to ship slaves and the operation of their financial arrangements.[39] That is not to say that in an African context economic issues do not matter; they illustrate the problems of economic development which hamper African societies today, the origins of which may be related to the nature of the economic exchanges connected to the Atlantic slave trade and the trajectory of agricultural production in Africa (cf. Chapter 3). Yet the cultural, political and social consequences of that trade matter as much, if not more, from an African perspective. For if, as Stephan Bühnen notes, in the second half of the sixteenth century 20 per cent of all New World slaves came from just one Upper Guinean people – the Brame – one must ask why.[40] This is a question which debating Curtin's figures or analysing the credit operations in the European banking system will never answer. It is a question which forces us to go beyond the narrow focus of "number".

[36] Mendes (2007: 15): "*les réponses sont plus complexes que ne le laisse entendre la compilation des chiffres monstrueux de la traite atlantique*". This is also recognised in Eltis (2000: 2).
[37] Eltis/Richardson (2008b).
[38] Eltis (2000: 284).
[39] This is the subject of a book very soon to be published by Maria Manuel Ferraz Torrão of the Instituto de Investigação Científica Tropical of Lisbon, who in her research also deals with issues of quantification, destinations of slaves in the Spanish Americas and the interplay of Portuguese and Spanish empires in the early Atlantic.
[40] Bühnen (1993: 101); see also O'Toole (2007) for more data on the Brame in Peru and for a nuanced picture of Brame "ethnicity" in the Americas.

CREOLISATION AND THE SLAVE TRADE IN WESTERN AFRICA

Bühnen suggested that the reason for the predominance of Western Africa in the Atlantic slaving networks of the sixteenth century lay in local factors, and surely he is right.[41] Yet we must also go beyond local explanations to look at a more pervasive Atlantic phenomenon: that of creolisation. For the beginning of this major phenomenon in world history – the trans-Atlantic slave trade – cannot be separated from the development of one of the first Creole societies in the Atlantic world.

In this book, I support the culturally centred body of literature on Atlantic slavery mentioned in the previous section through the development of creolisation. By looking at the phenomena of creolisation and the slave trade together, we see how the two were related. The relevance of local factors to this process may relate to how existing cultural formations in Western Africa facilitated the rise of what was, along with São Tomé, the first Atlantic Creole society. By also showing the importance of Western Africa to the early trans-Atlantic slave trade, I argue that this region's experience created patterns which helped to set the tone for the trade from West-Central Africa to the Americas recently analysed by Heywood and Thornton.[42]

Indeed, the importance of these early developments in Western Africa emerges most fully when we consider the broad influence this period had. As Curtin wrote with regard to plantation slavery, this period "established the relationships that continued into the period of more extensive trade that was to follow".[43] Yet the relevance of the sixteenth century is not confined just to practicalities. It also relates to ideological transformations, as the English borrowed wholesale from the Iberians in their ideas concerning the New World. Explorers such as Raleigh borrowed Spanish phrases such as *"tierra firme"* to describe their findings.[44] From the early sixteenth century onwards, they discussed widely with the Spanish in the Americas.[45] Once installed in Barbados in the 1620s, the English turned to Brazil to borrow both the techniques of sugar plantation and refinery as well as the use of enslaved African labour to maximise sugar

---

[41] Bühnen (1993:102).
[42] Heywood/Thornton (2007).
[43] Curtin (1998: 43). Torrão (2010: 1) also holds study of the sixteenth century as key if we are to understand how the systems of the seventeenth century emerged.
[44] Hakluyt (1904: Vol. 8, 298): "we arrived upon the coast, which we supposed to be a continent and firme lande".
[45] Ibid., Vol. 10, 2, on English presence in Puerto Rico in 1516. On the early influence of the Spanish on the English in America, see Elliott (2006: 11–12, 15).

mill profits.[46] Barbados was the first mass sugar production site for the English in the Caribbean, and many of the most influential early colonists of South Carolina came from this island.[47] Subsequently, these North American colonists even borrowed the Spanish word *negro* to refer to their own African slaves.[48] Thus, the way in which the trans-Atlantic slave trade took shape during its first century, and its connection to the parallel development of creolisation, was pivotal to the subsequent economy and ideology of the Western hemisphere.

However, there are problems with the concept of "creolisation", particularly with its varied uses in African and Atlantic contexts. In discourse related to African Americans, it has come to relate to the question of whether or not there was any cultural continuity from Africa in the diaspora.[49] In Herman Bennett's analysis of imperial Mexico, the term refers to the development of a legal consciousness by African slaves.[50] In Sierra Leone, the Krio culture refers to that which developed following the arrival of freed African American slaves from the late eighteenth century onwards.[51] A different meaning still is employed by Megan Vaughan, whose use of the term derives from the fact that Mauritius was an unsettled island prior to the early modern period.[52]

Modern Creole studies emphasise an overriding linguistic phenomenon, which is the formation and use of a vernacular Creole language.[53] This is how I use the term "creolisation" here. In this interpretation, the cultural process implied these days by creolisation – of the development of hybrid societies – is given an empirical historical basis by its connection to a definite historical process demonstrated through linguistic change. It is a more precise term than "hybridity", being grounded in the context of the specific power relations which went with the creation of Atlantic Creole languages.[54] Indeed, as this book shows, Western Africa was a key site in which the power relations related to Atlantic creolisation were first developed. By looking in detail at this process, we may see

---

[46] Dunn (1973: 72).

[47] Ibid., 111–5.

[48] Jordan (1974: 35).

[49] See Price/Mintz (1992); Berlin (1996; 2000); Carney (2001); Heywood/Thornton (2007); Fields-Black (2009).

[50] Bennett (2003: 2–3).

[51] Wyse (1989) has one of the best analyses of the Krio of Sierra Leone.

[52] Vaughan (2005: 2).

[53] Woolford (1983: 5).

[54] On this conceptual distinction between creolisation and hybridity, see Cohen/Toninato (2010a: 14).

what characterised these relations and how the conditions arose in which they evolved.

Western Africa was one of the first sites to see the development of an Atlantic Creole language, and it is because of this that I use the term "creolisation". The latest research suggests that Caboverdean Kriolu had already become a "pidginised" *lingua franca* by the end of the fifteenth century; it was a vernacular in Cabo Verde by the middle of the sixteenth century and a vernacular of the trading settlements of Upper Guinea by the early seventeenth century.[55] Thus Western Africa offers a historical example of Atlantic linguistic creolisation in the period examined in this book. There are other debates to be had with regard to processes of identity formation and the degree to which the Creole language was constitutive of a new collective identity for some.[56] However, where the question of language formation is concerned, the evidence is comprehensive. Indeed the very idea of linguistic creolisation emerged in Western Africa, where it was first used by Jajolet de la Courbe in 1685.[57] The region thus has a certain chronological primacy in both the development of Creole societies and the development of the idea of the "Creole", and so it is difficult to study its cultural histories in an Atlantic context, as this book proposes, without reference to this idea.

This process of Creole language formation is, however, deeply connected to associated socio-cultural changes, and it is this which makes it an important prism for assessing the trans-Atlantic slave trade from a more cultural perspective. The development of a new language may reflect new social forces. Where social interactions and exchanges are intense, linguistic change follows.[58] In a social context creolisation may, as Wilson Trajano Filho suggests, therefore be a metaphor "to refer to the processes of social and cultural change involving a mass of people with different ties of social and political belonging".[59] It is in this sense

[55] Lang (2006: 57) argues convincingly that the large number of grammatical features in Kriolu deriving from Wolof point to this periodisation, as the vast majority of Jolof slaves coming to Cabo Verde arrived in the foundational period of the colony. See also Jacobs (2009; 2010) and Veiga (2000: 37) for this periodisation. Jacobs (2009: 352) shows that Kriolu had become a vernacular in Upper Guinea by the 1620s.
[56] On creolisation as involving the development of a new collective identity with an ethnic referent, see Knörr (2010: 353). Seibert (forthcoming, 2012) argues that this creolisation did not occur in Upper Guinea.
[57] Holm (1988: Vol. 1, 15).
[58] Woolford (1983: 1–2).
[59] Trajano Filho (2003: 4): "*uma metáfora para...referir aos processos de mudança social e cultural envolvendo uma massa de gente com diferentes laços de pertenecimento social e político*".

that cultural theorists have used the term over recent decades, as a sort of "master metaphor" for processes of cultural mixing in the era of globalisation.[60] In this book we will see that mixed cultural practices did develop in Western Africa in the sixteenth century and that they were connected to the very early forms of economic globalisation that developed at the same time, which illustrates how, as in our contemporary era, economic globalisation and cultural hybridisation often go together.[61]

Although secondarily employed as a metaphor for such mixtures, however, creolisation in this book is primarily tied to the specific historical situation which, although allowing such cultural mixtures to occur, also facilitated the rise of this early Atlantic Creole language. The key point is that that historical situation was associated with the rise of the trans-Atlantic slave trade, which occurred earlier in Western Africa than elsewhere in the African Atlantic, and thereby laid down early markers for the process in the wider Atlantic world.

Back in the 1970s, the Jamaican writer Edward Kamau Brathwaite suggested that the study of creolisation was inseparable from the study of slavery. This book thus does as Brathwaite did for Jamaica, and interconnects the study of creolisation and slavery, though this time in a Western African historical context.[62] Such work has been undertaken by Heywood and Thornton for Central Africa, but it remains to be completed in Western Africa.[63] At its most exciting this "creolisation model" can show that "Africa was a place where the Atlantic trade had produced deep historical transformations that were not just the result of European imposition, but of the internal dynamics of African societies".[64] However, it must also emphasise the differences which emerged. Within Western Africa we will find that the processes of creolisation varied in the different locales of Santiago, Fogo and Upper Guinea (something itself illustrated by the different Kriolu dialects of these locales today). Moreover, there were important cultural differences between Western Africa as a whole and the Kongo/Angola region. Linguistic diversity was much richer in Western Africa than in Central Africa.[65] This warns us against loose use of terms such as "Creole," which mar the otherwise interesting work of Heywood and Thornton.

[60] Hannerz (1996: 66); Cohen/Toninato (2010a: 5–7).
[61] Gruzinski (2002: 4).
[62] Brathwaite (1971: vii).
[63] Heywood/Thornton (2007). Though note Nafafé (2007), whose work provides a thorough basis from which to continue in this area.
[64] Naro/Sansi-Roca/Treece (2007b: 3).
[65] Heywood/Thornton (2007: 56).

Thus a core point to emerge from a culturally centred analysis rooted in the idea of creolisation is the greater differentiation of the Atlantic export slave trade in an African context. The work of Hawthorne and Martin Klein has illustrated that the old "predatory state thesis" which saw the slave trade as bolstering expanding African slaving empires requires revision.[66] There was not one Atlantic slave trade, but many trades wreaking many different effects, and indeed the African capacity to influence the early Atlantic emerges in this diversity of African-European relations.[67] Detailed analysis of developments related to the trade in one particular context can help to remind us of the need to differentiate our understanding, and not to fall into the trap of generalisation which so often means, as Claude Meillassoux eloquently put it, that African societies become the "laboratories for retarded fantasies".[68]

RETHINKING AFRICAN AGENCY IN THE ATLANTIC WORLD

Atlantic history is one of the fastest-growing fields of historical research. As David Armitage has put it, "we are all Atlanticists now".[69] Studying the Atlantic allows historians to examine the way in which the trading networks developed in the early modern world were forerunners of the interconnected systems which underpinned the rise of the global industrial economy of the nineteenth century.[70] It illustrates how global factors affected particular societies and how the rise of a "world history", characterised by multiple connections linking disparate locations required this integration of global and local forces. However, in this new literature the role of African societies has been conspicuously absent. The recent dearth of studies by Africanists on the early modern period is a major cause of this, but more general narratives have also failed to give an adequate account of the place of African societies in the Atlantic.[71]

This book shows that this situation is inadequate. By studying the first century of Atlantic history in detail through events in Western Africa, we see not only the importance of Western Africa in the developing picture

---

[66] See Hawthorne (1999; 2001; 2003); Klein (2001).
[67] A point made by Eltis (2000: 164).
[68] Meillassoux (1991: 21).
[69] Armitage (2002: 11).
[70] Bailyn (2005).
[71] Abulafia (2008) is an egregious recent example. There are exceptions to this picture, such as Thornton (1998), the more recent work of Law (2004), and an important article co-authored by Law and Mann (see Law/Mann [1999]). See also Green (2009). But in general there are very few publications on "the African Atlantic".

of Atlantic slavery and creolisation, but also how African societies helped to shape the early Atlantic. In particular, it is argued that mercantile diasporas in the Iberian Atlantic emerged in part through the contact which members of those diasporas had with societies of Western Africa, in which such cross-cultural trading diasporas had long exerted influence. Because recent works have emphasised the role of mercantile diasporas and ideas of shared identity in the rise of the Atlantic system, it becomes clear that the importance of diaspora trading networks to the Atlantic world cannot be separated from the contact which those networks had with African societies.[72]

For students of African history, the importance of African contacts in the emergence of early global diasporic networks may come as little surprise. In general, the recognition by scholars such as André Gunder Frank of the importance of diasporas in pre-industrial trade was stimulated by research on African history by scholars such as Abner Cohen and Paul Lovejoy.[73] Curtin's path-finding work on the importance of diasporas in cross-cultural trade focussed significantly on diasporas in African history.[74] Subsequently, debates between Avner Greif, Jeremy Edwards and Sheilagh Ogilvie on the role of private reputation and corporate identity in long-distance diaspora trade, and the significance of this for understanding the place of cultural patterns in economic development, developed out of the data on "Maghribi" traders and their commerce in medieval North Africa.[75] Yet in spite of the importance of African history for the study of diasporas in cross-cultural commercial networks, historians have not before seen the connection of trans-Saharan histories to the emergence of Atlantic connections.

This book argues that this connection is central, and therefore reasserts the centrality of African societies to the study of early modern diasporas and to the early Atlantic world. Such an emphasis is important in a context where the place of diasporas in early modern cross-cultural trade is an increasingly important question for historians. In an influential work concentrating on the Sephardic Jews of Livorno, Francesca

---

[72] See especially Herzog (2003); Studnicki-Gizbert (2007); Ebert (2008).

[73] Frank (1998: 62); A. Cohen (1969; 1971); Lovejoy (1973; 1978).

[74] Curtin (1984).

[75] Greif (1993; 2008); Edwards/Ogilvie (2008). Ogilvie and Edwards have disputed Greif's assertion that the reliability of these early trade networks was assured by private reputation and a form of "coalition" shared by people with a collective identity, rather than through legal mechanisms; Greif (2008) argues convincingly that their view of the place of legal mechanisms in the trade of "Maghribi traders" is a poor interpretation of the facts.

Trivellato has criticised both Curtin and Greif for embracing a static view
of culture.[76] Although appearing to derive many of her ideas on the role
of diasporas in transmitting reliable information from Greif, she chides
him and Curtin for arguing that there was a tendency among members of
diasporas to become absorbed by their hosts and cease to be able to act
as go-betweens.[77] However such a view appears to draw from an essentialist view of "culture" and an over-concentration on the place of the
eighteenth-century Sephardic diaspora which she analyses. Trivellato's
failure to engage with African histories means that her argument cannot
acknowledge the ways in which, as this book shows, in African and New
World contexts the cultural frameworks of various diasporas – including the New Christians, themselves closely related to the Sephardim (cf.
Chapter 4) – did become absorbed into one another in the early modern
period. Such mutual reciprocity was a by-product of the development
of long-distance trade networks on the one hand; and, on the other, of
the long-standing history of cultural pluralism in West Africa which meant
that trading communities characterized by the ability to retain distinctive
original cultural features and yet also adopt traits of the host culture were
widespread (cf. Chapters 1 and 8). Such a combination of distinctiveness
and hybridity seems contradictory from a Eurocentric perspective, but from
the African point of view it is in keeping with the long-standing "interpen-
etrating multiculturalities that characterize so much of the region".[78] Thus
this book's focus on these African-Atlantic contexts shows that a more
nuanced view of cross-cultural trade is required, one which is alive to the
cultural distinctiveness and influence of each region of the world; from this
perspective, the maintenance of cultural distinctiveness, mutual influence
and absorption of one culture by another, and simultaneous distinctiveness
and reciprocal influence were all equally strong possibilities.[79]

   Thus returning to an analysis of the African diasporic movements from
which many of the contemporary debates on cross-cultural trade derives
is important, for it offers a reminder of how the persistent failure of so
much mainstream historiography of the early modern period to engage

[76] Trivellato (2009).
[77] Ibid., Chapters 6–8 on the importance of reliable information for the functioning of
long-distance diasporas; 17, 276 for these critiques of Curtin and Greif.
[78] The phrase is from Farias (1999: 164). On Africa as a part of the emergent global economic system that predated European expansion, see Bayart (2000: 218), and as in some
ways more open commercially than Europe, see Mendes (2007: 9).
[79] See Antunes/Silva (2011) for an argument that Western Africa did offer a different
context for cross-cultural trade in the early modern era.

with African history limits the available perspectives, and also supports this book's more general argument as to the centrality of cultural perspectives to an understanding of economic networks. To compound this issue, this African role in early Atlantic history was moreover concealed by ultra-nationalist ideologies for many decades. For far too long the historiography of Western Africa was dominated by the colonial perspective of Portugal's mid-twentieth-century Salazar regime, which saw African history as beginning with the Portuguese "discoveries" of the fifteenth century.[80] In this narrative, "history" began with Nuno Tristão's passing of the River Senegal and Dinis Diaz's arrival at the Cape Verde peninsula in 1444. However, the experiences which the Portuguese sailors had on the African coast depended on preceding exchanges and historical events dating to an already distant past. In Upper Guinea, peoples had come under pressure since the thirteenth century from the Mandinka of the famous Mali empire in their push towards the coast, a pressure which had affected the structure of their societies and the way they responded to newcomers (cf. Chapter 1); with the arrival of the Portuguese, the peoples of Upper Guinea would find themselves between Mandinka and Atlantic powers, a situation which brought new changes.[81]

Yet Salazarist historians tended to pass over preceding African forces in these exchanges. Along with historians of the other European colonial powers in the twentieth century, they created a narrative in which "active" Europeans helped to shape a new African reality. There was little reconstruction of earlier African histories which may help to grasp how Africa affected the early Atlantic.[82] Thus as a new wave of historians of the region such as Brooks, Fields-Black and Hawthorne have shown, a full account of the emergence of the Atlantic system here must begin with events before 1440.

In order to illustrate one way in which narratives of Atlantic history may be "Africanised", I begin before the 1440s with events in Western Africa which helped to shape the first African-European exchanges. I argue that the cultural framework found by European navigators in

[80] An example of this trend is the work of Antonio Brásio (e.g., Brásio 1962). This is a serious problem because Brásio's published collections of documents (MMAII) remain the best available source of published documentation for Western Africa. On the ideological problems related to the region's historiography, see Green (2007b: 5–16).

[81] Barry (1998: 27). "Mandinka" is the ethnonym used specifically in the old Kaabu region by people known more widely in West Africa as "Mande" or "Malinké". It is therefore the ethnonym used in this book except where the discussion is more widely of Mande peoples in West Africa.

[82] On the importance of this, see Ballong-wen-Menuda (1993: Vol. 1, 79–83).

the fifteenth century influenced the nature of their exchanges, the places where they settled, and their ability to form the settled trading communities which were essential to the operation of the trans-Atlantic slave trade in the sixteenth century. By then integrating this picture with important new documentary finds related to early African-European relations, I show how the "pre-Atlantic" history of Western Africa was decisive in the emergence of these early Atlantic communities.

Indeed, this is where the question of African "agency" in the Atlantic world intersects with the idea of creolisation we looked at in the previous section; for the nature of the mixed societies which emerged here in Atlantic West Africa depended on the pre-existing frameworks of both partners. From the African perspective, as we have just seen, this involved Upper Guineans who had adapted to the Mandinka expansion, and from the European side, New Christians, who were descendants of Jews who had been forced to convert to Christianity by Manoel I in 1497. New documentary evidence discussed here shows that sixteenth-century European settlements in Upper Guinea contained a majority of New Christians, and, in collaboration with Peter Mark and José da Silva Horta's work on Jewish communities in seventeenth-century Senegambia, I advance the argument that it was the quality of adaptability inherited by both Upper Guineans from their relation to the Mandinka and by members of the New Christian diaspora from their pre-existing position in Portugal that helped to mould the Creole societies of Western Africa[83]; by illustrating the nature of the Atlantic slaving networks of the sixteenth century and how they were connected to these Creole societies, this book also offers a suggestive mechanism as to how the phenomenon of creolisation as developed in Western Africa subsequently influenced developments elsewhere in the Atlantic world.

Indeed, integrating the New Christians into the picture decisively connects the patterns of creolisation in West Africa to the wider Atlantic world, which makes the case for the importance of the history of African diasporas mentioned earlier. It turns out that the pre-existing frameworks of diasporic trade connections common among both the trans-Saharan and New Christian traders were crucial in integrating the Atlantic networks

[83] See Mark/Horta (2011: 17); like Mark and Horta, this book therefore foregrounds the importance of the theme of diaspora in understanding this history (ibid., 15). There is no significant published study of the New Christians in this region, although in addition to this work by Mark and Horta there are recent studies of the Sephardim in seventeenth-century Senegambia by Mendes (2004), Mark and Horta (2004; 2005; 2009;) and Green (2005; 2008a and 2008b).

of interest to many scholars today.[84] Indeed, the New Christian networks in the early Atlantic may well have been directly connected to the functioning of earlier trans-Saharan networks (cf. Chapter 2). Western Africa became part of what I call the "pan-Atlantic", where African experiences affected how Europeans perceived and "discovered" the New World before events in the New World in turn affected Africa. A further key finding to emerge from this book is thus that this "pan-Atlantic" emerged earlier than historians generally allow.

The accommodation of New Christian diaspora networks within West Africa was vital to the process of forging this pan-Atlantic in the sixteenth century. The development of creolisation in Western Africa, it turns out, was facilitated by the existing practices of both African and New Christian diaspora merchants. One of the most important aspects of this analysis of African and New Christian diasporas is that it moves beyond traditional binaries – Black/white and dominant/subaltern – and beyond current polarised disputes to posit a mixed past.[85] However, the apparent paradox is that this history of commercial and cultural mixing – the mixture that helped to create linguistic creolisation – occurred at a time of the first stirrings of modern racism. For Africans, this saw the association of slavery and skin colour leading to increasingly institutionalised prejudice in the wider Atlantic world beyond the African coast, whereas for New Christians the emphasis on Old Christian ancestry – so-called *limpeza*, or "purity of blood" – saw their growing marginalisation within Iberian society.[86]

Although ideas of race remained unfixed in the sixteenth century, they were beginning to harden. Thus as this book unfolds, one of its ironies is the need at times to integrate this latent and essentialist discourse of "race" into an understanding of how the mixed cultural and linguistic communities of Atlantic Western Africa developed in the sixteenth

---

[84] Trading diasporas have long been important to West Africa and indeed still are. For the trade diaspora of the Wangara in Central Sudan in the sixteenth century, see Lovejoy (1978); for the trade diaspora of the Hausa of post-colonial Nigeria, see A. Cohen (1969). For the scholarship on early Atlantic networks of New Christians, see for example Wachtel (2001); Israel (2002); Schorsch (2008).

[85] Prime among these polarities is the "Black Athena" debate. See for example Bernal (1991); Lefkowitz (2008).

[86] On the developing association of skin colour and slavery in fifteenth-century Valencia, see Blumenthal (2009). However, Blumenthal agrees with Medeiros (1985) and Russell-Wood (1978) that this picture, though nascent, was not institutionalised until later in the sixteenth century; a contrary position on this is taken by Sweet (1997). For new perspectives on the growing marginalisation of New Christians in the Iberian Atlantic, see Schwartz (2008); and Yovel (2009).

century. Because of its contrary register to the discourse of creolisation, the question of race emerges only in a minor key in this book. However, in the final chapters I draw on the marked changes by 1600 to argue that these conflicting discourses of mixed creolisation and emergent and essentialist racism were connected in the early Atlantic world, and that the connection lay in the hyper-mobility and rupture with previous labour patterns which distinguished the early Atlantic from the worlds that preceded it, and from which both discourses emerged.

Through engaging with these themes, this book illustrates how peoples of Western Africa had an important place in building the Atlantic world, and that this was indeed a relevant location in the birth of economic and ideological currents associated with modernity (see especially Chapter 4). This sort of argument, of course, runs counter to the ideas concerning the historical place of African societies which emerged in the colonial era, and now, in the twenty-first century, different ideologies challenge these ideas. Many cavil at talking about African agency in these centuries for fear of blaming the evils of slavery on Africans themselves; and indeed, some scholars, in a desire to demonstrate such agency in the early Atlantic, come dangerously close to abetting this position.[87] However, debates on African agency do not have to get caught up in the issue of blame for the Atlantic slave trade. Indeed, almost all large-scale societies have practised or benefited from some form of forced labour. To hold that African societies cannot or should not have done so is thus to hold a paternalistic myth of the noble savage and thereby to replicate, unconsciously, older historiographies. This is not to say that Africans were to "blame" for the slave trade, but rather that the export of slaves emerged through a complex process in which Africans most certainly were not without agency.[88] Nor is it to give European sugar consumers and slavers absolution from the greed which was a key driver of the trade. It is to accept that people often behave badly and to seek to understand how the behaviour of all parties here helped to shape the emergent modern world, at the same time acknowledging, as I do in this book, that far from having "complete control" over the slave trade, it was always those African societies who were most under pressure from a combination of local and Atlantic forces that experienced its most pernicious effects (cf. Conclusion).

---

[87] See for example Thornton (1998: 74): "the slave trade ... grew out of and was rationalised by the African societies who participated in it and had complete control over it until the slaves were loaded onto European ships".

[88] The very association of the ideas of "guilt" and "blame" with this subject today itself reveals statements of value rather than fact, the importance of which probably derives from narratives of guilt and redemption which emerged with the Abolitionist movement.

Indeed, what this integration of the question of agency to that of Atlantic slavery and creolisation may show us is precisely the limits of that agency, ideologically and historically. We need to recognise the acuity of Walter Johnson's analysis: that the very idea of agency itself smuggles in a notion of the universality of liberal ideas such as freedom and independence which were vital to the self-identification of white elites in the nineteenth and twentieth centuries; on Johnson's analysis, therefore, the idea of agency itself in some senses represents what he describes as a "white" form of address in a Black conversation.[89] For although this book shows how and why societies of Western Africa influenced the emergence of the Atlantic world, it also points up limits to that agency through the cycles of violent disorder which the Atlantic in turn brought to bear on Western African societies. It emerges that although pre-existing African cultural and economic patterns were vital to shaping the formation of the early Atlantic, within a few decades the demand side of the Atlantic economy had begun radically to affect the way in which African communities defended themselves, built alliances and structured their societies. Here the book supports the work of Walter Rodney, who more than forty years ago argued for the influence of this early Atlantic trade on cycles of violent disorder and practices of enslavement in Western Africa.[90] This book shows in detail how these cycles of violence developed and how they affected the cultural, political and social frameworks within which peoples lived in Western Africa.

So although for ideological reasons related to perceptions of African history in the epoch of twentieth-century imperialism we must recognise African agency, we should at the same time not be afraid to see the limits of this idea; we must recognise that even its positing is in some senses a response to the earlier assumptions of white racism. Otherwise, as Rosalind Shaw recognises, "when we celebrate the agency of those who have been the objects of transregional European enterprises (via colonization, missionization, or the Atlantic slave trade) without adequately distinguishing the very different agency of colonizers, missionaries or slave traders, we risk writing neorevisionist histories".[91] Thus as this book shows, of course we must recognise the role and autonomy of African societies in this period, but we must do so whilst also grasping the very real constraints which the institution of Atlantic slavery imposed on both slaves and the African societies from which they came.

[89] W. Johnson (2003: 115, 120).
[90] Rodney (1965); idem., (1966). Rodney's ideas were strongly disputed by Fage (1969b).
[91] Shaw (2002: 19–20).

SOURCES AND STRUCTURE

This book draws on several extended periods spent in the Casamance, Guinea-Bissau and Cabo Verde between 1995 and 2011. It includes material derived from interviews and observations relating to cultural practices there.[92] Such experiences formed my initial entrée into thinking about the region, and subsequently I have followed them up with archival and library work to complement them. I have also drawn on published collections of oral traditions of the peoples of Upper Guinea.

For written sources I have used archives in Colombia, Gambia, Portugal, Spain and the Vatican. Much published material has also been consulted. I have drawn from the Spanish accounts of their conquest of the Americas in the late fifteenth and early sixteenth centuries. These sources have not been examined before in writing the history of Western Africa, but they supplement the published accounts of André Alvares d'Almada, André Donelha and the documents published by António Brásio.

The evidentiary base includes tables of slave "ethnicities" in Spanish America (1548–1600; see Tables I.1 and I.2). These tables offer the most complete picture yet of slave "ethnicities" in the Americas in the sixteenth century. They draw on findings from Nueva España (now Mexico), the Nuevo Reino de Granada (now Colombia) and Perú, as well as from Panamá and the Caribbean islands. They are thus fairly representative, bearing in mind that different African peoples were used for different labour tasks in the Americas. They allow us to reinterpret Almada and Donelha, corroborating some of their observations and permitting new interpretations. Though there are problems with these "ethnic" identifications, scholars are broadly agreed as to their value.[93]

This evidentiary base is supplemented by new findings from the Archive of the Indies in Seville and the inquisitorial archives in Portugal, which permit a re-examination of changes in African polities and societies in this period. Some readers may worry as to the reliability of inquisitorial sources, but there is a general consensus among scholars of the Inquisition that such information cannot be discounted.[94]

This approach is analogous to Ray Kea's combination of archival and published oral histories for the Gold Coast.[95] However, it retains

---

[92] An illustration of one aspect of my experience of Upper Guinea is Green (2001).

[93] For a good discussion of the value of these identifications, see Hawthorne (2010b: introduction).

[94] Gitlitz (1996: 77–8) suggests that "most of what [the inquisitors] wrote is mostly accurate". See also Green (2007b: 335).

[95] Kea (1982: 8).

TABLE I.I. *Upper Guinean Origins of Slaves in the Americas, 1547–1560*

"Ethnic Group"	Numbers Recorded
Bainunk (known as Bañol)	27 = 6.12%
Biafara	101 = 22.90%
Bioho	3 = 0.68%
Brame (known as Bran)	88 = 19.95%
Cocoli	4 = 0.91%
Criollo de Cabo Verde	1 = 0.23%
Kassanké (known as Casanga)	12 = 2.72%
Jolof	84 = 19.05%
Pullo (known as Fula)	2 = 0.45%
Mandinga	39 = 8.84%
Nalu	5 = 1.13%
Sape	39 = 8.84%
Sereer (known as Berbesi)	36 = 8.16%

Sources: Archivo General de las Indias; Archivo General de la Nación (Bogotá); Carroll, Blacks in Colonial Veracruz; Inchaustegui, Reales Cedulas ... de Santo Domingo; Lockhart, Spanish Peru, 1532–1560; Millares Carlo/Mantecón, Índice y Extractos ... de Notarías de México.

This table illustrates the origins of Upper Guinean slaves in the Americas in the mid sixteenth-century. Four hundred forty-one slaves' origins are annotated, most of whom were tabulated by Carroll and Lockhart, but some of whom have been located by myself in the archives. I have also used records collated by Incahustegui and Millares Carlo/Mantecón. The major American colonies are covered in this picture, Carroll focussing on Mexico and Lockhart on Peru, whereas Incahustegui's data covers Hispaniola.

Readers should note, however, that although Spanish scribes did note down with reasonable accuracy what they perceived as the ethnicities of slaves arriving in the Americas, sold in deeds of sale, etc., that these identifications in themselves are not watertight. Sometimes the "ethnicity" was more a representation of the area from which a slave had been taken than a precise "ethnic" identity. Indeed, Spanish scribes usually noted that an individual came from the "land of xxxx" (*tierra de x ...*). With this caveat in mind, however, this information can still tell us much about the areas which traded most heavily, and is in all likelihood as good a window as we can have onto how this picture fluxed over the course of the sixteenth century. Those wishing to engage further in the question of the reliability of these ethnic identifications are advised also to consult Hawthorne (2010b: *Introduction*).

a dependence on external written sources. Some readers may feel that dependence on these sources weakens this book. Personally, I prefer the approach of Mendes, who argues that "the sources produced by Portuguese colonists should not be automatically dismissed under the heading of Eurocentrism, but rather interpreted in their context and interrogated as

TABLE 1.2. *Upper Guinean Origins of Slaves in the Americas, 1560–1600*

Group	Numbers, 1560–1567	Numbers, 1568–1577	Numbers, 1578–1589	Numbers, 1590–1600
Arriata	0	1 = 0.13%	0	0
Baga	0	1 = 0.13%	0	0
Bainunk	10 = 2.17%	37 = 4.81%	64 = 8.38%	54 = 10.59%
Balanta	0	7 = 0.91%	0	6 = 1.18%
Biafara	52 = 11.28%	167 = 21.72%	172 = 22.51%	143 = 28.04%
Bioho	8 = 0.67%	36 = 4.68%	18 = 2.36%	21 = 4.18%
Brame	70 = 15.18%	212 = 27.57%	187 = 24.48%	155 = 30.39%
Cocolí	1 = 0.22%	7 = 0.91%	5 = 0.65%	7 = 1.37%
Criollo de Cabo Verde	0	10 = 1.30%	2 = 0.26%	2 = 0.39%
Floup	0	3 = 0.39%	0	6 = 1.18%
Jalonké	0	0	1 = 0.13%	0
Jolof	25 = 5.42%	30 = 3.90%	48 = 6.28%	18 = 3.53%
Kassanké	9 = 1.95%	32 = 4.16%	40 = 5.24%	8 = 1.57%
Lamba	1 = 0.22%	0	0	0
Mandinga	30 = 6.51%	45 = 5.85%	59 = 7.72%	35 = 6.86%
Nalu	7 = 1.52%	27 = 3.51%	14 = 1.83%	19 = 3.73%
Pepel	0	2 = 0.26%	0	0
Pullo	2 = 0.43%	2 = 0.26%	2 = 0.26%	0

Sape	190 = 41.2%	130 = 16.91%	99 = 12.96%	28 = 5.49%
Sereer	20 = 4.33%	14 = 1.82%	53 = 6.94%	4 = 0.78%
Susu	30 = 6.51%	6 = 0.78%	0	0
Volon	6 = 1.3%	0	0	0

Sources: Archivo General de las Indias; Archivo General de la Nación (Bogotá); Bowser, The African Slave in Colonial Peru; Navarrete, Cimarrones y Palenques en el Siglo XVII; Tardieu, Origins of Slaves in the Lima Region in Peru (Sixteenth and Seventeenth Centuries)

This table tabulates the ethnic origins of slaves from the Upper Guinean region in the Americas between 1560 and 1600. Two thousand five hundred individuals are tabulated here, giving an average of roughly 600 per decade or 60 individuals per year. This is not an inconsiderable statistical sample.

The sources are varied. I have put together Bowser's and Tardieu's figures for Peru with Navarrete's figures for Colombia. The only possible overlap (i.e. individuals who may have been cited twice) is between the figures of Bowser and Tardieu, and this is unlikely to be statistically significant because Tardieu's figures cite far higher proportions of Brames and Sapes than do Bowser.

To these figures I have added 1,150 transcriptions of my own from the Archivo General de la Nación in Bogotá and the Archivo General de las Indias in Seville.

The main documents used in Bogotá for this table were the following:

Archivo Histórico de Boyacá, Notaría Primera de Tunja: Legajos 1–69, Rollos 1–20
Archivo Notarial de Santander, Notaría Primera de Pamplona Rollo 1507294
Negocios Exteriores, Legajo 4, fols. 714 – 784
Negros y Esclavos, Antioquia, SC43/Legajo 1, fols. 997–1018
Negros y Esclavos, Antioquia, SC43/Legajo 4, fols. 731–745
Negros y Esclavos, Cundinamarca, SC43/Legajo 8, fols. 686–924
Notaría Primera de Bogotá: Vols. 1 – 5B, 9–11A, 13

The main documents used in Seville for this table were the following:

Contaduría 1174, No. 6, fols. 12v – 16v
Escribanía 2A, fols. 471v-473r, 493v – 498r
Escribanía 165A, fols. 107r, 109r, 111r, 113,5, 115r
Justicia 518, No. 1, fols. 36v – 44v
Justicia 996, No. 2, Ramo 3
Panamá 33, no. 83
Patronato 234, Ramo 6, fols. 416v – 419r

The statistics compiled here may usefully be compared to Alejandro de la Fuente's for the period 1570–94 for Havana (Fuente 2008: 106). These are given in percentages, but broadly bear out the numerical spread provided by my own research.

to their reliability".[96] There is a sense in which texts inscribe memories, and rather like photographs, *become* memories of events. Although they only give a partial view of an event, questions of identity and the past are often increasingly caught up in the way in which that past is presented in texts, and thus the use of texts is undeniably important.

Moreover, passing archival sources over for the exclusive use of oral history is impractical. As Peter Mark and Donald Wright have argued, oral history before the eighteenth century becomes too sketchy to provide detailed and reliable accounts.[97] The material from the Oral History Archive in the Gambia used in this book has allowed the integration of African perspectives into aspects of the text, and my hope is that to some degree it balances the preponderance of written records which I have used, but even the voluminous material stored there is too vague in terms of chronology, and too focussed on various key events, to be used in isolation from other sources. Keepers of oral histories are just as open to ideological diversion as writers of modern history, and both Charlotte Quinn and Wright have noted how the griots of the region around the Gambia River appeared unreliable as sources of factual information.[98] Hawthorne uses oral information for aspects of the seventeenth century, and Robert Baum for the eighteenth century, but very few authors argue that specifics beyond there emerge in oral data.[99] Fields-Black's linguistic research has proved rich for analysing the *longue durée* of the Nunes River region, but such methods cannot analyse detailed decade-by-decade changes such as this work attempts.[100] This is not a situation confined to Western Africa. Some decades ago Miller noted for the Imbangala and Mbundu of West-Central Africa (present-day Angola) that oral traditions for the sixteenth and seventeenth centuries have little to say about individuals and rather deal largely with institutional changes.[101] It is of course possible to use oral information to recover some aspects of the distant past, if not its year-by-year details, and where possible I have done so, but this approach could not serve as a replacement for written information.

This book is the first in an anticipated two volumes dealing with the trajectories of West African societies and the trans-Atlantic slave trade

[96] Mendes (2007: 60): "*les sources produites par le colon portugais ne doivent pas être machinalement invalidées au titre d'un européo-centrisme, il faut les replacer dans leur contexte et poser leur fallibilité*".

[97] Wright (1991); Mark (1985: 2).

[98] Quinn (1972: xvii); Wright (1991: 401–3).

[99] Baum (1999); Hawthorne (2003).

[100] Fields-Black (2009).

[101] Miller (1976a: 12).

between 1300 and 1700. This first volume commences circa 1300, with the Mandinka expansion into Upper Guinea and Senegambia, and ends in 1589. This date marks an important moment with the construction of the Portuguese fort at Cacheu, a move which followed the first in a series of terrible droughts afflicting Cabo Verde between 1580 and 1610. This building project was undertaken by Caboverdeans fleeing famine and migrating to the coast, bringing with them their Kriolu language and implanting it as a vernacular in the Cacheu region, which was subsequently taken across the Atlantic to form the kernel of the Papiamentu Creole of Curaçao.[102] Hereafter, although the trans-Atlantic slave trade remained important in Western Africa, the main accent moved gradually to West-Central Africa. This was therefore a watershed in the history of the region's creolisation and of the Atlantic slave trade as a whole, and thus marks an appropriate point to end the volume.

The book is divided into two parts. Part 1 is a regional history of the emergence of creolisation in Western Africa (1300–1550), throughout which the importance of Atlantic slavery and slave production is emphasised, and the socio-cultural context for the commercial networks which facilitated the rise of the trans-Atlantic slave trade is elucidated. Here we see how the pre-Atlantic relationship between Upper Guineans and Mandinka rulers shaped attitudes of cultural accommodation and receptivity to diaspora traders (Chapter 1); how this history influenced the first exchanges between Africans and Europeans in the second half of the fifteenth century (Chapter 2); how this was in turn influenced by the settlement of Cabo Verde and the development of regional networks and identities spanning these islands and the coast (Chapter 3); how this picture was then affected by the arrival of the New Christian diaspora in the early sixteenth century (Chapter 4); and how all this led to the emergence of an alliance between New Christians and the Kassanké of Casamance, which accompanied something like a creolised situation in parts of Western Africa by around 1550 (Chapter 5).

Part 2 spans the years 1492–1589 and integrates this regional history with wider global factors involving the Atlantic world. This half of the book deals in detail with both the trans-Atlantic slave trade and its cultural, political and social consequences in Western Africa. We see both how the emergence of creolisation in Western Africa influenced the Atlantic world and also how Atlantic factors in turn affected events in Western Africa. Part 2 shows how the "pan-Atlantic" emerged early and

---

[102] The exciting new evidence for this is detailed in Jacobs (2009; 2010) and Quint (2000).

how extensive the trans-Atlantic trade was by the 1540s (Chapter 6); how there was an explosion in contraband in the slave trade and the intensification of pan-Atlantic connections in the second half of the sixteenth century (Chapter 7); how these events influenced cycles of war and trade in Western Africa (Chapter 8); and how the emergence of a "Creole" identity in the late-sixteenth-century in Western Africa was therefore the result of this fusion of local and global forces related to the birth of the trans-Atlantic slave trade in the sixteenth century (Chapter 9).

The book thus offers a thematic structure around a broadly chronological base, allowing us to see how creolisation and slavery were connected. By integrating the regional development of creolisation in Western Africa with global forces, the shape of the book illustrates one of its key points: that the emergence of what we may call world historical connections in the sixteenth century was a consequence of the interaction of analogous local and global forces on all sides of the Atlantic world. This structure indeed shows how events in Western Africa served, in part, as a prototype for what followed.[103] For not only was this the first locale of Atlantic creolisation, but Cabo Verde, together with São Tomé, formed the first locale in which slavery ceased to be multi-racial, as had always hitherto been the case in Europe and North Africa.[104]

We cannot shirk this history. As Patrick Manning suggests, "the influence of slavery has extended beyond the economy to transform human emotions and trouble the human spirit".[105] What are we to make of the fact that in the 1970s, in the Douala region of Cameroon, informants of the French priest De Rosny still dreamt of being led off by strangers, their hands tied, to the sea?[106] Is it a coincidence that the word long used in English to describe slavery, "bondage", now refers to a form of sexual fetish involving forced restraint and whipping?[107] Such questions force us to confront the enormity of these issues and the deep-rooted influences they may still have on the psychological and physical reality of being alive today.

[103] T. Hall, (1992: Vol. 1, 48).
[104] Ibid., Vol. 2, 632.
[105] Manning (1990: 1).
[106] Cit. Argenti (2007: 106).
[107] This relates to the work of the Brazilian sociologist Gilberto Freyre, who believed that the dynamics brought about by master-slave relations decisively affected Brazilian sexuality. See Sweet (2003: 66).

PART ONE

THE DEVELOPMENT OF AN ATLANTIC CREOLE CULTURE IN WESTERN AFRICA, CIRCA 1300–1550

Culture, Trade and Diaspora in Pre-Atlantic Western Africa

Western Africa is a region marginalised in the world's geopolitics. Yet it was not always so. The coast stretching from the baobab-sprinkled scrubland by the Senegal River down to the creeks and forests of Sierra Leone saw exchanges between Africans and Europeans in the fifteenth century which formed a prototype for the relationships between European imperial emissaries and others that have defined so much subsequent world history.

The cultural world established in Western Africa at the time of these exchanges did not spring from nothing. Rather, it developed from antecedents which had shaped fifteenth-century societies on the Upper Guinean coast. By the 1440s, this was a region where already for several centuries there had been a tradition of accommodation to the presence of powerful and at times violent outsiders who represented the commercial and political interests of the empire of Mali.

To understand the historical picture which emerged by the fifteenth century, it is important to know something of the different groups which lived there at this time. There were two main geographical sub-regions of continental Western Africa. To the north, the Senegambian region between the Senegal and Gambia Rivers was Sahelian in character. The land was dry. The Jolof lived in the interior to the north, the Mandinka settlements were along the Gambia River, and the Sereer inhabited the creeks of the Saluum delta along the coastline north of the Gambia. Some way inland along the Senegal River, the Pullo established themselves at Fuuta Tooro in the late fifteenth century: The Pullo migrated in search of pastures for their cattle and were also to be found in number throughout the region. Because there were no tsetse flies communicating sleeping

MAP 2. Map of Peoples and Cultures in Upper Guinea, and the Zones of Their Territories.

sickness, horses and cattle were able to live there. In general, this was an area of fairly centralised polities. By the time of the Portuguese arrival in the fifteenth century, the Jolof polity consisted of five sub-kingdoms, each with a viceroy, whereas the Mandinka presence operated as an arm of the powerful trading empire of Mali.

To the south of the Gambia River lay a more fertile forested area that stretched south to Sierra Leone, generally known as Upper Guinea. In contrast to the Senegambian region, this area was characterised by smaller-scale, decentralised political units that flourished in an area of marshland and swamps, which made centralised control hard to impose. Tsetse flies were found south of the Casamance River, which made cattle-raising and maintaining cavalry difficult. All this made political units smaller and contributed to an area of great human and political complexity. "In less than twenty leagues [approximately 100 kilometres] there are two or three nations [to be found]", Almada wrote in the 1590s.[1] There were numerous small polities in the coastal regions of present-day Guinea-Bissau, and their oral histories describe migration from regions farther inland following the Mandinka expansion of the thirteenth century. Among the more important groups were the Bainunk-Kassanké, Balanta, Biafada, Bijagó, Brame, Cocoli, Floup, Landuma, and the Nalu. However, in spite of the difficulties of centralised control, the Mandinka related to Mali exercised hegemony over some of the groups living there, who as a consequence exhibited some acculturation to the Mandinka and also shared some cultural and productive practices. Inland from the coast, occupying much of the plateau inland from the coastal belt that straddles the borders of present-day Gambia, Guinea-Bissau and Senegal, was the Kaabu federation, a loose-knit collection of Mandinka states which asserted independence from Mali in the late fifteenth century. South of the borders of present-day Guinea-Bissau lived numerous groups, including the Baga, Jalonké and Volón, who intermingled with the Mandinguised Susu and the lineages of Sierra Leone called Sape by the Portuguese.

This chapter examines the relationships that these peoples had both with one another and with the Mandinka in the centuries preceding the creation of the Atlantic world. It underlines the role of trans-Saharan trading diasporas in aspects of commercial and cultural practice in Senegambia and Upper Guinea in this era, and suggests that this pattern was significant when European mariners arrived, assisting in the

---

[1] On tsetse fly distribution, see Fields-Black (2009: 45–6); for Almada, see MMAII: Vol. 3, 231.

formation of communities vital to the success of early trans-Atlantic trade. Its primary contribution to the historiography is to foreground the role diasporas had in the historical process in Western Africa and to connect this pattern to subsequent developments in the early Atlantic era. However, although I place the role of diasporas within the political paradigm of the Mali empire, I am also wary of understanding this era through what might be called an imperial straitjacket; the personal connections and shared values of diaspora networks were, as this chapter and book show, just as significant as the policies of centralised powers in shaping patterns of change in the late medieval and early Atlantic eras.

The pattern linking Senegambia and Upper Guinea to Mali dates to the latter half of the thirteenth century. The social situation which developed then in Upper Guinea has been called "primary creolisation".[2] Although we should recognise that this era offered a very different historical context to that in which Atlantic creolisation occurred, there are certain shared characteristics which make this term a useful comparator, particularly when trying to see how events in pre-Atlantic Africa may have influenced the early Atlantic. By looking at this primary creolisation, this chapter shows that analysis of the Atlantic Creole world in Western Africa must acknowledge the influence of this preceding history.[3]

In writing this pre-Atlantic history there are methodological problems. Direct written sources are scant. While one or two historians have reconstructed elements of pre-fifteenth-century history through mixing oral and written traditions or through ethno-linguistics, this is a notoriously difficult enterprise; and as we saw in the Introduction, some historians doubt that detailed histories of this type can be constructed.[4] Moreover, such written sources as do exist are problematic. Most were written between the eleventh and fourteenth centuries by Islamic scholars for whom, as Paulo Farias argues, the lands of the Sahel were simultaneously objects of desire and dread.[5] Thus these sources do not offer objective accounts of Sahelian societies. Meanwhile, fifteenth-century Portuguese accounts

---

[2] For the term "primary creolization", see Trajano Filho (2003: 13–4).

[3] This role of Western Africa's earlier history is touched on in Mark/Horta (2005: 48–50). On landlord-stranger relationships, see Brooks (1993b).

[4] The unquestioned exceptions are Boulègue (1987a) and Fields-Black (2009); even here, though, the detail for pre-fifteenth-century events is limited.

[5] Farias (2003: cxv). See also Farias (1974) on the silent trade as a myth exposing this sort of dread: The attractiveness of the myth of dumb barter was that one did not actually have to engage with these "others" in order to reap great profits from their lands through the trade in gold. See CEA 21, 28 and 29 for accounts from the tenth and eleventh centuries by Arab scholars of the gold of Ghāna.

of Mali may well have been projections of the Portuguese intuition about their own power and authority rather than an objective account of power relations.[6] Archaeological evidence can be helpful in constructing patterns, but the best that can be developed is a general overview.

Rather than offering a detailed chronological account, therefore, this chapter presents a wider pattern. Although oral sources may not be reliable on specifics, they help to understand fluxes of migration and exchange. The extensive collection of oral histories held in Fajara by the National Council of Arts and Culture of The Gambia offers an important window onto these processes. They can be blended with such written sources as we do have and help in developing persuasive hypotheses. This chapter therefore synthesises these oral traditions, other published oral accounts, and ethno-linguistic considerations with these written sources, coupled with oral traditions from my own interviews. The resulting analysis works towards an explanatory paradigm for social change along the Western African littoral prior to the Atlantic era.

DIASPORAS OF COMMERCE AND RELIGION: GHĀNA, MALI AND THE MANDINKA EXPANSION OF THE THIRTEENTH CENTURY

"We originated from Tumbuktu in the land of the Mandinka: the Arabs were our neighbours there ... All the Mandinka of the West came from Mali to Kaabu".[7]

Thus begins the *Ta:rikh Mandinka de Bijini*, a source from a village near Bafatá in present-day Guinea-Bissau. As with this text, all known oral traditions there describe the arrival of the Mandinka in Upper Guinea from the east and their formation of the kingdom of Kaabu in the plateau between the Fouta Djalon mountains and the creeks and forests of the coast. This expansion is said to have begun in the second half of the thirteenth century.

Mandinka expansion into Upper Guinea and Senegambia had far-reaching consequences. After a century or more of fragmentation following the collapse of the empire of Ghāna in the mid-eleventh century, Mandinka power was consolidated into the empire of Mali under the rule of Sunjata Keita (*fl.*1235).[8] There then followed the migration

---

[6] Horta (2000: 116).

[7] Giesing/Vydrine (2007: 51): "*Nous sommes originaires de Tumbuktu dans le pays des Mandinka: les Arabes y étaient nos voisins ... Tous les Mandinka de l'Ouest sont venus du Mali jusqu'au Kaabu*".

[8] On the likely historical existence of Sunjata, see Wilks (1999: 47, 53).

of Mandinka into Kaabu under Sunjata's general, Tiramaghan Traore, with the intimate connection of Kaabu to Mali indicated by the fact that "Kabou" means "region" in the Soninké spoken by the migrants.[9] Mandinka influence near the coast thus post-dates the middle of the thirteenth century, although it had probably been preceded by the arrival of smiths and traders. Between 1100 and 1500 there was a dry period which saw geographical boundaries shift, and this may have encouraged the migration of smiths who possessed important ritual power for Mande peoples.[10] According to some accounts, the smiths went first to prospect new gold deposits with their iron manufactures and were followed by traders connecting this product to the caravans of the Sahara.[11] Some oral traditions indeed recall that there were Mandinka already living in the Kaabu region when Tiramaghan's followers arrived.[12] The Mandinka smiths formed new ritual power associations. Their arrival in increasing numbers may have enabled the consolidation of Mali's power in the region. Although it is important to recognise that the evidence for this movement of smiths is scant and debated, the importance of smiths to the gold trade and political power in Upper Guinea may be reflected in the widespread oral traditions that hold that the Mandinguised Bainunk king Gana Sira Bana always sat on a gold chair.[13]

The renewed Mande unity which accompanied the rise of Mali and the migration of smiths to areas such as Upper Guinea may have been a response both to the changing climatic conditions and to the increasing importance of the trans-Saharan trade, which most accounts see as beginning to flourish in the tenth century, and which expanded rapidly from the late eleventh century onwards.[14] It was the trans-Saharan trade that allowed connections between the gold fields of Upper Guinea, the Bambuk uplands in the foothills of the Fouta Djalon to the south, and Mediterranean products to the north; these connections were provided

[9] Ba (1981: 23–4).
[10] Brooks (1993b: Appendix A) established this climatic periodisation; see also Fields-Black (2009: 91–2). On the ritual power of Mande smiths, see McNaughton (1988). Hawthorne (2003: 31), like Brooks, sees smiths and merchants leading this migration as due to the dry period. However, Colleen Kriger (1999: 9) suggests that the evidence for this passage of the smiths southwards is limited to a projection from twentieth-century ethnographic research and is very hard to prove.
[11] Brooks (1993b: 46–51).
[12] NCAC/OHAD, Cassette Transcription 466B, page 56.
[13] According to an oral tradition which I collected from a Balanta elder in Simbandi-Balante, Casamance, in March 2000; confirmed subsequently from an interview with Seydhou Fall in Goudomp, Casamance, in April 2011.
[14] Nixon (2009: 220).

through the itinerant Mandinka traders known as the *dyula*. The growing strength of the smiths reflected an increase in trade and demand for
gold. However, gold was not the only commodity in demand, and this
expansion cannot have been entirely separated from the trans-Saharan
slavery which accompanied the gold trade; indeed Meillassoux suggests
that Mandinka unity against brigandage and this slave trade was also
important to the rise of Mali.[15]

However, it is difficult today to say how relevant the trans-Saharan
slave trade was to the relationships which Mandinka smiths may have
had with Upper Guineans. Some oral traditions do suggest a connection,
with Tiramaghan Traore's success in the eyes of Sunjata being proved
when he arrived at the latter's court with "countless slaves" following a
war against the Jolof.[16] As this account suggests, considerable violence
must have accompanied the selling of slaves into the trans-Saharan trade.
This violence may well have affected smaller political units in areas such
as Upper Guinea, whereas Mande unity against this problem may have
been a factor in political developments.[17] Yet admitting this is not the
same thing as declaring that this practice of slavery involved people selling
members of their own lineage, which is Meillassoux's suggestion. Some
historians have cast doubt on this account, interpreting it instead as a projection of nineteenth-century slave-raiding history among the Mandinka
onto the foundational myths of the Mandinka past – something which
may confirm the difficulties of using oral histories as guides to such distant events.[18]

Instead of seeking certainty, therefore, we must trace general patterns.
Clearly, the rise of Mandinka power in the Sahel and their influence in
Upper Guinea was contemporaneous with the expansion of the trans-
Saharan trade following the eleventh century. This coincidence was probably significant. Moreover, because the selling of people into slavery was a
significant part of that trade, the direction and channelling of the violence
associated with trans-Saharan slavery, together with the mining activities
and ritual power which the Mande smiths accrued in new territories, may
have been important to Mali's influence in Upper Guinea.[19] The empire

[15] Meillassoux (1991: 143–7).
[16] NCAC/OHAD, Cassette transcription 566, page 11.
[17] On the importance of the trans-Saharan slave trade to Ghāna and Tekrur, see Bovill
(1958: 83–4); Lydon (2009: 58).
[18] Farias (2007: 295).
[19] Ibn Battuta's 14th-century account is clear on the large numbers of slaves in Mali – CEA,
304–5.

of Mali formed under Sunjata Keita thus filled a power vacuum that had emerged in the Sahel following the demise of Ghāna; it began to influence peoples in Upper Guinea through its increasing power, and it did so as trans-Saharan connections intensified.

In this picture, the place of religion and religious trading diasporas in the Sahel is important.[20] Ghislaine Lydon has argued that the activities of trans-Saharan traders were structured and organised through Moslem religious practice.[21] As Curtin saw, this Islamic religious practice could have both an exclusivist and a proselytising character. It was important for members of the initial trading communities to secure conversions among their host communities, but in time the adoption of an exclusive and distinctive religious practice also became important to maintaining the corporate identity of the trading communities.[22] How this worked in practice can be traced through the trajectories of the trading polities such as Ghāna and Mali, which influenced areas like Upper Guinea through their demand for the region's products.

Ghāna's wealth had been founded on its gold and the trade with Islamic merchants from North Africa that this produced. One of the consequences of this trade was the emergence of a complex approach to Islam in Ghāna. Prior to the adoption of Islam, under pressure from the Almoravids in 1076–7, the capital was divided into two towns, one of which was Moslem and one of which was not (although it contained a mosque).[23] Moreover, although the king himself was not Moslem, many of his advisers were.[24] Islam was thus influential and important in Ghāna, but it was not a state religion. Until the 1076–7 conversion in Ghāna, the influence of Islam was exerted through trading diasporas and acculturation.[25]

In these circumstances, the character of the Islamic faith practised in sub-Saharan Africa was distinctive. Far from being simply North African

---

[20] Ibn Battuta suggested that Sunjata Keita converted to Islam at the same time as founding Mali (ibid., 295). However Bovill (1958: 86) places the conversion of Mande leaders to Islam to the early twelfth century (cf. also below in this chapter, for oral data to support this latter view).

[21] Lydon (2009: 3).

[22] Curtin (1984: 49).

[23] One of the best sources for the rise of the Almoravids is Al-Bakri, (CEA: 70–3). See ibid., 98, on the adoption of Islam. Ibn Abī Zar' (ibid., 235–48) also discusses the Almoravids. For the division of Ghāna's capital into an Islamic and a non-Islamic town see ibid., 79–80 – the account of Al Bakri; recent archaeological finds would suggest that a similar pattern pertained at Djenné in present-day Mali.

[24] Ibid., 80.

[25] Farias (2003: cxix–cxxi).

expatriate centres, trading settlements tended to be mixed.[26] There was a definite space for the old non-Islamic religious traditions, and indeed the strategy adopted by Islamic trading diasporas of incorporating aspects of their host cultures into their practices was integral to their success.[27] A certain cultural and religious interchange became inevitable, and this history was decisive in the way that members of long-distance and outsider trading diasporas were viewed in West Africa.

In spite of this hybridised religious practice, however, Islam was key to the expansion of trade and political centralisation. As Lydon has argued, Islam's promotion of literacy was key to the ability of merchants to draw contractual agreements and dispatch commercial letters.[28] Such activities were far from being confined to groups of itinerant North Africans. Mandinka were swift adherents to Islam after the collapse of Ghāna, making the religion part of their spiritual and cultic practices without erasing all older beliefs and rituals. The religion's spread from Ghāna was rapid, with oral traditions putting the arrival of Islamic Mandinka in the Gambia at the mid-twelfth century.[29] Islam was essential to the acceptance of the Mandinka by diaspora traders from North Africa whose commerce brought so much power and wealth. Its adoption by the Mande ruling caste reflected the growth of plural identities among ruling circles, where one (Islamic) religious face was presented to members of this powerful trading diaspora and another (hybrid) ritual face was presented to populations at home. This strategy cemented the place of cultural flexibility as an important strategy of power brokering in the Sahel.

The centrality of this nuanced approach to Islam to the rise of Mali emerges in the foundational myth of the empire of Sunjata Keita. Over the next two generations following the arrival of Islam in the Gambia region circa 1150, Mande peoples forged the empire of Mali, some of them claiming descent from Bilāl Ibn Rabāh, Mohammed's Black companion and the first Muezzin of Islam.[30] Such claims, incorporated in the epic of Sunjata, provided an orthodox Islamic heritage and revealed the importance of Islam to Mali's ideology; and yet even here this Islamic

---

[26] Nixon (2009: 220 and 244). Nixon's excavations at Essouk-Tadmakka in northeastern Mali show that this important trading settlement also contained a mixed community of Islamic and non-Islamic traders.

[27] Farias's (1999) analysis of the Gesere praisesingers in the Borgu and their incorporation of Islamic and non-Islamic dating for the practices of some ceremonies is revelatory here; on his analysis, this dates to the sixteenth century.

[28] Lydon (2009: 3).

[29] Cissoko/Sambou (1974: 111–15).

[30] Levtzion (1980: 54–5).

idiom co-existed with local cultural forms and the idea of occult power.[31] Although visitors from North Africa such as Ibn Battuta saw a blending of Islamic and non-Islamic forms in the practices he observed, religious traditions in West Africa are open to co-existence of different spirit shrines and practices, and such co-existence reflects a plural approach to religion, such as that suggested by the strategy of the Mande ruling caste, rather than necessarily a blending.

On this interpretation, the rise of the Almoravids in the mid-eleventh century led to important cultural and political changes in the Sahelian region. Historians have long held that there were material effects also, because the flow of gold and slaves from the Sahara northwards rapidly increased, doubtless facilitated by the Almoravid presence in Morocco and Spain.[32] The Almoravid rise in the southern Sahara coincided with the fall of the Soninké empire of Ghāna, where African religions predominated, and the Soninké dispersal into fragmented states.[33] As it was the Islamic Almoravids who oversaw the Saharan trade from then on, it is apparent that successful trade in the Sahelian region was connected to contact with the Islamic world.[34] To underline this, the Almoravids appear to have cut out important and culturally mixed trading centres on the southern fringes of the Sahara, such as Tadmakka and Tegdaoust, and established their own centres farther south.[35] Fervent religious belief and messianic zeal were ever the companions to ruthless trade in medieval West Africa, as they would be later in the sixteenth-century Atlantic world.[36]

Yet this connection of proselytising Islam and the growth of the trans-Saharan trade was particular to this phase of Sahelian history. Subsequently, the emperors of Mali did not proselytise producers of gold.[37] This gold production depended on the smiths associated with

[31] For an analysis of how the Sunjata epic is syncretic of the Islamic concept of grace laced with power and the Mande concept of occult power, see J. Johnson (1999: 18). Interestingly, such strategies are used by other groups today to claim an orthodox Islamic heritage. Some Bainunk claim that the first Bainunk came from a quarter of Mecca called Baynounka – from an interview with Ansumane Manga in Singuère, Casamance, April 2011.

[32] Levtzion (1980: 41); Lydon (2009: 72); Nixon (2009: 248–9).

[33] Levtzion (1980: 45–7).

[34] On the connection between the rise of the Almoravids and the collapse of Ghāna, see Mota (1954: Vol. 1, 135). On the Almoravids, see Farias (1967).

[35] Nixon (2009: 249).

[36] Or as Subrahmanyan (1993: 49) puts it: "[T]hose who were so religiously motivated could often be equally the persons in whose breasts the most fervently mercantilist spirit resided".

[37] See for instance the account of Ibn al-Dawādārī (CEA, 250). Mansa Musa, on his famous pilgrimage to Mecca in 1324–5, recounted in Cairo that whenever they had tried to conquer the land where the gold was produced, the gold production had disappeared.

the practice of non-Islamic rituals and cultic practices, whose influence was, as we have seen, already significant in Upper Guinea. These rituals were probably related to the actual production and mining of gold, and thus Mali could not insist on the conversion to Islam of miners or smiths and preferred receiving gold in the form of tribute payments. This attitude towards non-Moslems was an acknowledgement of the complex ritual and religious situation of the Sahel and of the co-existence of both the exclusivist and proselytising versions of Islam in the region; it was an expression of the plural cultural outlook that was one of the consequences of the arrival of diaspora merchants from North Africa.

Following the expansion of trade under the Almoravids in the twelfth century, a strong imperial force emerged in the Sahel in the thirteenth century as Mali was founded. Trade and religion were the keystones to new Mande power. Diasporas of "outsider" merchants who were distinguished by their difference from the predominant religio-cultural practices of the Sahel were thus an important feature of this period. It was indeed precisely the distinctiveness of these diaspora communities that was most important, for it was this which allowed them to act as cultural go-betweens bridging the Sahara; as Curtin noted, without this difference, the capacity for diaspora traders to act as cross-cultural brokers vanished.[38]

Such connections spread. The diaspora of Wangara merchants linked areas such as Gao, in the far east of present-day Mali, with the Borgu (borderlands of present-day Niger and Nigeria) from perhaps the late thirteenth century until the rise of the Songhay empire in the late fifteenth century. Indeed, the strength of the Wangara diaspora may have influenced the rise of Songhay.[39] The importance of diaspora merchants to the caravan trade emerges in the fact that the very gold fields which underpinned the trans-Saharan trade were thought by North African traders to lie in a land called "Wangara".[40]

The importance of the Wangara who operated within Mali illustrates the commercial orientation of the empire and shows how a strong connection had developed in West Africa between long-distance trading diasporas and religious belief. This connection is underscored by the fact that Jews residing in North Africa and the Saharan oases were also

[38] Curtin (1984: 38).
[39] Farias (1996: 263); idem., (2003: clxxii); Lydon (2009: 64–5).
[40] Bovill (1958: 67).

important long-distance traders in the caravan trade. The cloths made by teams of Jewish weavers in North Africa were an important product in the trans-Saharan trade, and both Jews and their Islamic counterparts developed what Lydon calls a "paper economy of faith".[41] The interconnection of diasporas of religion and trade would prove greatly significant when a new long-distance mercantile diaspora, that of the New Christians, arrived in the region in the sixteenth century.[42]

As the Almoravids pushed the sites for the main trading settlements related to the Saharan trade farther south, these developments came to affect the communities that lived in Upper Guinea, and thus this interconnection of religion and long-distance trade became significant there. However, in contrast to their kin in Mali, the Mandinka who arrived in Kaabu in the thirteenth century, following the smiths, retained the old non-Islamic rites.[43] Indeed, some oral traditions hold that the founder of Kaabu, Tiramaghan, only left Mali when it adopted Islam.[44] Other traditions, meanwhile, give Tiramaghan himself an orthodox Islamic heritage, claiming fancifully that he married Mohammed's grand-daughter.[45] Such divergences suggest that Islam was a complex factor in the formation of Kaabu, and could have been a faultline of sorts between the peoples of Kaabu and Mali. This is also implied by Sereer oral traditions, which, according to Henri Gravrand, suggest that the migration of Guelwaar princes from Kaabu to the Siin region north of the Gambia river occurred circa 1335–40, following the Battle of Trubang in which the issue of religion may have been a trigger.[46]

However, as we have seen here, Islam was not as purely observed in West Africa as such a polarising narrative might suggest. It may well be that one of the major differences between Kaabu and Mali was not so much ritual – though this undoubtedly must have been important – as commercial, given the connections we have seen between Islam and long-distance trading diasporas. For while the Soninké of Kaabu remained

[41] Lydon (2009: 3); Lydon even talks of a "Jewish era in the Sahara" (ibid., 69). On the Jewish clothmakers and the trans-Saharan trade see Prussin (2006: 333, 344–5).

[42] On the role of religion in African trading diasporas, see Farias (1996) and Lovejoy (1978) for the fifteenth and sixteenth centuries and A. Cohen (1969; 1971) for more recent manifestations.

[43] Thus Niane (1989: 12) concurs with the seventeenth century French traveller Jajolet de la Courbe, who called Kaabu a pagan kingdom. However by the seventeenth century it was very tolerant of Islamic *dyula* traders – this tolerance may itself have been because the *dyula* themselves leavened their Islam with non-Islamic rituals.

[44] For this version see Niane (1989: 19 n7).

[45] NCAC/OHAD, Transcribed Cassette 020, page 16.

[46] Gravrand (1981: 50).

animist, the traders were Islamic, as in Mali.[47] Thus the trigger of the battle of Trubang could just as easily have been commercial as religious. It may, therefore, have been the connection of religion to trade which was the source both of the cohesion of Mali in the thirteenth century and of the differences which developed between Kaabu and Mali.

Following the rapid expansion of the Mandinka under Sunjata Keita during the thirteenth century, matters had stabilised by around 1300. By that time, political and cultural influence from Mali was strong on the Atlantic coast. Writing in the second half of the fourteenth century, Syrian-born historian Al 'Umari referred to "Takrur" – the lower valley of the Senegal River – as being under the control of Mali.[48] In his passage through Cairo in 1324–5, Mansa Musa, emperor of Mali, told how his empire stretched to the Atlantic.[49] Linguistic evidence confirms Mandinka influence at this time among the Jolof of Senegambia, because the Mandinka word *fará* was used to designate numerous dignitaries.[50] Oral traditions of the Balanta suggest raids also dating from this era on their coastal villages by Mandinka horse warriors.[51] Although these raids did not lead to direct political control, they expressed the potential of Mandinka power. Thus in the coastal regions of Casamance and present-day Guinea-Bissau, although decentralised polities of the mangrove creeks and channels of the coast were never subordinate to the Mandinka and retained their own structures of authority, Mandinka power from Mali was always proximate.[52] Such traditions illuminate how the expansion of Mali allowed Mandinka in Upper Guinea to develop a sort of hegemony in the area.

Mali's influence spread from the Lower Senegal as far south as the area occupied by the Biafada, near the Rio Grande in present-day Guinea-Bissau. That this was the southern limit of Mandinka influence is shown by the fact that when the Italian sailor Alvise de Cadamosto arrived there in 1456, he was unable to find a common language.[53] Writing in the first

---

[47] Person (1981: 63).

[48] CEA, 261–2; Boulègue (1987a: 44). This observation must not be taken as definitive, because Islamic scholars frequently referred to "Mali" as "Takrur" in their texts.

[49] CEA, 267

[50] Boulègue (1987a: 45).

[51] Personal communication from José Lingna Nafafé.

[52] Hawthorne (2010b: Ch 2) explicates the interplay of Mandinka elites in the interior plateau region of Guinea-Bissau and their relationship with coastal peoples.

[53] Hair (1966: 14–5). Hair suggests that the common language between the first Portuguese sailors and the peoples of Senegambia and Upper Guinea was Arabic. Some Portuguese sailors would have spoken Arabic following the long history of Islamisation of Iberia, and the Mandinka *dyula* traders brought Arabic into the towns in which they traded.

decade of the sixteenth century, Duarte Pacheco Pereira noted that the Biafada were subordinate to the "king of the Mandinkas" and suggested that many of them were Moslems.[54] Writing at about the same time, Valentim Fernandes described how the peoples of this river were subject to Mali and observed that most rulers in the area were Moslem.[55] By contrast, south of this region the influence of Sape lineages was stronger, and writing towards the end of the sixteenth century, Almada noted how the Nalu, immediately to the south of the Biafada, were very different to them "in language and clothing and everything else".[56] The source of these differences may have related to the absence of Mandinka influence, and from what we have seen here this was a pattern which had developed some time before.

However, although there was little political influence from the Mandinka south of Biafada territory, there were connections between this region and Mali. Similar crops were grown in Sierra Leone under the Sape lineages as in the Mandinka-influenced areas of the Grande – rice and millet – and the iron used to produce tools to clear mangrove swamps was produced by Mande groups.[57] There was much iron in Sierra Leone among the Mande Susu people, and this was likely produced by analogous associations of smiths as those we have seen farther north.[58] Iron was also found on the coast of present-day Guinea-Conakry, but it was brittle and of inferior quality to that produced by the Mandinka smiths, which was probably sought after and may have been exchanged in small quantities in markets.[59] Biafada markets were famous, and

Moreover both Portuguese and the languages of Senegambia and Upper Guinea contained words of Arabic origin. The absence of a common language in the Rio Grande region demonstrates that this was the limit of the Mandinka influence.

[54] MMAII: Vol. 1, 648: "*sujeitos a el-rei dos Mandinkas*". Brooks (1993b: 260) suggests that this was an error and true only of the *dyula* traders encountered by his informants.

[55] MMAII, Vol. 1, 721.

[56] For Fernandes on the Sapes, see ibid., Vol. 1, 722; for Almada on the Nalu, see ibid., Vol. 3, 339 – "*são mui diferentes no linguagem e no trajo e no mais*".

[57] Ibid., Vol. 1, 648, 656. Pacheco Pereira says that the Sapes and Cocolis in this area were subject to Mandinka hegemony and grew these crops.

[58] On the iron among the Susu, see Pacheco Pereira (ibid., Vol. 1, 655); Fernandes also noted the large amounts of iron in Sierra Leone in the fifteenth century (ibid., Vol. 1, 734). Fields-Black (2009: 145–54) shows decisively that Susu iron technology was important to Nalu and Baga peoples in their agriculture from the fifteenth century onwards; she disputes, however, that such tools were always imperative to rice production, but holds that they were in widespread use by 1500.

[59] Fernandes describes the brittle iron produced north of Sierra Leone – MMAII: Vol. 1, 722. Fields-Black (2009: 99) shows that iron was known by the distant ancestors of fifteenth-century Baga, Sape and Temne peoples, but as local knowledge was apparently supplanted by Susu smiths this would seem to confirm Fernandes's account here.

as markets are often in border areas, it was probably here that these exchanges occurred.[60]

What emerges from this picture of Mandinka expansion is therefore a complex mosaic of influences. The formation of a strong Mandinka power in the mid-thirteenth century was related both to the expansion of the trans-Saharan trade in gold and slaves and the rise of Islam in the Sahel. By the fourteenth century the political power of Mali stretched to the lower Senegal valley, and by the fifteenth century (and perhaps earlier) as far south as present-day Guinea-Bissau. Cultural influences accompanied the spread of political power, and Mandinka words entered the languages of the Jolof around the Senegal valley. Religion also acted as a vector of political and commercial acculturation; embedded Mandinka cultural influences, with Arabic vocabulary accompanying Mandinka into the languages of Upper Guinea, were testament not only to the spread of the Mandinka, but also to the acculturation which the Mandinka themselves had displayed towards the diaspora merchants from North Africa. The power of the Mandinka and of their shared outsider religion was expressed through the growing ritual significance of amulets made by itinerant scholar-traders by using Islamic script, which were known as *gris-gris* and were used throughout Upper Guinea.[61]

Thus several interlocking factors were at work. The formation of Mali, the expansion of trade, the presence of diaspora merchants professing an outsider religion, and the growth of that religion itself were all interconnected. This meant that the ritual power associations formed by the smiths who produced the iron used to work the gold deposits were deeply connected to the expansion of trans-Saharan trade. For it was the increasing demand for gold which enhanced the smiths' power and influence in the economy of Mali as a whole and, perhaps, thereby helped to enhance the reputation of their power associations and magical powers in Upper Guinea.[62] Who else but people with extremely powerful magical aides could withstand the pressure of the emperor of Mali to adopt Islam, when Islamic adherents themselves were increasingly perceived as holders of strong occult powers?

Two consequences of great importance emerged from this constellation of factors. The first was the way in which economic utility and power

---

[60] I am grateful to Olukoya Ogen of Osun State University for this point.

[61] Green (2001). On the prevalence of these gris-gris in the late fifteenth century, see HGCV: CD, Vol. 1, 123.

[62] For the role of gold in the medieval Mediterranean economies, see Godinho (1969: 101–33).

became associated with ritual power in Upper Guinea, something which, as Baum has shown among the Diola of the Basse Casamance, was a connection that continued throughout the Atlantic era.[63] A second and equally long-lasting effect of this pattern was the emerging importance of diasporas in the mercantile culture of West Africa and the strong connection which diaspora members had to new or foreign religions. Under these conditions, membership of an alien religion such as Islam, far from being a handicap, was a trading advantage. Yet the process of cultural accommodation flowed in two directions, as aspects of the diasporic trading religion themselves were influenced by local ritual practices, and it was this complex interplay of reciprocal cultural influences from both host and guest cultures which was to be of fundamental importance when the first Atlantic traders began to arrive.

ACCOMMODATION AND EXPANSION
IN THE FORMATION OF KAABU

The relationship of commercial and cultural accommodation which developed between members of North African trading diasporas and West African rulers and their peoples continued in the thirteenth century. It was transferred with the Mandinka migration towards the Atlantic coast and the formation of Kaabu. Kaabu was the most important polity of the pre-colonial era in Upper Guinea. In time, it grew into a large federal structure spreading from the southern Gambia River states to the Grande River and across the plateau between the coastal lowlands and the Fouta Djalon mountains. Its heartland was between the Upper Casamance, around the present-day town of Vélingara, and the northeastern reaches of present-day Guinea-Bissau. It was here that its capital, Kansala, was located.

Many different peoples co-existed in this zone. The creeks and forests of the coast were impossible to subdue because of the difficulty of using mounted armies there. They were populated by groups whose oral histories recount their movement from further inland in part as a response to the Mandinka migrations. According to oral traditions, at the time of the Mandinka arrival in Kaabu in the thirteenth century, the land in the creeks and forests of what is today Guinea-Bissau was all bush.[64] Some

---

[63] Baum (1999) illustrates how certain shrines among the Diola of the Casamance emerged in response to the trans-Atlantic slave trade.

[64] NCAC/OHAD, Transcribed Cassette 566, page 11; Transcribed Casstte 491B, page 6. Confirmed also in an oral interview with Antonio da Silva Mango, Bula, Guinea-Bissau, April 2011.

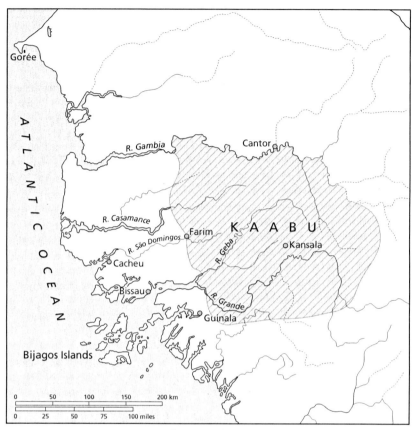

MAP 3. Map of Extent of Kaabu Federation.

traditions hold that the villages of the Bainunks who lived there then were five days or more distant from one another.[65] Doubtless what human settlements existed were concentrated in the dispersed settlements known as *moranças*, a type of settlement which persisted into the sixteenth century in some communities.[66] This influenced the peoples who migrated, the "Balantoos, Naloos, Kanyabatiis, Karooninkaas, Joolaas, and Mankaanyis and the Papeloos".[67] Traditions describe how these groups, together with the Bijagó and the Floup, arrived all together in what is now Guinea-Bissau.[68] Finding themselves surrounded by jungle and swamps, many of

---

[65] NCAC/OHAD, Transcribed Cassette 566, page 11.
[66] Hawthorne (2003).
[67] NCAC/OHAD, Transcribed Cassette 491B, page 6.
[68] Oral interview with Antonio da Silva Mango, Bula, Guinea-Bissau, April 2011.

these groups worked together. The Brames, who later became Mancanha, Manjaco, Papel, joined together to form an empire known as Tancabaceira around a capital of Cobiana, in the area south of the later Portuguese settlement of Cacheu.[69] Soon villages were constructed and a new pattern of human settlement emerged in the region.

Gradually, a definitive settlement pattern was constructed during the late thirteenth and early fourteenth centuries. At the farthest west were the Bijagó, who inhabited the archipelago of the same name in the Atlantic ocean. The numerous islands found here make it a mistake to see the Bijagó as one "ethnic group". There were, and still are, important differences between the islands, and two major languages were spoken on the archipelago by the early seventeenth century, and probably earlier.[70] The identification of Bijagó as one group probably has more to do with the geographical unity of the region than with political and cultural realities.[71]

On the mainland, opposite these islands, were the Biafada and Brame, and also at this early stage perhaps the Floup, whose traditions suggest that they later migrated north to present-day Casamance. The Brames possessed many different lineages which came to live largely under Mandinka hegemony, and they tended to define themselves according to specific regional origins (whether from Cacheu, Baserral, Bajola or the island of Pecixe).[72] As the pre-colonial period went on, the multiplicity of Brame lineages coalesced into three broad "ethnicities" of Mancaigne, Manjaco and Pepel, but this in turn saw the fragmentation of allegiance to a broader "Brame" identity. Farther north in the Casamance were the Bainunk, on many accounts the oldest group of the region.[73] Like the Brames, many (though not all) of the Bainunk accommodated Mandinka authority, and one of their lineages, the Kassanké, acculturated significantly to the Mandinka and became the most powerful group in the region. This accommodation did not categorise all groups however, and Balanta and Floup groups, who had the most decentralised forms of political organisation, remained outside significant Mandinka influence.

---

[69] Ibid.

[70] Sandoval (1627: 93) emphasises the different languages spoken in the Bijagos islands.

[71] Thus islands in the Orangozinho and Orango region today have separate kings or lineage heads. Thefts occur between members of the different lineages, and hospitality is not always shown to people from one island by those of another.

[72] Sandoval (1627: 92) describes this in detail.

[73] NCAC/OHAD, Transcribed Cassette 566, page 11; confirmed in an interview with Ansumane Manga, Singuère, April 2011.

Kaabu was therefore founded in a situation of great human complexity. Owing to its Mande roots, Kaabu has widely been seen as the western outpost of the Mali empire, even though, as we have seen, there were differences in religious emphasis between Kaabu and Mali. To add to these religious differences were strong discrepancies in other cultural practices which developed with this Mandinka migration. The notion of an "imperial" Kaabu and of its relationship to Mali may indeed be more a projection of imperial narratives onto African history rather than an account of what this polity was like, because Kaabu emerged from the blending of many traditions rather than the imposition of a few.[74]

The establishment of Kaabunké hegemony in Upper Guinea may have been gradual. Oral tradition holds that Kaabu's power lasted for 606 years until its fall to the Pullo of the Fouta Djalon in 1867.[75] Naturally this cannot be taken as a precise time span, but if we take a figure of around six centuries, this would put its formation circa 1250–80, which is in keeping with the tradition we saw earlier that the kingdom was founded by Tiramaghan, a general of Sunjata Keita's army and, by some accounts, his cousin.[76] Yet it is unlikely that the establishment of Kaabu came from immediate conquest. Oral histories suggest rather a gradual spread of influence through the formation of alliances. Tiramaghan's army followed the earlier migration of Mandinka smiths and traders who themselves had probably formed alliances with lineages from the region.[77] A similar pattern of kingdom building through the development of voluntary alliances has been suggested for the formation of other important African polities of this early pre-colonial era, notably by Thornton for the Kingdom of Kongo.[78]

This pattern of cross-lineage alliance building by the Mandinka smiths was replicated by Tiramaghan's army. The oral histories of disputes which accompanied the marriages of Kaabunké men to women from the local area reveal both that the Kaabunké compromised and that these alliances were common.[79] Thus the arrival of the Mandinka led to changes in lineage patterns in Upper Guinea and the formation of new alliances. The oral histories of mixed marriages between Kaabunké and

[74] Hawthorne (2003: 30).
[75] See for instance Innes (1976: 113).
[76] Niane (1989: 19 n7).
[77] Mark (2007) offers a useful primer on the unreliability of narratives of "conquest" for Western Africa at this time, suggesting again that what seemed rapid to outside observers often may have masked a longer-term process.
[78] Thornton (2001: 110); see also Randles (1968: 57–8).
[79] See for example the story recounted by the griot Bamba Suso in Innes (1976: 77–9).

local groups indicates that there was a certain realignment of lineage, and such realignments were fundamental in shaping the ways in which the new polity was constituted.

Following this line of thought, a reasonable suggestion is that the waves of Mandinka began to exert a growing influence after their arrival with Tiramaghan, and that by the fourteenth century they were in political control of what was to become the Kaabu federation of states, in part through the multiple new lineage alliances that they had made.[80] On this account the formation of alliances was much more relevant than any idea of absolute Mandinka authority. Such a picture, as we shall see later in this chapter, is in keeping with the importance of lineage to comprehending the social composition of societies in Africa at this time.[81] The idea of the imposition of some absolute Mandinka power may be more a hangover of imperialist historiography than a representation of what happened.[82]

Kaabunké influence was soon widespread in Western Africa. Nowhere is this better exemplified than by the formation of the Sereer kingdom of Siin to the north of the Gambia.[83] It was in the fourteenth century that, according to Gravrand, the existing Sereer-Cosaan of the Siin-Saluum delta fused with Kaabunké incomers known as the Gelwaar, forging the Sereer group who became important Atlantic trading partners in the sixteenth century with the foundation of the state of Saluum *circa* 1500 under the eleventh king of Siin, Mbeyan Ndor.[84] Although Kaabunké specialists have seen the resulting culture as reproducing Kaabunké organisation, this may reflect over-reliance on Gelwaar traditions which minimise earlier Sereer achievements: archaeological evidence shows that the Sereer-Cosaan made large amounts of pottery, and may have traded smoked fish and oysters for iron and cotton cloth from the interior.[85] Certainly, neither the Sereer-Cosaan nor the Kaabunké group was absorbed by the

---

[80] This outline would fit with Cissoko/Sambou's (1974: 5) view that Kaabu's control over Upper Guinea dates to the fourteenth century.

[81] On lineage, see Miller (1976b: 76–7).

[82] See Fields-Black (2009: 112–15) on how such models have unconsciously influenced accounts of the Mande in Upper Guinea.

[83] Gravrand (1983: 239). Known in the earliest Portuguese sources as the "Berbesins", "Berbesin" was a corruption of the Wolof term for the Sereer king, *Buur-ba-Siin* (Boulègue 1987: 16, 58; Horta 1996: 78).

[84] Gravrand (1983: 52–3). On Mbeyan Ndour, see the explanations provided by Hassoum Ceesay at the National Museum of the Gambia.

[85] Ibid., 39; C. Lopes (1999: 57, 93). On the pottery and trade of the Sereer-Cosaan, see the explanations provided by Hassoum Ceesay at the National Museum of the Gambia in April 2011.

other. The new Sereer people retained the Sereer name and language but adopted Kaabunké culture, religious rites and chieftaincies.[86]

The creation of this culture in the fourteenth century thus represents, on the one hand, a continuation of Mandinka expansion beyond the borders of the Mali empire.[87] Yet on the other hand this expansion was tempered by the adoption of some characteristics of the people of the Saluum delta. Thus events in the Saluum may illustrate the sort of primary creolisation which was mentioned at the start of this chapter. Given the oral histories of the mixing of Mandinka and local peoples in what became the Kaabu heartland, this strategy in the Saluum was probably a continuation of that previously adopted there.

Oral history from Kaabu confirms this hypothesis. On these accounts, as we have seen, the Mandinka mixed rapidly after their arrival there, living in the same villages and taking the names of their Bainunk wives. The Traoré clan of Tiramaghan adopted the name Sané in this process, and the new arrivals adopted the matrilineal inheritance characteristic of the region and different from the traditional patrilineal inheritance of other Mande groups.[88] Thus the processes which accompanied the consolidation of the Kaabunké did not simply involve the forcible imposition of an external culture and ideology. Rather, as with the earlier incorporation of North African trading diasporas into the Sahel, there was a two-way interaction. Although the Mandinka did impose a strong veneer of their own customs in Upper Guinea, they also adapted to those which they found – an analogous process to that which occurred among the Sereer-Cosaan.

We can therefore learn much about the Upper Guinea region of distant times from oral history. We do not learn the specifics of events and dates but rather glimpse changing patterns. Mandinka adoption of matrilinearity, intermarriages and the formation of new lineages suggest cultural accommodation. Whereas all societies have within them a capacity for such accommodation and syncretism, these qualities can emerge more strongly at certain times; in this case, the connection to long-distance trade in key commodities and the political power associated with incomers appear to have been pivotal both for the Mandinka of Mali in their

---

[86] Gravrand (1983: 160).

[87] Boulègue (1987a: 47).

[88] Niane (1989: 39); Person (1981: 62). Oral traditions on the matrilinearity of Kaabu are many – see, for instance, NCAC/OHAD, Transcribed Cassette 553A, page 9; Transcribed Cassette 550A, page 7. On the patrilineal inheritance typical of Mande societies in the region of the present-day republic of Mali, see J. Johnson (1999: 11–12).

relationship to North African diasporas and for Upper Guineans in their relationship to Mandinka ones.

The key finding to emerge is that right from the start cultural change was a two-way process, and was not characterised by the simple imposition of Mandinka practices. Yet at the same time, this should not blind us to the fact that the Mandinka rapidly came to constitute a dominant influence. Their language became the key to trade, and, as we shall now see, a certain process termed the "Mandinguisation" of culture began. Although the Mandinka themselves accommodated themselves to the practices and rituals of those who lived in Upper Guinea, so too the peoples of Upper Guinea learnt to adapt to the powerful newcomers.[89] It was this legacy which would prove crucial with the onset of Atlantic trade in the fifteenth century.

ACCULTURATION IN UPPER GUINEA

This section of this chapter seeks to understand this process of acculturation to the Mandinka and what it may have signified for subsequent events. As we have seen, intermarriage of Mandinka and other groups was one important factor in the spreading of the Mandinka cultural world. The development of new shared kinship entailed some sort of identification with Mandinka practices. Added to this was the role of diaspora traders in spreading commerce and ideas, bringing with them as they did the goods and symbols of the rich trans-Saharan trade.

Yet the idea of Mandinguisation needs to be treated with care. The view of early sixteenth-century Portuguese writers such as Pacheco Pereira, that peoples in Upper Guinea had adopted Mandinka customs, may reflect Portuguese perceptions regarding the superiority of "imperial" peoples such as the Mandinka (and themselves) rather than reality. Indeed, the very idea of Mandinguisation was invented by Portuguese colonial officials who may have seen their role in a similar light.[90] The views of writers like Pereira may also reflect the fact that the Portuguese contact with peoples in Upper Guinea was often mediated by the Mandinka themselves or by groups that had heavy Mandinka influences, such as the Kassanké, as is evidenced by the fact that, as we shall now see, the Portuguese often adopted names for groups in the region with Mandinka derivations. So we must begin from the realisation that, whilst the political and economic

---

[89] On Mandinka as a language of trade, see Horta/Dias (2005: 475).
[90] The key to this was Carreira (1947).

power of the Mandinka gave them a pre-eminence in exchanges in Upper Guinea through the role of Mali, it was not the sole factor.

When we cast around to see what characterised these changes, an important clue may lie in language. In Upper Guinea in the fourteenth and fifteenth centuries, Mandinka was certainly a lingua franca, if not a vernacular among non-Mandinka groups. Even today it is perhaps the most common second language in the Casamance and parts of northern Guinea-Bissau. By the eighteenth century this situation was identified by outsiders for trading transactions with Kaabu, and it probably developed much earlier.[91] Just as the widespread power of English in the early twenty-first century is testament to the global hegemony of the United States, so the adoption of Mandinka as a language of cross-kinship communication is testament to Mandinka power in Upper Guinea. The role of language in the spread of Mandinka culture is very important. It reveals that Upper Guinea of the thirteenth and fourteenth centuries really was a place in which intense cultural exchanges are demonstrated by linguistic changes. Although this did not lead to the formation of a vernacular Creole, it does emphasise that the term primary creolisation is appropriate, at least as a metaphor for cultural mixing of the sort discussed in the Introduction.

Although the economic and political power of the Mandinka must have constituted a major factor in this process, we must not lose sight of the perceived ritual power of the Mandinka and particularly their smiths. The magic powers held to reside with the power associations formed by Mandinka smiths would certainly have influenced the acceptance of Mandinka customs. The political importance of ritual power is suggested by the very many oral histories which depict the role of ritual in political conflicts, the most famous of these being that between Sunjata Keita and Sumunguru for control of Mali.[92] The connection of ritual to political power is discernible today by the fact that many in Guinea-Bissau still hold the Mandinka as having the strongest marabouts, which are said to be found near Gabú in the old Mandinka heartlands.[93]

Thus in Upper Guinea a combination of economic, political and ritual factors saw acculturation to the Mandinka in the fourteenth and fifteenth centuries, although some local practices were adopted by the Mandinka.

[91] Havik (2004b: 123) and Mané (1978: 120).
[92] This is by no means the only example. A Balanta story of their incursion into Bainunk territory also describes a war fought through magic powers – in a tradition I collected from Balanta elders in Simbandi-Balante in March 2000.
[93] For more detail on this see Green (2001).

Some specialists have described how Kaabunké cultural qualities eventually spread to "all the other ethnic groups of the region, in forms of political organization, social structures, the economy, cultural symbols, [and] linguistic borrowings".[94] Certainly, there was strong acculturation to the Mandinka by the time of the Portuguese arrival.[95] As Cadamosto wrote on his arrival in Casamance in 1456, "we were told that this river was called Casa Mansa which meant that the river belonged to a black Lord called Cassamansa".[96] As *Mansa* is the Mandinka term for "ruler" or "lord", Mandinka influence in the Casamance at this time is clear. The "Casa Mansa" whom Cadamosto was told about referred to the ruler of the Kassanké, a Bainunk lineage.

It is clear from the Mandinguised name of their ruler that the Kassanké had adopted Mandinka practices. Yet for some specialists the Kassanké dynasty was, like the Gelwaar of the Sereer, originally a Mandinka dynasty which had adopted local customs, in this case Bainunk ones.[97] Most others see the Kassanké as a kinship line of the Bainunk who had heavily Mandiguised themselves and their practices.[98] This is probably most consistent with linguistic findings that show the languages of the Bainunk and Kassanké are mutually intelligible dialects.[99]

Cadamosto's evidence on Casamance thus indicates a strong Mandinka influence over the Kassanké, whose Mandinguisation accompanied their political power. Moreover the influence of the Mandinka on Bainunk peoples stretched beyond the Kassanké kinship branch. The Bainunk themselves began to practice a sort of federal structure of kinship analogous to the federation of allied states found in Kaabu, and their acculturation to the Mandinka can be seen in the fact that according to Carlos Lopes, many Bainunk today pretend to be Mandinka.[100] A dictionary compiled by French traders in the late seventeenth century shows that many Bainunk words were Mandinka in origin, further emphasising the dominant position of the Kaabu Mandinka in this relationship.[101]

---

[94] C. Lopes (1999: 23): "*todas as outras etnias da região; formas de organização política, estruturas sociais, económicas, signos culturais, intercepções linguísticas, etc.*".

[95] See G. Midlo Hall (1992: 29), who holds that by the fifteenth century "all of Upper Guinea had long exhibited a lamina of Mande civilization".

[96] MMAII: Vol. 1, 364: "*Dissene che questa fiumara se chiamava la fiumara de Casa Mansa zoe a dir la fiumara de un signor nominado Cassamansa negro*".

[97] Boulègue (1980: 482); Gaillard (2000a: 14).

[98] Niane (1989: 32); Roche (1976: 24–5).

[99] Mota (1954: Vol. 1, 233).

[100] On federal structure, see Lespinay (2000: 211); on Bainunk pretending to be Mandinka, see C. Lopes (1999: 60).

[101] Lespinay (2000: 210).

This interconnectivity between Bainunk and Mandinka reached a deep level in Bainunk affiliations. Oral histories collected in the 1970s by Christian Roche suggest strong identification by Bainunk of their past with Mandinka migrations, with some traditions claiming that the Bainunk were forced out of their lands by the Kaabunké.[102] On this account the Bainunk king Gana Sira Bana Biaye was obliged to move to Casamance, but as the name Gana Sira Bana is itself Mandinka, the level of Mandinka influence even at this time of supposed forced migration was clearly intense.[103] Another oral tradition holds that an ally of Gana Sira Bana in Ingore (present-day Guinea-Bissau; just twenty miles/thirty kilometres across the Senegalese border from Brikama, site of the Bainunk court) was a Bainunk king called Nunkuntamba, also a Mandinka name.[104] Nothing expresses it more clearly than the fact that the name "Bainunk" may derive from the Mandinka words *abaï*, meaning "hunt him," and *nunko*, meaning "he who has been hunted".[105] Moreover it is significant that this was the ethnonym adopted by the Portuguese themselves, revealing that often when they thought they were describing peoples of the African coast in their own terms, they were in fact using the eyes of other powerful outsiders, the Mandinka.

The influence of the Mandinka in Casamance stretched beyond the Bainunk. It has also been identified by specialists on the Floup of Casamance as transforming their cultural practices.[106] We can surmise that this influence was important along the entire littoral between the Senegal and Cacheu Rivers from Fernandes's observation that "the Mandinka can be differentiated from the Jolof in their language, but in their faith and their customs they are identical".[107] Of course, this assertion may reflect an inability to differentiate in the eyes of Fernandes's informants, but we have seen earlier in this chapter that the influence of the Mali empire on the Jolof of the Lower Senegal was intense by the

---

[102] Roche (1976: 22).

[103] Ibid., 22–3.

[104] From a tradition I collected from a Balanta elder in the village of Simbandi-Balante in March 2000.

[105] Roche (1976: 22). Brooks (1993b: 87) holds rather that "Bainunk" may be a generic term for "trader". Some of today's Bainunk elders prefer an etymology which sees them originating from a quarter of Mecca called Baynunka – from an interview with Ansumane Manga, Singuère, Casamance, April 2011.

[106] Linares (1992: 147). Known more widely today as the "Jola", this ethnonym only became widespread in the nineteenth century; "Floup" was more common in the period which this book deals with.

[107] MMAII: 700: "*Os de Mandiga sõ differeciados cõ os de Gyloffa em a lingua, mas em a fē e custumes som huũs*".

latter fourteenth century, and therefore Fernandes's claim is not to be dismissed out of hand; rather, it may well illuminate the same process which has been observed here for Casamance.

Mandinka influence in Upper Guinea in these centuries matters greatly when we try to understand the first African-European exchanges of the mid-fifteenth century. The arrival of outsiders bearing goods and political and religious changes through long-distance trade was nothing new. The capacity of the peoples of Upper Guinea to adapt to such outsiders and incorporate them into society was also nothing new. Accommodation to a powerful external force and incorporation of some of its practices were precisely the qualities which exchanges with the Kaabunké had inculcated. Yet, as we have seen so far in this chapter, this accommodation was not just an acceptance of a dominant power; rather, it was coupled with the imposition of local values as new lineages were formed, and these new kinship lines developed their own loyalties and practices which derived from local custom.

In Senegambia and Upper Guinea, Mandinka power derived both from their connections to the trans-Saharan trade and from the ritual power associated with it. As we have seen, key to the development of this power by Mali had been its receptivity to and treatment of trading diasporas, as well as its accommodation to the Islamic religion professed by diaspora members. It is surely significant, then, that in Upper Guinea the Mandinka themselves came to constitute a sort of diaspora, thereby replicating the pattern which emerged in the trans-Saharan trade. Mandinka groups spread heavily to the Gambia and influenced the Sereer-Cosaan, Kassanké and Biafada. Thus did the importance of diasporas in Western African culture and commerce spread from their role in the trans-Saharan trade to Upper Guinea through the intermediaries of the Mandinka.

In the Casamance, the Mandinka brought trade and with it a hint of the great world beyond. Social structures changed through a growing commercialisation and opening to the outside world. At the time of the European arrival, the Bainunk were famed for their markets, which were held every eight days, and to which people came from as far off as fifteen leagues (approximately forty-seven miles/seventy-five kilometres); there were also markets farther south among the Biafada.[108] These markets formed a powerful means of furthering Mandinka influence. Here, members of groups who had not acknowledged some form of Mandinka

---

[108] Mark (1985: 12); Nafafé (2007: 78). On the Biafada and the Mandinka, see Mota (1970: 6–9).

political authority, such as the Balanta, the Bijagó and the Floup, were able to secure goods from the *dyula* from the trans-Saharan trade and also perhaps some iron products forged by local smiths. Thus Mandinka political, cultural and ritual power was expressed at these markets to groups not under their direct control, because the ritual power of the smiths was well-known and the commercial and political power of the Mandinka was asserted in the long-distance trade practised by the *dyula*. In this way trade and exchange formed a powerful means of spreading Mandinka influences even among those groups of Upper Guinea who were not politically subordinate to them.

Equally as important as trade in terms of Mandinka influence on society was production. Fields-Black has shown that rice-growing technology was ancient in Upper Guinea already by the fifteenth century.[109] Rice was grown by Mandinka lineages in the Gambia area by the fifteenth century, and probably long before.[110] The ability to farm rice in large quantities derived increasingly from the iron made by the smiths, and thus greater agricultural production affirmed both Mandinka ritual power and enhanced the power of Mandinka.

Thus the ritual power of the smiths, the trans-Saharan trade and the social changes produced by changing agricultural techniques were all interconnected. Mandinka influence had partially integrated Upper Guinea into the trans-Saharan trade of gold and slaves in return for horses and other commodities; and it had prepared the ground for the region's willingness to participate in what at first appeared to be a similar trade with the white and bearded people who emerged from those strange ships that began to appear from the sea.[111]

PRIMARY CREOLISATION AND ATLANTIC CREOLISATION

The sort of primary creolisation described in this chapter proved a foretaste of the creolisation which accelerated with the formation of Atlantic communities in the fifteenth and sixteenth centuries. Such exchanges, however, were not just between Mandinka and others, but they also

---

[109] Fields-Black (2009).
[110] Hawthorne (2003: 155).
[111] The importance of horses in this context emerges in an oral tradition that the Bainunk king Gana Sira Bana was so powerful that he could point his horse in any direction and the forest would part for him – this illustrates how horses, power and trans-Saharan trade were interconnected in the pre-Atlantic world. From a tradition I collected in Simbandi-Balante in March 2000.

characterised the relationships between many of the decentralised groups of the region.

We can begin examining this pre-Atlantic primary creolisation by looking at Casamance. Drawing on informants whose knowledge of Casamance probably stretched back to the 1480s, Fernandes wrote in 1506 that "the Casamance River is a great trading river ... in this kingdom people of all nations [*gerações*] are mixed together, Mandinkas, Floups, Balantas and others".[112] In other words, by the fifteenth-century Portuguese arrival, this was what would be termed today a multi-cultural zone, where peoples from different kinship lines co-existed under the rule of the Kassanké, following the Kassanké's own heavy acculturation to the Mandinka.[113] Oral traditions confirm this view, stating that peoples from different groups would often intermarry, with Balantas, Floups and Papels all intermarrying.[114] This would imply that Mandinka power had created a situation where those living under that power co-existed in a large political space. Co-existence in this space precipitated a sharing and mixing of local cultures. Such cultural mixing of different groups has indeed often been a feature of large polities, which of their nature tend to embrace many different peoples.

Evidence for a long-standing sharing of practices exists. In addition to Fernandes, we should look at Almada, who in his prologue described how "the kingdoms of the blacks and their languages are as many and various as their diverse customs, because everywhere in less than 20 leagues [approximately sixty-two miles/one hundred kilometres] there are two and three nations all mixed together, with some of the kings minor and others powerful, the one subject to the other, and ... their sects and customs and the laws of their government and oaths come, for the most part, to be all as one".[115]

As with Fernandes's description, Almada talks of different nations [*nações*] being mixed together and moreover draws a connection between this multi-cultural mixing and the sharing of customs (which come "to be all as one"). Elsewhere, he gives a specific example of a practice shared by

---

[112] MMAII: Vol. 1, 712: "*Ryo de Casamansa he huu ryo de muyto resgate ... E neste reyno ha gēte mesturada de todas gerações como Mandinkas, falupes, balan[t]as etc...*".
[113] This point is made well by Nafafé (2007: 75).
[114] NCAC/OHAD, Transcribed Cassette 466B, page 7.
[115] MMAII: Vol. 3, 231: "*Os reinos dos negros sejam tantos e as linguagens tão várias como os costumes diversos, porque em cada espaço em menos de vinte léguas há duas e três nações, todas misturadas, e os reinos uns pequenos, e outros grandes, sujeitos uns aos outros, e ... suas seitas e costumes e as leis do seu governo e juramentos venham, pela maior parte, a ser todos uns*".

Jolof, Mandinka and Sereer, describing how a Jolof king had once decided that because kings had many wives and that the wives' children could not all be the king's, it was possible that one of these children would inherit the kingdom illegitimately, and that for this reason the king's nephews – his sister's sons – should inherit the kingdom, "a law, which until today is kept in the kingdoms of the Jolofs, Sereers and Mandinkas".[116] Almada's description here is of the matrilinearity which, as we have seen, was a practice adopted by the Kaabu Mandinka in contrast to the patrilinearity of other Mande groups. Whatever the general accuracy of Almada's text, it surely does convey the reality of this shared practice among Jolof, Mandinka and Sereer.[117]

To complement this evidence from Almada and Fernandes, ethnographic material suggests the sharing of practices. This can be noted for instance among the Brame. As a whole, the Brame have a history of shared linguistic and cultural practice, and in the fifteenth century this was intense.[118] Moreover, the Brame sub-group known today as the Pepel have linguistic and cultural similarities with the Floup. The two exhibit a linguistic affinity which is indicative of some past shared history.[119] Even the distinguishing regalia of ritual leaders observed among the Pepel in the late seventeenth century were identical with those used by their counterparts in Floup communities north and south of the Lower Casamance River: a red cap and an iron staff of office.[120] Wider similarities can also be found between the Floup and other groups in the region: Manjaco and Bainunk ritual offerings and shrines resemble in general those of the Floup.[121] South of the Grande River, Fields-Black has identified strong sharing of cultural practices between the Nalu and Baga peoples of present-day Guinea-Conakry in the *D'mba* masquerade.[122]

Meanwhile, there were shared practices across the whole region between Casamance and the Rio Grande. Almada described how all

---

[116] Ibid., Vol. 3: 238: "*uma lei, que é até hoje guardada nos mais Reinos dos Jalofos, Barbacins e Mandinkas*".

[117] The texts of Almada and Donelha are analogous sources to the oral histories which modern historians use for the nineteenth and twentieth centuries. Horta (2000: 120, 122) makes the important point that these texts were primarily collations of oral histories and accounts, indicators of an oral culture in Upper Guinea.

[118] Mota (1954: Vol. 1, 147, 164–5).

[119] Carreira (1964: 241). Indeed, some oral traditions of the Manjaco (a sub-group of the people known as the Brame in the sixteenth century) claim that they descend from the Floup – see NCAC/OHAD, Transcribed Cassette 434C, page 3.

[120] Mark (1985: 9).

[121] Ibid.

[122] Fields-Black (2009: 130–1).

noblemen [*fidalgos*: or perhaps, lineage heads] wore iron rings and a type of rattle on their hands, exemplifying the role of iron in ideas of power in the region.[123] He noted how in all Guinea paternal uncles were "held as fathers of their nephews".[124] Among the Bainunk, Bijago, Brame and Kassanké, meanwhile, it was the custom for the *fidalgos* to ride cows or oxen using ropes as a bit.[125]

In short, it is clear that the spread of Mandinka power into Upper Guinea and the formation of a powerful loose-knit federation of states overseen by the Kaabu Mandinka coincided with cultural exchanges and borrowings not only between the Mandinka and others, but also between the peoples of the region.[126] Such practices were also common among peoples not under their authority, such as the Nalu and Baga. To the north of the Grande River, it may have been that the creation of a larger political space encouraged this process by breaking down the boundaries between the different lineages and facilitating their co-existence. Thus it was the strength of Mandinka power in West Africa as a whole, cemented through the long-distance trade and adhesion to Islam, that facilitated the potential for cultural flexibility in the Upper Guinea region.

Indeed, even those groups who resisted the Mandinka in some sense defined themselves culturally through this resistance. We have already seen how the ethnonym "Bainunk" may derive from Mandinka words relating to "he who has been hunted". The Balanta illustrate the same phenomenon. The Balanta are thought to derive their ethnonym from the Mandinka "balanto", or "those who resist and do not reciprocate".[127] In the Balanta case, the nature of this resistance varied. Though some Balanta clearly did resist the Mandinka expansion and fled to the creeks of the coastal areas, others – now known as the Balanta-Mane – stayed farther inland and intermarried.[128] Nevertheless, the oral traditions of both Balanta-Mane and other Balanta coincide in seeing their origins as having been in the east and in conflicts with Mandinka invaders.[129]

---

[123] MMAII: Vol. 3, 327.

[124] Ibid., Vol. 3, 326. This custom continues to this day.

[125] Ibid., Vol. 3, 327.

[126] Hawthorne (2010b) concurs with the idea mooted here of a "cultural zone" of shared practice and belief in Upper Guinea.

[127] Havik (2004b: 95); Hawthorne (2003: 32); Roche (1976: 47).

[128] See Hawthorne (2003: 32–3) for a good summary of these different responses to the Mandinka push from the east.

[129] In Simbandi-Balante in March 2000, I witnessed this myself. My informant, a Balanta-Mane wearing Mandinka dress, described the typical Balanta origin story concerning their migration from the east.

Thus though many Balanta did resist the Mandinka, the very name they used to describe themselves did so in terms of their relationship with the Mandinka.[130]

When we consider the Mandinka meanings of these two ethnonyms, Bainunk and Balanta, we perhaps reach to the core of what we have called here primary creolisation. We must recognise that this was not the same process as that which occurred in the Atlantic, for vernacular Creole languages did not develop and Mandinka remained a language largely of trade; here certainly the concept of creolisation is invoked as the sort of "master metaphor" so popular among cultural theorists. Yet at the same time, events here foreshadowed the process of cultural exchange in the Atlantic, for this primary creolisation both facilitated the exchange of practices and, as in the Atlantic, was also predicated on violence. The way in which hunting, resistance and subordination are implied in these ethnonyms make it clear that exchanges with the Mandinka were not exactly peaceful. Violence escalated with primary creolisation, both among these peoples and others of the region. On one foundation story, the founder of the Sereer culture, Waal Paal, was an escapee slave who had been seized by Kaabunké slave raiders and forced to work as a goatherd before returning to the king of Siin and establishing himself.[131] Because, as we have seen, Sereer culture was itself a hybrid of Sereer-Cosaan and Kaabunké culture, this story may well reveal the violence which accompanied this process of accommodation and may hint at events elsewhere. Moreover, as we have seen, the trans-Saharan commerce itself involved a heavy trade in slaves, some of whom may well have come from victims of the violence which accompanied these processes of change. When asked how ancient Kaabu lived prior to the arrival of the Europeans, one informant described how "by then there was only war. The Soninkés fed on that".[132]

Thus this pre-Atlantic pattern also offered a foretaste of the cycles of violent disorder which Atlantic trade would begin in Western Africa. It is difficult to imagine how things could have been any different. The imposition of new cultural and economic realities such as the Mandinka embarked upon in Upper Guinea in the thirteenth and fourteenth centuries

---

[130] It should be noted, however, that the origins of this name are unclear, with some sources pointing to the Balanta as soldiers of the Pullo warrior-king Koli Tenguella (cf. Chapter 2), who refused to accompany him back north from the Fouta Djalon to Fouta Tooro. Cf. Ba (1981: 25); and also information from an interview with Seydhou Fall, Goudomp, Casamance, April 2011. However, these sources tend to be external from the Balanta's own narrative, which define their resistance in relation to the Mandinka.

[131] Gravrand (1983: 28–33).

[132] NCAC/OHAD, Transcribed Cassette 550A, pages 58–9.

has always been accompanied by violence, whether there, in the Atlantic world of the early modern era, or in Africa again in the colonial era. The Bainunk and Balanta namings and the Sereer foundation story imply that Mandinka expansion was accompanied by slave-raiding. Certainly, in the mid-fifteenth century the sale of slaves into long-distance trade was not a new phenomenon.[133] Thus primary creolisation meant both a sharing and a violence; this was a legacy which was to have its own consequences through mutual suspicion and people hunting when the era of Atlantic trade began.

CREOLISATION, LINEAGE AND NAMING IN THE PRE-ATLANTIC AND ATLANTIC WORLDS

The casual visitor to Western Africa today may pick up a guidebook describing the peoples of the region. For Senegal, for instance, they will find out about "the Wolof", "the Sereer" and "the Diola". Here is a projection of the ethnic essentialism which engulfed African and European societies in the era of colonialism. Yet this chapter has shown how the historical reality of the peoples of Senegambia and Upper Guinea is infinitely more composite than ethnic nationalism can allow.

As we have seen, from the thirteenth to the fifteenth century barriers to inter-cultural mixing were never so high that they could not be overcome. The peoples known with ethnic labels today had ancestors in these times who would not have recognised themselves in these labels. Identity was not perceived in terms of "ethnicity", an invention of racist anthropologists of the nineteenth century.[134] Lineages and kin connections were of far greater importance in determining how people related to one another, and these could and did cut across imposed Western "ethnic" boundaries. This was of particular significance in Upper Guinea because, as Martin Klein and Paul Lovejoy have pointed out, lineage structures in Africa are in general more pervasive in non-Islamic societies.[135] Thus if we want to understand the ways in which Creole communities formed in Upper Guinea, the place of lineage becomes key.

It becomes clear that lineage, and not some form of proto-ethnic identity, matters most here when we recall that the very names which the

[133] Mendes (2007: 11).
[134] On "ethnicity" as a primordialist and racist invention, see Amselle (1998: 22–6) and Banks (1996: 158, 190). On the development of "ethnicities" in Upper Guinea, see Brooks (1993b: 28).
[135] Klein/Lovejoy (1979: 185).

Portuguese used to denote the peoples of the region were themselves projections. As we have seen in this chapter, the likelihood is that early communication between Africans and the Portuguese was carried out using the Mandinka as intermediaries and the shared language of Arabic, which some Mandinka and Portuguese held in common. This being the case, the names by which the Portuguese learnt to call the peoples of the region were likely imparted to them by the Mandinka, a hypothesis substantiated by the fact that many of these names are Mandinka in origin.[136] These names were themselves imprecise attributions which ignored differences between some of the peoples to whom they were attributed. Both Bainunk and Kassanké, for instance, claimed that the Portuguese used the name indiscriminately to describe what were in reality several distinct groupings in the Casamance region.[137]

Powerful and expansionist societies have often found it useful to classify their foreign subjects, and such classification is of its nature artificial. What was true of the British in the nineteenth century was also true of the Portuguese in the sixteenth century, and, it would appear from this discussion, the Mandinka before them.[138] The history of the "naming" of the peoples of Upper Guinea thus fits well with the hypothesis that this was a region which was the meat in the sandwich between two powerful forces, the Mandinka and the Portuguese. Both collaborated together in giving the names by which the peoples of the region are known today.

This was a history which, on an ideological level, saw the Atlantic turn into a battleground between the imperial typology of classification on the one hand, and on the other what Jean-Loup Amselle calls "mestizo logics," which accept "original syncretism" rather than trying to create artificial differences on a classificatory basis.[139] In many areas of the Americas, the Caribbean and Europe, the typology of classification was in the ascendant, with the well-known legacies of institutionalised racism and sociopolitical hierarchies which persist to this day. However, in Senegambia and Upper Guinea "mestizo logics" offered a stronger governing principle for the peoples who lived there, meaning that people were quite able to hold flexible and even multiple identities; they could be affiliated both with particular villages and lineages, and also to wider political units such

---

[136] This hypothesis was made by Mota (1954: Vol. 1, 144–5).
[137] Ibid. The point that the term "Bainunk" encompassed several different groups is made by Rodney (1970: 8).
[138] On how this process worked for slaves taken by the Portuguese to America, see Mellafe (1964: 158).
[139] Amselle (1998: 10).

as that of Casamance. There would of course have been major perceived caste differences between those who were and were not involved in the long-distance trade, in the religious and ritual differences this implied, and in the blacksmithing art; but such distinctions would have been less intense for many Upper Guinean groups who relied on the Mandinka for their connections to this wider world and who, as this chapter has shown, were more willing to share in one another's practices.

This matters to this study on the level of articulation of and identification with difference. Although all cultures are hybrids of different linguistic and social habits from different groups, not all cultures recognise this and articulate it in their social identity. Classificatory cultures ignore this reality and try to bury it beneath artificial differences. Areas where "mestizo logics" prevail do articulate this syncretism, however, and this chapter has shown that Senegambia and Upper Guinea were such places. As I have suggested, it was the particular constellation of factors surrounding the trans-Saharan trade, the role of diasporas, and the power of the Mandinka which may have generated the tendency towards primary creolisation at this time. West Africa was doubtless no more or less inherently disposed than any other region of the world towards such cultural exchange; rather, the economic, political, religious and social conditions that prevailed in the pre-Atlantic era had shaped a particular outlook which would be of great importance. In a region where the distances between ecological zones north and south of the Sahara were much larger than the ordinary and where long-distance trade in the early modern era was generally conducted by diasporas, the particular socio-cultural and political features associated with such cross-cultural trade were liable to be especially accentuated.[140]

Conceptualising how this syncretism was articulated in the psychologies of the pre-Atlantic world thus requires a move away from the idea of "ethnicity". The much more African-centred ideas of kinship relations and lineages is more useful. Thus when looking at the Bainunk and Kassanké, it may be more appropriate to think of them not as cultures more or less acculturated to the Mandinka, but as different lineages who had taken the decision to acculturate to or resist the Mandinka.[141] It may be that the terms "Bainunk" and "Kassanké" themselves encapsulated more than one lineage involved in such a decision, but the key factor would seem to

---

[140] Curtin (1984); on the importance of diasporas in the early modern era, see Frank (1998: 62).

[141] The idea of Bainunk and Kassanké as competing lineages is in Mark (1985: 15).

be that differences between the Bainunk and Kassanké were not articulated on the level of culture or language (which were very closely related); boundaries and loyalties were instead provided by kinship ties, and as the Kassanké intermarried with Mandinka the ties between them and the Bainunk would have lessened.

These ideas are also helpful when looking at some of the other groups of the region. Writing in the early seventeenth century, Manoel Alvares described how the Brames were "like the Bainunk" and had "many kings".[142] More accurate might be to see these "kings" as heads of lineage, something which would also fit with how the Brames are now seen as subdivided into Mancanha, Manjaco and Pepel. Indeed, this way of understanding Upper Guinea was not entirely foreign to informed observers of the time: Alonso de Sandoval, a Jesuit based in Cartagena de las Indias, described in 1627 how "under the caste and name of Balantas there are many different castes of this nation, of whom some don't understand others".[143]

The advantages of understanding the pre-Atlantic Upper Guinea coast through lineages rather than cultures emerge most strongly with the Floup. The Floup are now generally known as the Diola, but according to Baum, the Diola did not use the term as a mode of identification until the onset of the colonial era and their increasing integration into a multi-ethnic Senegal. Until the twentieth century, they only used the name of their sub-group and did not consider themselves to be truly "at home" outside of their quarter of their home town, which exemplifies how lineage, home and identity were all closely connected and demonstrates that "supra-lineage" national identities existed mainly in the eyes of outsiders.[144]

These observations confirm the accuracy of Bennett's view that "in [Upper] Guinea of the fifteenth through sixteenth centuries ... individuals largely identified themselves on the basis of lineages and occasionally state structures, both of which were tenuous".[145] When we consider how this affected the historical context of the African entry into the Atlantic world, it is perhaps most important for us to note the very fluidity highlighted by Bennett here, the fact that lineages of their nature may change rapidly, and with them, allegiances. For as identities changed with new lineages (as with inter-marriages with Mandinka for instance), so

[142] SG, *Etiopia Menor...*, fol. 20v.
[143] Sandoval (1627: fol. 61v).
[144] Baum (1999: 27, 62–3).
[145] Bennett (2003: 6).

practices inevitably became more open to these new allegiances. Thus the flexibility of the fourteenth and fifteenth centuries may have developed not only from changes deriving from Mandinka influence, but also because this acculturation was articulated through a framework of lineage.

A second important consideration for us of this ideology of lineage is the concept of what Africanists have called "wealth in people". This is the concept of accumulated value most current in pre-Atlantic societies of the west coast of Africa, and may have been dependent as Miller suggests on the high mortality of the region and the consequent fragility of future claims to wealth not predicated on a guaranteed supply of labour.[146] This created an entirely different economic rationale to that of Europe, where land constituted the primary form of revenue-producing property.[147] In Africa wealth derived from control of people, not from control of land. Some have argued that this perspective is vital to understanding African participation in the Atlantic trade because lineage chiefs and rulers rapidly began to acquire more followers through their acquisition of new trade goods from the Atlantic.[148]

The ideology of lineage was probably fundamental to the development of the concept of "wealth in people". Supra-kinship national identities such as those imposed from the outside would not necessarily have lent themselves as easily to this worldview; in the framework of lineage, however, it is clear that the larger and more extensive the lineage, the greater the degree of wealth in that lineage. Hence this discussion illustrates another way in which perceiving the exchanges of pre-Atlantic Africa and their influence on the early Atlantic requires conceptualisation through the notion of lineage.

Understanding that external ideologies cannot explain how Western African societies saw the Atlantic turn also helps to elucidate one of the central themes of this chapter, that of the role of diasporas. We have seen how the mercantile diaspora of Islamic merchants from North Africa was crucial in creating a flexibility of outlook among the Mandinka ruling clans, and also how the subsequent migration of Mandinka towards the Atlantic created similar tendencies among the peoples there. In each of these two cases, the incoming diaspora brought powerful ideas, rituals and wealth, and forced a certain amount of cultural accommodation. Yet this accommodation could not override local practices and beliefs, which

---

[146] Miller (1988: 47–8).
[147] Thornton (1998: 74).
[148] This is the general argument of Miller (1988).

remained very strong and which today provide the greatest explanatory power when we try to interpret how these changes were perceived.

The argument of this chapter about the flexible identities and growing openness of peoples in Senegambia and Upper Guinea to external influences emerges most strongly in this context of diaspora and lineage. The mixture of cultural practices was facilitated particularly by the organisation of society according to lineage lines, where inter-marriage with the Mandinka would create kinship ties which themselves brought the cultural mixtures highlighted here. Thus although the context of this world was often violent, the creation of new lineages and the allegiances these brought with them would have gone some way to promoting acceptance of this situation. Moreover, the fact that these lineages were themselves connected to centres of wealth and political power through the Mandinka diaspora of merchants must have been attractive and fostered accommodation.

The importance of lineage also brought the willingness to consider forging new alliances if other emissaries of a powerful external force arrived – as soon they did. In 1455, the Genoese sailor Alvise de Cadamosto navigated down this flat coastline that had seen so many changes over the preceding two centuries. South of the Cape Verde peninsula there were still trees and evidence of fertility where today there is arid scrub filled with gnarled and twisted shapes of baobabs. Then he reached the Wolof kingdom of Cajor, where the Damel or king welcomed him and offered him "a young girl aged 12 or 13 and very beautiful ... for service in my chamber, which I accepted".[149]

Of course even by this time Europeans were not a novelty. Their ships had been coming for ten years. Extensive changes can occur in such a short period of time, as human beings have seen in our days with the growth of the Internet from a position of relative unimportance in the late 1990s. In the light of those ten years, the Damel was probably already aware of how the new seaborne traders could be worked to his advantage in his relationship with the Jolof ruler farther north. It would obviously be to his benefit if he could forge a new alliance.

Such nuances were lost on Cadamosto, who doubtless would not also have imagined how events during the preceding two centuries in Senegambia and Upper Guinea could have influenced his reception. Yet clearly these changes had shaped the way in which Cadamosto and those like him were received. And when we think of the Damel's offer of a

[149] MMAII: Vol. 1, 322.

pretty girl for service in Cadamosto's chamber, we may not be too far from the mark if we imagine that he had in mind a new kinship alliance which could transform his lineage's prospects. The Damel may have been playing the long game, but Cadamosto and others like him had more immediate desires for personal riches and gratification. Over the coming centuries it would be these desires which would be served by the forces which oversaw the rise of the Atlantic world.

2

The Formation of Early Atlantic Societies in Senegambia and Upper Guinea

Although the Atlantic world began in Western Africa, this important fact is rarely to be gleaned from most works of Atlantic history. Yet the Spanish settlement and conquest of the Canary Islands in the late fifteenth century only gathered pace as a direct response to Portuguese activity there.[1] Almost thirty years separated the Portuguese arrival at the Senegal River in 1444 from their arrival at what became the Gold Coast (present-day Ghana) in 1471.[2]

The birth of this Atlantic world in Western Africa was multifaceted. Primary creolisation in Upper Guinea and the process of state formation in medieval Portugal shaped an early Atlantic economy influenced profoundly by violence and its legacies. Yet on the other hand, these conditions had enabled a tradition of cultural sharing to develop in Western Africa. It was this combination of violence and flexibility which came to characterise Creole societies both here and elsewhere in the Atlantic world.

This chapter begins the examination of how this position developed and offers new perspectives on these vital first African-European exchanges. A variety of written sources is used. Chronicles of European mariners, with their inevitable quota of bias, are mixed with accounts by Islamic scholars. Oral traditions collected by sixteenth-century writers, and others stored in the Oral History Archive in Fajara, are also used. The chapter shows that the first encounters in the 1440s were not between peoples that were unknown to each other and that, in fact, continuity

[1] Elliott (2006: 16).
[2] For explorations of the Gold Coast, see Vogt (1979: 7–9).

with the previous trans-Saharan and Mediterranean economies was a key factor in shaping initial exchanges.

Thus I suggest here a need for a new perspective on the early Atlantic world in the phase before the Spanish voyages to America. My argument is that neither Africans nor Europeans saw this world as being revolutionarily new. Indeed, elements of continuity enabled the first steps towards the creation of a mixed society to be taken on the West African coast. It turns out that the long-standing role of diasporas and outsider groups in the region's trade and the influence which such conditions had had in creating a sort of cultural receptivity were vital stages in the development of the Atlantic's first Creole communities. We also see how pre-existing political configurations determined patterns of settlement for Europeans and the shaping of these very early mixed communities, as well as how these configurations were then influenced by the patterns of the new Atlantic trade.

In examining these exchanges, I place the importance of the slave trade in the foreground. Historians have traditionally seen the motivation of the early Portuguese trade as having been to procure better supplies of gold, but in contrast to this earlier emphasis, this chapter shows that the strongest early impact in Western Africa was in exacerbating cycles of violence and political instability that had already emerged with Mandinka expansion and the trans-Saharan slave trade. We see here how the earliest steps towards mixed societies in the African Atlantic occurred within the prism of a trade in slaves, which makes apparent the interconnection of Atlantic creolisation and slavery examined throughout this book; we also see how the demand side from the Atlantic influenced the development of patterns of violent disorder in Western Africa, as Rodney argued in the 1960s. Thus the chapter shows how the continuities between trans-Saharan and Atlantic long-distance trades facilitated the intensification of violence that was heralded by Atlantic trade and that contributed significantly to political and social changes in Western Africa. The suggestion is that this contribution was as strong, if not stronger, as the process of climatic change previously highlighted by George Brooks.[3]

THE IMPORTANCE OF CONTINUITIES IN THE FIRST ATLANTIC EXCHANGES IN WESTERN AFRICA

The first exchanges between Africans and Europeans in Western Africa were not those of strangers. As early as 1413 Iberian officialdom knew

[3] Brooks (1993b).

something of sub-Saharan African polities. In that year, a document written in Seville referred to "*un negro de jelofe Mandinka* [a Black of Jolof Mandinka]", which, although a confused statement, illustrates some knowledge of the peoples south of the Sahara.[4] Then in 1415, during their conquest of Ceuta in Morocco, Bartolomé de las Casas wrote in his *Historia de las Indias* that the Portuguese heard of the extent of Africa beyond Fez into the desert, where the Azenegues lived, "and that these people bordered with the blacks of Joloph".[5] Therefore, although the sea beyond Cape Bojador in southern Morocco was frightening and unknown to the Portuguese, this was not so of the land and the peoples who lived there.[6] By the time of their arrival among the Jolof thirty years later, the Portuguese also appear to have known that the desert was the world of Arab and Berber groups and that Black Africans lived beyond it. Zurara, author of the earliest account of the Portuguese presence in Africa, wrote that when the Portuguese ships reached two palm trees by the River Senegal "they knew that there began the land of the blacks".[7]

Not only were the Jolof known to the Portuguese at least by name when their ships arrived on the Senegal River in the 1440s, but the cultural context in which they lived was also familiar. As in Europe, the Jolof world was one of expansionist monarchs with large mounted armies.[8] The prevalence of Islam and the presence of North African diaspora traders were resonant both of the Portuguese trading outposts in North Africa and also of Castille, which would not complete the conquest of Granada for almost fifty years. The long-standing presence of Jewish diaspora traders in Sahelian regions would also have been a source of familiarity.[9] Religious familiarity brought with it linguistic familiarity. Not only did North Africans speak Arabic, but some of the Jolof did also; the Portuguese language contains many words of Arabic origin, and there remained then many Arabic speakers in Iberia.

There was also much continuity in this early coastal African trade with the commerce of the trans-Saharan caravan route.[10] Indeed, the Portuguese

---

[4] Mathieu (1982: 183). This statement could even refer to the tributary status of the Jolof to Mali.

[5] Las Casas (1966b: Vol. 62, 174): "*y estos confinaban con los negros de Joloph*". Las Casas may have been projecting sixteenth-century knowledge into the fifteenth century; he may, alternatively, have had access to sources now lost.

[6] On fears of what lay beyond Cape Bojador, see Delumeau (1978: 42) and Green (2006: 27).

[7] MMAII: Vol. 1, 27: "*pellas quaes conheceron que ally se começaua a terra dos negros*".

[8] This point is made by Abulafia (2008: 92).

[9] A good discussion of this presence is in Lydon (2009: 65–70).

[10] Mendes (2007: 6).

knew this. As Mendes has discovered through groundbreaking archival research, the Portuguese base established at Arguim, in present-day Mauritania, relied on the same trans-Saharan networks that had supplied the ports in North Africa, which hitherto had traded with Lagos and Lisbon in Portugal and with Genoa and Venice in Italy.[11] Moreover, not only were these networks themselves continuities, but the traders who operated them had a foot in both the Iberian and West African worlds. Mendes has shown that the principal agents in the early Portuguese cloth trade at Arguim – one of the main articles of exchange – were Moroccan Jews descended from the Sephardic Jews who had fled Spain following the anti-Semitic riots of 1391.[12] Meanwhile, the Portuguese commissioned textiles in their enclaves in Morocco, such as Safi and Azemour for sale in Arguim and Senegal, from Sephardic Jewish weavers who had previously been involved in preparing cloth for the trans-Saharan trade.[13] New research by Mark and Horta also suggests links between the Sephardic Jewish sword-makers in late-fifteenth-century Morocco and Western Sahara with a subsequent trade in weapons that developed in West Africa in the sixteenth century.[14] The presence of Iberian Jews connected to these trans-Saharan trading networks also is shown in the maps of Jewish cartographers of Majorca of the late fourteenth century, which depicted the empire of Mali with relative accuracy (and notable even-handedness).[15]

As this evidence suggests, some of the continuities that emerged in this early Atlantic trade came through the Iberian Jewish community. Iberian Jews had had increasing connections to the trans-Saharan trade following the large-scale migrations to North Africa which followed the 1391 riots. Even before 1391, the Jewish traders of Barcelona and Aragon had long offered Spanish monarchs access to West African gold through a network with the Jews of Tlemcen (Algeria) and Sijilmāssa (southern Morocco); and after 1391, Iberian Jews settled throughout Morocco and their connections quickly spread south of the Sahara.[16] The extent of the interconnections between Iberian Jewish trading networks and the trans-Saharan trade may emerge through the work of Ismaël Diadié Haïdara, who has

[11] Ibid., 377.
[12] Ibid., 448.
[13] Prussin (2006: 345).
[14] Mark/Horta (2011: 125 n.61).
[15] On these connections see Bovill (1958: 113–4). For a more recent discussion of Cresques' 1375 Catalan Atlas, see Nafafé (2007) and Prussin (2006: 329).
[16] Lydon (2009: 69–70).

developed an interesting theory concerning the origins of Mahmūd Kâ 'ti, the author of the earliest written history of Mali and Songhay, known as the *Tārīkh al-Fattāsh* (written in the early sixteenth century).[17] Haïdara argues that Kâ 'ti was in fact a member of the Cota family from Toledo, and although his genealogy of Kâ 'ti is open to doubt depending on the reading of an Arabic text without diacritic markers, it is certainly known from his work that Kâ 'ti's father migrated from Toledo to Tumbuktu in 1468.[18] The Cotas were infamous New Christians [converted Jews] in Toledo, and the tax collector Alonso Cota had been a source of public rage during the 1449 riots in the city; these led to the establishment of the first discriminatory statutes against New Christians in Iberia, known as the statutes of *limpieza de sangre*, or "purity of blood".[19]

This suggestive role of the Iberian Jews illustrates that across much of West Africa at least some familiar networks integrated the old Mediterranean trade with the new Atlantic African one.[20] Moreover, just as the Jolof and their mercantile culture of trans-Saharan links influenced by Islamic and Jewish traders were not alien to the Portuguese, the reverse was also true. Writing of his arrival at Cantor [Kantora, later the northernmost tip of Kaabunké power] on the Upper Gambia in 1448, Diogo Gomes told how "soon word spread throughout the land that the Christians were at Cantor, and people came from everywhere, from Tambucutu [Tumbuktu] in the north and in the south from the Gabei hills [perhaps the Fouta Djalon mountains of Guinea-Conakry] and from Quioquum, a large walled city [probably Kukyia, near Gao in the far east of present-day Mali]".[21] Naturally, there was hyperbole in this statement – it cannot be true that people travelled well over a thousand miles from Gao to the Upper Gambia just to see Gomes (they could have travelled a similar distance northwards across the Sahara to do the same, and done some trade into the bargain). Yet Gomes's report may contain some

[17] Haïdara (1999: 22–4); See also Lydon (2009: 86).

[18] Hofheinz (2004: 156,164); the doubt concerns whether or not Kâ 'ti's father, whom Hofheinz calls "Ali the Goth", was in fact a Moslem leaving Toledo rather than a member of the Cota family.

[19] On Alonso Cota, see Green (2007a: 25–6).

[20] This mirrors the situation for the distribution of sugar produced in the Atlantic in the sixteenth-century European economy, which followed the existing redistribution networks linking Portugal with Flanders and northern Italy – Ebert (2008: 17–20).

[21] MMAII: Vol. 1, 194: "*logo soou a fama por todo o país que estavam os cristãos em Cantor, e correram de toda a parte para ali, a saber, do norte de Tambucutu, e moradores, do lado do sul, para a Serra Gabei; e vieram gentes de Quioquum, que é uma grande cidade cercada de muralha ...*". Kantora is thought to have lain approximately 25 miles/40 km east of the modern town of Basse Santa Su.

accuracy in the description of people coming to see him, albeit not from such a great distance. Clearly, therefore, people knew what a Christian was and would travel just to see one. Probably the many diaspora traders had told of the world north of the Sahara, and many people in West Africa had also travelled across the desert. For at this date Mali was an outward-looking region, more so than many parts of Europe.

We know for instance that Mansa Musa was said to have slaves from Turkey and other Mediterranean regions in the early fourteenth century.[22] For centuries there had been deep commercial and cultural connections between centres such as Gao, Timbuktu and the Islamic kingdom in Granada, with architects from Al-Andalus coming to the Sahel to work for the Emperor of Mali, and books and commodities all regularly changing hands.[23] People from Mali commonly passed through North Africa, and by the mid-1450s there was an annual caravan of pilgrims from Mali making the pilgrimage to Mecca.[24] Such traditions dated at least back to the first quarter of the fourteenth century, when the entourage which accompanied Mansa Musa on his famous pilgrimage to Mecca was said to have included 14,000 slave girls alone.[25] The cosmopolitan nature of the region is confirmed by notarial records linking the Genoese and the trade from Ceuta via Sijilmāssa to Senegambia, which indicate the presence of goods in the Sahel from as far afield as China, the East Indies, Turkestan and Flanders.[26]

Thus there was considerable knowledge of the worlds north of the Sahara in Mali, certainly among members of the ruling lineages. Diogo Gomes's information corroborates this. People there knew of the Christian world beyond the Sahara and they probably also knew that some of the goods which they traded across the desert were further traded on to it. They were interested in this world. However, it probably also frightened them. Surely members of the ruling circles in contact with diaspora traders would have heard of the Portuguese inroads in Morocco and of their raids on the desert coast of the Sahara following the conquest of Ceuta in 1415. To peoples of West Africa, members of the North African trading diasporas represented a powerful culture. News that the Christians

[22] CEA, 265 for the slaves from Turkey – the account of Al' Umarī.
[23] Haïdara (1997).
[24] CEA, 360–1. Here, Ibn Taghrī Birdī describes such a caravan departing Cairo in 1455 and then states that in 1456, owing to brigandage, "none of the Maghrībīs or Takrūrīs made the Pilgrimage". See also Godinho (1969: 122).
[25] CEA, 351; the evidence of Al-Maqrīzī: doubtless an exaggeration, but even so it suggests a large number.
[26] Lydon (2009: 76).

had defeated representatives of this culture at Ceuta must have been disquieting. Thus though the arrival of Christians was not necessarily unexpected, it probably was alarming.

So when we think of these exchanges beginning so swiftly and easily between Africans and Europeans, we should begin from the realisation that what today is often projected as an unexpected encounter was not like that at all. Each had already found out something of the other through the traders which linked them both, both the North African Moslems and members of the Ibero-Moroccan Jewish diaspora. Moreover, not only did they know something of one another, but they were peoples who had much in common.

The first exchanges were concentrated in Senegambia, therefore, not only because of geographical proximity, but also precisely because of these points of familiarity. As we saw in the previous chapter, the limit of mutual intelligibility between Africans and Europeans was at the Rio Grande in Upper Guinea where the Biafada lived. The fact that communication was easier in the area to the north of this must have shaped the fact that trade was most intense there at first. Although historians have seen the failure of Portuguese navigators to go beyond the coast of present-day Liberia between 1462 and 1471 as caused by internal Portuguese politics, this ignores the fact that the Portuguese certainly found Senegambian cultures more accessible than those farther south.[27]

Moreover, the Islamic influence in Senegambia was vital in the beginnings of the slave trade to Europe. Those deemed legitimately enslaved in Iberia in the 1450s were generally war captives purloined in frontier raids with the Moslems of Granada or in North Africa.[28] War had always been the main justification for enslavement, and in medieval Iberia this custom, inherited from the Romans, had altered to concentrate on the capture of those belonging to a different faith.[29] The fact that Jolof were Moslem meant that the purchase of slaves from them could easily be reconciled with existing practices of enslaving Moslems from Granada and North Africa.[30] Most slaves in fifteenth-century Iberia were Islamic, and in Valencia, to take one example, Moslems were the only group that could be penally enslaved.[31] Indeed, some scholars hold that

---

[27] For a statement of the traditional view, see Ballong-wen-Menuda (1993: Vol. 1, 45–6).
[28] Franco Silva (1979: 17).
[29] Ibid., 37–8.
[30] Jolof slaves arriving in Valencia in the 1480s included two named Ali and one named Amet (Cortes 1964: 223, 230).
[31] Blumenthal (2009: 14).

the earliest Portuguese chronicler of West Africa, Zurara, deliberately portrayed Africans in the guise of Moors and the military skirmishes through the traditional religious language of the *reconquista*, so as to justify enslavement.[32] Such ideological trickery continued even after the procurement of African slaves. Once they reached Europe, the Jolof were said to have warlike tendencies and not to be of peace even though they had been bought and not captured; maintaining this fiction and the appearance of a just war against an Islamic foe provided a continuity with the older slave system and also served as a segue to the commercial orientation that followed.[33]

Continuities thus turn out to be important in both practical and ideological terms in the formation of the first Atlantic-African connections. Islamic influence created a point of cultural contact between Jolof and Portuguese and shaped the ideological and practical contours of the early slave trade to Europe. However, for the Portuguese, Islam was a barrier as well as a bridge. The importance which diaspora merchants professing Islam had for the Jolof in the trans-Saharan trade meant that there was no desire to break this connection. The king, or *Damel*, of Cajor encountered by Cadamosto in 1455 (and called Budomel by him) may have been friendly and receptive, but he was in no hurry to adopt the sailors' religion; his court was filled with "Arabs who he has continually in his house almost as we do our priests because it is they who show him the [Islamic] law".[34] The Portuguese never shifted this pattern.

Thus in Senegambia there was never any doubt that Islam was an entrenched religion of trade which had circulated through the mercantile activities of the trans-Saharan trading diasporas. This related to the circumstances of the Jolof rise to pre-eminence. As we saw in the previous chapter, the Lower Senegal River was subordinate to Mali in the fourteenth century, and thus the growth of the power structure encountered by the Portuguese in Senegambia was related to Mali's rise, which as we saw in the previous chapter itself related to the acceptance of a version of Islam as a religion of trade. If by the fifteenth century the Jolof had freed themselves of Mali's authority, therefore, this does not mean that the Islamic religion was not related to ideas of kingship and authority that European sailors found among them.[35]

[32] Baxter Wolf (1994: 468); Blumenthal (2009: 41); Saunders (1982b).
[33] Franco Silva (1979: 38): The slaves were described as "*de buena guerra e non de paz*". See also Blumenthal (2009: 20).
[34] MMAII: Vol. 1, 326–7: "*arabi chel tien continuamente in chassa quasi como dissamoli nostri preti perche sono quelli che li mostra la leze*".
[35] On Jolof's independence from Mali in the fifteenth century, see Boulègue (1987a: 23).

There was a further corollary of this situation which would affect Portuguese engagement with this world. The relationship between peoples in Western Africa and Islam meant that religion itself – and specifically, as we have seen, a monotheistic religion brought from outside the region – was deeply connected to the activities of foreign trading diasporas in a context often connected to the transport of slaves.[36] This would be important when members of a new trading diaspora holding to a monotheistic faith also arrived, in the shape of the New Christians. Moreover, these New Christians had trading ties, and probably family connections, to the Jewish traders in Morocco who, from their workshops in the Portuguese enclaves in Morocco, controlled the trade in cloth near Arguim.[37] Probably, they were also connected to other centres of recent Jewish settlement in the Saharan region following the 1391 riots in Spain and the migration of Jews to North Africa. These two factors placed these New Christians in a very advantageous position when another trade for slaves through the medium of cloths was initiated for the Atlantic trade. There would soon be striking similarities between the two trades, and some scholars argue for a definite historical link between the indigo-dyed cloths made by Jewish weavers and used in the trans-Saharan trade on the one hand, and on the other, the prevalence of this later cloth trade from Cabo Verde and the subsequent development of indigo-dyed fashions in the region of present-day Guinea-Bissau.[38]

THE BEGINNING OF AN ATLANTIC SLAVE TRADE TO EUROPE

In spite of the continuities which existed, however, Atlantic trade brought ruptures to Senegambia. The most immediate impact was through the Atlantic slave trade to Iberia, which began at once. Of course there had been already a long-standing trade in slaves across the Sahara, as we saw in the previous chapter. However, the addition of the Atlantic vector in trade to the existing Saharan one intensified cycles of violence

[36] On the connection of the trans-Saharan diaspora to the slave trade, see Seck (forthcoming, 2012).
[37] This can be deduced from the ground-breaking work of Mendes (2007: 448–50), who shows how New Christian merchants of Antwerp had strong links to Sephardic Jews of Taroudant, Morocco, an important caravan centre in the 1530s. The New Christians of Antwerp also had strong connections to sugar mills in São Tomé and to subsequent New Christian and Jewish families of the Senegambian region, and thus it is very likely that they also were connected to the New Christian families trading in Western Africa in the early sixteenth century. See Green (2008a: 87–8, 91); Mendes (2007: 371).
[38] Prussin (2006: 345–7).

and instability in the region by placing an even greater emphasis on the demand side.

The traditional view has been that it was gold, not slaving, which was the primary focus of these Portuguese voyages.[39] Yet although the Portuguese voyages were motivated in a macro-political sense by the desire for gold, on the micro level of the motivations of the sailors themselves, things were very different.[40] After a failed attempt to seize slaves near the isle of Gorée in 1445, Rodrigo Annes was quoted by Zurara as having said to his men: "You already know that the people of this land are not as easy to enslave as we wished".[41] The detail may not be accurate, but Zurara captured here the ordinary sentiment of sailors, revealing how private motivations and enterprise shaped early African-European exchanges more than state design and policy.[42]

Although gold may have been the political motivation for Portuguese expansion, this was not how this expansion was perceived in Senegambia. The impact of slaving on the Atlantic coast itself was certainly transformative. Around 1445 the first slaves were being taken in the region of the Senegal River.[43] Yet already by the time that Zurara was writing, probably in the late 1450s, the villages by the shore had been "depopulated by those who went there in ships from our country".[44] This illustrates the impact the Atlantic trade had already had in Senegambia. Ships involved in this early trade may have become targets for pirates. In 1452 some brigands from the Andalusian ports of Seville, Moguem and Palos robbed a Portuguese caravel returning from Africa with sixty-six slaves on board.[45]

Thus just ten years after the European ships arrived in Senegambia, there had been significant changes in levels of security, at least for those Africans living near the coast. That this sort of insecurity was widespread was shown by Cadamosto, when he recounted in 1456 near the Gambia that people "do not stray far from their country because they cannot go safely from one country to the next for fear of being seized by the blacks and sold by them as slaves".[46] For those outside the elites of Senegambian

---

[39] Voiced by, for instance, Fage (1969a: 54–5).

[40] The key work on the role of gold in this trade is Godinho (1969: 149–63).

[41] MMAII: Vol. 1, 39 – "*Já sabees que a gente desta terra nom hé assy ligeira de filhar como nós deseiamos*".

[42] On the importance of private enterprise in Portuguese navigation, see Ballong-wen-Menuda (1993: Vol. 1, 45–9).

[43] MMAII: Vol. 1, 187.

[44] Ibid., Vol. 1, 50 – "*despovoradas per os que lá foram em os navyos desta terra*".

[45] Albuquerque/Santos (1993: Vol. 1, 36).

[46] Ibid., Vol. 1, 358: "*non se alargano molto dal suo paexe perche non vano securi da um paexe al altro per non esser prexi pur da negri et esses vendudi per schiavi*".

society – slaves used in agriculture and as members of the royal household, for instance – the increase in violent disorder was perilous. Naturally, this related to the trans-Saharan trade, but, like the emptying of the villages on the coast, it most likely also related to the new seaborne trade. This is supported by Cadamosto's 1455 account of the Jolof king's slave trade:

> He maintains himself with many robberies and he always has many slaves which he gets partly from his own country and also from neighbouring countries and he uses these slaves in many ways, principally in sewing crops in lands which belong to him and also by selling many of them to the Azenegue [Western Saharan] merchants who trade horses and other things with him, and by selling them to Christians ever since they have started to trade in the lands of the blacks.[47]

This passage suggests that the Jolof trade in slaves through Azenegue merchants to the Portuguese at Arguim and in Senegal had already diverted some of its exports from the trans-Saharan trade. We should of course be wary of assuming that this new trade led to an increase in slave exports. We can, however, look to other indirect signs that there may have been such an increase. Given Cadamosto's assertion that the Jolof king procured his slaves from both his own country and from his neighbours, any increased supply would have to have been accompanied by increased war against his neighbours and a cycle of military procurement. In Senegambia military procurement required cavalry, and by 1462 there is evidence that there was an increased demand for cavalry from many groups. This demand for cavalry was accompanied by increasing political instability, which is suggestive of military confrontations. Taken together, the rise in military procurement and political instability suggest that there had been an increase in wars and thus in prisoners of war who, as Cadamosto's evidence suggests, were often sold as slaves.

The evidence for this comes from an expedition of Diogo Gomes in 1462. Gomes had been sent by King Afonso V of Portugal to the Saluum delta occupied by the Sereer to take authority over any Portuguese ships he found trading there. Afonso was worried about uncontrolled trade in slaves for horses, a fear underlined in a letter of March 28 of that year when he had referred to the "many people buying horses and embarking

---

[47] Ibid., Vol. 1, 316: "*Questo se mantien con altre robarie chel fa et ha sempro molti schiavi negri chel fa pior si nel suo paexe como neli altri paexi vexini a lui e de questi tal schiavi el se ne servie in molti modi e principalmente lo i fa lavor a seminar certe terre e possessione deputada a lui e ancho molti de loro ne vende azanegi merchandanti che capitano de li con cavali e altre cosse e ancho ne vende a christiani depoi che hano comenzado i diti christiani merchandar nele parte de negri*".

them for Guinea".⁴⁸ When Gomes arrived in the Saluum delta, he indeed found that the price for which the Portuguese could sell their horses had halved from twelve slaves per horse to six.⁴⁹ Gomes himself sailed with ten horses, enough, so he said, to purchase one hundred to one hundred fifty slaves. Arriving among the Sereer he found two ships, both of which had brought horses to trade. He also found the Jolof king Buur Gebil sheltering there, having fled after an attack from a rival.

It is thus clear both from Afonso V's letter and from Gomes's account that the Sereer were buying horses hand over fist in these years, and also that there were upheavals among the Jolof elites. These factors were connected. Although for many people in Senegambia the new coastal trade had brought instability, lineage heads saw it as an opportunity. The Sereer were buying horses, and the new cavalry offered them a chance to fight on more equal terms with the Jolof who hitherto had much better access to horsepower. At the same time, such possibilities wrought instability among the Jolof, allowing figures such as Buur Gebil to be challenged and also subsidiary Damels on the coast to get direct access to cavalry and thus begin to threaten the central authority. That this trade was increasing is suggested also by the fall in value of the horses brought by the Portuguese from one horse for twelve slaves to one horse for six, suggesting an increasing demand for slaves and thus an increasing number of horses required for the trade.

Thus this evidence supports the hypothesis of an increased cycle of military procurement and the increased political instability which this cycle had helped to create, an instability whose by-products included prisoners of war that could be sold into the slave trade. The rapidity with which subsidiary Jolof Damels and Sereer lineage heads engaged with the Portuguese illustrates how much they had learnt from the way in which Jolof and Mandinka elites had built up their own power through the trans-Saharan trading diaspora. That is, it shows the importance of access to long-distance mercantile diaspora traders in Senegambia. Here we may see an early example of what Jean-François Bayart has called extraversion in African polities, whereby political power was wielded through the "control of the economic benefits flowing from dependence on the exterior environment".⁵⁰

⁴⁸ Albuquerque/Santos (1993: Vol. 1, 116) – "*achamos que hora novamente muitos comprão cavallos e os embarcão para Guinee*".
⁴⁹ MMAII: Vol. 1, 202; and also for the rest of the information in this paragraph.
⁵⁰ Bayart (2000: 231). Farias (2003: cxvi) sees early trans-Saharan trade as a form of extraversion.

Worlds can change swiftly with a new discovery or technology. Initial changes following the opening of the Atlantic coast for trade depended on the importance of existing political balances in Senegambia. As we have seen, the European arrival affected the balance of slave exports and most likely exacerbated the conflicts which contributed to the supply cycle. However, although demand increased, the initial mechanism of supply was merely the intensification of the violence that underlay the slave-procurement process already in existence for the supply of the trans-Saharan trade. It was in this sense a continuation of what had gone before. There was nothing revolutionary about slavery or slave-trading in the African and Mediterranean worlds of this era. These practices were utterly normal.

Thus the Portuguese trade initially capitalised both on this existing process and on existing tensions. Soon after their arrival the centre of Jolof power in the middle Senegal valley was challenged by their subordinates on the coastal periphery. According to Münzer – writing in the mid-1490s – the Damel of Cajor was already in conflict with the Jolof king at the time of the Portuguese arrival and used the new supply of horses to expand his campaign.[51] This may or may not be true, but certainly Münzer's evidence implies that the Damel must have capitalised on the Portuguese presence almost at once to fulfil his ambitions. The cycle of war which developed was to have a major impact on the profile of slaves traded to Europe in the second half of the fifteenth century, with nearly 85 percent of the slaves shipped to Valencia between 1479 and 1516 said to be from the "land of Jolof".[52] Some Mandinka slaves were also recorded, but no slaves were recorded from areas farther to the south prior to 1497.[53]

The impact of this trade on Senegambian society emerges in a petition to the Portuguese king made by the Parliament of Évora in 1472. Here the king was urged not to allow slaves to be exported outside Portugal, "because, Master, [the slaves] constitute an important population in your Kingdoms, and they are the cause of new lands being opened and woods being cleared and marshes being opened and of other benefits".[54]

---

[51] MMAII: Vol. 1, 235–6.

[52] The figures are 2,487 out of 2,944 with a specified provenance. See Hair (1980). The ethnonym referred to the land of provenance and thus generically to Senegambia; the slaves themselves may have been Jolof, Mandinka, Pullo or Sereer.

[53] Cortes (1964). Soares/Torrão (2007: 137) concur with this reading of the evidence, noting that only after 1497 do Sapes begin to emerge in the documentation, with Sereer found after 1502, Cocoli after 1505, Pullo after 1506 and Biafada after 1509.

[54] MMAII: Vol. 1, 453 – *"porque senhor, fazem grande povoaçam em vosos Reynos, e sam causa de se fazer terra novas e romper os matos e abrir pauuys e outros proveitos"*.

This is evidence both of a large volume of slaves being shipped from Senegambia and also of their impact in a Portuguese society still coping with the effects of depopulation following the Black Death of 1348.[55] It reveals that labour needs brought on by the population shortage must in part have driven the expansion and slaving activities of the Portuguese elite, which was accustomed to subsisting within a predatory, militaristic paradigm.[56]

These internal tensions among the Jolof were soon superseded by other symptoms of the trade. Beginning in the 1460s Pullo migrations transformed the region, leading to conflicts in areas as different as Fuuta Tooro on the banks of the Senegal in the north and Kaabu and the Rio Grande in the south.[57] The Pullo migrated with large numbers of cattle and may also have had some horses deriving from a trade with the Portuguese on the Upper Senegal River.[58] By the 1480s there was a line of Pullo power running between the Fouta Djalon mountains and Senegambia. Equally important, these migrations also helped catalyse the independence of Kaabu from Mali.[59] On their way to the Fouta Djalon, the Pullo fought the Kassanké in Casamance, and the experience which the Kaabunké had in defending themselves from the Pullo enhanced their military status and their independence from Mali, whose power was then being eroded by Songhay.[60]

The Pullo migration was largely prompted by a desire for new pastures, perhaps to satisfy increasing livestock herds.[61] These increasing herds coincided with the last decades of the dry period between 1100–1500, when competition for pastures in arid areas by the River Senegal was intense. Many Pullo melted away en route as they found good grazing land, and the army was finally defeated by the Biafada at the Grande

---

[55] For the contribution of slave imports to redressing the labour shortage following the Black Death, see Godinho (1981: Vol. 4, 152). The Senegambian origins of these slaves can be deduced from the Valencia evidence and the fact that, as we saw at the start of the chapter, the Portuguese had only reached the Gold Coast the year before this petition, in 1471.

[56] Estimates of numbers of slaves imported to Portugal at this time range from 33,500 before 1492 (Curtin 1969: 115–16; almost certainly an underestimate) through 80,000 before 1492 (Russell-Wood 1995: 148) and to 150,000 from 1441 to 1495 (Godinho 1981: Vol. 4, 161).

[57] On the Pullo migrations and their effects on the region, see Niane (1989: 55–61).

[58] Brooks (1993b: 127).

[59] Barry (1998: 20–1).

[60] On the conflict between the Pullo king and the Kassanké in these years, see Sandoval (1627: 38v). The decisive break of Songhay from Mali was in 1489.

[61] Brooks (1993b: 199).

River before dispersing. At the Gambia River, it was later said, the Pullo had been so many that each soldier had thrown a stone into the river and thereby created a ford.[62] This oral tradition implied more the size of that wave of migration than an actual event, and it is a tradition often associated with cycles of power and migration in Upper Guinea.[63] There was a need for new stories to make sense of the countless changes brought on by the Atlantic, for even with these events far from the coast, Atlantic trade had played a role. Although as Brooks argues, climatic stresses were key, a part of the success of the Pullo migrations must have stemmed from divisions among the Jolof triggered by Atlantic trade; and meanwhile, as the Mandinka of Kaabu and the peoples of Casamance who had acculturated to the Mandinka looked beyond Mali for support in their conflicts with the Pullo, they turned to the new power on the horizon, the Europeans in their ships.[64]

Thus the Pullo migration marked a watershed, encouraging both the political independence of Kaabu from Mali and greater alliances between peoples south of the Gambia with seaborne traders. The success of the Pullo army and the growing insecurity of the region attested to by Cadamosto meant that self-defence, and the iron needed to fashion the weapons to achieve this capability, was increasingly important. Demand for iron following the Pullo migrations and the ability of Atlantic traders to supply this played a major role in the expansion of links to Upper Guinea from the 1480s onwards. Thus were new alliances formed in an attempt to deal with the new relationships which maritime traders had themselves helped to bring about by arriving on the coast with horses to trade for people who themselves were seized in the wars which the new horses were used to fight. By 1480, with the Pullo migrations in full flow, the violent circle of Atlantic trading and slavery had begun.

Indeed, whereas the impact of the early trade on the region has to be inferred from a complex reading of sources such as Cadamosto and Diogo Gomes, by this point in the later fifteenth century the picture becomes clearer. Jean Boulègue estimates that by the second half of the fifteenth century eight hundred to one thousand Senegambian slaves were being sold annually from Arguim, and this was a considerable increase

---

[62] Ibid.

[63] See NCAC/OHAD, Cassette 566, page 12, for an account of Tiramaghan crossing the Gambia River in this manner. Some Bainunk traditions also hold that their king, Buba Manga, built a bridge across the Casamance River near his court at Brikama in the same way – from an interview with Ansumane Manga, Singuère, Casamance, April 2011.

[64] See Brooks (1993b: 199) on the role of climatic stresses.

on the previous trans-Saharan trade to Morocco.[65] By 1480 the trade had spread into other regions, with Mandinka slaves reaching the slave markets at Seville.[66] These Mandinka probably came from the Gambia region, and their presence is reflective of this extension of exchange beyond the Damel of Cajor and the Sereer. Here, then, were new cycles of violence and power which had swiftly carved their own space in African society.

RELATIONSHIPS BETWEEN WESTERN AFRICANS AND THE PORTUGUESE IN THE FIFTEENTH-CENTURY ATLANTIC

In order to consolidate this new slave trade, the Portuguese required several types of engagement. Although the first fifty years of African-Portuguese relationships were initially characterised all too often by fear and misunderstandings, as the commercial and political changes precipitated by the Atlantic trade were cemented, the seeds of what became the first mixed communities connected to Atlantic trade also emerged in Africa.

On the institutional level, the first type of engagement needed by the Portuguese was that of political relationships with African rulers. Such diplomatic missions were feasible in areas of centralised government such as among the Jolof and in Mali, and, farther south, in Benin and Kongo. This need was swiftly understood, and the Portuguese monarch João II (1481–95) embarked on a sustained programme of diplomacy in Africa among the Jolof of Senegal, the Obas of Benin and the rulers of Kongo; he also sent ambassadors inland to Mali, Mossi, Songhay and Timbuktu.[67] The embassy to the Court of Mali was still recalled by that emperor's grandson fifty years later.[68]

However, it is important to realise that the political engagement of the Portuguese did not stem from some proto-colonial policy. The changes which Portuguese rulers hoped to impose on African societies related essentially to the hope of diverting some of the existing trade. There was no attempt to found colonial outposts in this early period, and indeed as we shall see in subsequent chapters, the Portuguese monarchy tried to

---

[65] Boulègue (1987a: 88). If accurate, this estimate confirms the earlier supposition that the birth of the Atlantic trade had increased the quantity of slaves being sold from Senegambia.

[66] Documents illustrating this are found in Albuquerque/Santos (1993: 257–8).

[67] On this policy of João II, see Mota (1954: Vol. 2, 10) and Ryder (1969: 28–9). On the embassies to Mali and Timbuktu, see João de Barros – MMAII: Vol. 1, 561–2.

[68] As recounted by Barros – ibid., Vol. 1, 562.

impose draconian penalties on those who did settle on the African coast. Although lip service was paid to the desire to bring about ideological change, this was not a priority. There was a pretended zeal of Christian evangelisation throughout, and although this became important in Kongo, it was not essential to the Portuguese. When it became clear that the Islamic Jolof could not be conquered and would not convert, trade went unimpeded. Indeed, one of the main Christian and political goals – the formation of an alliance against Islam if the mythical Christian King "Prester John" could be found – related far more to shoring up the political situation against the perceived Islamic threat in Portugal than it did to changing Africa.

At the political level, the most concerted attempt at Portuguese official engagement in Senegambia occurred in 1488 with the case of Bumi Jeléen (known in Portuguese sources as Bemoim). Bumi Jeléen was a Jolof prince who came on a caravel to Portugal in 1488 to seek assistance in a civil war that had developed between himself and a rival for the kingship.[69] The occurrence of a civil war among the Jolof again confirms the growing cycle of instability that has been traced for this period in the preceding sections of this chapter. Bumi Jeléen's decision to seek support in Portugal indicates how far strategies of extraversion had already been diverted from the pre-existing trans-Saharan trade into an Atlantic dimension. It also offers a very early example of what was to become a long-standing policy of the Portuguese in Kongo and Angola, whereby the Portuguese supported claimants to the throne in the hope of installing puppet rulers.[70]

Bumi Jeléen was well received in the Portuguese court; he was treated as a visiting king and dressed in the clothing of a Portuguese nobleman. This was during the monarchy of João II, who, in line with his active policy of diplomacy in Africa, sent Bumi Jeléen back to the Senegal River with a Portuguese fleet of twenty armed caravels. However, on their arrival at the mouth of the Senegal River, the captain-general of the fleet, Pero Vaz de Cunha, stabbed Bumi Jeléen to death, claiming treason; other accounts simply said that Cunha was afraid of dying of disease and killed the Jolof prince so that he could turn back.[71] The Portuguese mariners had shown

---

[69] Indeed, Russell (1995: 162) sees this event as pivotal in the history of relationships between the Portuguese and African kings in this era.

[70] See for instance Hilton (1985: 53–5).

[71] The main accounts of the Bumi Jeléen affair are all collated in MMAII: Vol. 1, 529–63. See also Francisco de Lemos Coelho's account in Peres (1953: 96). On Bemoim as Bumi Jeléen, see Boulègue (1987a: 75).

that they would not treat an African prince as a superior, and indeed João II failed to punish the culprits on their return to Portugal because of the serious penalty he would have had to impose.[72] Meanwhile, Bumi Jeléen's Jolof companions on the return voyage to the Senegal River were left on the Caboverdean island of Santiago.[73]

In many ways, therefore, this Portuguese diplomatic intervention was a failure. By siding with Bumi Jeléen only to kill him, they had destroyed their chances of building up a relationship of trust with future Jolof monarchs; their alliance with him could not have been pleasing to his now-unimpeded rivals. Moreover, the affair had emphasised how many barriers of both fear and discrimination there were to the creation of partnerships between Africans and Europeans. Those who had not spent long periods in Western Africa, such as Bumi Jeléen's killer, Pero Vaz de Cunha, were afraid of diseases and other potential threats. Certainly, the Portuguese voyages in Africa were accompanied by extraordinary levels of mortality; in a letter of circa 1497 to the *Reyes Católicos* of Aragón and Castile, Ferdinand and Isabela, Christopher Columbus wrote that over half the population of the kingdom of Portugal had died in the exploration of Guinea.[74] Many of these sailors doubtless also articulated these fears through a discriminatory discourse. Although scholars such as Debra Blumenthal do not believe that racism was a fully articulated ideology in Iberia at this point, and although there were both positive and negative images of Africans in Europe, there is an important body of evidence that in the late fifteenth century there was an increasing connection between negative ideas of slavery and skin colour in Iberia.[75] This too must have directed the ways in which Portuguese sailors accompanying

[72] See Rui de Pina's account – MMAII: Vol. 1, 549.
[73] According to Lemos Coelho – see Peres (1953: 96).
[74] Las Casas (1966b: Vol. 62, 255) – "*si se cuenta la gente del reino de Portugal, y las personas de los que son muertos en esta empresa de Guinea, se fallaría que son más de la mitad del reino*". In this passage Las Casas quotes in full a letter of Columbus's to which he had access. This can only be an exaggeration, but it is probably indicative of a gruesome reality, or – just as importantly – of how reality was perceived.
[75] Sweet (1997: 166) emphasises the pre-existing racial stereotypes in Iberia inherited from Moorish culture and suggests that these were becoming universalised by 1492. Blumenthal (2009) argues forcefully against this position, suggesting that although the large number of African slaves in Iberia in the fifteenth century began to see an association between skin colour and slavery, this was not universalised by the end of the fifteenth century – a picture supported by Medeiros (1985) and Russell-Wood (1978), who both share this view but argue that colour racism quickly came to predominate by the end of the sixteenth century. On the positive and negative images of Africans, see Nafafé (2007: 28–31).

Bumi Jeléen perceived Senegambia, and contributed to the barriers to partnerships between Africans and Europeans.

Whereas Europeans feared death, Africans feared enslavement; they compartmentalised this fear by associating Europeans with cannibalism and witchcraft. When Cadamosto reached the Gambia River in 1455, he was told that people did not want to enter into friendship with the Europeans since they had learnt that the "Christians ate human flesh and that we bought blacks only to eat them".[76] The accusation of cannibalism was symbolic of the fear with which the new European traders were seen. It further showed also that Europeans were perceived through the prism of witchcraft, because in Western Africa cannibalism was associated with witchcraft.[77] Here were white witches who had come literally to "eat" others by taking them away.[78]

From an African perspective, such barriers to mixed communities thus existed at the level of discourses of enslavement-related ritual. However, prejudice stemming from fear of these foreign traders appears to have been less marked than they were for many Europeans. This was largely because Sahelian communities were accustomed to light-skinned outsider traders and, indeed, as we saw in Chapter 1, had already incorporated them into their social frameworks. Although it is likely that there was some familiarity with race as a marker of difference in the medieval Sahel, this was not generalised; according to Bruce Hall, "race" itself had a more cultural meaning than it developed in the subsequent Atlantic world.[79] Comparatively light-skinned North Africans were common

---

[76] MMAII: Vol. 1, 348 – "*christiani manzavemo carne humana e che compravemo negri salvo per manzarli*". This belief ran deep in Senegambia. When Geraldini visited the Damel of Cajor in 1519, he was told that "a century ago a legend was told that those of our hemisphere were white and that we ate blacks from Africa; but that around 30 years ago this nonsense had been rejected, once commerce with the Portuguese had begun" (Geraldini 1977: 87) – "*corría, de siglo atrás, la leyenda de que los de nuestro hemisferio éramos blancos y que nos comíamos a los negros Etíopes; pero que hacía 30 años que habían abandonado tal patraña, al comerciar con los portugueses.*" When juxtaposed with Cadamosto's evidence, the likelihood would be that this idea only dated from the start of Jolof-Portuguese exchanges.

[77] Thus according to some traditions, Tiramagahan Traoré's father, Daamansa Wulading, began to accrue power when he defeated a great witch called Duukamisa who used to eat more than one thousand people per year – NCAC/OHAD, Transcribed Cassette 566.

[78] On cannibalism and witchcraft, see Hawthorne (2010b: Chapter 6). Moreover, we know from both Angola (Miller 1988: 4–5) and Cameroon (Argenti 2007: 55) that this accusation of cannibalism was widespread in the African Atlantic. For a Eurocentric perspective on cannibalism in the Atlantic world, see Abulafia (2008: xvi).

[79] B. Hall (2005).

enough in Senegambia and Upper Guinea, and Diogo Gomes met one from the Algerian town of Tlemcen on the Gambia River in 1448.[80]

Thus one of the greatest barriers to the creation of mixed trading communities in Western Africa was Africans' and Europeans' mutual fear of one another, a fear grounded in various combinations of mutual difference, the ubiquity of mortality, and the challenges of these new exchanges.[81] What such barriers revealed was that there was a deep need for trust at a more localised level between African and European traders. This was a sort of trust which could only be built up if each was prepared to learn more about the other. Such communities could only develop if Europeans were prepared to spend some time living in the region and Africans were prepared to receive them, and it was in the last fifteen years of the fifteenth century that this first began to occur to any significant extent.

As we have seen, the first Portuguese exchanges in West Africa were largely confined to Senegambia. However, this pattern changed in the 1480s. The two major contributing factors were the Pullo migration and the resultant need which Upper Guineans had of new allies, and the fact that the Portuguese had damaged their links with the Jolof monarchy following their failed support of Bumi Jeléen. Both these factors meant that it was at about this time that Portuguese first began to live among African communities south of the Gambia River and intensify trading relationships there. Allied to this was the increasing understanding among the Portuguese of the importance of rivers to successful trading along West Africa's coast; there was a much greater preponderance of rivers south of the Gambia.[82]

Writing in the first decade of the sixteenth century, Valentim Fernandes wrote of the "many Portuguese Christian merchants visiting and trading with the Blacks" in the area of the Casamance River.[83] The same pattern pertained in the São Domingos river.[84] Fernandes was dependent for his work on informants who knew the region, and therefore one can surmise that this information refers to exchanges which must have developed some time before. He compiled his work at the end of the first decade of

---

[80] MMAII: Vol. 1, 195.

[81] On the role of fear in early exchanges in Atlantic Africa, see Green (2006).

[82] For example, at around this time, in 1499, Álvaro de Caminha, the captain of São Tomé, described his achievements to Manoel I as including the discovery of "many new rivers, in which there are many slaves and [there is] much ivory" – "*descobryndo muitos Ryos Novos, em os quaes há muitos escravos e muito marfim*": MMAI: Vol. 1, 167.

[83] MMAII: Vol. 1, 712 – "*muytos christãos estātes mercadores q tractā cō aquelles Negros*". See also Mark (1985: 17).

[84] MMAII: Vol. 1, 717.

the sixteenth century, thus these settlements probably began well before the year 1500.

The initial establishment of these settlements had depended on multiple factors. From the African perspective, the political changes and growing instability prompted by ecological fragility and Atlantic trade prompted rulers in Upper Guinea to seek new sources of support. However, this decision was shaped also by the long-standing tradition in the region, which we saw in Chapter 1, in which diaspora traders were well known and accepted in the region. Thus proximate environmental and political causes were necessary conditions for the first seeds of mixed communities in Western Africa, but they alone were not sufficient; without the preceding cultural and economic histories tied to the Mandinka expansion, the authorities of the Casamance and São Domingos regions might have opted for a very different course of action.

From the European side, meanwhile, the development of these mixed communities grew out of the perceived need for slaves to feed growth in both the wider Mediterranean economy and, as we shall see in the next chapter, the local Caboverdean one. Not only were African slaves an important source of labour in underpopulated Portugal, as we have seen, but they also increased Portugal's commercial links with other parts of southern Europe. The establishment of the *Casa dos Escravos* and of an *Almoxarife dos Escravos* in Lisbon in 1486, which showed the increasing importance of slaving to Portugal, centralised a trade which had hitherto been confined to the Algarve.[85] Large numbers of these slaves were re-exported from Portugal to different cities in Spain, enhancing Portugal's economic strength in the region.[86] If this growth was supported by the slave trade, few saw any need to question the moral basis of this new expansion. Why after all should we expect Portuguese mariners to have valued the lives of Africans whom they seized or bought for slaves when they did not appear to give much value to their own lives? The vast mortality of these early voyages shows that had they done so, they would not have embarked from the Mediterranean port of Lagos in the first place.

CHANGING POLITICAL AND TRADING RELATIONSHIPS IN WESTERN AFRICA, CIRCA 1490–1510

The advent of these commercial settlements on the West African coast in the 1490s was symptomatic of wider changes in Western Africa in

[85] Vogt (1973a: 2–4).
[86] An excellent study involving data on this trade to Valencia is Blumenthal (2009).

which the accent of Atlantic engagement switched from Senegambia to Upper Guinea. Although the Atlantic slave trade continued to be strong in Senegambia for a while yet, as the sixteenth century developed the focus there would switch away from slaving to trade in commodities such as hides, ivory and wax sold to English and French traders. Such trade does not, however, appear to have involved much residence on the part of Europeans in Atlantic trading settlements of the coast. Creolised communities living in mainland Africa came to be connected to the slave trade, which increasingly was conducted south of the Gambia from Upper Guinean ports on the Casamance, São Domingos and Grande Rivers.

By 1500, the extent of the slave trade was significant. Duarte Pacheco Pereira, writing in 1505, gave estimates for the whole region from the Senegal River to Sierra Leone of 3,500 slaves exported annually.[87] He described a flourishing trade on the River Senegal, in Cajor, among the Sereer, in Casamance and on the Rio Grande.[88] His figures have been criticised by Ivana Elbl as obviously exaggerated.[89] But this view depends on the idea that the account books kept by royal officials were accurate. Because they did not allow for cheating and contraband, this is a problematic assumption.[90] Indeed, we know that around this time, as early as 1505, there were accusations of contraband by the slave traders of São Tomé, and so it is a reasonable assumption that such practices had already taken hold in Western Africa. Given the greater longevity of the trade in this region, it is possible that this practice had indeed been borrowed from Western Africa by traders in São Tomé.[91] In fact, Pereira's figures are broadly in keeping with other estimates of the time.[92] Certainly, Cocolí, Jalonké, Sape and Sereer slaves began to be recorded in Europe from 1497 onwards with relative frequency, which confirms his remarks regarding the increasing sourcing of African slaves from areas south of Senegambia.[93]

---

[87] MMAII: Vol. 1, 658.

[88] Ibid., Vol. 1, 630–48.

[89] Elbl (1997: 68).

[90] See Newson (2006: 157) on the unreliability of early slave export figures from Africa and the connection of this to contraband.

[91] MMAI: Vol. 1, 206 – "*os rendeyros e tratadores que ora som da Ilha de Sāthomé, nó g[u] ardam cõ muta parte os taxas ordenadas do que devē mādar dar por peça*". The practice was widespread enough for the crown to ban all slaves being taken from Kongo other than in the royal ships in 1519 (ibid., Vol. 1., 429).

[92] Elbl herself cites two of these estimates, one by Chá' Masser that at least 2,000 slaves arrived annually in Portugal in the 1500s, and the other of the port inspector Bernardo Segura of 1516 that the total slave-trading potential is 6,750 in 1517 (MMAI: Vol.1, 379) – see Elbl (1997: 35).

[93] Cortes (1964: 293, 306, 338, 347, 363, 383, 428, 432, 433, 444, 457).

Changes in social organisation may be better indicators of the impact of the slave trade than the game of guestimating export figures. We have already seen something of this in this chapter with the rise of the Pullo and the growing independence of Kaabu from Mali, both related in part to the onset of Atlantic trade. The evidence is that these processes accelerated at the end of the fifteenth and the start of the sixteenth centuries, reinforcing the picture of how the birth of the Atlantic trade was a necessary but not sufficient condition of political fragmentation and civil strife.

The clearest example of this is among the Jolof. Although there still appears to have been a united Jolof political unit in the late fifteenth century that included the provinces of Jolof, Cajor, Waalo, Bawol and Siin, it was unravelling. The Sereer polity of Saluum was founded around 1500 from a constellation of Gelwaar/Sereer chieftaincies which previously had been preyed on by the Jolof cavalry for slaves.[94] The independence of the Sereer derived from their strengthened military capacity, a result of their new ability to procure horses in the trade for slaves. Meanwhile, the Jolof empire fragmented into its constituent kingdoms following uprisings on the coast and the rise of Pullo power in Fouta Toro circa 1510.[95] The weakness brought about by competing power interests bolstered by the Atlantic trade had precipitated a decisive shift in political organisation in Senegambia. Kingdoms like Cajor and Siin had new access to horses and could free themselves from the old Jolof heartland.

The effects of this on the Jolof are expressed through the evidence that the vast majority of slaves in early America were Jolof, most likely war captives procured through attacks from Cajor and the Sereer.[96] The first major slave revolt on Hispaniola, which took place in December 1521, was undertaken by slaves who were mostly Jolof.[97] The Jolof quickly gained a reputation for being "arrogant, disobedient, agitators and incorrigible, responsible for uprisings among the [B]lacks and for the deaths of some Christians"; in 1532 a law was passed decreeing that Jolofs should no longer be taken to America.[98]

---

[94] Curtin (1975: 10); Boulègue (1987a: 17).

[95] Boulègue (1987a: 160).

[96] That there were regular slave raids from Cajor in this era is shown by Geraldini (1977: 79), who recounts in 1519 that while in Cajor the king had "occasion of making ... certain expeditions [i.e. raids]": "*ocasión de hacer ... ciertas expediciones*".

[97] Saco (1879: Vol. 1, 131); Deive (1989: 33).

[98] Saco (1879: Vol. 1, 158): – "*soberbios, inobedientes, revolvedores, incorregibles y autores de los alzamientos de negros y de las muertes de algunos cristianos*". However, the evidence from Tables I.1 and I.2 proves that this law was routinely ignored.

That these changes in the balance of political power were connected to the rise of the Atlantic world is accepted by historians.[99] The Jolof themselves recognised this all too well. Awareness that the Atlantic trade had precipitated the growing weakness of Jolof power may have been manifested in sporadic hostility directed at Portuguese ships, particularly around the Cape Verde peninsula. Portuguese ships bound for India in 1505 were refused water there and instead sailed on to Cajor, where they were supplied.[100] Two years later, fifteen sailors aboard Vasco Gomez d'Abreu's fleet bound for India were seized, again in this region, and were only ransomed with difficulty; and yet again, the fleet was well received in Cajor.[101] Clearly, the Damel of Cajor saw the Portuguese as vital, and indeed he had an ambassador at the Portuguese court in Lisbon in 1515, but perhaps those loyal to the traditional seat of Jolof power resented the Portuguese disruption, their alliance with Cajor, and their recent support for Bumi Jeléen as well.[102]

Political changes were not limited to the unravelling of Jolof's concentrated power. South of the Gambia River, they also included the independence of the federation of Kaabu from Mali. The association of Kaabu's rise with Atlantic trade is apparent in both oral and written histories. By 1500 Kaabu was a political force, referred to by Pacheco Pereira as a powerful kingdom.[103] Historians see Kaabu's independence from Mali towards the end of the fifteenth century as connected to an increasing autonomy derived from the growing commodity and slave trade with the Atlantic, and perhaps also with the need for greater self-reliance which followed the Pullo migrations of the 1470s and 1480s.[104]

Thus the political instability and reorientations which developed from the 1460s to the 1480s continued at the end of the fifteenth and beginning of the sixteenth centuries. With some kingdoms, such as Jolof, this precipitated fragmentation, and yet with others, such as Kaabu, there was rather political consolidation. Moreover, just as the political effects varied, so did the nature of the slaving economy. In Senegambia most slaves appear to have been captured through war, as the evidence we looked at earlier in this chapter from Cadamosto made clear. As we also saw earlier, Geraldini witnessed the Damel of Cajor embarking on a military

[99] This is the general argument of Boulègue (1987a). See also Fage (1980: 302).
[100] Castanheda (1979: Vol. 1, 211).
[101] Ibid., Vol. 1, 308–9.
[102] On the ambassador in Lisbon, see MMAI: Vol. 15, 29.
[103] See C. Lopes (1999: 77–8); for the passage from Pereira, see MMAII: Vol. 1, 642.
[104] Havik (2004b: 21); Barry (1998: 20–2). See also Rodney (1970: 12); Curtin (1975: 8).

campaign in 1519, and though this was clearly a regular occurrence, these Jolof derided the peoples of Guinea (i.e., south of the Gambia) who lived "without the least security, since there brothers and relatives ... sell one another to traders from far distant lands".[105] This suggests that raids between neighbouring villages, perhaps related through kinship, were not unknown south of the Gambia. Whereas in Senegambia wars between large groups were the major source of slaves, in Upper Guinea slaves were already being procured through intra-lineage and village raids of the sort which came to be much more widespread in later generations.[106]

What emerges from this complex pattern is that effects of the new Atlantic trade were not uniform and depended on pre-existing social and political configurations. On the social level, as we have seen, the very possibility of mixed Atlantic trading communities depended on the willingness of Upper Guinean elites to welcome and make some accommodations with members of trading diasporas as they had learnt to do previously with the Mandinka. On the political level, meanwhile, the nature of political organisation and how centralised power was structured in a given area was particularly important.[107] In previously centralised regions such as that of the Jolof, the tendency was towards fragmentation, with existing political structures unable to control their representatives, who had new access to sources of military strength such as cavalry, in far-flung peripheries. In broadly decentralised regions, however, such as those in Upper Guinea, the smaller political units meant that rulers could retain control, but that in order to do so they needed to make alliances with the newcomers. It was the combination of both pre-existing cultural and political factors which thus facilitated the settlement of Europeans in these areas and allowed the first steps to be taken towards Atlantic Creole communities on the African mainland. Meanwhile, the new configurations allowed for the rise of new centralised states like Kaabu in areas where these had not been so strong previously; the new patterns as a whole were embedded through the intensification of cycles of violent disorder precipitated by the labour demands of the new Atlantic economy.

When we try to imagine what the atmosphere of such a distant time and place was like, the historical record is not our friend. First-hand

---

[105] Geraldini (1977: 135): "*sin seguridad alguna, ya que allí los hermanos y consanguíneos ... venden a mercaderes de remotísimas naciones a sus proprios hermanos y consanguíneos*".

[106] Baum (1999); Hawthorne (2003).

[107] On the relationship of the slave trade to centralised and decentralised societies, see Hawthorne (2001) and M. Klein (2001).

accounts of actual arrivals and exchanges or dialogues on the Western African coast are few. However, there may be aides to help us imagine some of these exchanges. With the colonisation of the Caribbean island of Hispaniola in the 1490s, connections rapidly sprang up between Western Africa and the Caribbean (cf. Chapter 6), and the atmosphere of exchanges among the Spanish in Hispaniola may convey something of what was then going on in Western Africa. When Las Casas arrived in Hispaniola for the first time, in 1499, he wrote:

> We cast our anchors in the port of Santo Domingo, and before any man among us had jumped ashore some of the residents here came down to the beach, and some of those on the ship who had been here before asked those who they recognized in a loud voice ... "What news? What news is there in the land?", to which the others answered, "Good, good, there is much gold, a grain of so many pounds was found, and there is war with the Indians which means that there will be many slaves". There was much happiness and rejoicing among those on the ship when they heard the news.[108]

Turning from the Caribbean to Western Africa, we know from casual accounts that there was a constant back and forth of ships along the coast. Diogo Gomes came upon two ships trading among the Sereer when he arrived in the Saluum in 1462, and Amerigo Vespucci came upon another two when he reached the Cape Verde peninsula in 1501.[109] Also, of course, these sightings of sails would have led to exchanges of news among the sailors. With a slaving culture as embedded as it was, and with the wars between Sereer, Jolof and Pullo that had developed partly as a consequence of this, it is not too ahistorical to imagine that exchanges similar to this one observed by Las Casas may have taken place, where slavers rejoiced at the wars of African peoples and the prospect of the captives which would be sold to them as a result.

---

[108] Las Casas (1966b: Vol. 63, 178) – "*echamos anclas en este puerto de Sancto Domingo, ántes que hombre de nosotros saltase en tierra, llegáronse a la playa algunos de los aquí vecinos, y los de la nao, algunos que habían estado acá, preguntando a los que cognoscían, á voz alta ..."Qué nuevas, qué nuevas hay en la tierra?", responda, "buenas, buenas, que hay mucho oro, que se cogió un grano de tantas libras, y que hay guerra con los indios porque habrá hartos esclavos, etc." De las cuales nuevas hobo en la nao harta alegría y regocijo*".

[109] On Vespucci, see Formisano (1992: 19). On Gomes, see MMAII: Vol. 1, 202.

3

The Settlement of Cabo Verde and Early Signs of Creolisation in Western Africa

In his account of the settlements on the Casamance and São Domingos Rivers discussed in the previous chapter, Valentim Fernandes stated that the main trading partners of these settlements were Caboverdeans.[1] Here we get a glimpse of how, as we shall see in this chapter, the settlement of Cabo Verde from the 1460s onwards was a key factor in both the development of Creole communities in Western Africa and in the emergence of the trade networks of the early African Atlantic.

The ten large islands and numerous islets of Cabo Verde were initially settled by European sailors in the 1460s. In the sixteenth century there were two main inhabited islands, Santiago and Fogo. The archipelago offered a base for Europeans trading in Africa and swiftly became connected to the African coast, so that both islands and the coast were integrated into a single geopolitical zone. Economically, neither can be studied alone in this early period.[2] Thus while recognising the priority of pre-existing African factors in shaping Atlantic exchanges in Upper Guinea, we must also accept the integration of Cabo Verde into the picture. This is particularly important for the understanding of the development of Creole communities; the Creole culture which emerged in Western Africa was one that spanned both the islands and the coast and did so because of the heavy interconnections between the two zones.[3]

This chapter explores the first settlement of Cabo Verde. Although traditional historiography has tended to emphasise settlement and

---

[1] MMAII: Vol. 1, 717.
[2] A point made by Torrão (1991: 237).
[3] Horta (2000: 101); Mark (2002: 14).

colonisation, by looking in detail at economic data I show how dependent the settlement on Cabo Verde was on slave labour and thus how crucial slavery was to this very early colonial settlement. Slaves were essential to the labour provided on plantations, which provided the cotton that Cabo Verde grew to weave the cloths that were used for exchange on the African coast. They were also needed for labour in the construction of a colonial outpost which had to be built from scratch in these desolate islands. In this chapter, this analysis is linked to the relationships which Caboverdeans began to develop in Upper Guinea in the late fifteenth century and to the new emphasis on slaving which this required there.

This process turns out to be central not only to the emergence of the first Atlantic slave trade to Europe which we saw in the last chapter, but also to the emergence of a Creole culture. By the late fifteenth and early sixteenth centuries, the earliest signs of a Caboverdean Creole language emerged. This was still a pidgin language of communication, not yet a fully fledged vernacular. However, as Caboverdeans travelled to and from West Africa for trade, they took both this mixed language and the mixed cultural forms that were developing on the islands with them. Thus as we see in this chapter, the islands developed a key role in the emergence of an Atlantic Creole society in Western Africa in the early sixteenth century, thereby offering an early indication of just how far the processes of creolisation and slavery would be connected in the Atlantic world.

Yet at the same time, as we saw in the last chapter, this role was only made possible by the pre-existing commercial and cultural configurations of Upper Guinea, which determined which areas of the African mainland were open to this process. Thus the most important new aspect of the argument I put forward here is that the development of creolisation across Western Africa was made possible through a combination of internal and external factors, and not by the subordination of the internal to the external as an earlier historiography once suggested. It was because of a fusion of local West African factors and wider, more global ones that the Creole world born in Cabo Verde could be transferred to the African mainland.

THE SETTLEMENT OF CABO VERDE AND EARLY TRADE WITH THE WEST AFRICAN COAST

When the first Portuguese ships reached the Senegal River in the mid-1440s, the islands of Cabo Verde had not even been spied by European mariners. However, around 1460 Cabo Verde was settled by Genoese and Portuguese sailors.[4] Simultaneously way-stations to more distant points of the Atlantic and Indian Oceans and bases from which to trade with the nearby African coast, without these islands the subsequent history of Western Africa would have been very different. The intensification of the slave trade in Senegambia and Upper Guinea in the late fifteenth century was partly facilitated by the settlement of the islands and the more frequent exchanges which this settlement facilitated. Thus to understand how Creole society here evolved with Atlantic trade, we must also understand how Caboverdean society evolved and was interconnected to the African mainland. This is particularly important given the meaning I ascribe to creolisation in this book, with the latest research demonstrating that the Kriolu language itself developed on Cabo Verde before being transferred to Upper Guinea.[5]

One of the first Europeans to set foot on Cabo Verde was Diogo Gomes. He described a verdant scene: "There were many fish there. On land we found many strange birds and rivers of fresh water ... There were many ducks there. There was also a large quantity of figs ... there are large numbers of these trees. And we also saw much pasture there".[6] Yet such pastoral scenes were not to last. The sixteenth century saw over-exploitation of the islands' delicate ecosystem and their desertification. From the moment the process of colonisation began, this outpost of the nascent Portuguese empire was set on a collision course with nature and history.

Cabo Verde was permanently occupied by the Portuguese in 1462 with the founding of the settlement of Ribeira Grande, the first European city built in the tropics.[7] The principal focus was to settle the islands, but this was not easy. In 1466, trading privileges had to be given by the Portuguese crown to residents of Ribeira Grande to encourage settlement, thereby instituting a mechanism for population which was later copied

---

[4] There is a tedious literature relating to the discovery of the islands and who was the "first" to set foot on them. Caboverdean historians have challenged the view that the islands were unknown before the Portuguese "discovery" of them. A useful summary of this literature is Green (2007b: 5–7).

[5] Jacobs (2009: 320 n.1 and 352 n.51; idem., 2010).

[6] MMAII: Vol. 1, 203 – "*Havia ali grande pescaria. Em terra, porém, achamos muitas aves estranhas e rios de agua doce ... Havia aí muitos patos. Também era grande a fartura de figos ... destas árvores há grande número. E ali também vimos farta pastagem*".

[7] AG, Vol. 11, 32: Carta de Privilégios dos Moradores da Ilha de Santiago, June 12, 1466: "*como averia quatro anos que elle começara povorar a sua ilha de Santiago...*"; see also J. Barreto (1938: 65).

on São Tomé.[8] This had some effect. Three years later the *capitanias* or captaincies of Ribeira Grande and Alcatraz were founded on Santiago, and the Portuguese crown made the first contract of trade for the Guinea coast with Fernão Gomes.[9] Thus one can say that the first administrative and human settlement of the islands took roughly ten years, from their "discovery" in 1460 to an effective level of settlement and their administrative organisation in 1469. These ten years must have involved intense maritime trade because the majority of the materials used to build houses in Ribeira Grande were imported from Portugal: lime, floor, roof and wall tiles, calc for mortar and plaster, limestone for door and window frames, columns, arches and rib-vaults, marble for tombstones, and wood for construction.[10]

One should not underestimate the psychological importance of this process of settlement, for what went on in Cabo Verde was very different from events in the other Atlantic archipelagos already settled by the Portuguese, the Azores and Madeira. Whereas these other islands had familiar geographical and climatic conditions, the "island Sahel" of Cabo Verde belonged to a different register.[11] It may not have been the heat itself which was so alien – the summers of the Iberian plains were every bit as hot as the conditions in the African Atlantic – but rather the aridity. The desolation of this desert necklace of islands cast adrift in the Atlantic was discouraging to Europeans, and the Portuguese were unable to settle the islands alone. Many Catalans and especially Genoese joined the Portuguese among the Europeans who lived there.[12] One of the first two captains of the island, Antoni di Noli, credited with having discovered them by the Portuguese crown, was Genoese. Indeed the Genoese,

---

[8] AG, Vol. 11, 32: Carta de Priviliégios dos Moradores da Ilha de Santiago, 12 June 1466. For São Tomé, see MMAI, Vol. 1, 50–1 (a decree of 1485); for the letter of privileges in ibid., Vols. 1, 183 and Vol. 4, 21 for 1500.

[9] For the dates of the *capitanias*, see J. Barreto (1938: 67). Gomes's contract dated from November 1469 (for more details, see M. Silva 1970: Vol. 25, no. 97, 27); Gomes had previously been the receiver of all slaves and goods from Guinea since 1456 – Vogt (1973a: 2), Ballong-wen-Menuda (1993: Vol. 1, 47 n.8).

[10] Richter (2009: 156) and also in personal communication. This process thus prefigured the export of large amounts of construction materials to Elmina for the construction of the Portuguese fort there in 1482; following the Elmina expedition, similar shipments of such materials followed to Kongo.

[11] On the different ecological conditions of the Atlantic islands, see Crosby (1986: 72–3) and Henriques (2000: 31). The phrase "island Sahel" is Correia e Silva's – see the title of Correia e Silva (1996). For a discussion of how this different register affected the psychologies of the colonists, see Green (2006).

[12] T. Hall (1992: Vol. 2, 599) is good on the Genoese links. See also Bentley Duncan (1972: 19).

operating under the aegis of powerful merchants such as Bartolomeu Marchionni, dominated the early supply of slaves from Senegambia to Lisbon and Cabo Verde.[13] Thus from the very start, control of the islands and the operation of the slave trade from mainland Africa were connected.

Once a process of efficient settlement had begun by 1470, attention turned to integrating Cabo Verde into the economy of the new trading zones which had already opened up on the African coast. Here, the royal privileges granted in 1466 were fundamental. The Portuguese crown allowed the islanders to trade anywhere between the Senegal River and Sierra Leone, but the area beyond Sierra Leone was granted in exclusivity to Fernão Gomes in his 1469 contract. The Portuguese crown also stipulated that only goods and crops from the Caboverdean islands themselves could be used in trade to the African coast. Very rapidly the islanders settled on horse-breeding and the cultivation of cotton, selling horses and weaving cloths known as *panos di terra*, which were used as items of exchange on the coast where good-quality cloths were a valued commodity and a sign of prestige.[14] Both strategies in the formation of this early Atlantic commercial circuit were continuities from the existing trans-Saharan trade, in which horses and the trade in cloths through Morocco had been important for many years (cf. Chapters 1 and 2). Thus the first development of the Caboverdean economy involved continuities with the old long-distance trading economy of Western Africa, just as the first Portuguese exchanges in Arguim, Cajor and Siin had done.

There was however a hiatus in the early formation of Caboverdean society, with a Spanish attempt to seize the islands in the mid-1470s. The late 1470s saw the Spanish trying to encroach on Portugal's African trade at every point between the Cape Verde peninsula and the Gold Coast, but these tensions were resolved by the 1479 Treaty of Alcaçovas and thereafter Cabo Verde's integration into the geopolitical and cultural space of Western Africa was secured.[15] The trade of the islands had been sufficient for the first *almoxarife* – or administrator of state property – to be established in 1471, and an accountant followed the Alcaçovas treaty

[13] Mendes (2007: 342–51).

[14] On cotton see E. Lopes (1944: 52); J. Barreto (1938: 70); on horse-breeding, see Brooks (1993b: 127), and on the importance of horses in general, see T. Hall (1992). Law (1980: 53) suggests that the value of horses in the slave trade declined because a horse-breeding system was established in the Senegambia and Upper Guinea regions. However, perhaps more likely is that the value declined as the demand for slaves increased in the sixteenth century.

[15] Rumeu de Armas (1956: 103); Castillian attacks on Cabo Verde ran from 1475–77.

in 1480.[16] This suggests that the development of both horse-breeding and cotton plantations took place throughout the late 1460s and the 1470s and was sufficient for the trade with the coast to be profitable by 1480. The cotton plantations required slaves to labour in the fields and in cotton processing, and thus a significant trade in slaves with the coast must also have been under way by the early 1470s at the latest. The importance of slaving to early society may be underlined by the fact that the phrase *"largo do pelourinho"* ("Pillory Square") also means "marketplace" today in the Kriolu of Santiago Island, which shows how slave sales and markets were seen as synonymous from very early in the colony.[17]

Thus very quickly Cabo Verde was integrated into the picture of slave trading which we saw in the previous chapter for Senegambia. This illustrates why the early history of Western Africa may provide clues as to the origins of various aspects of the subsequent Atlantic and African Atlantic worlds. By 1471, the year in which Portuguese mariners first reached the Gold Coast, the economic space of Western Africa had become more or less integrated. Clearly the processes by which that space was formed affected how Portuguese sailors then developed exchanges on the Gold Coast, in Benin, Kongo and elsewhere in the Atlantic and Indian Oceans.[18]

Cabo Verde's economy was very rapidly seen as a prize. By as early as 1469, two Sevillian traders, Joham and Pero de Lugo, were trading cudbear (a lichen) from Cabo Verde to Portugal.[19] Ships from Madeira were being provisioned by people in Cabo Verde and sent to trade in Upper Guinea by 1472, whence slaves were most likely despatched to work on Madeira's sugar plantations.[20] These years saw a boom in the sugar industry on Madeira. Whereas circa 1450 the island did not consume more than one-third of its wheat production, by 1479 Madeira had become an importer of wheat, largely because land which previously had been used to cultivate wheat now held sugar plantations and vineyards.[21] Although this sugar boom was not entirely dependent on slave labour, the availability of African slaves played a part.[22]

---

[16] Z. Cohen (2007: 72).

[17] Richter (2009: 69).

[18] One could compare Cabo Verde's swift integration to subsequent events in São Tomé. This island only developed its first sugar plantations after 1486, and yet by 1499 it was pivotal to the Portuguese trade linking Benin and Elmina – see Ballong-wen-Menuda (1993: Vol. 1, 161–3, 330–4).

[19] HGCV: CD, Vol. 1, 23.

[20] Ibid., Vol. 1, 25 – a document of February 8, 1472.

[21] Godinho (1981: Vol. 4, 233–5).

[22] Mendes (2007: 356) shows that slavery was not the only aspect of this development on Madeira.

The profitability of this early trade between Cabo Verde and the African coast is underlined by the number of illegal traders. In 1474 the crown passed a law concerning the illegal trade of inhabitants of Cabo Verde in "Guinea".[23] Yet with Cabo Verde so distant from Portugal, the crown was impotent. The authorities on the island of Santiago mentioned the illegal trade again in 1481, and individuals were accused in both 1484 and 1490 of trading illegally from Santiago to Sierra Leone for gold, slaves and ivory.[24] Meanwhile, the French traveller Eustache de la Fosse found a further two ships at the Cape Verde peninsula in 1479.[25] Thus a generation after the first European ships arrived at the Senegal River in 1445, European trade operating through Cabo Verde was a fixture of the commercial pattern of life in Western Africa, stretching from Senegambia south to Sierra Leone.

We have already seen in the previous chapter that the development of this new Atlantic commercial space in Senegambia had contributed to a cycle of violent disorder. The increasing insecurity was naturally also related to how Caboverdeans integrated into the framework. It is no coincidence that the earliest specific reference of the peoples with whom Caboverdeans traded, from 1484, points to the "river Gambia in the straits of Banhuine [Bainunk]".[26] This fact may be related to the Pullo migrations. The Gambia was a Mandinka-dominated area, and thus the Bainunk referred to here were almost certainly the Mandinka-influenced Kassanké with whom the Pullo fought during their migrations (cf. Chapter 2). Very likely, this openness of the Kassanké to trade with the Caboverdeans in the 1480s was related to a need to create new alliances in the new circumstances. Here, we see concrete evidence to support the argument made in the last chapter, that the Pullo migrations led to peoples in Upper Guinea turning to Atlantic traders in order to make alliances: The nearest Atlantic traders were of course Caboverdeans, and it was people from these islands who were in the best position to take advantage of this new situation as it developed.[27]

---

[23] AG, Vol. 2: 487–9.
[24] Torrão (1991: 245–6).
[25] MMAII: Vol. 1, 468.
[26] Albuquerque/Santos (1993: 380); this document refers to a journey up the Gambia in 1483–4, mentioning the "*rrio de Guambia no estreito de Banhuine...*".
[27] Cf. Brooks (1993b: 199), who cites Almada's assertion that the Pullo ravaged every Mandinka community they passed on the north bank of the Gambia, and says that the implications of the migration remain to be assessed. One of them may have been this increased commerce south of the Gambia with the Caboverdean and Portuguese traders.

When Caboverdeans entered into the economy in force, the accent of regional trade in Upper Guinea shifted towards slaving and away from the commodity trade in goods such as kola and salt, which hitherto had predominated. For what Caboverdeans needed above all else was labour to forge their new economy. They demanded slaves. As we saw in Chapter 1, although oral histories do suggest that Kaabunké raided for slaves in areas of Upper Guinea in the pre-Atlantic era, Rodney made a strong argument that slavery cannot have existed as an institution here prior to the arrival of the Europeans, because it was not mentioned by any of the early Portuguese sources which otherwise noted the practices of African societies in some detail.[28] In an interesting gloss on this point, Trevor Hall later noted that some of these early accounts did, however, cite the existence of slavery as an institution in Islamic societies of Senegambia, but not among non-Islamic societies farther south along the coast.[29] To this one could add evidence from West-Central Africa, where again early Portuguese reports from Kongo note the existence of slavery. These details thus support Rodney's argument here and suggest that the emphasis on slaving which emerged with the connections to Cabo Verde represented a change in the practices of Upper Guinea.

One wonders if this emphasis of the new Caboverdean trade disturbed the lineage heads who were involved. They were probably more concerned with shoring up the security of their lineages than worrying about the individuals who were sold as slaves. Yet we should not pass over the role of ritual and belief here. Many people in Senegambia and Upper Guinea believed that their spirits would return home on their deaths even if they were sold into slavery.[30] Lineage heads shared this belief. Probably they thought that by sacrificing some of their number or capturing members of rival lineages, they were strengthening their lineage in return for a sacrifice which, for the individual and the lineage concerned, would not be permanent. Human beings throughout history have shown an extraordinary facility in choosing moral positions that justify their behaviour; for the lineage heads, this could have constituted a moral discourse which legitimised the practices that evolved as the slaving economy and consequent cycles of insecurity expanded with the

---

[28] Rodney (1966: 433–4).

[29] T. Hall (1992: Vol. 1, 74 n.48).

[30] Brooks (1993b: 262). Hawthorne (2010b: Chapter 6) notes how "the spirits of both the good and the evil, most all thought from the seventeenth through the nineteenth centuries, continued to live on earth, affecting the living on a daily basis". The lives of the dead and the living are still believed to intersect today – see Green (2001: 227–8).

development of trans-Atlantic trade and the consolidation of the links with Cabo Verde.

In the previous chapter, we saw how the first development of mixed Atlantic communities in Upper Guinea began as a consequence of these African-European exchanges. It became clear that preceding African cultural and political configurations were essential in this process. However the formation of mixed Atlantic communities required both African and European partners, and the European partners came from Cabo Verde. By the 1490s, when the first seeds of mixed European-African communities had emerged in Casamance, they had already had thirty years to develop as Cabo Verde was colonised.

It was in this period that the first signs of creolisation developed on the islands, something which the Caboverdeans took with them as they plied to and from the settlements in West Africa for slaves. Proximity shortened the length of trading journeys and enabled Caboverdeans to carry them out more frequently than could mariners from Portugal, accelerating exchanges between Africans and others. The origins of this emerging mixed society in Cabo Verde are therefore very important to understanding the nature of early creolisation in the Atlantic world. As we shall see here, these origins were fundamentally connected to the processes of slavery and institutional violence which were constitutive of the historical condition of Creole societies in the Atlantic.

The cultural world of Cabo Verde in these early years was mixed. Not only were Europeans a mixture of Aragonese, Genoese and Portuguese, but there were also of course a large number of Africans from diverse origins. As the necessity of slave labour increased to build this new society and consolidate its trading links in the last years of the fifteenth century, the first traces of the Kriolu language developed, initially as a pidgin to ease communication between the African and European architects of this new society.[31] With this mixed language went a certain mixture of cultures, and by 1501 there were accusations that people from Cabo Verde were travelling to the African coast to sell fake charms in imitation of

---

[31] Lang (2006); Jacobs (2009: 352 n.1). This argument follows from the large number of Wolof words in Santiago Creole and the fact that Wolof slaves only predominated in the trade to the islands in the fifteenth century.

those adopted locally, which indicates how ideas travelled from Africa to Cabo Verde and affected the ideas of both Africans and Europeans who lived there.[32]

This Atlantic cultural and linguistic framework was still very new. It went with other changes which were equally irreversible. Most apparent of these were the mixed-race children who were born of the sexual relations between male masters and female slaves. This population was an inevitable consequence of the colonial condition of Cabo Verde; on the practical, physical level, this was due to the absence of European women on the islands, and on the ideological level it was due to the belief in fifteenth-century Iberia that, as Blumenthal has shown, "it was a master's prerogative to have sex with his slave women ... an enslaved woman's body was at the complete disposal of her master".[33] Naturally, there were important correlations for both gender relationships and the status of the new mixed-race class.

In the Salazar era there used to be a tendency among some historians of Cabo Verde to romanticise the early exchanges of Africans and Europeans on the islands. In an influential book on the island of Santiago, the esteemed historian Ilídio do Amaral wrote of how the island's Creoles were "born of the harmonious fusion of the White with black slaves" (sic, including capitalisation).[34] However, the notion that the skewed power relations of male European slavers and their female African slaves could possibly have led to a harmonious fusion is difficult to sustain.[35] The evidence of Blumenthal and the work of scholars such as Thomas Burnard on Jamaica and James Sweet on Brazil make the relationship between slavery and sexual exploitation in the Atlantic world abundantly obvious.[36] It is difficult to see how Cabo Verde could have been any different, and thus the emergence of this first mixed society was predicated on violence, just as the primary creolisation of Upper Guinea had been in the pre-Atlantic era.

Part of the consolidation and codification of this violence emerged through the administrative structure which developed on the islands. R. I. Moore has suggested that the expansion of the administrative class in the medieval period was related to the development of structures of

---

[32] HGCV: CD, Vol. 1, 123.

[33] Blumenthal (2009: 87–8).

[34] Amaral (1964: 19): "*nascido da fusão harmoniosa do Branco com os escravos negros*".

[35] The sexual exploitation by European colonists of their female African slaves in the early Caboverdean colony is cited also by T. Hall (1992: Vol. 1, 294–5); this is of course not to stigmatise the society that followed, but rather to place it in a broader context.

[36] Burnard (2004); Sweet (2003).

persecution in European societies.[37] In Cabo Verde administrative structures developed very rapidly, coinciding with the initial violence which characterised both the slave trade on which the islands were founded and the sexual exploitation of female slaves. The consolidation of settlement in Santiago through the 1470s helped in the settlement of the nearby island of Fogo; the first church was built there in 1480.[38] The accounts of the 1490s imply growing efficiency.[39] By 1495 there was a sufficient slave population on Santiago for a church to be built for the Black African confraternity, *Nossa Senhora do Rosário*.[40] By 1500 there would be a public jail in Ribeira Grande with an employed jailer.[41]

This administrative consolidation related to the new slave trade. This was the real economic motor of the region; violence and conditions of inequality were fundamentally connected to creolisation in the Atlantic from the beginning.[42] Integrating into a new administrative structure, and developing a legal consciousness regarding it, has been seen by Bennett as an indicator of Creole identity in the Atlantic world.[43] On Cabo Verde, administrative control was a precondition for establishing the institutional framework of slavery within which creolisation developed. The historical conditions of the development of a Creole community on the islands were thus inseparable from these developments, just as the voluminous sources of the voyages of slaving ships used to build the Trans-Atlantic Slave Trade Database also testify to the fundamental relationship that linked bureaucracy and slavery. Thus administration of the islands' slave population and of the profits of its labour reflected the institutionalisation of violence and its connection to the process of creolisation in the Atlantic world.[44]

[37] Moore (1987).

[38] Cerrone (1983: 14).

[39] See the accounts of the Almoxarife of Cabo Verde, Afonso Annes do Campo, of 1491–3, producing for the crown 1,914,050 from the sale of slaves (AHP, Vol. 1, 95), and the accounts of Pisival Machado of monies received in Cabo Verde owing to the king (AHP, Vol. 5, 240).

[40] Richter (2009: 132). The church was built from 1495 through to the 1510s (ibid., 250). It is today the best-preserved church in *Cidade Velha*, the modern name for the old city of Ribeira Grande.

[41] HGCV: CD, Vol. I, 123–4, 131–2, 139.

[42] S. Hall (2010: 29) emphasises the place of the condition of inequality in understanding Atlantic creolisation.

[43] See Bennett (2003: 2–3).

[44] Of course I draw here on Michel Foucault's well-known work on the history of institutions of violence. Historians dependent on the records of such institutions cannot themselves escape a relationship with this violence even as they seek to understand it.

Thus as with the genesis of the cultural world of Upper Guinea in the fourteenth and fifteenth centuries, the Creole society which began to emerge in Cabo Verde in the last decades of the fifteenth century was characterised by violence and flexibility. The violence of the imposition of the new society emerges casually and on many levels. It is apparent of course in the fact of slavery and also from the first recorded account that we have of African *grumetes* in Cabo Verde, dating from 1463.[45] According to a letter of Afonso V of December 18 of that year, some *grumetes* had rebelled against their shipmasters when arriving at Cabo Verde and had fled ashore after killing some of them.[46] These were probably the very first escaped slaves on Cabo Verde.

Yet among this violence there was also fluidity and accommodation. The adoption of elements of African languages within the early pidgin which developed on the islands and of some African ritual practices show that the violence of Atlantic slavery was tempered by elements of reciprocity. Even sexual relationships were complex and not always characterised by violence, especially on the African coast. Cadamosto's "acceptance" of a "beautiful girl" of twelve or thirteen offered by the Damel of Cajor may not meet modern standards of gender relations, but nor was it necessarily a case of sex through the imposition of the Venetian's will.[47] This was indeed a general pattern in West Africa. Farther south, in Elmina, the Frenchman Eustache de la Fosse pretended a prudish outrage when a young girl asked him if he wanted to *choque-choque*.[48] According to Valentim Fernandes, whites were offered women to sleep with among the Mandinka of Gambia and Casamance, "and this from friendship and not by force".[49] As we have seen, on Cabo Verde, where master-slave hierarchies characterised relationships in a way that they did not in Africa, sexual relations were probably more coercive. However, these three pieces of evidence should warn us against assuming that it was always so, or that the violence which characterised some aspects of this world characterised all of them.

In Cabo Verde at the end of the fifteenth century, two human experiments coalesced: the birth of the Atlantic slave trade and the first stirrings of an Atlantic Creole society. These factors gave this locale an unusual

---

[45] *Grumetes* were servants/attendants of Caboverdean and Portuguese traders in Upper Guinea.

[46] Albuquerque/Santos (1993: 136).

[47] For Cadamosto's account of this, see MMAII: Vol. 1, 322.

[48] Ibid., Vol. 1, 472.

[49] Ibid., Vol. 1, 702 – "*por boa amizade, e nã por força*".

importance as the Atlantic world was born. The islands' strategic value was recognised swiftly. When the Treaty of Tordesillas was drawn up in 1494 to delineate the "dominions" of Portugal and Spain, Cabo Verde became the reference point for the line of demarcation.[50] These isolated volcanic slabs represented the westernmost extremity of the known world. When Columbus developed his rationale for a voyage to the West, he noted that the last unknown space of the sea was between the "far east and the said islands of Cabo Verde".[51] However, the islands represented not only the last physical outpost of the Old World; they were also the first step towards the social realities of the New.

THE PLACE OF SLAVERY IN EARLY SIXTEENTH-CENTURY CABOVERDEAN SOCIETY

In order to understand just how closely the expansion of Atlantic slavery and the development of creolisation were connected, it helps to look further at the intensification of Cabo Verde's slave economy in the early sixteenth century. For if this was the era when mixed societies in Western Africa were just beginning to develop on both Cabo Verde and in Upper Guinea, it also saw the expansion of this economy and of the connections which it required across the region.

That slavery was the lynchpin of the Caboverdean economy was widely known. After Columbus visited the islands on his third voyage to the New World in 1497, he wrote in 1498 to the Spanish monarchs, the *Reyes Católicos* Ferdinand and Isabela, that "in these past days when I went to Cabo Verde, where the people have a great trade in slaves and are always sending ships to obtain them and receiving them in the port, I saw that even the cheapest slaves in the worst condition were being sold for 8,000 maravedís".[52] However, by the 1490s the Caboverdean economy appeared to have diversified substantially. Affonso Annes do Campo, *almoxarife* of Cabo Verde, recorded receiving taxes between 1491 and 1493 paid in slaves, ivory, rice, millet, cotton, biscuit brought from Portugal, horses and pepper.[53] Similar records for 1498 reveal taxes paid in horses, gelded goats, cotton, goat and ox hides, and slaves.[54] Writing in

---

[50] This point is made by Ameal (1966: 105).

[51] Las Casas (1966b: Vol. 62, 56) – "*entre el fin oriental y las dichas islas de Cabo Verde*".

[52] Ibid., Vol. 63, 323 – "*estos dias que fuí á las islas de Cabo Verde, de donde la gente dellos tienen gran trato en los esclavos, y de continuo envian navíos á los recatar, y están á la puerta, yo ví que por el más ruin demandaban 8.000 maravedís*".

[53] AHP, Vol. 1, 95.

[54] Ibid., Vol. 5, 240.

1505, Pacheco Pereira described how Cabo Verde exported goatskins and cowhides to Portugal and how cotton was cultivated both on Santiago and the other islands.[55] The desire to diversify economic production was underlined by attempts to grow sugar by the end of the fifteenth century, although the aridity made this industry impractical.[56]

The taxes due to the Caboverdean *almoxarifes* were paid by Caboverdean ships that traded in Guinea. These tax records thus imply a diversity of production. However, on closer analysis we can see that many of these productions required a servile population in Cabo Verde, for instance in the harvesting of cotton and sugar and the butchering of goats and oxen for hides. Thus by the end of the 1490s the hierarchies required for the social organisation of a slave society were in place on the islands to ensure the regular payment of taxes. That this social organisation depended on reliable ties with African polities is shown by the fact that these slaves were fed in part by the millet and rice brought over from the mainland, part of which was paid in taxes to the state treasury.[57] Thus, of the fourteen ships officially logged as returning from Upper Guinea to Cabo Verde in 1514, ten brought millet or rice; the following year eleven out of sixteen did so; and by 1528 all the fourteen ships returned with millet and seven of them also brought rice.[58] By the early sixteenth century, this role of Western Africa in the provisioning of the new Atlantic economies was increasing rapidly; by 1504, ships plying between Elmina and Lisbon apparently stopped in the region of Upper Guinea to provision with rice, while by 1514 at the latest slave ships plying from São Tomé to Portugal also stopped in the Senegambian region for provisions to feed their slaves.[59]

Already, therefore, the Caboverdean – and wider African-Atlantic – economy was extracting surplus produce from African agricultural units and using it to feed its slave-oriented production and export system. This may have been a continuity of existing practices feeding the trans-Saharan trade, in which caravans also required provisions; there is some evidence of the transference of foodstuffs and culinary skills from sub-Saharan Africa to the north.[60] Yet this Atlantic extension created new pressures

---

[55] MMAII: Vol. 1, 637.

[56] Schwartz (1985: 12–3).

[57] This very early reference to taxes in rice confirms Fields-Black's (2009) argument on the longevity of rice growing in Upper Guinea.

[58] Torrão (1991: 265–7).

[59] On ships from Elmina, see Mark/Horta (2011: 140); on the São Tomé trade, see MMAI: Vol. 4, 76.

[60] See Seck (forthcoming, 2012), who holds that couscous was a grain originating in sub-Saharan Africa.

on local production systems. This extra demand for food supplies may have been influential in accelerating processes of change in production techniques in Upper Guinea and the labour systems used for cultivation; we know that the arrival of the Portuguese was connected with new tools used in cultivation.[61] Moreover, this system did not only lead to changes in agricultural organisation; it also created a direct link between extracting both "surplus" produce and "surplus" labour from Africa and the development in Atlantic islands of a productive system based on slavery.

In this light, it emerges that the socio-economic impact of the development of the slave mode of production in Cabo Verde stretched well beyond the islands themselves. The consequence of the new system was that these African productive surpluses requisitioned for the Caboverdean economy were essentially lost to Africa in exchange for non-productive items of consumption, display, and military apparel, and were transferred instead to the economic systems being built by Europeans in the Atlantic. As this economic system grew, it required the development of the trans-Atlantic slave trade in the sixteenth century, and the nature of this dependence on surplus African production accelerated through the demands of provisioning ships for the Middle Passage (cf. Chapter 7). This is of the first importance in understanding the economic trajectories of African and European societies in the early modern period. Over thirty years ago, the historian Jan de Vries argued influentially that one of the keys to the broader growth of the European economy that prefigured industrialisation, in the period between circa 1650 and 1750, was that agriculturalists increased output substantially without this increase being wiped out by population growth.[62] In England, for example, increased output and a stable population ensured low grain prices and the diversification of the non-agricultural sector.[63] Although De Vries's argument overplayed internal factors in growth at the expense of understating the influence of imperial systems of economic (and, indeed, agricultural) exploitation, his work made a strong argument that this process of successfully harnessing the fruits of enhanced agricultural production was one of the catalysts of the Industrial Revolution.[64] But in Africa, although there were indeed increased outputs, much of the surplus represented by the increase was lost to the local economy and could never be re-invested there. Though the same dynamic did not pertain everywhere on the continent, this may prove to be an important consideration when trying to

[61] Hawthorne (2003: 43–8).
[62] Vries (1976: 47).
[63] Ibid., 76–82.
[64] For a strong counter-argument to this perspective, see Inikori (2002).

answer the question posed by Inikori and raised in the Introduction as to why the discrepancy between African and European economic outputs had become so marked by the dawn of the colonial era in the late nineteenth century.

Thus although there clearly were other factors in the decline of production and manufacturing diversity, such as the rise in wars and consequent instability in harvests, this factor is obviously significant in understanding the evolution of production in Atlantic Africa in the early modern period.[65] Moreover, it is important to emphasise that the growth of the Atlantic economy in the sixteenth century would have been impossible without the appropriation of these surpluses from productive systems in Africa. By the seventeenth century, the centrality of securing provisions for slaves was apparent to all those involved in this aspect of the Atlantic economy. In 1643 Dutch officials in Luanda, Angola, were forced to curtail slaving voyages to Calabar because of the lack of provisions to feed the slaves.[66] Moreover, it was the consistent absence of sufficient provisions for the slaves and the Dutch colonists there which was one of the main causes for the failure of the Dutch to retain the colony, leading to its recapture by Portuguese from Brazil in 1648.[67] Without these agricultural surpluses, it was simply not possible to feed slaves sufficiently on the Atlantic crossing, or, in the local Caboverdean context, those on the arid islands of the archipelago. Thus without the use of these surpluses, it would have been impossible for the European colonies in the New World to grow.

The transfer of these labour and production surpluses was therefore key to the construction of Caboverdean society in these years and to the development of the social hierarchies which permitted a diversified economy. For although diversification of sorts is implied through the different productive occupations of Cabo Verde, in the raising of wild cattle for hides and the cultivation of cotton and sugar, it was impossible without slavery. Statistical and personal records show that the new economic and social systems were underpinned in their entirety by slavery. When on October 24, 1512, the residents of Ribeira Grande on Santiago protested

---

[65] On these other factors in an Angolan context, see for instance Parreira (1990: 26–7).

[66] Jadin (1975: Vol. 1, 428).

[67] See the repeated complaints in the documents published by Jadin; ibid., Vol. 1, 323, 390; Vol. 2, 644, 883, 1077. Similarly, accounts of slave voyages note both their purchasing of provisions from coastal peoples in Africa and that they frequently had to cut short slaving expeditions due to shortages of provisions – see the account of a trip to Calabar in the 1640s in Anguiano (1950: 180).

about a new decree that all slaves had to be brought directly from the coast of Guinea to Lisbon, not via Cabo Verde, they emphasised that "the said island [Santiago] does not have any other merchandise or trade except for the bringing of slaves, because cotton is only a merchandise which is offered to the merchants who come from [Lisbon]".[68] According to the petitioners, the new decree would have a devastating effect: "It is very damaging to the said island and is ruining everything. And it will also affect many other merchants and squires, knights and even poor noblemen who earn their livings through [the trade]".[69]

This petition emphasises the place of slaving in the islands' economy. Cotton, the petitioners said, was only used to sell to merchants from Lisbon – the "other merchants and squires" – who used it to buy slaves in Africa. Its economic importance derived from the slave trade. That was all the trade that there was, and so profitable was it that the accounts of the *almoxarife* of the Guinea trade for the years 1510–13 showed that, after Elmina, the African locale from which the Portuguese crown derived the greatest profit was Cabo Verde. The Cabo Verde contract was sold for 3,130,999 reis, as opposed to 1,616,000 for Sierra Leone, 1,363,500 for the Gambia River and 1,212,000 for the "rivers of Guinea" (present-day Casamance and Guinea-Bissau).[70] When we consider this information, the central place of slaving in the Caboverdean economy is overwhelming.[71]

Indeed, the Portuguese crown itself was well aware of this reality, and the authorities emphasised that slaving should be the main business of the Caboverdean traders. In February 1517, Manoel I protested that residents of Santiago were going to Sierra Leone to procure "ivory, wax, iron and other forbidden goods".[72] He ordered that they should not go to Sierra Leone, but to the areas where they were permitted to go (the Senegambian and Upper Guinean locales to the north), where they should only "trade for slaves for their service and work".[73] In other words, it was royal policy to limit the trade of the Caboverdean islanders in goods such as wax and

---

[68] MMAII: Vol. 2, 54 – "*Por que da dita Ilha nõ teē outras mercadurias que trazer soomente espravos, porque o algodão nõ hē mercadoria que faça soomente pero os mercadores que vaom da dicta cidade [de Lisboa]*". For the decree see ibid., Vol. 2, 51–2.

[69] Ibid. – "*é muito danoso à dita ilha e lança em tudo a perder. E ainda a outros muitos mercadores e outros muitos escudeiros, cavaleiros e ainda fidalgos pobres que nela se remedeiam a sustem sua vida*".

[70] AHP, Vol. 2, 440–1.

[71] T. Hall (1992: Vol. 1, 288) emphasises the importance of slaves to the early Caboverdean economy.

[72] MMAII: Vol. 2, 139 – "*marfym, çera, ferro e outras mercadorias defesas*".

[73] Ibid., Vol. 2, 143 – "*onde nam resgataram senam escravos pera seu serviço e trabalho*".

ivory. Slaving was heartily encouraged.[74] This was emphasised six years later, when the factors of the Casa de Mina in Lisbon complained to the council of Santiago that they were sending too much ivory and that they should concentrate on procuring slaves instead, as many as possible.[75] Thus there is no question that the economic motor which accompanied the rise of the first signs of Caboverdean creolisation examined in the previous section was the slave economy, and that this was widely accepted. This was, moreover, a widespread Portuguese royal policy in Africa. When in 1526 João III of Portugal insisted that all slaves sent from Kongo to São Tomé (and thence Elmina or Portugal) were to be carried in official boats, these boats refused to carry any exports other than slaves from Kongo in spite of the protests of the *Manikongo* Afonso I.[76]

In Cabo Verde, the result of the profitability derived from slaving and the transfer of these labour and productive surpluses from Africa was that the local economy expanded, and in the first decade of the sixteenth century all the Caboverdean islands were colonised. By the end of the fifteenth century, Fogo was well settled by residents of Santiago and their slaves in order to cultivate cotton.[77] By 1499 the population was sufficient for Spanish ships to restock there en route to the Indies.[78] In the first decade of the sixteenth century, colonists irradiated out from Santiago to most of the other islands. By 1504 there were cattle herds on the island of Maio, and by 1505, also on Boavista.[79] In 1509 even remote Brava was colonised, with the New Christian Francisco de Afonseca given a licence to cultivate cotton there.[80] Just how new this process of colonisation was is revealed by the fact that just twelve years before, when Columbus visited in 1497, it was clear that Brava had not even been fully explored; he was told that it was thought there might well be islands beyond it to the west, whereas in fact there is just an empty and desolate sea all the way from Brava to America.[81]

Thus expanding economic requirements allowed Caboverdean society to grow and consolidate the new social structures which underpinned it. An economy which could produce cotton and breed horses,

---

[74] Z. Cohen (1994: 350).
[75] MMAII: Vol. 2, 185: "*fareis por tyrardes dos Ryos este ano todas as peças que poderdes*".
[76] Hilton (1985: 57); MMAI: Vol. 1, 484.
[77] Ribeiro (1954: 94).
[78] Las Casas (1966b: Vol. 63, 453) – this was the voyage of Diego de Lepe.
[79] MMAII: Vol. 2, 11, 15.
[80] HGCV: CD, Vol. 1, 183–5.
[81] Las Casas (1966b: Vol. 63, 225).

to be exchanged for slaves, ivory and food in Western Africa, was one which required cheap labour and a hierarchical system of production. This development of an economy based on slave labour in Cabo Verde required new systems of social organisation which, like the shift to a new pattern of economic organisation, were predicated on violence. As we have seen in this chapter, this violence was codified and legitimated by a rapidly expanding administrative structure, which developed further in the early sixteenth century with the establishment of new *almoxarife* posts in Alcatrazes in 1501 and on the island of Fogo in 1506.[82]

Yet in spite of the crown's intentions, royal authority on the islands was partial at best. Papers were stolen from the council [*câmara*] of Ribeira Grande, and as early as 1512 escapees from justice had only to flee to the hills of Santiago to find sanctuary.[83] The failure of the crown to control the hills of Santiago was symptomatic of wider trends. Metropolitan Portugal could not control social developments in the African Atlantic, and this was a world which Caboverdeans and Africans would build themselves.[84] Although the new social order had been founded on violence, alliances had to be formed. In Cabo Verde incentives had to be offered such as the freeing of slaves – *alforría* – in the wills of their owners, which encouraged good behaviour and thereby increased productivity.[85] Indeed, by the 1520s residents of Cabo Verde saw the *alforría* as an important aspect of their society, and they objected to those who did not respect it. When a freed slave called Rodrigo Lopez was smuggled onto a ship and sailed to Hispaniola in 1526 to be sold, it provoked outrage in Ribeira Grande.[86] The importance of such practices were testament to the sort of accommodation which always formed a subtext to relations between masters and slaves in the Atlantic world, an accommodation which went with the flexibility also associated with creolisation. Thus had the institutional violence of slavery and the flexibility associated with creolisation developed together in Cabo Verde by the early sixteenth century.

[82] On the jail, see HGCV: CD, Vol. I, 123–4, 131–2, 139. On the *almoxarifes* in Alcatrazes (which moved to Praia in 1515) and Fogo, see Z. Cohen (2007: 77–8).
[83] On stolen papers, see MMAII: Vol. 2, 38. On escapees to the hills of Santiago, see HGCV: CD, Vol. 1, 215.
[84] T. Hall (1992: Vol. 2, 424–32).
[85] On how the freeing of slaves underpinned master-slave relationships on Cabo Verde, see the will of Catarina Fernandes of 1632 at IAN/TT, Jesuitas, Cartório, Maço 37, doc. 18, fols. 2v, 4r.
[86] AGI, Justicia 11, no. 4, fol. 10r. Lopez was freed by his master Ruy Lopez, the royal accountant in Cabo Verde, but then sold by Ruy Lopez's nephew.

The testimony in this case of Rodrigo Lopez shows that the freed Black population was important in Cabo Verde by the 1520s. Not only did the case cause murmurings on Santiago, but numerous witnesses described how Lopez was recognised as free in Cabo Verde and indeed had moved between the islands of Fogo and Santiago.[87] Lopez was part of a community of growing importance, members of which were used as crews on ships plying to and from the West African coast. By 1546 their size and strength was such that a group of them wrote to the crown to ask for permission to apply for official posts.[88] Interestingly, this process also occurred on the island of São Tomé, farther south in the African Atlantic, where the religious brotherhood of the Irmandade da Nossa Senhora do Rosário de Homens Pretos was established in 1526 by former slaves.[89] Yet although the presence of an active free Black population developed through the institution of the *alforría* was testament to the negotiations inherent in the emergence of creolisation within the system of Atlantic slavery, there was also a way in which it gave moral legitimacy to the entire structure; it rewarded pliant and co-operative slaves with the eventual possibility of freedom and thereby ensured the success of the institutions which oppressed them.

This emerges in the way in which the procurement of slaves became an activity in which everyone on Cabo Verde, *senhores* and even their slaves, had a stake. Ships from Cabo Verde carried slaves themselves as agents of masters who had been sent to procure more slaves.[90] This indicates that the slave class on Santiago was itself stratified, with some slaves entering into the confidence of the *senhores* and being trusted with commercial expeditions in Upper Guinea. This practice imitated the use of African slaves in contemporary Portugal, where urban slaves were frequently sent on commercial errands by their masters, and also the way in which Portuguese resident in Kongo and Angola later used their own slaves – the *pombeiros* – as agents for them in the markets of the hinterland. Instead of a generalised *senhores/escravos* opposition, there were gradations in both classes, which are testament to a more complex process of social formation than traditional narratives of Atlantic slave societies have usually allowed.[91]

[87] Ibid.
[88] Saunders (1982a: 11); IAN/TT, Corpo Cronlógico, Maço I, Vol. 78, No. 17
[89] Personal communication from Gerhard Seibert, Centro de Estudos Africanos, ISCTE, Lisbon.
[90] Torrão (1991: 268).
[91] This consideration also challenges Torrão's hypothesis here (ibid.) that the presence of these slaves is indicative of a commercial interest in the process of slaving, as otherwise

It is worth hypothesising as to what qualities allowed these slaves to be trusted. Almost certainly, these must have been the individuals who were the most willing to adapt to the Portuguese culture of the slave-masters and accept their place within the hierarchy. Otherwise, the *senhores* would not have trusted them with important missions. Therefore these slaves had probably adopted the Catholic religion, at least outwardly, and learnt enough Portuguese – or the Kriolu which, as we have seen, was already being developed by this time – to communicate freely with their *senhores*. The corollary was that there were strong incentives to accept the system of slavery for new arrivals and to adapt to the emergent Creole society. The fact that new arrivals saw trusted slaves being granted a degree of freedom meant that there was every incentive for them to adapt.[92] The institution of slavery – both through how slaves were procured in Upper Guinea and how they were socialised on Cabo Verde – therefore encouraged the acceleration of the creolising process. The new language was used as a means of communication, and adoption of mixed cultural and ritual forms became a means of social advancement.

LANÇADOS AND THE FORGING OF MIXED COMMUNITIES ON THE UPPER GUINEA COAST

In order for the growing coincidence of slavery and a very early form of creolisation to move beyond the islands of Cabo Verde, agents of transference were required. Although as we have seen there had been exchanges between the islands and West Africa since at least the 1470s, exchanges which had grown ever more intensive as the need for slaves expanded in Cabo Verde, it was not until Caboverdeans settled permanently among the peoples of Upper Guinea that the emerging mixed society and language on the archipelago began to find a home on the African mainland. These settlers were known as *lançados* by the Portuguese, from *lançar*, meaning to throw: here were people who had literally "thrown themselves into" African society and "out" of the European orbit.

By the early 1500s the Portuguese crown had no control over the large number of Caboverdeans settling on the African coast. In the 1510s

there was nothing to stop them escaping. Equally as likely is that their privileged status within the slave corps was more attractive than returning to a society in which they had been deprived of the opportunities and reciprocities of kin relations as a result of being sold as a slave, and in which it would have been much harder for them to achieve a comparable position of privilege.

[92] I am grateful for this point to António Leão Correia e Silva, *Vice-Reitor* of the Universidade de Cabo Verde.

Manoel I attempted to demonstrate control by issuing a spate of royal decrees. Following up his decree of 1512 ordering that all slaves be taken directly from Upper Guinea to Lisbon, in 1514 he ordered that no one should go and live among the Africans in Guinea and that no iron should be taken from Cabo Verde for trade in Africa.[93] Yet this prevented neither these prohibited trades nor the settlement of *lançados* on the African coast. In December 1517 he ordered that the property of all *lançados* should be confiscated, and the following month issued a law prohibiting any ships sailing direct from Santiago, Cabo Verde, to Upper Guinea because of the damage to the royal treasury.[94] In March 1518 he wrote to the inhabitants of Ribeira Grande, accusing them of ruining royal trade to Africa.[95]

This legislative activity occurred in the wider context of the Portuguese crown's desire to regulate West African trade in these years. In 1509 a new rubric, or *Regimento*, for the running of the Casa de India and Casa de Mina was published, whereas 1512–13 saw new ordinances and laws published concerning the whole Guinea trade, including lists of prohibited trade goods and the prohibition of all private commercial transactions.[96] Like his predecessor João II, Manoel I clearly recognised the importance of the African trade and wished to regulate it as much as possible. In this light the prohibitions on *lançado* activity gain a richer complexion. Yet prohibition cannot occur if there is nothing to prohibit, and the slew of royal legislation from the 1510s reveals both how widespread *lançado* activity was and that the crown could not control it.

This royal legislation on *lançados* was not proactive but rather reactive. By the first decade of the sixteenth century there were active communities of *lançados* dating from at least the 1490s, as we have seen. The attempted prohibition of these *lançado* settlements was therefore fifteen or twenty years behind the times. The same goes for another prohibition attempted by Manoel I in the 1510s, on the Caboverdean trade in iron, which was also at least fifteen or twenty years old by the time that the Portuguese crown tried to stop it. The very first recorded instance of a *lançado*, concerning one Gonçallo de Paiva, dates from 1499 and accuses him of using iron to buy slaves in the "rivers of Guinea". Paiva not only used iron to trade, he also brought some escaped murderers from the hills

---

[93] MMAII: Vol. 2, 89, 72.

[94] Ibid., Vol. 2, 143, 144.

[95] Ibid., Vol. 2, 149. On this legislation against the *lançados*, see J. Barreto (1938: 75), Boxer (1963: 9), and M. Silva (1970).

[96] Ballong-wen-Menuda (1993: Vol. 1, 175).

of Santiago Island so that they could live in the "land of the Mandinkas"; these fugitive *lançados* also brought iron with them to buy slaves.[97]

This document is very informative about African-European relationships and the first mixed communities which were beginning to emerge by 1500. The implication would be that this expedition had been to the Casamance region, because this was the part of the "rivers of Guinea" with the strongest Mandinka influence. We know that other *lançados* in this period settled with the Kassanké, as Mendes has located evidence that a *grumete* did so in 1503 in Bugendo, the main Kassanké port for Atlantic trade.[98] Pacheco Pereira describes an intensive trade in these years, and this would be consistent with sufficient acculturation of Africans and Europeans to one another to permit small numbers of Europeans to live among the Kassanké.[99]

The trading culture which had developed in Casamance after two centuries of acculturation to the diaspora trading merchants of the Mandinka must have influenced the areas in which the *lançados* sought to settle. As we have seen, this culture was very influential in the region. In his collation of eyewitness accounts, Valentim Fernandes noted how the Mandinka "trade a lot of merchandise ... they trade their goods a long way into the hinterland and much more so than any other group of that land".[100] Later he observed that the people in the São Domingos region were "very disposed and given to trading in markets and they go to many different places where markets are held and in the same way others come to this place to their markets from other places"; the markets were held every eight days, and people came from as far as twenty leagues (one hundred kilometres) away, seven to eight thousand at a time.[101]

Fernandes's account, as we have seen, refers to customs and events from at least the 1490s, and so very likely this trading disposition described here far predates the arrival of the European mariners. The effect of this

[97] MMAII: Vol. 2, 3 – "*A nós diseram ora que hūu Gomçallo de Paiva, cavaleiro, armara o anno passado de lRix, da Ilha de Cabo Verde pero [hir] aos Rios de Guiné hūa sua caravella, em a quall elle passara çerta soma de ferros que lá resgatou aos negros... e que bem assy pasara na dita caravella çertos christãos omiziados que andavam na Serra pera terra de Mandinka, os quaaes outrosy comsiguo levaram muyta soma de ferro e a resgataram aos negros*".
[98] Albuquerque/Santos (1993: Vol. 2, 314).
[99] MMAII: Vol. 1, 645.
[100] MMAII: Vol. 1, 705 – "*tractā muyta mercadoria...tractā suas mercadorias muy lōge pello sertão e mais que nenhūa outra geraçã daquela terra*".
[101] Ibid., Vol. 1, 718 – "*muy disposta e muyta dada pera tractar em feyras e vam pera muytos lugares onde se fazē feyras e assi mesmo vem pera esta terra e suas feyras de outros lugares*".

long-standing Mandinka influence in the Upper Guinea region prior to the mid-fifteenth century had been to create a sort of "multi-culturalism" in which the arrival of one new caste – in this case the *lançados* – could be accommodated. Thus this pattern in turn shaped the locales in which communities connected to Cabo Verde, sharing rituals and practices and speaking the emergent (and still pidginised) Kriolu, emerged over the course of the sixteenth century.

The African role in the trade with Cabo Verde went much deeper than simply in helping to shape *lançado* settlement patterns. The importance of iron in trade by the end of the fifteenth century also shows how the existing requirements of African societies helped to shape the early Atlantic trade. Iron was probably being traded to Upper Guinea by 1490 if not earlier, because a royal provision barring the trade of iron was passed in 1497.[102] The prohibition from trading iron was routinely ignored. Recorded cases of people flouting the rule can be found for both 1499 and 1514, and these were certainly very numerous from 1510 onwards.[103]

The African desire to acquire iron in Atlantic exchanges has often been ascribed to the use of iron in making weaponry.[104] It has indeed long been recognised that in the rivers of Guinea this was the key commodity which African peoples wanted to buy in the sixteenth century in exchange for slaves.[105] Iron was used for the making of weaponry for the conflicts which produced slaves for export and to defend lineages from predatory attacks motivated by the Atlantic trade. Yet it also enabled the creation of new and more efficient agricultural implements which could enhance production. Research by Hawthorne has shown that the advent of iron-edged tools among smaller decentralised groups in Upper Guinea only came with the Portuguese, and that this coincided among some groups in the region with a boom in high-yielding crops such as rice.[106] Although as we have seen in Chapter 1 some small quantities of iron were procured before from Mandinka smiths, the Atlantic trade offered a decisive new opportunity. High-yielding crops could help create a stronger and larger population to face down the new threats brought on by Atlantic trade.

By accepting Caboverdean *lançados*, peoples of Upper Guinea were thus extending both their possible trading networks to procure iron as

---

[102] Torrão (1991: 244).
[103] MMAII: Vol. 2, 3, 72; Torrão (1991: 247).
[104] See for example Torrão (1991: 244).
[105] Carreira (1983: 83); Rodney (1965: 311).
[106] See Hawthorne (2003: 43–8). Fields-Black (2009) argues that rice production was already long-standing but that iron increased production.

well as the traditions regarding diaspora traders which had grown up under Mandinka hegemony. This influenced not only the success of these trading networks, but also the way in which the mixed culture which had developed in Cabo Verde with the advent of a slave economy could extend itself into Africa. Although this process was still young, by the second decade of the sixteenth century it had already laid down roots which became very important.

Thus although the combination of institutionalised violence and accommodation shaped the first stages of creolisation in Cabo Verde, an analogous preceding history in Upper Guinea shaped the areas in which the emergent Creole culture of Cabo Verde was able to develop in West Africa. These historical processes led to the development of a shared cultural zone across the region and also to influences far beyond. For, as we will see in the next chapter, from the Atlantic side a key group shaping the development of these communities were the Iberian New Christians, who had wide-ranging connections to America and Europe. Meanwhile, Alida Metcalf has argued that *lançado* status as insiders and outsiders in West Africa, as well as the strategies they adopted in order to integrate, were soon borrowed by other "go-betweens" in Brazil, paving the way for the colonisation process there.[107] Thus in this way, the plural identities which had such a long history in West Africa became important not only to the development of creolised communities there, but in the use of such strategies elsewhere in the new Atlantic world.

---

[107] Metcalf (2005: 58–9).

4

The New Christian Diaspora in Cabo Verde and the Rise of a Creole Culture in Western Africa

The last forty years have seen a significant body of work done on the New Christian diaspora in the Iberian Atlantic world. It has become clear that the New Christians were perhaps the key mercantile community linking the trading economies of Africa, America and Europe in the early Atlantic era to circa 1640. Their networks in the Low Countries helped to integrate the trade of Atlantic sugar for Northern European textiles and Baltic wheat exchanged between Iberia and Flanders. The early establishment of a community in Antwerp and the opening of a Sephardic Jewish community in Amsterdam in 1596 opened the way for Dutch trade and influence in the Caribbean and Brazil.[1] The links with New Christian families in Portugal and Spain encouraged the spread of New Christian communities throughout the New World.[2] Scholars still dispute the place of this diaspora in the overall emergence of Atlantic trade, but there is no question that it was significant.[3] In this work, the picture of the New Christian diaspora in West Africa has only recently come to the fore.[4] Yet as we shall see in this chapter and the next, this

---

[1] Key works on the New Christians in Brazil include Mello (1996); Novinsky (1972), Salvador (1969; 1978), Wiznitzer (1955; 1960) and Wolff and Wolff (1986; 1989).

[2] For Colombia, see MesaBernal (1996) and Splendiani (1997); for Mexico, Liebman (1970), and Toro (1932; 1944); for Chile, Böhm (1948; 1963); for Peru, Guibovich Pérez (1998) and Millar Carvacho (1997).

[3] Ebert (2008) disputes that the New Christian monopoly in the sugar trade from Brazil to the Netherlands was as strong as some scholars suggest. Whatever the nuances in the argument, though, the overall significance of the question has placed the subject within mainstream historiography, following works by Kagan/Morgan (2009), Schorsch (2008), Israel (2002) and Wachtel (2001).

[4] Green (2007b); F. Silva (2002; 2004).

diaspora was extremely important in the early period in Western Africa, at the very same time as the first signs of an Atlantic Creole community were emerging there.

Caboverdeans themselves are well aware of this strand of their early history. A second wave of Sephardic migration from Morocco in the nineteenth century has contributed to a sense of the significance of this first wave for the islands' cultural identity.[5] A researcher looking for residues of this often finds gratifying results. During a chance discussion in 2003 at a bar in Praia, the national capital, all three of my interlocutors claimed Jewish ancestry, and one of them had the surname Ben-Simon; at another bar, the landlady said her surname was Levi; and as I was shown by Januário Nascimento, then president of the Caboverdean-Israel Friendship Society, headstones with Hebrew inscriptions can be found in the main cemetery at Praia and in the highlands of Santiago island in the back yards of small farmsteads.

Such connections run deep. This chapter collates previously unused archival and published sources to offer the first detailed overview of the formation of the New Christian diaspora in Western Africa in the 1520s and 1530s. The arrival of New Christians in increasing numbers in the years after 1500 accelerated the processes which we have seen emerging in the previous chapters. As the pre-eminent Atlantic traders of the region, New Christians facilitated not only the Atlantic opening of Upper Guinea, but an atmosphere in which exchanges developed: diaspora traders have often been intermediaries in the cultural exchanges which accompany creolisation.[6] This chapter's main goal is both to discuss this new evidence and to show how the New Christian diaspora contributed to the emergence of a Creole society in Western Africa. Yet although the evidence shows that the New Christian presence was important in this process, it does not show that this presence was alone sufficient. As Chapters 1 and 2 have shown, early Atlantic Creole society in Western Africa was shaped by the region's pre-existing commercial and cultural patterns and the plural identities which these patterns encouraged. Thus the plural identities which New Christians developed in the sixteenth century, and which, I argue here, were important in nascent patterns of modernisation, did not represent a new departure in Western Africa, but rather a continuity.

---

[5] On the second wave, see Correia (1998).
[6] Trajano Filho (2003: 15). We saw this also in Chapter 1 relating to the diasporas of Mandinka and North African traders in West Africa.

To talk of modernity in this early period is to raise some important issues. Here, following the well-known work of Arjun Appadurai, Serge Gruzinski, Ulf Hannerz and many others, I see issues of mobility and flows – of people, resources and ideas – as central to how what we might call "modernity" began to be constituted.[7] Clearly, as has also been widely recognised, it is the increasing speed of these flows and exchanges which distinguishes the current manifestation of such global interconnectedness from that of the period examined here.[8] My argument in this chapter and the one that follows, however, is that the beginnings of this process of global flows, and associated changes in identity and cultural forms, can be seen in the emergence of an Atlantic Creole culture in Western Africa in the sixteenth century; this was of course not the only location where this process occurred in this period, but the evidence presented here shows that it was, undeniably, an important one.

I also argue in this chapter that, where this early proto-modernity is concerned, other aspects are very important beyond those of increasing flows and global interconnectedness. The chapter provides evidence for changes in conceptualisation that accompanied experiences in Western Africa and promoted a new mathematised and spatialised worldview; I further argue that these were all related to the processes of ideological, linguistic and psychological abstraction which accompanied modernisation in Iberia and the early Atlantic world. Also significant to these first stirrings of modernity, as we saw in Chapter 3, was the refinement of administrative systems of control relating to slavery and the development of proto-"national" identities in the sixteenth century; these developments, I argue in this chapter, make self-consciously modern categories such as the "transnational" relevant even to this distant time and place. Moreover, the presence of large numbers of New Christian refugees from the violence of the Inquisition and anti-Semitic riots in Iberia raises the connection which violence had to the emergence of modernity. I argue here that the New Christian experience of the violence of proto-modernity in Iberia helped to shape their responses to both creolisation and slavery in the African Atlantic.[9]

This chapter shows how the circulation of these experiences of proto-modern violence was related to the birth of a Creole society in Western

---

[7] Appadurai (1990); Gruzinski (2005: 13–4); Hannerz (1996 : 17).

[8] Appadurai (1990: 16); Smith/Guarnizo (1998a: 17); Vertovec (2009: 3).

[9] Or, as Mendes (2007: 15) puts it, "was not this massive slavery but the mirror of the inherent violence of modern society?" – "*cet esclavage massif ne fut-il que le miroir des violences inhérentes à la société moderne?*"

Africa. By the 1520s and 1530s the pidginised version of Kriolu which had developed on Cabo Verde by the end of the fifteenth century was consolidating into a vernacular language for communication between slaves and their masters and among the slaves themselves. Slaves speaking Kriolu are cited in a document of 1558, and linguistic evidence suggests that the vernacularisation of the language was completed on the islands before the 1560s.[10] Yet as the linguistic changes circulated, the mixed societies which emerged with them varied. "Creolisation" was a distinct experience in Upper Guinea to that on the islands of Santiago and Fogo. All three differed and produced Creole societies whose discrete characters can still be discerned.[11] This is exemplified by one saying on Fogo today: "If you annoy someone on Santiago, they kill you; if you annoy someone here, we kill ourselves".[12] The cultural character of each locale varied. and although this may sound axiomatic as every culture depends on its formation for different characteristics, what turned the Western African region into one where this mattered was that certain similarities ultimately did create a shared Creole culture that spanned the region and co-existed alongside existing Upper Guinean societies.

It was exactly the Creole society of Western Africa which had the largest role in engaging with the new commercial demands of the Atlantic world; thus this picture of creolisation cannot fit the classical nineteenth century model in which hybrids were seen as degenerate.[13] Their own pre-existing tendencies towards adaptability were crucial for the New Christians when they arrived at a cultural situation where such adaptability had long been practised by peoples neighbouring the Mandinka. This chapter shows for the first time the fusion of these pre-existing trends and how they worked together to form Creole society in Western Africa in the shadow of the rise of the slave trade at the dawn of the modern age.

MODERNITY, AFRICAN EXCHANGES AND THE CREATION OF THE NEW CHRISTIAN IDEOLOGY

In order to understand interactions between Upper Guineans and the Portuguese New Christians in the early sixteenth century, we must

---

[10] Ladham (2003: 145); Seibert (forthcoming, 2012).
[11] Thus in Creole studies it is generally accepted that "no single historical mise-en-scène will fully account for the genesis of all creoles" (Grant 2001: 81). See also ibid., 107–8.
[12] Personal communication from E. Akintola Hubbard, São Filipe, Fogo, May 22, 2008.
[13] See Bernal (1991: 29–32) for an outline of Victorian historiography as seeing creative civilizations as "racially pure". See also Holm (1988: Vol. 1, 1) on how until the 1950s traditional Creole studies saw Creole societies through this prism as "deficient".

understand the New Christians' complex and violent history. The Portuguese New Christians were descended from Portugal's long-standing Jewish community, from the New Christians who fled the Spanish Inquisition for Portugal in the 1480s until this migration was made illegal by João II in 1488, and from the Sephardic Jews who were expelled from Spain by the *Reyes Católicos* in 1492.[14]

The influx of Spanish New Christians in the 1480s had created unrest in Portugal. This was compounded by the 1492 arrivals. Estimates of the numbers of Jews who arrived in Portugal in 1492 range from 10,000 to 250,000.[15] With their arrival the Jews constituted, according to some estimates, 10 percent of Portugal's population.[16] The refugees from Spain had a mixed fate: six hundred families were given leave to remain on payment of a large tax, many moved on to Italy and North Africa, many died in unsanitary conditions in camps near the Spanish border, and yet others were enslaved.[17] Taken together, Spanish New Christians and Jews were widely blamed for the plagues which afflicted Portugal every year between 1477 and 1496.[18] Demonisation gathered pace, and in 1497 the vast majority of Jews in Portugal were forcibly converted to Christianity by Manoel I.[19]

Though initially protected from inquisitorial investigations, these Portuguese New Christians were eventually persecuted by inquisitors just as their forebears had been in Spain. Many fled to the Ottoman Empire, Italian principalities, the Low Countries and North Africa, where they reverted to "open" Judaism. Others, however, remained in Iberian possessions, both in Europe and in the New World, and in these areas some of them secretly practised elements of their Jewish faith. It was these so-called crypto-Jews who were at the forefront of many later inquisitorial investigations in both Western Africa and Latin America.[20] Indeed,

---

[14] On the relationship of João II and the Spanish New Christians (or *conversos*), see Soyer (2007: 98–101).

[15] The estimate of Loeb was 10,000 (1887: 181–2), and that of Herculano was 250,000 (1854: Vol. 1, 197); Andres Bernaldez estimated around 93,000, Damião de Góis 100,000. For a summary of the various estimates, see Tavares (1982: Vol. 1, 253).

[16] Révah (1971: 483).

[17] Soyer (2007: Chapter 2).

[18] Tavares (1982 : Vol. 1, 425); Herculano (1854 : Vol. 1, 108).

[19] Almost all the Jews converted – see Soyer (2007: 229–31) – though some did escape according to Tavim (1997: 83–4). For a summary of the Jewish and New Christian experience under Manoel I, see Yovel (2009: 191–206).

[20] For a more detailed account of the Inquisition of Spain, see Netanyahu (1995) and N. Roth (2002). For the Portuguese experience, a superb general account is Bethencourt (1994; idem. 2009). See also Green (2007a).

although many influential studies still see the Sepahrdic networks in the Mediterranean basin as key to the formation of Sephardic communities in the early modern period, it has become clear that the sixteenth-century Atlantic diaspora was also very significant, particularly in Amsterdam.[21]

When the New Christians began to arrive in Western Africa early in the sixteenth century, therefore, they brought with them the legacy of important recent experiences which helped to shape their interactions with Africans. First and foremost was the experience of violence. In Spain, the Jews had been expelled and lost much of their property, and the New Christians had been persecuted by the Spanish Inquisition at its most ruthless and violent.[22] In 1497 those who had left for Portugal with the expulsion had all their offspring aged fourteen or more seized and taken to be educated by Christian families. Some mothers had killed their children rather than have them taken away, others had committed suicide, and the 20,000 Jews who had reached Lisbon hoping to depart and save their faith had been refused permission to leave, whereupon many more had killed themselves.[23]

However, supplementing this experience of violence was the adaptability that force and fear of force can create. Prior to the traumas of the 1480s and 1490s, many Spanish Jews had converted to Christianity in the late fourteenth and early fifteenth centuries, and subsequently incorporated Roman Catholic images into their religious practice, although Jews saw this reverence of images as idolatry.[24] Eventually, even those Jews who had tried to preserve their faith in Spain, and who had then migrated to Portugal, had been forced to convert to Christianity. Having thus adapted their outward practices and faith, these Portuguese New Christians were peculiarly well-versed in their recent experience in how adaptability could become a strategic benefit. Their long experience of adaptability both in Portugal and elsewhere in the Jewish diaspora had shown them how accommodating themselves to the cultures of their hosts brought advantages.

To this can be added a third and more complex strand of their recent experience. The violence directed at the New Christian class in Spain and

---

[21] Trivellato (2009: 112) offers a recent example of the claim that the Atlantic only became important to Sephardim after 1650. This view is seriously challenged, though, by evidence on the importance to the early Amsterdam community of the Brazilian New Christians and trading centres in Senegambia (Green 2005; 2008a; Mark/Horta 2011).

[22] For a general account, see Green (2007a: 17–44).

[23] Góis (1949: Vol. 1, 42); Osorio (1944: 81); Soyer (2007: 226–7).

[24] Pereda (2007).

Portugal in the late fifteenth century was a product of the growing modernisation of existence and of the abstraction of thought that went with it, and thus the New Christians who came to Western Africa brought with them acute understanding of these trends. This connection of New Christians to modernisation emerges most clearly in the economic factors frequently used as an explanation for the anti-Semitism of Iberia in the fifteenth century.[25] For most Jews in Portugal in 1497 were not large-scale financiers in Lisbon, but rather petty merchants and craftspeople.[26] There were strong divisions between the oligarchy of Portuguese Jewish society and the rest of the community.[27] Furthermore, the arrival of the Jews from Spain was not, as François Soyer has shown, totally disruptive.[28] In fact, it brought great wealth into Portugal, and the receptor of the entry taxes from the Spanish Jews collected 8,951,312 *reais* in Évora alone.[29]

Thus in Portugal, popular anger at economic injustices fastened on a scapegoat for frustration rather than on the root cause of it. The protests about the Jews' wealth really reveal something else: the growing importance of material concerns to Portuguese society. This pecuniary turn reflected social changes, in particular urbanisation and the change in perspectives of value which foreshadowed the modernity discussed in the introduction to this chapter; capital became mobile and in turn increased human mobility, which contributed to urban drift. The notion that Old Christians worked in the fields while New Christians luxuriated in the towns was frequently cited as a cause of hatred, something which really reveals resentment of urban life.[30] The development of wage labour that resulted from urbanisation led to changes in lifestyle that caused widespread discontent.[31] Migration to cities was usually reluctant and the source of unhappiness, thus new forms of proto-racism were themselves urban phenomena.[32] Such feelings were at bottom the product of anger and fear: a visceral anger at being separated from the land and fear of the new way of life in the towns, which in migrants' minds was most ostentatiously expressed by the Jews.[33] Above all, it was the fear of change, for humans cope badly with sudden change.

[25] See, e.g., Herculano (1854: Vol. 1, 101, 109–10); Azevedo (1922: 17–20).
[26] Tavares (1982 : Vol. 1, 330).
[27] Ibid., Vol. 1, 125–6; Azevedo (1922: 22).
[28] Soyer (2007).
[29] AHP, Vol. 3, 472.
[30] See, e.g., AG, Vol. 1, 105–6.
[31] Baechler (1975: 14–5).
[32] On the urban nature of racism, see Carneiro (1983: 53); on the role of separation from the land in the rise of anti-Semitism in Spain, see Green (2007b: Appendix A).
[33] On conflicts between town and country in Iberia, see Gilman (1972: 410–11).

As these changes occurred in the fifteenth century, there was a growing abstraction of thought: a distancing process such as is often produced by fear.[34] This can be observed through changes in both linguistic and mathematical conceptualisation. Changes in language are very important here. The term *descobrir* was first used to signify the discovery of new lands in 1472, whereas the more abstract term for "discovery", *descobrimento*, surfaced in 1486 – the abstraction residing in the fact that the latter was not predicated on an agent to undertake the discovering.[35] The African Atlantic had thus itself become a "space to discover"; a geography dominated by *places* (occupied by humans) was superseded with one occupied by abstract *spaces*.[36] Indeed, there was no word in medieval European languages to signify the modern term "space"; this developed specifically along with the Atlantic voyages.[37]

Crucially to the ideas of this book, experiences in Western Africa were necessary conditions for these changes, for the voyages along the African coast were essential in changing the conceptual lexicon of late medieval Portugal towards this more abstract, spatially aware and mathematised worldview. In an important work, Joaquim Barradas de Carvalho illustrated these changes by showing how the advances in numeracy and mathematisation were made possible by the experience of new worlds catalysed by the Portuguese voyages of "discovery"; he argued that confrontation with the new precipitated growing interest in quantification.[38] Although the use of Arabic numerals and ordinary mathematical symbols such as "+" and "x" remained unheard of in the fifteenth century – and indeed, in the case of the latter, were still unusual until the end of the sixteenth century – by the early sixteenth century, when three Portuguese mathematicians published new works, all of them used Arabic numerals.[39] These mathematical changes were accompanied by important scientific breakthroughs also related to spatial and mathematical concepts. In the first place, there was a new dependence on astronomical observation for navigation in the second half of the fifteenth century, where previously European sailors had never travelled out of sight of land.[40] Such spatial awareness led to the growth of cartography in Portugal and the

---

[34] See Green (2006).

[35] On the contrast of places and spaces, see L. Fonseca (1995: 15).

[36] Ibid., 15–16. See also Tzvetan Todorov's analysis of Columbus's journal from 1492, which shows more interest in lands than in people "*[une] préférence pour les terres plutôt que les hommes*": Todorov (1982: 39).

[37] Richter (2009: 55–6).

[38] J. Carvalho (1981).

[39] Ibid., 51–69.

[40] Albuquerque (1983: 31–41).

introduction of a latitude scale on maps in the early sixteenth century.[41]
One may reasonably say, therefore, that the experiences of navigation in
the waters of Atlantic Africa were fundamental in shifting the perception
of experience onto a more scientific footing.

There were many consequences of this shift for which, again, events in
Africa were relevant. Key to the new conceptualisation of quantification,
for instance, was the growth of the importance of coinage in Portugal following the exploitation of Elmina's gold. Such was the flood of gold from
Elmina that by 1495 it provided a public revenue of 120,000 *cruzados*, in
comparison to 126,688 *cruzados* from other sources, and it dramatically
increased the amount of coinage available in the Portuguese economy.[42]
The gathering importance of gold in the years leading up to the forced
conversions of the Jews in 1497 then allowed for the abstraction of value
and perception.[43] Such abstraction was a central element of emergent
modernity, often represented in monetarised economies by the equiva-
lence objects of production are granted by their exchangeability through
a system of universal value constituted by money.[44] Thus the urbanisation and monetarisation of the Portuguese economy that expanded along
with the explorations of the West African coast were accompanied by
a sense of abstraction and alienation, and it was precisely the new economic horizons that had opened up in West Africa which consolidated
these changes. The voyages along the West African coast had therefore
not only brought the economic liquidity to catalyse growing abstractions
in monetary terms; they had also helped to create new concepts which
were vital to this new, more theoretical and scientific worldview.

In Iberia this process of abstraction was replicated ideologically in
the awareness and articulation of regional identities. Medieval Iberia
had represented an Islamic (and thus North African and Middle Eastern)
model of place, with different communities co-existing.[45] The new Iberia
of the 1490s, however, was a culturally purified space purged of its
non-Christian communities, tied spatially to the rest of Europe through
its geography, and conceptually by this new mode of abstract thought

[41] Ibid., 62–70.
[42] Godinho (1969: 829). In this seminal work Godinho also showed how the hyper-inflation
of the late fourteenth and early fifteenth centuries, produced by a chronic shortage of
gold, had been one of the spurs to the voyages to Africa.
[43] The connection between monetarisation and alienation is discussed by Marx in the
Grundrisse – see McLellan (1971: 60–1).
[44] Simmel (1990: 120, 128–9).
[45] On this Islamic model of place, see Perceval (1997: 88–9); N. Roth (2002 : 41); Marques
(1972 : Vol. 1, 82–3).

developing along with the voyages of discovery. The end of the previous model of place perhaps came when the forced conversions of 1497 tied Portugal culturally to this new vision of reality.[46] Thus in the urban spaces of Iberia in the fifteenth century, several levels of abstraction were at work: physical (from the land to the towns), economic (with the growing value of money, which can be seen in the emphasis placed on materialism in the envy of the Jews), and psychological (with the new conceptual armoury and the shift in Iberia's conception of itself). Many of these changes were symbolised by the new importance of urban centres, and thus it was the anger at the death throes of the previous worldview which was directed at the New Christians.

This analysis shows why the New Christians who came to Western Africa did so with acute experience of the forces which soon engulfed the Atlantic world. These New Christians had been the very first targets of this process, in which modernisation required scapegoats in order to legitimate and drive forward the changes which growth through the forcible appropriation of economic surpluses required. It was an inevitable condition of Jewish life in Iberia that they should be part of this bourgeois vision, barred as they largely were from significant landholdings and the status this provided in feudal societies.[47] They could therefore easily be identified with the new system: they were the perfect scapegoats. Yet as well as being scapegoats for resentments felt at the new system, as urban dwellers and traders they were active participants in it. Those New Christians who went to Western Africa would bring these experiences with them, and the new ways which the forces of modernisation and alienation found to present subjectivity would make Western Africa a key testing ground in the formation of new types of belonging.[48]

THE EARLY NEW CHRISTIAN DIASPORA IN WESTERN AFRICA

The New Christian diaspora in Western Africa emerged from the role of the New Christians' Jewish forebears in the Portuguese economy. In the fifteenth century Jews had been used by the Portuguese kings to collect the royal tax revenues, not only in Portugal but also, in the late fifteenth

---

[46] See Castro (1954), especially 85–135, on how different Iberia was from the rest of Europe.

[47] Tinhorão (1988: 20 n.9); see also Simmel's (1990: 224) analysis of the importance of money to strangers in societies, as it can easily be exported outside the group.

[48] On the role of Upper Guinea in finding new ways to present subjectivity, see Nafafé (2007: 2).

century, in the nascent overseas trade.[49] The Portuguese crown may have felt it wise to use an unpopular class to carry out an unpopular task. However, as the overseas trade grew, there was also a growing structural segue between the way in which international trade transcended boundaries and the ways in which the Jewish diaspora did likewise in the Mediterranean world.[50]

Diasporic peoples were well suited to the strategies needed for successful trade as transnational trading worlds opened up in the early Atlantic. Some readers may feel uncomfortable with the use of a term such as "transnational," which has been comprehensively reworked in recent decades and applied to the era of industrial globalisation.[51] Christopher Bayly has argued that the idea of the transnational is of limited relevance to the era before the formation of nation-states.[52] Yet scholars recognise that many of the key features of contemporary transnationalism existed in previous eras, such as mobility, diasporas, long-distance networks, and maintenance of connections with the place of origin.[53] These features all apply to the early New Christian Atlantic traders, and indeed Patricia Seed has suggested that this New Christian diaspora offers an example of transnationalism preceding what we think of as modernity.[54] Clearly, there were major differences between these New Christian groups and contemporary transnational networks, but the transnational category is nonetheless useful in forming an understanding of them.[55]

This usefulness becomes clearer when we consider how scholars have started to explore the possibilities of some form of transnational identity among other diasporas of the early modern Atlantic; indeed one of the benefits of using this term here is to see how the events analysed in this book show many of the characteristics of an incipient form of modernity.[56] Portugal and Spain in the sixteenth century were proto-modern states characterised by their global reach and new institutions such as the Inquisition which were notable for their use of extensive

---

[49] Salvador (1981: 2); by around 1472 they were involved in the sugar trade with Madeira together with Genoese merchants – see also Soyer (2007: 75), and Lobo (1979: 519).

[50] Correia e Silva (1995: 2).

[51] See for instance Hannerz (1996); Smith/Guarnizo (1998b); Vertovec (2009).

[52] Bayly et al. (2006).

[53] Vertovec (2009: Chapter 2). As Vertovec says, "transnationalism (as long-distance networks) certainly preceded the nation" (2009: 3).

[54] Bayly et al. (2006).

[55] On these differences, see Yovel (2009: 289–90).

[56] For an example of early modern transnational identity, see O'Toole (2007: 21) on the Brame diaspora of Peru.

bureaucracies and state-sanctioned punishment. When this point is fore-grounded together with the fact that the New Christians themselves began to be known as – and to call themselves – "Men of the Nation" (*hombres de la nación/homens da nação*) in the sixteenth century, and that this "Nation" was precisely defined by its dispersed nature, the rele-vance of the transnational category to the early New Christian diaspora becomes clear.[57]

The dispersed nature of New Christian trading communities was vital to their early success. In the African Atlantic, as among the Jewish Mediterranean communities, this quickly became essential, and, com-bined with pre-existing knowledge, helped to cement the New Christian status there. As we have seen, Sephardic Jews were already involved in the trans-Saharan trade, and these Moroccan communities probably had commercial and family contacts with traders in Iberia (cf. Chapter 2). The Portuguese New Christians were thus ideally placed to become involved in the Atlantic trading diaspora plying to and from the West African coast. A further continuity lay in the fact that the early *rendeiros*, or tax farmers, of Cabo Verde were New Christians, just as the Jews had been tax collectors in Portugal.[58] Continuity was key to the organisation of this new trade as it had been in Senegambia.

The role of the New Christians in early Caboverdean history is underlined by the mechanism used by the Portuguese crown for putt-ing the Caboverdean contracts out to tender. When bidding for the new contract was announced in Lisbon in 1507, the factor of the Portuguese islands and *almoxarife* of the slave house sent someone down the Rua Nova shouting for bids from "whoever wants to take up the contract of the islands of Santiago and Fogo and the rights of the island of Maio".[59] After the events of 1497, the old *judiarias* or Jewish quarters of Portugal were called "*vilas novas*" or "*ruas novas*" and re-occupied by their former inhabitants.[60] By asking for bids for the Cabo Verde

---

[57] On the global and modern nature of the Inquisition, see Green (2007a) and Bethencourt (2009); on the use of the term "nation" for the New Christian diaspora, see Bodian (1997) and Arbell (2002).

[58] Z. Cohen (2002: 89, n.89) notes this; see also idem., (1994: 346).

[59] HGCV: CD, Vol. 1, 171 – a document of 6 February 1507: the whole passage reads: "*E o dito feitor [Gonçalo Lopes] e eu, escrivão [Álvaro Anes], ... mandamos [a Diogo Fernandes, porteiro do concelho] que se fosse per a Rua Nova e per as ruas acustumadas e que afron-tasse que se havia logo d'arrematar. E o dito porteiro começou de dizer altas vozes quem quizer lançar nas ilhas de Santiago e do Fogo e nos direitos da ilha de Maio*".

[60] Tavares (1987: 43); Amador de los Ríos (1960: 747); Soyer (2007: 198). In Lisbon, the Rua Nova had formerly housed the largest synagogues, and after 1497 it remained inhabited largely by New Christians – see Lipiner (1977: 122–3).

contract in this way, the crown was guaranteeing that it would be taken up by New Christians.

That the Caboverdean contracts were typically parcelled out in this way is indicated by the identities of the *rendeiros* prior to this contract. In 1504 the contracts had been assigned to Duarte Rodrigues, Pero Francisco and Gil Álvares, whose guarantor had been Fernam de Loronha.[61] Loronha was Rodrigues's uncle[62]; he was also the head of a consortium of New Christians who had been given the first contract for Brazil after the voyage of Pedro Alvares Cabral in 1500.[63] Loronha was a well-known New Christian.[64] This has led some historians to assume that Loronha had converted in 1497[65]; in fact he was a member of the royal household by 1494 and had converted by this time.[66]

Nevertheless, Loronha's New Christian status is important in understanding the orientation of the traders who took up the Cabo Verde contract in the years after 1500. Although Loronha was not forcibly converted in 1497, he had active dealings with members of the Jewish community just before the forced conversions. Prior to 1497 he acted as receptor for rents due on cottages belonging to the royal household, and the sums involved included 495,495 *reais* that Salamam [Salomon] Negro owed to Afonso Fernandes dating back to the reign of João II, and which were charged to Loronha and his partners as they were also partners of Negro at that time; the Negro family was one of the Jewish families involved in high finance in Lisbon.[67]

Loronha's nephew Duarte Rodrigues had had a similar trajectory. A quittance from the receptor João Álvares Rangel of 1496 included monies received from Duarte Rodrigues as part of the dues from the factor of Guiné[68]; associated with Rodrigues was Yoçe Cabanas, Yoçe being a

---

[61] HGCV: CD, Vol. 1, 141–7.

[62] Z. Cohen (1994: 344).

[63] RD, Vol. II, Part III, 120–1. See also Lipiner (1969: 15); Carneiro (1983: 197).

[64] On Loronha's connection to the Caboverdean contracts and the assignment of these contracts in the *Rua Nova*, see Correia e Silva (1991: 365–7).

[65] See for example Thomas (1997: 111).

[66] Wolff/Wolff (1986: 141).

[67] AHP, Vol. 2, 351: "495: 495 rs que Salamam Negro devia a Afonso Fernandes, thesoureiro que foi de el rei que Deus tem, e foram aqui carregados ao ditto Fernam de Noronha e seus parceiros, por serem parceiros em o ditto Salamam Negro ao trauto das moradias de el Rei que Deus tem": tr. "495,495 reis that Salomon Negro owed to Afonso Fernandes, treasurer to the late king, who were charged to Fernam de Noronha and his partners, having been partners with the said Salomon Negro in the business of the late king [João II]'s cottages". Noronha and Loronha are variants of the same name.

[68] HGCV: CD, Vol. 1, 105.

typical transliteration of the Jewish name Yosef in Iberian documents of the time.[69] Thus, like his uncle Loronha, Rodrigues had also converted prior to 1497 – as evidenced by his Christian name – and also remained associated with members of the Jewish community at that time.

These factors are important when considering the Loronha-Rodrigues consortium of New Christians in Cabo Verde in the early sixteenth century. These figures clearly had strong connections with the New Christian communities of Lisbon. Furthermore, the activities of this consortium were widespread across West Africa. In 1502 and 1503 Loronha held the contract for the Rios dos Escravos (present-day Benin and Nigeria) and for the pepper from Guiné and Elmina, and therefore his dealings in Cabo Verde merely extended this interest.[70] This evidence suggests a need to reconsider the career of this well-known Atlantic consortium; Loronha is often presented in a Brazilian context, although his activities spanned the Atlantic, and he was equally as active in West Africa.[71]

This evidence of major New Christian traders taking a wide interest in Western Africa in the early sixteenth century is supported by other data. Loronha and Rodrigues were followed as contractors in Cabo Verde by Antonio Rodrigues Mascarenhas in 1510.[72] Mascarenhas was the son of João Rodrigues Mascarenhas, one of the leading New Christian merchants of Lisbon, killed by a mob during the riots of 1506.[73] João Rodrigues Mascarenhas had been involved in bartering in Upper Guinea, and he had been leased the *vintena* of the region from the years 1505 to 1507, prior to his untimely death.[74] His son Antonio's involvement in Cabo Verde continued until at least 1516, and thus New Christians and their agents on the Caboverdean islands were pivotal to the collecting of taxes throughout this period.[75]

The involvement of these influential New Christians is certain to have had an impact on the type of person to be found in Cabo Verde.

[69] Ibid.: "*500 [cruzados] que recebeo de Lopo Mendes e 1.580 rs. de Duarte Rodrigues e os 150 de Yoçe Cabanas...*".

[70] AHP, Vol. 2, 239: a document of 15 June 1509, detailing the dues owed by Loronha to the crown. See also Salvador (1981: 19); Thomas (1997: 112); Vogt (1979: 73).

[71] Though Salvador (1981: 19) recognises Loronha's equally important role in the African context. This evidence supports the argument of Metcalf (2005) regarding the importance of African experience in the colonization of Brazil.

[72] Barcellos (1899: 66).

[73] On the filial relation, see Salvador (1981: 19); on the murder of João Rodrigues Mascarenhas, see C. Roth (1959: 65).

[74] AHP, Vol. 4, 73; he had also previously held the licence to trade on the Gambia at Cantor/Kantora (ibid., Vol. 4, 72).

[75] Z. Cohen (1994: 343).

Following the riots of 1506 against Lisbon's New Christians, Manoel I had passed a law permitting their departure from Portugal without his permission in March 1507.[76] This facility, combined with the dangers of staying in Portugal, made their presence in Cabo Verde almost inevitable, particularly as the contracts were controlled by other New Christians. Already in 1501 New Christians were being exiled to Cabo Verde.[77] Then, in a well-known letter of 25 October 1512, the *câmara* of Ribeira Grande complained that the "New Christians who act as *rendeiros* [tax farmers] here" were damaging the interests of the court secretary, Antonio Carneiro.[78] In a letter dated the previous day, they had complained that the New Christians had misinformed the crown with damaging results.[79] Manoel I soon took account, and a decree of 8 May 1515, barred New Christians from living or passing through Santiago once the contract of Francisco Martíz had ended.[80]

As we saw in the previous chapter, the tax receipts handled by these New Christian tax collectors derived from the labour of slaves in Cabo Verde and the trade in slaves from West Africa. That is, the commercial exploitation of the region that had seen the development of such an early Atlantic slave economy and the first stirrings of a creolised society in the Atlantic was placed in the hands of the New Christian merchant class that was still coming to terms with the violence that they and their relatives had been the victims of in Spain and Portugal. Although from a metropolitan perspective continuities in the tax-collection process were clearly important, the New Christian experience of violence in Iberia may also have counted. We might ask: Can the *rendeiro* Antonio Rodrigues Mascarenhas's actions as a tax farmer in Cabo Verde really be separated from his experience of his father's lynching in Lisbon? Gaining income through tax receipts derived from a trade in human beings may have constituted some form of psychological transference for a group whose estimation of humanity cannot have been very high following recent events in Portugal.

This is not to play the old game of demonisation of the Jews. For one thing, New Christians had a complex attitude to religious matters, and

---

[76] Révah (1971: 488).
[77] Mendes (2007: 299–300).
[78] MMAII: Vol. 2, 57: "*se algũ mall se faz, os crystãos novos que quá sam rendeyros fazem todo esto*".
[79] Ibid., Vol. 2, 53: "*Ora, a requerimento de allgũos christão novos que a V.A. mal ynformarão*".
[80] Ibid., Vol. 2, 97: "*Acabado o arrendamēto da dita ylha que ora teem Francisco Martíz, ally por diante nã posam nella viver de morada, nem estar nhũs christãos novos.*"

whereas some stuck fast to the old Jewish beliefs, as many were devout Catholics and even atheists. The majority of New Christians did not become Atlantic traders at all, and many merely tried as best they could to assimilate into Portuguese society. Nevertheless, a minority did become Atlantic diaspora traders involved in the slave trade, and invoking previous experience as a partial explanation for this is simply to recognise facts about human nature and the responses which human beings may have to their experiences of violence. Naturally, not everyone responds in the same way, but certainly some people do respond to experiences of persecution by transferring it. Why should these *rendeiros* have shown any greater estimation for the value of human life than had been shown in their general experience?

On this interpretation, and as suggested in the introduction to this chapter and the subsequent analysis of anti-Semitism and proto-modernity in fifteenth-century Iberia, their participation in this trade was an expression of the violence which was one of the many aspects of the emergence of modernity. Yet the participation of New Christian *rendeiros* in the trade had its own nuances. The emergence of an Atlantic slave economy in Western Africa may have depended on violence, but, as in pre-Atlantic West Africa, this violence would bring with it a flipside of cultural accommodation in which the New Christians, although initially somewhat reluctant, came to play a pivotal role.

THE CONSOLIDATION OF THE NEW CHRISTIAN DIASPORA IN CABO VERDE

The New Christian presence grew swiftly in Cabo Verde throughout the first third of the sixteenth century. As New Christian families sought to escape the Inquisition in Portugal – instituted by papal bull in 1536, though not accorded comparable powers to its Spanish counterpart until 1548 – Cabo Verde became an attractive point of escape apparently beyond inquisitorial power.[81] Moreover, it was not only Western Africa that was attractive; by the 1550s, there were also many New Christians said to be living in Kongo and São Tomé.[82] Having shown adaptability in

---

[81] Mark/Horta (2011: 9) concur in seeing this region as a place of escape from the Inquisition for Jews and New Christians.

[82] See the letter of Belchior de Sousa from July 1553, MMAI: Vol. 2, 286; and the letter of Christovão d'Orta de Sousa from November 1561 claiming that five out of every six people in São Tomé are New Christian ("*as synquo partes da jẽte desta ylha sam cristãos novos...*") – ibid., Vol. 2, 475.

adopting some outward signs of Roman Catholicism, it may have been that the adjustments required in the African Atlantic did not seem too difficult to these new refugees.

In Western Africa, however, the importance of New Christian adaptability was not immediately apparent. Indeed, many of the earliest New Christians appear to have chosen Cabo Verde as a place where they would be free to maintain their ancestral Jewish rites unmolested. They were there not to adapt to new cultural rites but to maintain old ones. It was only by the end of the 1530s that patterns of adaptation began to emerge. Case studies help us to trace this pattern, and the inquisitorial archives allow us to trace individual cases back very early in time. The New Christian presence can be mapped through specific cases back to the 1510s.

The first recorded case comes from the remote island of Brava. Brava's first *rendeiro* had been the New Christian Francisco da Fonseca, who was nominated in 1509, with profits coming from cleaning cotton and preparing it for export.[83] There were also some cattle on the island, and the rights to the island were passed on to his sons Diogo and João in 1518.[84] Things continued thus until 1542, when both Diogo and João were accused of Judaic practices on a caravel.[85] Action was swiftly taken, and by 1545 the rights to Brava had passed on to João Pereira, a member of the royal council.[86]

Evidence from the Canariote Inquisition supplements the suggestion here of a Judaising tendency among Caboverdean New Christians from at least 1518. The first burnings by the Canariote tribunal were in 1526, and one of the main cases was that of Álvaro Gonçales and his wife Mencia Baez from Palma Island, who were burnt together with their son Sílvio.[87] Another son, Duarte, escaped with a *sanbenito* [penitential garment], which he was sentenced to wear for five years on Palma. However, his mother-in-law, Catalina Diaz, denounced him again to the Inquisition on 8 April 1527.[88] Duarte soon plotted to flee. He went to a certain Juan Diaz on the island to ask for help to leave, and Diaz also came to the Inquisition, saying that Gonçales had asked to be taken to Cabo Verde,

[83] HGCV: CD, Vol. 1, 183–5.
[84] Ibid., Vol. 1, 183.
[85] IAN/TT, Inquisição de Lisboa, Livro 52, 169v, 173r-v; abstract published by Baião (1921: 130).
[86] A good discussion of this case is Z. Cohen (2002: 131–2).
[87] Wolf (1926: 18–79); Millares Torres (1982: Vol. I., 88–9).
[88] Wolf (1926: 78–9).

where he had rich relatives.[89] Then on 29 July 1529, Catalina Diaz came
to the Inquisition to say that she had heard that Duarte had been living
with his uncle in Cabo Verde, but that he had died there.[90]

The cases of the Fonsecas and Duarte Gonçales corroborate the accusations of the 1512 letter from the council of Ribeira Grande concerning
the strong New Christian presence in Cabo Verde. Other cases support this
hypothesis, in particular that of Graviel [Gabriel] Rodrigues. Rodrigues
was accused of crypto-Judaism in February 1559 to the Bishop of Cabo
Verde, Francisco da Cruz.[91] He had not attended church for a whole
year.[92] An old man by 1559, he appears to have been one of the Spanish
Jews who fled to Portugal after the expulsion of 1492.[93] He could not
recite the Ave Maria, the Pater Noster, or the Credo and did not even
know if he had been baptised.[94] Moreover, his sole statement of religious
belief was that he believed in "God the All-Powerful Father and Creator
of the Heavens and Earth [*criador dos ceus e da terra*]", where the formulation "*Deus dos ceos*" was a standard one for crypto-Jews in the early
modern era.[95]

Rodrigues was transferred to Lisbon for trial.[96] There he said that he
was a widower and that his wife had fled from Lisbon with her relatives
many years previously when King João III of Portugal had given the New
Christians licence to leave the kingdom. Rodrigues had been in Cabo
Verde at the time, and on his return he had found them gone, which
shows that this New Christian had a long history of trade in Cabo Verde.
In his trial Rodrigues stated that he could not remember how long ago
this had occurred. New Christians suffered bans from leaving Portugal
in the periods 1532–5 and 1547–50, and given the long period of time
which must have elapsed for Rodrigues to forget when exactly his wife
had fled Lisbon, the likelihood is that this could have been around 1535,
and that this was when he had previously been present in Cabo Verde.[97]

---

[89] Ibid., 79.
[90] Ibid.
[91] IAN/TT, Inquisição de Lisboa, Processo 16034, fol. 2r – the first 5 fols. of this trial are
numbered but the remainder are not. I would like to express my utmost thanks to Filipa
Ribeiro da Silva who drew my attention to this file.
[92] Ibid.
[93] Ibid., fol. 2v.
[94] Ibid.
[95] Ibid; on the formulation "*deos dos ceos*", see Bodian (2007: 44).
[96] IAN/TT, Inquisição de Lisboa, Processo 16034; for the remainder of the detail of this
case there are no fol. numbers.
[97] On the dates of prohibitions of New Christians leaving Portugal, see Révah (1971:
495–521).

Rodrigues evidently had a history of repeated trips to Cabo Verde over a long period; it is also quite possible that this had not been his first trip to Western Africa and that he had been there previously in the 1520s.

A final case from this early period confirms both the Judaic practice of many of these first New Christian migrants and the way in which Cabo Verde was seen as a place of escape. In June 1539 evidence began to be received in Lisbon against Branca Dias, a New Christian accused of fleeing Lisbon for Santiago, Cabo Verde, out of fear of the Inquisition.[98] Four years later, on March 12, 1543, Dias was arrested in Praia on Santiago and taken to Ribeira Grande.[99] Witnesses claimed that she had come to Cabo Verde smuggled in a water barrel on a ship captained by her son and had then gone to Fogo before settling in Praia, where she baked bread.[100]

Branca Dias's case shows how the New Christian diaspora had spread in Cabo Verde beyond Ribeira Grande to Praia (also on Santiago) and Fogo. Moreover, as Dias's son Nuno Fernandes was a trader in Upper Guinea, one can also see here evidence of its spreading to the African coast.[101] Taken with the other three cases examined here, it reveals the longevity of the New Christian presence in Cabo Verde; individuals can be traced back through the records to the 1510s, 1520s and 1530s. Many of these New Christians appear to have identified strongly with the Judaic faith. The Fonsecas kept Jewish prayers aboard ship. Branca Dias was said to go to Jewish houses in Lisbon and, like Graviel Rodrigues, used a Jewish ritual formulation when she declared her belief in the "all-powerful God who created the stars and the earth" [*deus todo poderoso q criou as estrelas e a terra*].[102] Rodrigues himself, meanwhile, used these Jewish formulations of prayer and did not even know whether he had been baptised. Duarte Gonçales asked his wife to work on a Sunday – and so clearly did not keep the Christian sabbath – and his parents and brother were heavily involved in crypto-Judaism.[103] For these individuals, Cabo Verde was a place for personal and cultural preservation. People like them cannot have had much desire to engage in the cultural give and take which characterised the development of a Creole culture and language on the islands.

---

[98] IAN/TT, Inquisição de Lisboa, Processo 5729, fols. 2r, 15r.
[99] Ibid., fol. 17r.
[100] Ibid., fols. 17v-18r, 19r, 20r, 26v, 27v.
[101] Ibid., fol. 4r.
[102] Ibid., 15r, 4r.
[103] Wolf (1926: 78–9, 18–52).

However, we cannot understand the early New Christian diaspora in Cabo Verde solely through the desire to maintain Judaic practices. Crucial to the place of this emergent community was the role which Western Africa was beginning to take in the wider Atlantic world, as well as the interrelationship of regional and global factors which was developing. Cabo Verde was an attractive option for New Christians not only as a place of escape from the Inquisition, but also because of wider geopolitical dynamics and its place in the development of pan-Atlantic connections, at which we will look more closely in Chapter 6. Moreover it was relatively safe, as the Atlantic was not a key economic space for Portugal in the first half of the sixteenth century, a time when much of the Portuguese nobility was glory-hunting in India.[104]

As a space passed over by the nobility in the first half of the sixteenth century, the Atlantic was attractive for New Christians.[105] This may explain why they were able to use their long-standing experience of diaspora trading to forge such advantageous networks. In Cabo Verde, they rapidly developed connections not only to the Canaries (the Gonçales case) and the trading houses of Portugal (the Fonsecas, Rodrigues), but also to Brazil. According to a letter of 30 October 1544, written by the captain of Cabo Verde, António Correia de Sousa, all ships going to Brazil called there.[106] Indeed, as we have already seen from the Loronha trade consortium's twin interests in West Africa and Brazil, there had been commercial and maritime connections between the two sides of the Atlantic from the very start. In fact, the evidence for the early New Christian presence in Brazil is rich. By 1543 there were people in Brazil with children in the jails of the Inquisition for Judaising.[107] By 1553 people who had been accused by the Inquisition had fled to Brazil.[108]

As the mobile trading class of the pre-Atlantic Portuguese commercial system, it was inevitable that the New Christians would come to predominate commercially in the part of the overseas explorations largely passed over by the Portuguese nobility in the first half of the sixteenth century; they rapidly took over from the Genoese merchants who predominated in the late fifteenth and early sixteenth centuries.[109] As with the *rendeiros*,

---

[104] Azevedo (1929: 100–101).
[105] Schorsch (2008: Vol. 1, 49–51); Schwartz (2008: 99).
[106] MMAII: Vol. 2, 370: all ships going to Brazil (and São Tomé) "*per força ham de tocar ho dyto porto [de Santiago]*".
[107] Baião (1921: 141).
[108] AG, Vol. 9, 204–5.
[109] Using shipping contracts of the *Casa de la Contratación* in Seville, Mendes (2007: 471) sees the period from 1535 onwards as one increasingly dominated by New Christians.

140   *The Development of an Atlantic Creole Culture*

pre-existing practices were translated into the nascent pan-Atlantic world. But whereas initially the religious beliefs which went with those practices had tended towards a maintenance of old Jewish rites, as the first half of the sixteenth century developed, a more mixed form of identity began to emerge, and the old diasporic forms adopted new clothes as creolisation intensified. It was then that the tendency towards maintaining the old and secret Jewish rites became fused with the influences from West Africa.

The first evidence of this New Christian role in accelerating creolisation comes from 1546, when the council of Ribeira Grande wrote a letter to the inquisitorial officers of Évora denouncing many officials of the island as New Christians. This letter was first cited by Avelino Teixeira da Mota, and its purport was that about two hundred New Christians lived among the Africans of Upper Guinea, many having done so for ten, fifteen and even twenty years, and that they performed Mosaic and animist rites together with the Africans and had become polygamous.[110] The customs house of Ribeira Grande was singled out, with officials there accused of having despatched a known fugitive from the Inquisition in Lisbon to the Upper Guinea coast for his protection – this fugitive's father and brother were said to have been burnt in Lisbon.[111] The authors of the letter wrote that "so many of those who live here and who most rule the land are New Christians, especially in the customs' house, where the accountant, *almoxarifes*, scribes of the customs' accounts, scribes of the state and of the justices, and many others, [are all New Christians], very rich and powerful".[112] The council urged the king to establish the Inquisition in the islands.[113]

Some have seen this as a generic complaint grounded in economic competition rather than religious affiliation.[114] However, the evidence of

The evidence on the *rendeiros* considered here may even require this date to be pushed back, certainly as far as the Portuguese side of the trade goes.

[110] Mota (1978: 8). Mota gave the following citation for this evidence: *Inquisição de Évora, Livro de Denúncias de 1544–1550*, fols. 7–12v. However the indices for the Inquisition of Évora contains no book of *denúncias* corresponding to this period, and I was unable to locate the relevant document. T. Hall (1992: Vol. 1, 163 n.52) experienced the same difficulty in the 1980s.

[111] Baleno (1991: 169); also cited by Correia e Silva (1995: 4); Havik (2004a: 102) and Brooks (1993b: 158).

[112] Cit Z. Cohen (2007: 144): "*quatro partes dos que aqui moramos e dos que mais mandam [n]a terra especialmente na alfândega são cristãos-novos, como o contador, almoxarifes, escrivães dos contos almoxarifados, do público e do judicial e outros, muitos ricos e poderosos*".

[113] Ibid., and Brooks (1993b: 158).

[114] Baleno (1991: 168, 168 n.137).

this chapter suggests that this is not a sufficient explanation. We have seen how there was indeed a large New Christian contingent in the region. Moreover, shortly before the accusations of 1546, the *corregedor* of Ribeira Grande, Pero Moniz, had been accused by the captain of the colony, António Correia de Sousa, of targeting Old Christians with a disproportionate number of complaints.[115] Moniz, a graduate of Coimbra, had been appointed in 1533[116]; by 1543 his enemies had closed in on him and he had been forced to flee to the African coast.[117] Correia de Sousa clearly felt himself embattled on many fronts; he had known some of the details of the case of Branca Dias and of her flight from Lisbon hidden in a barrel and had been disgusted at this.[118]

All this evidence would suggest that far from masking a commercial bias, the denunciations of the council of Santiago were serious. For one thing, the fact that Moniz felt there was an established community on the African coast to which he could escape in the 1540s says something of that community's size and strength. For another, commercial ties within diasporas are often predicated on religious ties.[119] The fact that the accusations of the Old Christians of Cabo Verde were couched in religious terms does not mean that they were not also commercial. Just as the Islamic quality of trading diasporas had been an important vector in the growth of the trans-Saharan trade in the Sahelian region, the shared ethno-religious bonds of the New Christian networks in Western Africa may also have assisted their trading activities. To suggest that accusations of religious deviance must reveal economic competition may be a projection of present concerns; it certainly reveals a lack of understanding of how religious ties often bound trading diasporas together and, moreover, how fundamental this connection was to societies of the Sahel and Upper Guinea.

The 1546 accusation to Évora suggests that many New Christians had migrated from Cabo Verde to Upper Guinea and that, once there, their Jewish rites had hybridised with African ones, with the New Christians adopting polygamy and other African ritual practices. The increasing

---

[115] MMAII: Vol. 2, 370–3; a letter of 1544.
[116] IAN/TT, Chancelaria D. João III, Livro 38, fol. 3v.
[117] Domingues (1991: 112).
[118] IAN/TT, Inquisição de Lisboa, Processo 5729, fol. 19r.
[119] A. Cohen (1971). See also Green (2007b: Part 3) and Mendes (2007: 17) for the role of a shared religious identity in the success of the New Christian trading diaspora. Clearly, the importance of this in this case shows that arguments such as Trivellato (2009)'s view that boundaries between communities could be important to the success of long-distance trade in the early modern era are not universally applicable.

engagement with African peoples, which trading and living in Africa required, encouraged them to adopt plural identities and some African practices. New Christians had recent experience of such stratagems, for in Iberia they had adopted Christianity, and many among them had adopted the devotional styles of Catholicism in opposition to their recent Judaism.[120]

This 1546 accusation to the inquisitors of Évora is thus not anomalous. It is in fact key evidence to support the ideas put forward here: that by the end of the first generation of New Christian migration, the desire to preserve the Jewish religion was shifting in some quarters to the willingness to adapt. The accusation demonstrates, moreover, that the trading communities with which they were connected on the coast of Upper Guinea were developing the mixed practices seen as being constitutive culturally – if not linguistically – of creolisation. The dispersed nature of Caboverdean New Christian communities had opened them to the wider processes at work in sub-Saharan Africa, and their success in the region's trade allowed them to become themselves key agents in the development of these mixed communities.

FLEXIBILITY, MODERNITY AND "CREOLISATIONS" IN EARLY ATLANTIC TRADE

Why was it that New Christians excelled in these early pan-regional connections linking Cabo Verde and the West African coast? We have seen that they were the Portuguese commercial class *par excellence*, and this must have been a factor in their success. Yet elsewhere in the Portuguese empire, the Old Christian nobility offered very able rivals, as Goa attested. Understanding the reasons for the New Christian success in Western Africa will allow us to grasp something of the nature of the mixed communities that had emerged by around the 1540s, and how the New Christian role worked alongside the Upper Guinean one in the development of creolisation in Western Africa. Moreover, it will then connect these processes to the developing proto-modernity which was analysed in the first half of this chapter.

This New Christian success was influenced by the ideological changes which had overtaken the Iberian trading communities of the Atlantic, and which were related to the conceptual changes which, as we have seen, were revolutionising the Portuguese worldview at this time. The

---

[120] Pereda (2007).

accusation by the inquisitors of Évora cited by Mota suggests that the interactions of large numbers of New Christians with peoples in Upper Guinea dated back to the mid-1520s. It suggests that these interactions depended on the willingness of New Christians to adapt their own cultural practices to Upper Guinean realities. Bonds of trust and respect on which successful trade relies depended on this willingness to engage in cultural borrowing and the formation of lineage alliances throughout the African Atlantic. Beyond Western Africa, in Kongo, by the 1550s it was said that the Portuguese who had lived there for fifteen or twenty years were "worse than the Kongolese" for observing the rites and customs of Kongo.[121] However, this willingness to adapt may have been one which Old Christians, with an increasingly inflexible ideological outlook in which "intermarriage" was a positive slur on one's *limpeza*, were less able to countenance than New Christians.

This relates to how Africans in general were perceived by those outsiders who traded with them. As we saw in Chapter 2, ideas of race were not generalised in the early Atlantic, but they may have played a role in shaping the way in which some Iberians related to their African trading partners. This process continued in the early sixteenth century in West Africa, with Africans increasingly coming to share a similar status in the minds of Old Christians with that of the New Christians, something which confirms Jonathan Schorsch's suggestion that in the Ibero-Atlantic world as a whole, Jews and people of Jewish descent were often "confused in the Iberian imagination with other Others".[122] It may have been this association which made Old Christians less willing and indeed less able to make the cultural accommodations required for successful trade in Upper Guinea. By contrast, such conceptual confusions cannot have troubled New Christians and must have made it easier for them to make the required alliances and engagements which facilitated the development of these shared practices.

The classic example of the Old Christian conceptual confusion in Western Africa is the perception that the griots – the praise-singers of the area – were Jews. The earliest description is from Valentim Fernandes,

---

[121] MMAI : Vol. 2, 329 – "*Tam emtregues aa devasydão e gentilidades dela, que são jaa piores que os naturaes*".

[122] Schorsch (2005: 111). In the Americas, scribes frequently made orthographic errors, inserting "*judío*" in place of "*indio*" – ibid., 112; Lewin (1960: 60–2). Such elisions between Jews and the demonized also prevailed in Iberia; in the 1570s Alonso de la Fuente, scourge of the *alumbrados* – or illuminists – of Extremadura declaimed how of the 70 priests in the *alumbrado* hotbed of Zafra, 60 were "*judíos*" [i.e., *conversos*] (Huerga 1978: 363).

circa 1506: "In this land [of the Jolof] and among the Mandinka there are Jews called *Gaul* [gawol] and they are black like the people of the land although they do not have synagogues nor practice the rites of the other Jews. And they do not live with the other blacks but apart in their own villages".[123] Almada, who knew the region intimately, wrote how "throughout this land of the Jolof, Serer and Mandinka there is a nation held among them all to be Jews".[124] Even as late as 1684 Francisco de Lemos Coelho would refer to the griots as Jews.[125]

Thomas Hale has suggested that this misconception arose from Portuguese confusion with the term *Juddy*, a rendering of *jeli* that appears in some seventeenth century writings.[126] Yet far more likely is that the structural similarities of the separation of griots from the rest of the societies in Senegambia and Upper Guinea to the condition of Jews in Portugal created the misconception that they "had" to be Jews.[127] These were people, as Fernandes said, who lived apart in their own villages, just as the Jews of Portugal had lived in *judiarias* until 1497 and continued to live in separate quarters as New Christians. It is significant, moreover, that Fernandes's account is collated from the accounts of Portuguese sailors, for his summary does not indicate his isolated perception, but rather how the griots were generally perceived. There was in this confusion of griots with Jews a structural similarity in the perception of the condition of Africans and that of the Jews. From the outsider Atlantic perspective, therefore, there were key ideological reasons why New Christians were more likely to form successful trading communities in West Africa, and this situation was made all the more likely by their long-standing facility for long-distance trade.

At the same time, there were vital internal African factors which facilitated the emergence of these communities. Just as in the Gold Coast, in Upper Guinea the area chosen for the site of settlement and exchange was one that was densely populated and had a long history of commerce.[128]

---

[123] Mauny/Monod/Mota (1951: 8): "*Em esta terra e em Mādinga ha judeus e chamā os Gaul e sō negros como a gēte da terra porem nō tem synagogas nē usā de cerimonias dos outros iudeus. E nō vivē cō os outros negros se nō apartados sobre sy em suas aldeas*".

[124] MMAII: Vol. 3, 263: "*Há em toda esta terra dos Jalofos, Berbecins, e Mandinkas, uma nação havida entre eles por Judeus*".

[125] Peres (1953: 101).

[126] Hale (1998: 83).

[127] Or, as Francisco Bethencourt (1998: 104) puts it, "Racial preconceptions are the constant object of self-reference": "*os preconceitos raciais são constantemente objecto de um processo de auto-referência*".

[128] Ballong-wen-Menuda (1993: Vol. 1, 151–2).

Similarly, just as on the Gold Coast, in Upper Guinea the incoming Europeans were unable to outdo the Mandinka diasporic trade networks except with the advance of the slave trade.[129] As we have seen in previous chapters, the areas in which Atlantic traders concentrated their activities were those in which there had been a long history of interaction with members of long-distance trading diasporas distinguished by their religious affiliation. Moreover, these interactions had also involved accommodation to the Mandinka, which had promoted cultural exchanges and yet also violence. These circumstances meant that this would prove the ideal locale for generating trans-Atlantic trade; through the co-operation of members of mercantile diasporas, both Mandinka and New Christian, their work smoothed the running of the proto-imperial forces of the Sahel and the Atlantic.

The New Christian presence was thus an extremely complex factor in the changes which the Atlantic world brought to Western Africa and in the emergence of creolisation. As Stuart Schwartz has recently shown, although there was a vein of pluralism in Iberian religious life of the sixteenth-century Atlantic world inherited from the *convivencia*, this was increasingly in tension with the essentialist tendencies of Old Christian ideology, which were reinforced by the Iberian Inquisitions and the Council of Trent.[130] Thus although it helped further the internationalisation of Western Africa, New Christian willingness to live among African peoples and adopt some of their practices distinguished them from many of their peers.

As Schwartz implies, a willingness to adopt plural identities is very important to understanding this picture. Scholars such as Yirmiyahu Yovel have recently seen "a confused, ambivalent identity" as emblematic of the New Christian experience, which, Yovel argues, was characterised by the collapse of "compact identities".[131] Plurality of identity, although a new part of the New Christian ideological lexicon, was a strategy which Sahelian and Upper Guinean societies had long used in their relationships with Islam and local religious and ritual practices; it was a result of the importance of long-distance trading diasporas and the traditional role of plural identities in allowing members of these diasporas to act as cultural go-betweens.[132] Thus a fundamental aspect of New Christian success in

[129] Ibid., Vol. 1, 391–4.
[130] Schwartz (2008: 48–61).
[131] Yovel (2009: 78–80, 387).
[132] Curtin (1984).

Western Africa was their ability to adopt these plural identities at a time when the hegemonic institutions of the wider Iberian Atlantic increasingly militated against this strategy, coupled with the fact that this ability coincided with a West African cultural world in which such pluralism was already established.

This picture therefore also illustrates the importance of a nuanced understanding of how the development of a Creole society in Western Africa was related to the emergence of modernity, and of how this related to the development of cross-cultural trade. The changes brought about in the sixteenth century provoked multiple responses. Although some of these militated towards an increasing homogenisation of culture and identity, as in the Iberia of the Inquisition, elsewhere there was a growing pluralism of identity. Whereas in the New World this pluralism could often be circumscribed and, to a certain extent, controlled by the Iberian colonial institutions, there were other regions such as Western Africa where its emergence was in keeping with the existing "mestizo logics" referred to by Amselle.[133] Here, the pluralism of many New Christians was an advantage, and their capacity for this pluralism itself grew out of the forced changes to their identities which the violence of proto-modernity in Iberia had brought. In Western Africa, this increasing pluralism was matched to the growing mobility catalysed by their role as Atlantic traders – to flows of people, goods and ideas – and thus the new mixed communities of the African Atlantic grew out of some of the changes associated with this proto-modernity, even when at the same time, elsewhere, more hardened identities were emerging.

We should, then, conclude this discussion by looking for evidence of how this flexibility and pluralism of identity was emerging in the Creole society of Western Africa at this early period. Such flexibility can be discerned through the fact that, as mentioned at the start of this chapter, creolisation already was not a uniform process in Western Africa. On the coast of Upper Guinea and on the islands of Santiago and Fogo, three distinct types of creolisation were developing, a testament to the flexibility which is a hallmark of this cultural form. To begin with, we can examine these differences by comparing the New Christian role on the islands of Fogo and Santiago.

The willingness of New Christians to borrow from other cultures will be examined in more detail in the following chapter, although it is clear from the 1546 accusation cited by Mota that this was particularly intense

[133] Amselle (1998).

on the African coast. On Santiago and Fogo, meanwhile, different realities pertained. Although the alleged defender of New Christian interests in the early 1540s, Pero Moniz, was unpopular on Santiago, he was supported by the people of Fogo.[134] Some historians have seen this as indicative of an early New Christian concentration on that island.[135] As we saw earlier, New Christians such as Branca Dias had contacts on Fogo, and this factor combined with the Moniz evidence would support this view. One of the attractions of Fogo may have been that its lands had not been passed over by the crown to royal donataries as on Santiago, thus colonists outside the nobility (among whom the New Christians must have represented a significant proportion) could own land; they could not on Santiago.[136]

Even today various cultural vestiges specific to Fogo may hint at an early New Christian influence. There is for instance the remarkable absence of pigs on the island, which I observed during a visit in May 2008. During several long excursions on foot across Fogo I did not observe a single pig in spite of the widespread raising of other domestic livestock such as chickens, goats, and the like, although I was informed that there was one person who did breed them; on Santiago, by contrast, pigs abound and roadside stalls selling barbecued meat are usually selling pork. Furthermore, the custom in some areas of Fogo of stooping down and touching the floor before going into a house may relate to the Jewish practice of keeping a *mezuzah*, a small box holding the sacred *Shema* prayer, on the doorposts of a house; this practice continues and was something I observed.

This evidence combines with the documentary material examined here to suggest a New Christian presence on Fogo in the early colony. It is not unreasonable to suppose that this presence affected the culture which emerged there. Certainly, the balance of racial composition on Fogo was substantially different to that of Santiago, which must have led to different types of relationships among peoples and different cultural forms. Fogo had a significant European population for much longer than Santiago, and even today there are vestiges of this past in the form of the so-called white cemetery of São Filipe, the main settlement of Fogo.[137]

---

[134] MMAII: Vol. 2, 368–9 – a document which reveals his popularity in Fogo.
[135] Barcellos (1899: 120); Ribeiro (1954: 98).
[136] Brito (1966: 81).
[137] Andrade (1996: 52). In a visit of November 2003, I found differing opinions on the source of the cemetery's name. Some see it as owing to the white marble used and point out that many Blacks were buried there; others see it as a legacy of the racism developed by Fogo's large white population.

The dispute over Pero Moniz and the other material alluded to here suggests that such cultural differences had emerged as early as the 1540s. By this point, processes of creolisation may already have been divergent, ranging from hyper-flexibility in Upper Guinea to maintaining Jewish rites on Fogo. Key in shaping the different processes were the dominant atmospheres of each locale – ranging from African on the Guinea Coast to predominantly African on Santiago and to a more mixed environment on Fogo – as well as the comparative predispositions of both Africans and Europeans towards adaptability. Importantly for the purposes of the argument of this book, all three locales saw interactions occurring with growing intensity in the 1520s and 1530s, precisely because of the growing demand for slaves from the New World (cf. Chapter 6). Thus from the beginning, the mobility associated with the slave trade and the processes of creolisation were intimately related. Herein the physical violence of modernity was constituted, as were the associated psychological abstractions and distancing mechanisms which allowed people to dehumanise those they treated as animals as they shipped them across the increasingly mathematised space of the Atlantic ocean.

5

The New Christian/Kassanké Alliance and the Consolidation of Creolisation

By the middle of the sixteenth century, many of the themes that have emerged over the first half of this book had coalesced. The Kriolu language developed on Cabo Verde at the turn of the sixteenth century had been taken to the African mainland by landowners and slaves of landowners on the islands, and, increasingly, New Christian merchants. There, the Creole society emerging in Cabo Verde interacted with a far older set of communities in which plural identities were the norm, and it was from this interaction that an Atlantic Creole culture in Western Africa was consolidated.

The aim of this chapter is to bring together the two main strands which have characterised the first part of this book. Chapters 1 and 2 looked at the influence of trans-Saharan trade and diasporas of merchants in shaping cultural accommodations and political environments in Upper Guinea; they showed how a culture of receptivity towards outsider traders emerged among groups such as the Kassanké, and how this cultural accommodation was influential in the very first African-European connections in the Atlantic in the late fifteenth century. Chapters 3 and 4 then looked at how Atlantic trade based around Cabo Verde became integrated into this picture through the activities of New Christian diaspora traders, and how these developments accompanied the rise of an early form of Creole society on the islands; these chapters further showed how the economic infrastructure underpinning this process depended on slavery and was associated with ideological changes connected to an early form of modernity. In this chapter, we now see the way in which these New Christian diaspora traders built alliances with the Kassanké by the mid-sixteenth century, and how this consolidated a mixed cultural identity and a shared Kriolu language spreading across the Western African region.

What emerges is nothing less than an analysis of how existing African commercial and cultural links were fused with early Atlantic processes, thereby enabling the expansion of the Atlantic slave trade which is considered in the second part of this book; as we see towards the end of the chapter, just as the processes involved in the consolidation of Caboverdean society were predicated on slavery, so the expansion of pan-regional links in Western Africa depended on the expansion of trans-Atlantic slaving by 1550. The chapter builds this picture by assembling a wide array of sources to illustrate the trading alliance forged between Kassanké and New Christians in these years. Many of these sources are new to historical study of this subject and furnish important perspectives on the formation of what became a consolidated Creole culture by the middle of the sixteenth century.

The chapter begins by examining the evidence for the importance of Casamance to the Atlantic trade of Western Africa in the 1530s and the 1540s. Here we see the importance of the *lançados*, and the evidence shows how the expansion of Atlantic trade depended on the ways in which these *lançados* were accommodated within existing frameworks. Subsequent case studies provide an important weight of evidence that shows how intertwined Kassanké and New Christian interests were. When this evidence is considered, this reveals that early Atlantic trade in Western Africa depended in large part on such groups and the diaspora trading networks which they had learnt to operate. Empires could not operate alone in the sixteenth century Atlantic; they depended on trading intermediaries who had their own independent networks and often shared a facility for developing plural identities, which stood in contrast to the more monolithic and rigid senses of affiliation promoted in the Iberian world.

I conclude the argument of this first part of the book by showing in detail just how the pre-existing characteristics of both African and Atlantic actors enabled the expansion of Atlantic trade in the sixteenth century. Like other trading diasporas in Western Africa, the New Christians were adept at forming new ties whilst using old bonds to maintain collective identity and the control of certain trades.[1] This facilitated the plural nature of emergent Creole society, opposed to the ideals of cultural

---

[1] For an example of this among the Hausa of twentieth-century Nigeria, see A. Cohen (1969: 14–5).

and religious purity which went with Portuguese expansion. This mixed world was a challenge to the dominant imperial culture, as is evident in the vituperative denunciations of it.[2] Yet there was also a way in which, through the alliance of Kassanké and New Christian groups who were at least nominally subordinate to the more dominant political powers of the Mandinka and the Portuguese, the imperial discourse expanded as the alliance provided slaves for the New World. The Kassanké/New Christian alliance, whilst a partnership of subalterns who represented an ideological threat on one hand, extended Iberian empires on the other. Indeed, the interconnections which were the foundations of this alliance would not have been so strong without the labour demands of those empires. If modernity pointed in the direction of flexible and plural identities in the African Atlantic, elsewhere the bonds forged as a result contributed to a system of forced labour and production which was administered by people with a very different outlook. Not for nothing did Antonio Gramsci assert that "subaltern groups are always subject to the activity of ruling groups, even when they rebel and rise up".[3]

THE RISE OF LANÇADOS AND OF RECIPROCAL CULTURAL INFLUENCES IN ATLANTIC CASAMANCE

Nothing excites so much as prohibition, the old adage goes, and where the settlement of the *lançados* in Upper Guinea is concerned it seems to be true. Around 1540, just before the deposition to the inquisitors of Évora which claimed that hundreds of New Christians were *lançados* in Upper Guinea (cf. Chapter 4), João III of Portugal again tried to tackle the *lançado* problem. In 1539, he issued a decree aimed at confiscating all the property belonging to *lançados* in Sierra Leone and the rivers of Guinea, with a subsequent elucidation from the crown that this applied to residents of the island of Santiago.[4] Three years later, João III reiterated the decree, urging his officials to seize "all the property of those Christian people who are *lançados* in Guinea".[5]

Clearly, the *lançado* "problem" was growing. More and more people were settling among the peoples of Upper Guinea. It was this accelerated process of exchange which would lead, by the middle of the sixteenth

[2] See Bhabha (1994).
[3] Hoare/Nowell Smith (1971: 55).
[4] MMAII: Vol. 2, 324–5.
[5] Ibid., Vol. 2, 352 – "*todas as fazendas das pessoas christãos que andão lançados em Guinee*".

century, to the establishment of a genuinely pan-regional Atlantic Creole culture linking the Atlantic trading settlements of Upper Guinea with Cabo Verde. Most of these documents refer to the *lançado* presence only in Sierra Leone and "Guinea", and it was here, to the south of the Gambia River, that Kriolu would develop as a vernacular among the Luso-African and Caboverdean trading classes.[6]

In this region, the commercial opportunities offered by the Casamance, São Domingos, Grande and Sierra Leone regions were all important. In Sierra Leone, large numbers of slaves were drawn into the Atlantic trade from the 1540s onwards, following the wars between the Manes and the Sapes (cf. Chapter 8). However the primary zone for African-European relations was farther north, in the Casamance and São Domingos regions. A wide variety of evidence shows that *lançados* were concentrated here in the Mandinguised kingdom of the Kassanké. The evidence of *lançado* presence here is such that, as Philip Havik has put it, the land stretching from the Bintang creek south of the Gambia through to Ziguinchor "hosted all of the early Atlantic trade settlements in the region".[7] The three major *lançado* settlements in the sixteenth and early seventeenth centuries were at Bugendo, Cacheu and Guinguim, all associated with the Bainunk-Kassanké (especially Bugendo and Guinguim); the alliance between the Portuguese and Masatamba, king of the Kassanké from around the 1550s to the 1580s, was described in detail by the Caboverdean trader André Donelha.[8] There are some recorded cases of *lançados* jumping ship in Senegambia among the Sereer – in 1542, one Francisco de Costa did so at Porto de Ale – but the majority of *lançados* lived in Casamance.[9] The roots of the economic motor of Western Africa's trade and its interconnections to the wider Atlantic therefore lay in the alliances which they were able to form with the Bainunk-Kassanké.

Some of the best evidence for this comes from the inquisitorial trial dating from 1548 of Antonio Fernandes, who was appointed as factor at Bugendo on the São Domingos River in 1547. The trial related to a power struggle between Fernandes and his predecessor, Manoel Garcia.[10] In the course of the trial, several pieces of information were disclosed which can tell us much about the strength of the *lançado* presence in Casamance and of the nature of African-European exchanges. What emerges is how

[6] Jacobs (2009: 352).
[7] Havik (2004b: 101).
[8] MMAII: Vol. 5, 139–40.
[9] Torrão (1991: 254).
[10] IAN/TT, Inquisição de Lisboa, Processo 801.

reciprocal cultural influences had developed in Upper Guinea by this time, a reciprocity related to the expanding Atlantic trading economy.

In his defence against charges of falsely claiming to represent the Inquisition, Fernandes claimed that on his arrival in Bugendo in 1547 the "black elders [*fidalgos*] of the land had made a written petition to him" regarding Garcia, whom they accused of having attacked some of the principal people of the area a few days before.[11] The letter was appended to the inquisitorial case as evidence and leaves tantalising questions: who had written it, and what does the use of Portuguese as a language of petition in Upper Guinea tell us about African-European relationships by the 1540s?

Bugendo was on the São Domingos River, on the borders of what today is southern Casamance and northern Guinea-Bissau. It was controlled by the Mandinguised lineage of the Kassanké. However, the petition was written not from Bugendo but from Cacheu, at the southern limit of Kassanké control. The idea that the elders [*fidalgos*] might have petitioned the incoming Caboverdean factor regarding the behaviour of the outgoing one is certainly suggestive of the importance of Atlantic trade in Casamance. It implies that the factors were extremely influential in Casamance. Such power may partly have derived from better weaponry – the petition refers to Garcia's use of "bombardments" [*bombardadas*] – but Portuguese firearms were fairly useless during the prolonged rainy season when powder could not be kept dry, and thus the influence of the factors in Casamance cannot have been kept by force alone.[12] Moreover, because one of Fernandes's accusations was that Garcia had given "artillery" to the "infidels", it is clear that by this time firearms were no longer the exclusive preserve of the Portuguese.[13]

Most likely, this influence of the Caboverdean factors derived from commercial realities of the new Atlantic world. Slowly but surely, Upper Guinea was being drawn into a more international range of influences from the Atlantic side. Why else would the petition have been written in Portuguese? The use of this language by lineage heads implies that they had rapidly acculturated to the language of the Atlantic world and its trade, just as previously they had done with the Mandinka connected to the trans-Saharan trade, and just as the *manikongos* of West-Central Africa, who also composed letters in Portuguese at this time, were doing.

[11] Ibid., fol. 4r: "*os fidalgos da terra negros lhe fizerā por escripto hū requerimento*".
[12] On "*bombardadas*", see ibid.
[13] Ibid., fol. 14v.

Most likely, the letter was written by a scribe and not by the elders of Cacheu themselves; scribes commonly composed official petitions in this era. Nonetheless, the ability of elders from Cacheu to communicate with the scribe using both a language and type of discourse which they hoped would find favour with the Portuguese crown is indicative of an understanding of Portuguese power and of how to frame petitions to it, which is symptomatic of a heavy degree of acculturation.

Thus in Casamance in the 1540s, not only were *lançados* adopting African cultural traits, as we saw in the 1546 denunciation of the New Christians in the last chapter, but the opposite was also occurring. Members of local elites had acculturated sufficiently to the new outsider traders from the Atlantic to frame arguments in discourse which might find favour in Lisbon. The cultural influences were thus reciprocal. Here is evidence of the mixed cultural environment for which "creolisation", as we saw in the Introduction, is taken by many theorists today as a "master metaphor". Moreover, we see here how, far from preserving their cultural traits as an advantage, each of the groups involved in this cross-cultural trade borrowed from one another's practices in order to find a mutual territory of shared understanding and communication.[14]

Such reciprocity was no accident. *Lançado* settlement among the Mandinguised Kassanké lineage of Casamance was part of a wider pattern which saw the Portuguese settle in locales of Mandinka influence not only in Casamance, but also, when the subsequent alliance with the Kassanké had begun to fade, along the Gambia and in the Biafada territories along the Rio Grande.[15] This is a key point which expands the argument of previous chapters, connecting early areas of *lançado* settlement among the Kassanké to the previous pattern of diaspora traders in Upper Guinea. For it turns out that this pattern was not confined to Bugendo but was widespread; as we saw in Chapter 1, peoples in these areas had become used to cultural accommodation predicated on initially violent incursions and a subsequent establishment of commercial systems based on long-distance mercantile diasporas connected to the trans-Saharan trade.

Such existing patterns mattered deeply in how the new Atlantic trade was constructed and how it affected societies in Western Africa.

---

[14] This warns us to be cautious of the argument of Trivellato (2009: esp. 275–6), which suggests that preservation of distinctiveness was automatically an advantage in cross-cultural trade in the early modern era. This evidence shows that this was certainly not always the case.

[15] Rodney (1970: 81).

Commercial exchanges were essential in the establishment of a mixed cultural environment, and agents of commercial exchange were often agents of acculturation.[16] In the Atlantic world, however, as elsewhere, the agents of trade (and creolisation) could only begin their work once a certain disposition towards plural identities existed. They could only advance once the violent work of bringing people to some sort of wider accommodation to hegemonic societies had been achieved. This was a long-standing pattern in Western Africa, and thus trade was not "imposed" on Africa, but rather fitted into a pattern which Africans themselves had shaped, a pattern which suited the role of diasporas of commerce and the fundamental role of religion and ritual in Upper Guinean societies. If such a pattern facilitated violence through the expansion of the slave trade, then this did not illustrate anything particular to Upper Guinean societies, but rather indicated how quickly modernity had come there and how fundamental violence was to the construction of modernity. Indeed, it was by integrating this violence into a new pattern of enslavement and cultural pluralism that creolisation took shape in Western Africa, in a foretaste of events elsewhere in the Atlantic world.

CASE STUDIES OF KASSANKÉ/NEW CHRISTIAN INTERACTIONS

In order for a Creole culture to emerge across Western Africa, intense links between Cabo Verde and the African coast were necessary. In the previous chapters, we have seen how these had developed already by the end of the fifteenth century and had involved the exchange of people, livestock, textiles and foodstuffs. The increasing settlement of *lançados*, as evidenced in the 1530s and 1540s, accentuated this process. It was because of the connections that *lançados* had with Cabo Verde and the frequent trade linking the islands with the Atlantic trading settlements of Africa that a shared and composite culture emerged.

Antonio Fernandes's trial contains other details which confirm this picture of the links between Upper Guinea and Cabo Verde. Fernandes himself had come to Bugendo from the islands. In his trial he claimed that one of his accusers, Domingos Rodrigues, was the nephew of a certain Francisco Dias who had been Manoel Garcia's agent on the island of Santiago, and that Dias had prepared a ship on Santiago and sent it to Bugendo to rescue Garcia from his forced imprisonment by Fernandes.[17]

---

[16] Gonçalves (1996: 39); Trajano Filho (2003: 15).
[17] IAN/TT, Inquisição de Lisboa, Processo 801, fols.14r, 15v.

There were regular connections between Bugendo and Santiago: one of the witnesses, João Lopes, noted how he had heard about the case from many people on the island of Santiago who had come from the "rivers of Guinea".[18] Thus by the late 1540s – and probably considerably earlier – Cabo Verde and the trading settlements of Upper Guinea constituted a linked space, and this explains how the development of a Kriolu language on Santiago could very rapidly have been communicated to the trading settlements of the African coast.

As these connections increased, so did the role of the New Christians. It was through the expansion of the *lançado* class in this era and the increase in New Christian influence that the Atlantic dimension of cre-olisation in Western Africa, and the role of preceding events in Cabo Verde, began to have an influence on the communities of the mainland. Case studies are the most useful tool we have for examining the interactions between Kassanké and New Christians, for they illustrate both how deep-seated the alliances were and how influential they came to be in the construction of a Creole culture and language which spanned the whole Western African region.

Evidence for the Kassanké–New Christian alliance emerges earliest from the António Fernandes case.[19] On a superficial level the case appeared to be about trading disputes, but a close examination reveals that concern about New Christian activity and the extent of New Christian alliances with the Kassanké was fundamental. In his written defence to the inquisitors, Fernandes stated that Garcia was a "New Christian and of the caste of the New Christians and is recognized as such by the people who know him".[20] Fernandes added that Garcia and those conspiring with him were "very familiar with and very close and helpful friends of Garcia and also all of them like the said Manoel Garcia are New Christians".[21] Thus whether Garcia and his friends were New Christians or not, Fernandes perceived a New Christian conspiracy against him; indeed, one witness reported that Fernandes had told him that he would "seize the said Manoel Garcia on the authority of the Holy Inquisition and that he was a Jewish *tangomão*".[22] Fernandes also denounced many

[18] Ibid., fols. 37r-v.
[19] See Schorsch (2008: Vol. 1, 12) on the value of inquisitorial cases for assessing relations between subalterns in the early Atlantic world.
[20] IAN/TT, Inquisição de Lisboa, Processo 801, fol. 4v: "*he cristã novo e de casta de cristãos novos e por tal he tido das pessoas q o conhecem*".
[21] Ibid., fol. 13v: "*do ditto mel garcia seus muy mtos familiares e amiguos de muy estreita amizade e mta prestação e tãbem por serem todos como o dito mel garcia xpãos novos*".
[22] Ibid., fol. 36v: "*prendera ao dito Manoel Garcia polla Santa Inquisção e q era tangomão Judeu*".

of Garcia's witnesses as New Christians, including Vicente Nunes and Francisco Lopes.[23] Then, when Fernandes arrested Garcia by claiming to represent the Inquisition, he accused him of refusing to relinquish the "property of Pero Rodrigues ... which belonged to the King since the wife of the said Pero Rodrigues had been arrested by the Holy Inquisition and might already have been burnt".[24]

One of the most interesting aspects of Fernandes's denunciation of these New Christians is the close alliances which he suggests they had forged with the Kassanké. Garcia was accused by him of giving weapons to the "blacks and infidels inimical to our Holy Faith", of having widespread dealings with the "infidels", and of taking refuge with the [Kassanké] King of Casamance when Fernandes sought to arrest him.[25] In the time when Garcia had been factor at Bugendo, Vicente Nunes was said to have "lived as a *lançado* among the blacks adopting African customs [*feito tango mao*]".[26] Another man, Francisco Lopes, had also been "living cast in among the blacks in Guinea".[27] The fact that this evidence derives from the Kassanké trading port at Bugendo and the denunciation of Garcia as living with the Kassanké King offer strong support for the idea that the Kassanké lineage heads had welcomed these traders to Casamance and that the influence and exchange was reciprocal.

From the New Christian side, there is objective evidence that Manoel Garcia himself was a New Christian, and that therefore many of those accused by Fernandes probably also were. Garcia's nephew and associate, Bartolomeu, was married to Branca Dias. Dias was the daughter of Manoel and Miçia Dias, residents of Fogo, who acknowledged that they were New Christians.[28] Thus Manoel Garcia at least was a New Christian, and Fernandes's attribution of a New Christian identity to his colleagues living among the Kassanké seems plausible.

---

[23] Ibid., fols. 14r, 14v.

[24] Ibid., fol. 58v: "*fazenda de pero rodrigues q elle tinha em seu poder a qual pertençia al Rey e q a molher do dito pero rodrigues estava presa pola samta Inquisição e q não sabya se sabia queimada...*".

[25] Ibid., fol. 4v ("*dava aos negros e infieis inimigo de na sta fee cruzes douro e armas*"); fol. 10r, "*infieis*"; fol. 15v.

[26] Ibid., 14r: "*e do tpo em q o dto mel ga estava por feitor nos dtos Rios andava cõ os negros lancado feito tango mao*".

[27] Ibid., fol. 14v: "*deytado com os negros em guiné*".

[28] On Bartolomeu as Manoel's nephew and friend, see ibid., fols. 14r and 15v. On Bartolomeu as the husband of Branca Dias, see IAN/TT, Inquisição de Lisboa, Processo 6580, case summary; ibid., for Branca's relation to Manoel Dias. On Manoel Dias's acknowledgement of his New Christian status, see IAN/TT, Inquisição de Lisboa, Processo 7312 (there are no fol. numbers to this trial). Again, I must thank Filipa Ribeiro da Silva for bringing my attention to these trials.

This being the case, the importance of New Christian networks in Casamance becomes central to the narrative of African-European relations in the 1540s and the development of Atlantic Creole identities across Western Africa. For although Garcia had over ten witnesses in his favour in the trial, Fernandes had only two. This strongly suggests that New Christians outnumbered Old Christians among the *lançados* of Casamance. Moreover, these New Christians were accused by Fernandes of living among the Africans, supplying them with weapons, adopting their cultural practices, and damaging the royal trade there. These accusations were very similar to those made to the inquisitors of Évora from Cabo Verde in 1546 (cf. Chapter 4).

The Garcia case is just one of many which show how the Kassanké and New Christians formed a mutually beneficial trading alliance. We can return for instance to the case of the Dias family mentioned previously in connection to Bartolomeu Garcia. Documents relating to the Dias family reveal that the New Christian networks of Cabo Verde and Upper Guinea were thoroughly interconnected. Moreover, these documents tell us much about the belief systems of these New Christians; they illuminate the attitudes which they brought to their interactions in Upper Guinea and how these beliefs were transferred from Cabo Verde to the Atlantic trading settlements of the West African coast as a result of their trading activities.

Inquisitorial records are extant for both Manoel and Miçia Dias and their daughter Branca. The picture which emerges is of a family caught halfway between Christianity and Judaism, with the women the most resolute crypto-Jews. Manoel Dias made a fairly orthodox declaration of his belief in Christian ideals, stating that he believed that God had sent his son Jesus Christ to redeem humanity and making no use of crypto-Jewish formulations relating to "God creating the heavens and earth".[29] He appears to have been something of an early empiricist in the mould of New Christians like Francisco Sanches, the philosopher of Toulouse; one accusation professed outrage that he had declared that ill people got better because of the work of nature and not through commending themselves to the Virgin Mary.[30] There were no accusations against Dias for keeping Jewish rituals however, and the only piece of real evidence was that he was alleged to have said, whilst standing outside Fogo's jail, that it

---

[29] IAN/TT, Inquisição de Lisboa, Processo 7312 (there are no fol. numbers to this trial). All subsequent references in this paragraph come from this trial.

[30] The classic work of Sanches is *Quod Nihil Scitur*, "That Nothing is Known", written in 1580 – see Sanches (1998).

was "better to be a Jew than a Mulatto", something which Dias denied.[31] However the intolerable position in which someone like Dias found himself is revealed by his comment that "people all hold me to be a Jew as they do with all New Christians".[32] A New Christian who was a sceptic or who even tried to be an orthodox Christian was seen as a Jew and was thus cast into a double interior life, emblematic of the plural identities of New Christians emphasised by scholars such as Yovel.[33]

In contrast to Manoel, both his wife Miçia and their daughter Branca Dias were accused of Judaising. Miçia Dias was said to keep the Jewish Sabbath on Saturdays, wearing clean shirts, using clean sheets and resting in a room, and then working on Sundays and forcing her slaves to do likewise.[34] People said that she would not give alms to Old Christians, that she concealed crucifixes in cushions on which visitors sat, and that she secretly whipped another crucifix and made sacrifices to a cow.[35] One witness said that she sent for bread to be baked on Fridays so that she did not have to do so on a Saturday.[36] Both Miçia and her daughters were infrequent churchgoers, and witnesses described how Miçia did not lift her face to the sacrament when it was raised by the priest and that she filled her daughters' mouths with salt after they had gone to receive it.[37] Perhaps the crowning insult was when she had emerged one Sunday from her house with her backside pointing at the street.[38]

Similar accusations were levelled at Branca, together with some new ones. Branca Dias lit candles on Friday nights. She kept the Jewish festivals and fasted on Yom Kippur, the Day of Atonement. She worked on Sundays. When attending a Mass at the church in Alcatrazes, on Santiago, she had turned her face away and refused to look at the Host when the priest had raised it. She had a very poor knowledge of basic Christian prayers, and could not even recite the *Salve Regina*.[39]

---

[31] Something which, if true, confirms Schorsch's (2008: Vol. 1, 7) assertion that "many ordinary people seem to have been quite aware of racialist thinking, if not participants in it themselves".

[32] IAN/TT, Inquisição de Lisboa, Processo 7312: "*eu sou xpão novo e me temdão por Judeu como temdos a todos os xpãos novos*".

[33] Yovel (2009).

[34] IAN/TT, Inquisição de Lisboa, Processo 3199, fol. 10r. Indeed, her slaves protested at having to work on a Sunday (IAN/TT, Inquisicão de Lisboa, Processo 13107, fol. 3r).

[35] IAN/TT, Inquisição de Lisboa, Processo 3199, fols. 8r, 10r-v.

[36] IAN/TT, Inquisição de Lisboa, Processo 13107, fol. 3r.

[37] Ibid., fols. 3v, 4r.

[38] Ibid., fol. 9r.

[39] All these accusations are contained in the unnumbered trial at IAN/TT, Inquisição de Lisboa, Processo 7312.

Here then is a New Christian family with connections to three of the main nodes of Western Africa in the middle years of the sixteenth century. Manoel and Miçia lived on Fogo and had also lived on Santiago, whereas Branca resided in Santiago.[40] Branca's husband, Bartolomeu Garcia, had strong trading connections to the Kassanké of Bugendo, and had even sailed to try to rescue Manoel Garcia when Antonio Fernandes arrested him there.[41] The networks which had developed along with the trade between the islands and the coast, propelled by the slave economy of the islands, meant that New Christian groups became dispersed, and thus the cultural forms developing among them did so also. It was this that made them key agents in the accelerating process of Atlantic creolisation which had spread across the region, and which also makes understanding the cultural outlook of these actors vital in understanding how this process had developed by this time.

As we saw in the previous chapter, many of the first New Christian migrants to Cabo Verde sought to maintain elements of Judaism in their practices. The Dias case confirms this picture, as does the suggestion that it was contact with African societies which opened some of these New Christians towards mixing their practices and attenuating their adherence to Judaism. It is significant that the women in the Dias household were more steadfast in their Judaism than the men. The role of women is emphasised in Judaism because of the matrilineal religious inheritance. Yet this religious explanation for the women's adherence to Judaism needs to be supplemented by the experiential reality of the constant travels of the New Christian men such as Bartolomeu Garcia and Manoel Dias to and from the African coast and the long periods that some of them spent living there.

There is some strong evidence of how these New Christians traders adapted to life in Upper Guinea in the world of ritual. Valentim Fernandes described how the very word *tangomao*, which was used synonymously with *lançado* in the sixteenth century, derived from a priestly lineage in Sierra Leone that guarded and officiated at a spirit shrine there.[42] The use of this word interchangeably with the Portuguese *lançado* shows that adaptation to the rituals of West Africa was a key strategy of those who settled there. Corroboration for this emerges from the inquisitorial trails of the Dias family. It was well known, Maria da Cunha of Fogo said, that

---

[40] Ibid; IAN/TT, Inquisição de Lisboa, Processo 6580.
[41] IAN/TT, Inquisição de Lisboa, Processo 801, fol. 15v.
[42] MMAII: Vol. 1, 737; Nafafé (2007: 160–72).

Miçia Dias kept a "calf with many chains of gold and that each day she sacrificed chicken's blood to it through its mouth".[43] Certainly, if Miçia Dias did this it had nothing to do with Judaism and was probably a rite imported from West Africa, which is a testament to both the composite cultural framework that was emerging there and how practices were becoming mixed in the Atlantic trading communities of both Cabo Verde and mainland Africa.[44]

The existence of a case study like this Garcia-Dias nexus cannot alone stand as evidence of the importance of the Kassanké–New Christian alliance. However, when it is supplemented by additional examples, a pattern emerges. Other networks existed at the same time, and one of equal if not greater importance was that developed by the Leão and Carvajal families from the late 1540s onwards. The evidence on this network first emerges through the Carvajal family of New Spain (Mexico). Publication regarding the messianic crypto-Jew Luis de Carvajal *el mozo* (hereafter Carvajal *mozo*) has been widespread, but the case of his uncle, Luis de Carvajal *el viejo* (hereafter Carvajal *viejo*), has been bypassed.[45] Yet Carvajal *viejo*'s relevance to Cabo Verde is key. When his father died at the age of eight, his maternal uncle, Duarte de Leão, came to collect him from Benavente and took him to Lisbon. He spent three years there – he told the inquisitors during his trial in Mexico City in 1589 – before being sent to "Cabo Verde, in which island he spent thirteen years, and there he was Treasurer and Comptroller of the King of Portugal".[46] Leão was holder of the contract for Guiné, and it was this which meant that soon Carvajal was being despatched to Cabo Verde in the service of his uncle.[47]

Carvajal *viejo* declared that he was approximately fifty years old in 1589, which would put his birth date at circa 1539.[48] He added that his father had died when he was eight.[49] A time lag of three months followed, as he was collected from Benavente and waited in Lisbon, meaning that he

[43] IAN/TT, Inquisição de Lisboa, Processo 13107, fol. 5r: "*tinha hu bezerro com muitas cadeas douro e cada dia lhe llançava sangue da gallinha pella Boca*".

[44] For the role of the sacrifice of chicken's blood in Western Africa, see Hawthorne (2010b: Chapter 6).

[45] See Toro (1944) and M. Cohen (2001). The will of Carvajal *mozo* is published by M. Cohen (1971b).

[46] Toro (1932: 280–1): "*y luego murió su padre en Benavente y el dicho Duarte de León, que vino allí, lo llevó a Lisboa de donde lo envio luego de allí a tres meses a Cabo Verde, en cuya isla estuvo trece años, y allí fue tesorero y contador del rey de Portugal…*".

[47] Ibid., 279 – "*Contratador de los pueblos de Guinea, Por el rey de Portugal…*"

[48] Toro (1944: Vol. 1, 36, n.1).

[49] Toro (1932: 280).

would probably have sailed for Cabo Verde in the spring of 1548. Thus in the same year that the inquisitorial trial of António Fernandes was held, another New Christian network began to develop in Western Africa.

Once in Cabo Verde, Carvajal *viejo* was not alone. Whilst there, he interacted with many relations. Another uncle was Francisco Jorge, factor of Duarte de Leão at Bugendo, the very same port on the São Domingos that was controlled by the Kassanké and where António Fernandes and Manoel Garcia had clashed in 1548. Jorge lived in Bugendo, and thus the presence of Carvajal *viejo* in Western Africa and of his wider circle of family and trading partners was connected to the relationship which, as we have seen, had already developed between Kassanké and New Christians.

In the early 1560s, an inquisitorial trial developed in which Francisco Jorge and several of his (and Carvajal *viejo*'s) relatives were implicated. The trial centred around accusations of mockery of the virgin birth on Christmas Eve in 1562.[50] A group of New Christians was said to have gathered in Bugendo with "masks of paper and dressed in disguise".[51] Then Mestre Dioguo had appeared "dressed in women's clothes and with towels on his head ... calling himself Maria and saying that he was giving birth", and a send-up of the birth of Christ began.[52]

These events have been referred to by various historians.[53] The reliability of the testimonies has been questioned, because the numbers of New Christians present ranged in depositions between one and four dozen.[54] The account of transvestism is held to follow a pattern of demonisation of the other which places the testimony in doubt, given that transvestism was severely frowned upon by the Inquisition.[55] Yet when Mestre Dioguo was brought from Bugendo to the jail on Cabo Verde, he did not deny that the "farce" had taken place and in fact described it in great detail, claiming that he had merely danced at the house of Jorge in honour of

[50] Jorge's relationship to Leão is stated in IAN/TT, Inquisição de Lisboa, Maço 25, no. 233, fol. 42v and confirmed in Carvajal *viejo*'s genealogy, where Jorge is, like Leão, given as a maternal uncle: "*Franciso Jorge de Andrade, que fué en Guinea fator y capitan general por el rey de Portugal...*" (Toro 1932: 279).

[51] IAN/TT, Inquisição de Lisboa, Maço 25, no. 233, 4r: "*mascaras de papel e cõ vestidos cõtrafeitos*".

[52] Ibid., fol. 4r, "*en trajos de molher cõ toalhas postas na cabeça ... chamando maria q estava parida...*".

[53] Torrão (1995: 64); Havik (2004a: 104); Mark/Horta (2010).

[54] Torrão (1995: 64, n.3).

[55] Havik (2004a: 104). Such moral censure was related to the fact that transvestites were often seen to be engaged in sodomy: see for example IAN/TT, Inquisição de Évora, Livro 91, fol. 41r.

it being Christmas Eve.[56] It is clear that this whole network was related to New Christian identity, because Dioguo described Jorge as the "New Christian factor".[57] Moreover, the cross-dressing element is also given a greater hint of plausibility by the fact that today, at the annual carnival in Bissau and elsewhere in Guinea-Bissau, people from each gender frequently adopt the clothes and roles of the other; of course, this does not mean that this more flexible approach to gender was current in the sixteenth century, but certainly it may have been, and this piece of evidence could in fact indicate the mixed cultural framework of *lançado* communities in Upper Guinea.[58]

In this way, the Carvajal case is a continuity from the Dias/Garcia trials of the 1540s, showing that throughout this period there remained strong Kassanké–New Christian ties in Bugendo and that these were fundamentally connected to the adoption of shared practices by both groups. In both cases, New Christian families adopted some African cultural practices both in Africa itself and on Cabo Verde; in this Mestre Dioguo case, for instance, in addition to the issue of presentations of gender, the use of masks [*mascaras de papel*] may well have borrowed from the ubiquity of masquerades in the rituals of Upper Guinea. Both of the networks we have looked at had strong connections in Bugendo and the Caboverdean islands – where we should recall that Carvajal *viejo* served as royal accountant – which emphasises how the islands and coast did constitute a linked space. Furthermore, the two networks were almost certainly connected because Mestre Dioguo may well have been the brother of Miçia Dias; on October 17, 1559, Dias told inquisitors that she had one brother, "Mestre Dioguo", and Dioguo himself, like Dias, had strong connections to Fogo.[59]

A defining feature of both these networks was that they each had come to Western Africa because they saw it as a place of escape. On October 9, 1559, Manoel Dias claimed that "24 years ago he went to the Island of Cabo Verde [Santiago] where he has lived ever since, there and in

---

[56] IAN/TT, Inquisição de Lisboa, Maço 25, no. 233, fols. 24r-v: the folios in this trial are confused, and so although these folios represent those marked on the trial documents, they are not always sequential.

[57] Ibid., 42v: "*Francisco Jorge feitor xpão Novo...*".

[58] Transvestism was current in other West African societies of the time; see Sweet (2003: 53–4). The observation on cross-dressing in Guinea-Bissau is derived from my participation in the carnivals of Bissau and Gabú in February 2000.

[59] IAN/TT, Inquisição de Lisboa, Processo 3199, on the sibling relationship; IAN/TT, Inquisição de Lisboa, Maço 25, no. 233, fol. 46r, on Mestre Dioguo's previous residence in Fogo.

the island of Fogo."⁶⁰ That would place the arrival of the Dias family in
1535, just a year before the bull was issued establishing the Inquisition in
Portugal.⁶¹ Throughout the 1530s it had been increasingly apparent that
a Portuguese tribunal of the Inquisition was inevitable. A papal inquisitor
had been appointed to Portugal in December 1531, only to be rescinded
in October 1532. This had been followed by pressure from Charles V of
Spain, someone whom the New Christian emissaries in Rome were not
able to best.⁶² Given the violence which the onset of the Inquisition had
unleashed in Spain in the 1480s, Portuguese New Christians in the 1530s
must have feared that something similar would soon be directed at them,
and therefore the arrival of the Dias family in Cabo Verde in 1535 may
well be linked to these events.⁶³

A similar pattern held for the Leão and Carvajal families. The year of
the eight-year-old Luis de Carvajal's arrival in Cabo Verde, 1548, was
the very year in which the inquisitorial trials of two of Carvajal *viejo*'s
uncles, Alvaro and Jorge de Leão, came to a head, both of whom had been
arrested by the Inquisition of Évora in 1544.⁶⁴ Both were released under
the terms of the General Pardon of the New Christians, and this history
and the inauguration of the new Portuguese tribunal of the Inquisition
with full powers must have encouraged Duarte de Leão to seek alternatives for his young nephew.⁶⁵

Indeed, Western Africa was not just a place of escape for young
Carvajal *viejo*. Carvajal *viejo* had a large family network during his time
in Western Africa. According to Mestre Dioguo, one witness of the farce
was "Antonio Duarte, a relative of the factor [Jorge]".⁶⁶ Another cited
by Dioguo, Antonio Fernandes, was "nephew of the said factor [Jorge]",
and Fernandes was implicated by other witnesses too.⁶⁷ The presence of
so many members of this family, taken with evidence of inquisitorial persecution of members of that family in the 1540s, suggests that these New

⁶⁰ IAN/TT, Inquisição de Lisboa, Processo 7312: "*avera vynte e quatro annos q se foy pera
   a Ilha de Cabo Verde onde sempre morou ē na Ilha do Fogo*".
⁶¹ Green (2007a: 59).
⁶² Ibid., 59–60, for a more detailed account.
⁶³ The 1480s and the 1490s were the most violent in the history of the Spanish Inquisition.
   See ibid.: 8.
⁶⁴ The two brothers' trials are recorded at IAN/TT, Inquisição de Évora, Procesos 8779
   (Alvaro) and 11267 (Jorge). For more details on the trial of Alvaro, see Green (2007a:
   Chapter 2).
⁶⁵ On the inauguration of the Portuguese Inquisition, see Remedios (1895–1928 : Vol. 2, 50).
⁶⁶ IAN/TT, Inquisição de Lisboa, Maço 25, no. 233, fol. 38v: "*Antonio Duarte, parente do
   feitor*".
⁶⁷ Ibid., fols. 43r, 5r.

Christians were there in large part for fear of inquisitorial persecution: Western Africa was seen as a place of escape and therefore also outside the vectors of Portuguese military and cultural domination.[68]

Taken as a whole, this evidence makes a strong case that these were general patterns governing the settlement of New Christians in Western Africa. The interconnections between the islands and the coast were ever present. Just as numerous witnesses in the António Fernandes case knew both the islands and the coast, the same held for the 1562 trial of Mestre Dioguo following the farce in Bugendo. According to Dioguo's evidence, one of the leaders in putting on the farce, Antonio Henriques, was a New Christian from the islands.[69] One witness declared that also present was the son of Bras Fernandes of Fogo.[70] Moreover, numerous witnesses were residents of Ribeira Grande, such as Gaspar Rodrigues and Tristam de Mascarenhas, the *juiz dos orfãos*.[71] Thus as these New Christians plied back and forth between the islands and the coast, they took both mixed Caboverdean forms to Africa and African cultural forms to Cabo Verde, and the shared culture of the region emerged.

THE "RACIAL" DIMENSIONS OF NEW CHRISTIAN LIFE ON CABO VERDE AND THE ACCELERATION OF CREOLISATION IN WESTERN AFRICA

One of the most important things to emerge from this analysis of the New Christian community of *lançados* in Upper Guinea has been the role of African societies in influencing New Christian receptivity to different cultural influences. As we have seen, those Caboverdean New Christian men who had most contact with mainland Africa were the most likely to develop plural identities and practices, whereas those who remained confined to the islands were more likely to hold to crypto-Jewish practices.

---

[68] This evidence requires a revision of Rodney's view that the Portuguese in Upper Guinea all came as free men (Rodney 1965: 307). The New Christians may have been "free" in the context of slave societies, but they were not in the same psychological position as Old Christians, who did not live in fear of the Inquisition. As the sixteenth century developed, this attitude was increasingly extended to other parts of the Atlantic. There were also many New Christians in São Tomé by the late 1560s, with a decree of 1569 barring them from settling there (MMAI: Vol. 2, 570).

[69] IAN/TT, Inquisição de Lisboa, Maço 25, no. 233, fol. 42v: "*Antonio Henriques xpão novo morador no Cabo Verde*".

[70] Ibid., fol. 9r.

[71] Ibid., fols. 5r, 10r, 43r-v.

This is important not only to the understanding of how mixed cultural practices emerged in Western Africa, but also to grasping what may seem an unlikely phenomenon: the contribution of African peoples such as the Kassanké to the wider reconstitution of Jewish and New Christian identities in the sixteenth century and their increasing hybridity and incorporation of non-Jewish influences.[72] The identities of New Christians and Jews were porous and mutually receptive: New Christian communities in France and the New World were in touch with Jewish communities in Italy, and Jewish communities in Amsterdam were in touch with New Christians in Brazil and Iberia.[73] The growing flexibility of Jewish practices in New Christian culture, spreading as it did to the New World and then back to Europe, was an influential factor in the formation of trading communities in the Atlantic world of the late sixteenth and early seventeenth centuries. This flexibility had been influenced by experiences of New Christian traders among the Kassanké of Upper Guinea in the first half of the sixteenth century, many of whom, as we shall see in Chapter 7, had important American connections. Thus the increasing links between Cabo Verde and Upper Guinea affected not only the local region, but also began to have wider effects as international connections intensified over the course of the sixteenth century.[74]

This sort of plural identity was also relevant to the initial trading networks of Western Africa, with many New Christians active in both Cabo Verde and Upper Guinea. Gradually, however, the identities and practices of New Christians in Cabo Verde and Upper Guinea began to diverge. Those who were most connected to the exchanges on which Atlantic trade and Atlantic fortunes depended were prepared to hybridise their practices. On Cabo Verde, however, a more rigid caste identity connected to the wider Iberian ideas of race and purity developing in these decades began to emerge. Both communities existed in places where Kriolu was spoken and mixed cultural forms had developed, but the types of interaction were very different in both.

---

[72] Evidence of this hybridity is found in the way in which crypto-Jews of the late sixteenth and seventeenth centuries adopted key aspects of emerging Christian theologies. See Bodian (2007).

[73] On the connections of New Christians in the New World to Italy, see Israel (2002: 146); on the connections of Jews in Amsterdam to Iberia see Graizbord (2004), and on connections to Brazil, see Wolff and Freida (1989).

[74] This relationship between the Atlantic New Christians and subsequent Sephardic communities in Northern Europe thus again clearly warns against the under-representation of Atlantic influences in the formation of Sephardic communities before 1650 – see Trivellato (2009: 112).

One of the main differences may have lain in the political influence of the New Christian community. In Upper Guinea, this was limited. Although their connection to Atlantic trade gave them a certain power, for the rulers of Casamance the New Christians were a dependent client caste who were useful because of their international connections and their outsider status. Diaspora merchants in Sahelian societies were, like the New Christians in Upper Guinea, usually aliens who, though able to have a place in the royal courts, could never challenge royal power precisely because of their outsider status.[75] Moreover, as with the Mandinka *dyula* diaspora who created an identity through their shared religion of Islam, the New Christian trading caste possessed a shared religious experience through their old Jewish heritage and their more recent experience of the Inquisition.[76] Thus Kassanké monarchs could exploit their trading connections, but there was never any danger of New Christians usurping power in Africa; this aspect of power relations must have been very important in dictating how flexible New Christian *lançados* became in Upper Guinea.

In Cabo Verde, however, things were very different. As we saw in the previous chapter, there were strong and repeated complaints by the 1540s that the New Christians constituted the dominant mercantile class of the islands. The Portuguese crown took a particular interest in Cabo Verde, where the prominence of New Christians was well known. Between the 1540s and the 1560s, the newly established Portuguese tribunal of the Inquisition showed its greatest interest in West Africa. A provision of August 4, 1551, placed Cabo Verde within the jurisdiction of the Tribunal of Lisbon.[77] Straightaway the inquisitorial authorities sent a visitor to the islands.[78] In 1558 Antonio Varela was appointed prosecutor [*procurador*] of the New Christians living illegally there.[79] Further official inquiries were sent concerning the Caboverdean New Christians in 1563 and 1567.[80]

Official attempts to constrain New Christian activities on the islands went beyond the Inquisition. An example is the attack by Francisco Pereira on Diogo Barassa, the *escrivão dos órfãos e dos defuntos* [notary of orphans and the deceased] in Santiago in 1559, where Pereira claimed that Barassa was a "New Christian from Fronteira [in the Alentejo]".[81]

---

[75] Meillassoux (1991: 241).

[76] See Curtin (1975: 66) on the role of Islam in the itinerant *dyula* trading diaspora of Senegambia. See also Fage (1980: 295).

[77] Published in Baião (ed.) (1921: 70; Appendix of documents).

[78] IAN/TT, Inquisição de Lisboa, Livro 840, fol. 8r.

[79] Barcellos (1899: 139).

[80] IAN/TT, Inquisição de Lisboa, Livro 840, fol. 41r; ibid., fol. 53r.

[81] IAN/TT, Chancelaria de D. Sebastião e D. Henrique, Livro 1, fol. 278v; cit. Z. Cohen (2002: 88).

Barassa was accused of selling the goods of orphans for less than their true worth and stealing large sums by making false inventories of the goods of the deceased.[82] Barassa had previously lived on Fogo before settling in Praia on Santiago.[83] Whatever the truth of the accusations levelled against him by Pereira, the relevance of his New Christian origins was revealed in the context of an attempt to obtain his position and thereby to secure an economic advantage.

The Barassa family from Fogo were important New Christian members of the Caboverdean community. After the uniting of the monarchies of Spain and Portugal under Philip II (of Spain)/I (of Portugal) in 1580, Fogo refused to accept Philip's authority. During Fogo's rebellion against the coronation of Philip as Portuguese king in 1582, one of the ringleaders was Garcia Alvares Baraça, probably a relative of Diogo Barassa.[84] Another leading rebel in 1582 was Baraça's brother, Alvaro Gonçalves. Two of the five ringleaders may positively be identified as New Christians, and therefore the rebellion led by this group may have been related to Philip II/I's known patronage of the Inquisition.[85]

Thus there was no question but that New Christians constituted a political power on the islands with the potential of rivalling that of the bulwarks of Portuguese power, the crown and the nobility. In this situation, and in parallel to developments elsewhere in the Lusophone world in the sixteenth century, the caste identity of New Christians became entrenched. Whereas Old Christians discriminated against New Christians according to their ancestry, New Christians created a closed identity which acted as a barrier to the integration of others.[86] This helped to create a situation on Cabo Verde in which, in parallel to analogous developments elsewhere in the Atlantic world in this period, some kind of shared "blood" or caste bond – a sort of proto-racial identity – came to play an important role in ideas of inclusion and exclusion. Although the modern idea of race had not yet developed fully, such ideas were certainly important in the minds of those in places such as Cabo Verde that were fully connected to other parts of the new colonial world.

The caste identity of New Christians on Cabo Verde was widely apparent. In 1581 Pope Gregory VIII wrote to the Archbishop of Lisbon

[82] Ibid., fols. 278v-279r.
[83] IAN/TT, Chancelaria de D. João III, Livro 68, fols. 201v-202r.
[84] Barcellos (1899: 157).
[85] On Alvaro Gonçales, see ibid.
[86] For a detailed analysis of how this pattern played out in the seventeenth century, see Green (2009).

complaining of the behaviour of Bishop Bartholomeu Leitão of Cabo Verde, who "lives in sin and worldly prostitution not only with women of ill repute and those who are married, but even with Jewesses".[87] When one considers the lack of European women in Cabo Verde, these "Jewesses" must have been women with Jewish fathers, which shows not only that anyone with Jewish ancestry was perceived as a Jew, but also that those with Jewish ancestry were known and identified as such in Ribeira Grande. This is confirmed by the deposition of Francisco de Sequeira, the governor of Cabo Verde, to the Inquisition in 1614: Sequeira related the story of a young woman, Joana Coelha, whose great-grandmother had told her granddaughter not to marry Joana's father because he was an Old Christian, and instead had told Joana to marry "her own kind".[88] As Joana Coelha was old enough in 1614 to marry, this story regarding her mother can be dated to the end of the sixteenth century.[89]

This awareness of New Christian identity, so firmly embedded in the mind of Joana Coelha's great-grandmother, was thus a feature of Ribeira Grande throughout the middle part of the sixteenth century. This can be seen in the case of Miçia Dias, who was accused of not giving alms to people who were not New Christians (cf. Chapter 4). Both these pieces of evidence would confirm the reality of a Jewish ghetto in Ribeira Grande at this time. In the 1780s, an account of Ribeira Grande noted that the "first whites were so proud of their honour that they only allowed new arrivals from Portugal to live in one street – still [in 1784] called the Calhau – unless they were able to prove the *limpeza* of their lineage".[90] Such a street did indeed exist in Ribeira Grande in 1614, where two witnesses to a trial were recorded as living in the "Rua do Calhau".[91] Such evidence, when combined with the strong Old Christian/New Christian identity opposition made clear from the cases of Miçia Dias and the great-grandmother of Joana Coelha, suggests both that a ghetto mentality existed among

---

[87] Barcellos (1899: 154): "*vive deshonestamente na immundicieda prostituição não só com mulheres de perdida reputação e casadas mas até com judias*".
[88] IAN/TT, Inquisição de Lisboa, Livro 205, fol. 229v.
[89] Ibid.
[90] Anonymous (1985: 27): "*Estes primeiros brancos eram tão zelosos da honra que, aos que de novo vinham do Reino, não deixavam habitar senão em uma rua a que ainda hoje chamam Calhaū, enquanto não mostrassem a limpeza do seu sangue*". Mendes (2007: 26) suggests that the Rua do Calhau was on the seafront of Ribeira Grande and that New Christians could only move farther back from the sea into the heart of the city once the community had accepted them.
[91] AHU, Cabo Verde, Caixa 1, doc. 77: "*Manoel Ribeiro botticairo morador nesta cidade na Rua do Calhau...*" (fol. 7v); "*Simão Roiz Correa mercador e morador nesta dita cidade na Rua do Calhau...*" (fol. 8r).

New Christians on Santiago in the sixteenth century and that attempts to attenuate the influence here of New Christians were utter failures.

This increasingly rigid boundary is interesting when we consider how the wider space of Western Africa had evolved by 1550. Whereas New Christians in Upper Guinea were free to adopt plural identities and practices, in Cabo Verde they were confined to a rigid caste identity which, in general, mirrored developments elsewhere in the Iberian Atlantic. For some New Christians, this may have encouraged them to fall back on ancestral Judaic practices and keep to the crypto-Jewish identity which characterised many New Christians in the late sixteenth- and early seventeenth-century Atlantic. For others, however, it must have been stifling. Indeed, this may have been what encouraged many to stay on in Upper Guinea as *lançados*, thereby increasing the exchanges on the coast and contributing to the acceleration of the process of creolisation which characterised the region as a whole.

This leads to the suggestion that the rigidity of the emerging system of *limpeza* in the Iberian world contributed to the development of plural forms in Atlantic communities in West Africa and to the spread thither of Creole culture from its Atlantic origins in Cabo Verde. Increasingly rigid laws and worldviews encourage transgression in those who are braver or less willing to be constrained. Thus although there was a way in which the expansion of the Iberian world in West Africa depended on subaltern groups, the actions of these groups themselves were in turn influenced by resistance to and rejection of the very hegemonic forces which they found oppressive in the first place.

ELITES, SLAVERY AND THE BOUNDARIES OF CREOLISATION IN WESTERN AFRICA

If renegade New Christians were increasingly inclined to settle in Upper Guinea in an attempt to seek a certain amount of freedom and enhance their trading activities, their increased settlement must also have meant there was a growing willingness among some Upper Guineans to accept them. Yet although the case studies have indeed shown that there was an alliance between Kassanké and New Christians in the mid-sixteenth century, they have told us little about how this alliance was formed in the first place. Moreover, given the inevitable Eurocentric nature of these written sources, and although we have learnt much about New Christian patterns of settlement among the Kassanké, we have learnt much less as to why they were accommodated by Kassanké lineage heads.

Understanding how Kassanké elites and New Christian *lançados* came to forge this alliance is, however, vital if we are to grasp how Atlantic Creole cultures became consolidated in Upper Guinea as well as in Cabo Verde. In order for this to occur, it was not just sufficient for traders to ply back and forth between Cabo Verde and Bugendo. There had to be reasons for them to be accepted among the Kassanké, and cultural practices in West Africa themselves had to change. Thus in order to understand how this occurred we need to grasp how the alliance was formed in the first place, for this will show how deep-seated the changes were and which elements of Upper Guinean societies were affected.

Useful comparisons can be made here to other known events. It may help, for instance, to draw an analogy with the most famous *lançado* of the sixteenth century, known as Ganagoga, meaning "the man who speaks all the languages" in the Biafada language.[92] Ganagoga's Portuguese name was João Ferreira, and according to Almada he was a New Christian.[93] Almada describes how the lineage head (*Duque*) of the Gambia River port of Casão had asked Ganagoga/Ferreira to go to the court of the Pullo king of Fuuta Tooro on the banks of the Senegal River, and that once he was there he married the king's daughter and had a child with her.[94] Ganagoga was apparently an influential figure among the Pullo aristocracy. The English sailor Reynolds stated of the area of the River Senegal that there "no *Spaniard* or *Portugueze* use to trade; and only one *Portugueze*, called *Ganigoga*, dwelleth far within the River, who was married to a king's daughter".[95]

The way in which Ganagoga/Ferreira forged an alliance through marriage into the Pullo aristocracy is instructive as to how the Kassanké–New Christian alliance may have developed. This *lançado* was on good terms with the lineage head of Casão and spoke many languages, so clearly he was well versed in the customs of Upper Guinea. Most likely, his behaviour in Fuuta Tooro replicated a strategy that had already found success in Casamance and on the Gambia. Moreover, association by New Christians with ruling circles followed the pattern their ancestors had known from Portugal, whereby the status of Jews prior to 1497 had seen them as "the King's Jews", and what security they had depended on a good relationship with the monarch.[96]

---

[92] MMAII: Vol. 3, 253.
[93] Ibid.
[94] Ibid. See also Carreira (1972: 67–8).
[95] NGC, Vol. 1, Book 2, 245.
[96] On this status of the Portuguese Jews, see Soyer (2007: 240).

From the Kassanké perspective, the welcoming of this trading group related to the securing of position in a political situation, where, as we saw in Chapter 2, there was a great deal of complexity and change. There we saw how the need to secure alliances during the Pullo migrations pushed the Kassanké towards alliances with Caboverdean traders. Surely, it did not take long for the advantages of this strategy to become clearer. The alliances offered both prestige goods and access to the iron that could increase production and, consequently, the consumption of elites. Moreover, goods doubtless came not only from trade itself, but also from the ritual of gift-giving. Here, a further line of comparative interpretation emerges from the Gold Coast, where in the 1520s, the Portuguese at Elmina sent presents several times annually to the king of Eguafo.[97] Initial contacts between *lançados* and Kassanké were very likely constructed through similar means. By the use of gifts, sovereignty was recognised and interests of Kassanké lineage heads secured. Then, once this had led to a certain status for the new outsiders, marriage alliances were formed which solidified the new caste in Kassanké society. Very soon, the New Christian *lançados* could therefore have become an accepted mercantile class, much as the Mandinka *dyula* had been before them. This process may indeed be what their Caboverdean and Portuguese detractors decried when they referred to *lançados* adopting African practices.

What emerges most clearly from this analysis is the importance of continuity with previous systems of trade and the incorporation of outsiders in Upper Guinea. The creation of alliances with elites was something that Portuguese Jews were long accustomed to achieving, whereas in Upper Guinea marriage alliances with powerful outsider traders in the form of the Kaabunké had also been common for centuries. The continuity offered by the cloth trade in *barafulas* from Cabo Verde with the preceding trans-Saharan one was key to both the peoples of Upper Guinea and the New Christians. In the long run, it was the ability to use familiar strategies in a new commercial environment which shaped the solidity of these alliances and helped in the construction of something new.

Continuities were even evident in the effects which creolisation had on the peoples of Upper Guinea. People were by no means equally affected. As with the previous trans-Saharan trade, where it had been most particularly the elites who had adopted North African traits of language and religion, so it was the Kassanké elite who opened most readily to Atlantic influences. As mentioned at the start of this chapter, the most

---

[97] Ballong-wen-Menuda (1993: Vol. 1, 90).

famous Kassanké monarch of this era was called Masatamba. In a famous account, Donelha described how Masatamba was a perfect friend to the Europeans and that the Portuguese were safer with him than in Portugal.[98] The people of Masatamba's kingdom were so scared of the consequences of mistreating Europeans that they would bring something dropped on a road to the royal palace the following day.[99] Masatamba dined on table-cloths in the European style, and was clearly somewhat acculturated to European fashions.[100] However Masatamba's willingness to adopt elements of European culture was not universal among the Kassanké. In the same period, rebellions sprang up in the Casamance. Relations in Bugendo became increasingly fraught, with the residents robbing the Portuguese and attacking them in the 1570s. Eventually, Masatamba was forced to attack Bugendo himself, killing and enslaving many of those who had attacked the Portuguese.[101]

None of this suggests that all Kassanké would have adopted elements of Portuguese culture as enthusiastically as Masatamba. As noted in Chapter 1, the Kassanké and Bainunk probably represented competing lineages.[102] The attack of Masatamba on Bugendo suggests that there were conflicts as to the best way to interact with the *lançados*, probably relating to the benefits which different lineages accrued from the interactions. Masatamba and his lineage clearly derived considerable wealth, whereas other lineages among the Kassanké and their Bainunk associates and competitors did not. Such cost-benefit analyses may well have been linked to the degree to which lineages were prepared to acculturate and to the extent and influence which the Creole culture and language of the region was able to have beyond the narrow confines of the Atlantic trading settlements. Naturally the influence of creolisation spread beyond elites, as local traders willing to take advantage of the new commercial opportunities of the Atlantic trading settlements started to reside there.[103] Fundamentally, however, the influence of the Atlantic Creole culture that linked Cabo Verde and Upper Guinea was connected to those who thought they had most to gain from direct exchanges with the Atlantic traders.

Why, then, were some lineages so keen to build alliances with Atlantic traders and thereby consolidate Creole culture, and others so hostile? As

---

[98] MMAII: Vol. 5, 139.
[99] Ibid., Vol. 5, 140.
[100] Ibid., Vol. 5, 140–1.
[101] SG, *Etiopia Menor*, fols. 18r-v.
[102] On the way in which Bainunk and Kassanké constituted competing lineages, see Bocandé (1849: 316), and also Mark (1985: 15).
[103] Such residents were typically female – see Havik (2004b).

with events in Senegambia in the late fifteenth and early sixteenth centuries, this was connected to the cycles of violent disorder which had been precipitated by Atlantic trading activities. Just as lineages of the Bainunk-Kassanké were hostile to trade with the Caboverdeans and Portuguese, so were many of the Kassanké's neighbours. Most important were the Jabundo lineage, who lived around the estuary of the Casamance River and spoke Bainunk.[104] Almada described a pronounced hostility to the Portuguese and Kassanké in the Lower Casamance[105]; at the time when he was writing, Portuguese ships had not been able to travel up the river for twenty-five years because of the Jabundo and the Floup, both of whom seized their ships and killed the sailors if they could, and who were also fighting a war against the Kassanké king.[106]

This hostility of the surrounding lineages to the Kassanké kings stemmed from the fact that the Kassanké were the principal group trading slaves in these years. Many of these slaves were secured through violence, in an echo of the processes of proto-modernity that we saw in the previous chapter in Iberia. However, whereas in the late fifteenth century the cycles of violent disorder were connected to demand for slaves from Europe, this predatory trade in slaves was now linked to a new source: America. One of the witnesses in the 1548 trial of Antonio Fernandes, Julián Valderrama, had been in the "Indies of Castile" at the time of the row between Fernandes and Manoel Garcia, and as we shall see in Chapter 7 the Leão and Carvajal families had extensive connections to the Americas.[107]

Thus it was that by 1550, when the Creole society of Western Africa had been consolidated, its activities were impossible to dissociate from wider connection to trans-Atlantic trade. The development of a local Creole society connected to processes of enslavement in Western Africa became inseparable from the forces connected to the modernisation of global economies and the birth of the Atlantic world; by now, the forces which had shaped the emergence of Creole language and identity had developed a powerful trans-Atlantic dimension which also could not be separated from the institution of slavery.

---

[104] Hawthorne (2003: 95–6).
[105] MMAII: Vol. 3, 288–90.
[106] Ibid. See also Boulègue (1980: 485–6).
[107] For the evidence of Valderrama, see IAN/TT, Inquisição de Lisboa, Processo 801, fol. 44r.

PART TWO

CREOLISATION AND SLAVERY

Western Africa and the Pan-Atlantic, Circa 1492–1589

6

The Early Trans-Atlantic Slave Trade
from Western Africa

One of the principal tasks of humanists and intellectuals is supposed to be to come up with new perspectives on the nature of human existence. Yet anyone who gives the matter a moment's thought is well aware that it is very difficult to come up with anything new at all to say on such matters. For instance, the process of globalisation, touted so widely by economists and political scientists since the end of the 1990s, is hardly anything new. As scholars such as Janet Abu-Lughod and Serge Gruzinski have shown, globalisation really dates back to the sixteenth century, if not before.[1]

Most scholarship on this early period tends to deal with interchanges between Europe and the New World in the era of the Spanish conquest of America. Yet the omission of Africa from this picture is a grave mistake. As the locus of the birth of the first Atlantic Creole culture, Western Africa was vital in the earliest globalisation of economies and ideas influencing the wider Atlantic world.[2] Yet the channels of influence cut in both directions. As the epicentre of the first trans-Atlantic slave trade from circa 1520 to the 1580s, events here prefigured and influenced those which happened later on elsewhere, but were themselves determined in part by the cycle of demand from America and Europe.

This chapter traces these early global interactions and the connection which they had to the first trans-Atlantic slave trade. For by the time that

---

[1] Abu-Lughod (1989); Gruzinski (2002; 2005).
[2] An exception to this general rule is Antunes/Silva (2011), who note (49) that Western Africa was "a major contributor to the development of European Atlantic economies and a key player in the newly born Atlantic societies".

the alliance of Kassanké and New Christians was fully developed in the
1540s, truly global pressures were already influential in Western Africa.
The most important impacts thus far had been those emanating from
Europe via the Caboverdean and Portuguese traders. However, from the
1520s onwards, the conquest of the Americas and the new demand for
labour for the American colonies provoked a new range of forces. As the
need for slaves became increasingly trans-Atlantic, it became impossible
to separate the development of Creole society in Western Africa from the
increased trade in slaves which trans-Atlantic trade demanded. It may
indeed be no coincidence that the 1546 denunciation from Cabo Verde to
the inquisitors of Évora said that for up to twenty years New Christians
had been mixing with Africans in Upper Guinea (cf. Chapter 4); for it had
been precisely in the 1520s that the direct trans-Atlantic slave trade from
West Africa to America had really taken off.

This chapter traces the development of this early trans-Atlantic slave
trade and the influences it had on interactions in Western Africa. In order
to place subsequent events in context, it begins by offering a new perspective on the early Spanish voyages to the New World, showing for the first
time the importance of African perspectives in these voyages and arguing thereby that the development of what I call a "pan-Atlantic space"
occurred far earlier than historians generally allow. This earlier history
demonstrates how easy it was for direct trans-Atlantic slaving to influence
the regional orientation of Western Africa from the 1520s onwards.

This picture is constructed with substantial help from the early chronicles of Spanish exploits in America written by Columbus, Las Casas and
Vespucci. These chronicles are surprisingly informative on the development of African-European relationships prior to 1492 and offer a decisive
new picture of the emergence of pan-Atlanticism at this early moment in
Atlantic history. One of the elements to emerge from these sources is the
pivotal role of slavery in both early Western African and New World economic aims. By connecting this to the preceding analysis of creolisation,
this chapter reveals the fundamental interconnection of creolisation and
slavery in the trans-Atlantic paradigm right from the beginning, before
the direct shipment of slaves from Western Africa to the Americas had
even begun.

The importance of the regional history of creolisation we looked at in
the first part of this book emerges because of the centrality of the Western
African region to early trans-Atlantic trade. Slaves from Kongo and
Angola populated the plantations of São Tomé and were important in the
direct trade to Portugal; later, though only from around 1570 onwards,

they dominated the trade across the South Atlantic to Brazil.[3] Meanwhile, slaves from Benin were exchanged for gold at Elmina.[4] Thus it was from Western Africa that moves towards a pan-Atlantic creolisation began, and so it was that the regional interactions which characterised events in Western Africa up until the 1540s were gradually superseded by a more global paradigm in which this part of Africa affected, and was affected by, forces all over the Western hemisphere. Although Heywood and Thornton have argued that the birth of "Atlantic Creole culture" can be traced to West-Central Africa in the late sixteenth and early seventeenth centuries, this chapter argues for a more nuanced view[5]; not only was creolisation in the Atlantic world variegated and not homogenous, as indeed previous chapters have already argued, but the role of Western Africa in this early era of Atlantic trade was important in shaping its boundaries.

From a wider Atlantic and imperial point of view, economic factors shaped this role of Western Africa in early trans-Atlantic slaving. The other island outposts of the Atlantic world had their agro-commercial functions. The Azores and Madeira grew wheat and wine for the metropole.[6] São Tomé grew sugar. However, Cabo Verde, because of its precarious ecology, was ill-equipped for a productive, cash-crop economy. Moreover, it was by far the nearest archipelago in the African Atlantic to the early centres of the Spanish colonial economy in the New World, the Caribbean islands of Cuba and Hispaniola, and the mines and plantations of New Spain [present-day Mexico]. Geographical proximity and lack of profitable alternatives meant that Cabo Verde's role as a slaving entrepôt for the growing labour demands of the Americas made good economic sense.[7]

This economic situation was a necessary condition for the rise of the trans-Atlantic slave trade from Western Africa in the second quarter of the sixteenth century. However, it was not a sufficient condition, for economic impetus could not alone guarantee the supply of slaves. This was demonstrated in Benin, where the Obas refused to sell any male slaves to the Portuguese from around 1530 onwards, and the slave trade was confined to female slaves taken to Elmina.[8] The intensification of this cycle

---

[3] Couto (1995: 305). Godinho (1981: Vol. 4, 172) suggests that Angolan slaves arrived in Brazil from around 1570.

[4] Elbl (1997); Vogt (1979: 57–8, 70); Ryder (1969: 35–9, 59–63).

[5] Heywood/Thornton (2007).

[6] Godinho (1981: Vol. 3, 233–43).

[7] Mendes (2007: 271–2) emphasises the economic side in the importance of Western Africa in the early slave trade.

[8] Ryder (1969: 59–68); Miller (1988: 108).

of slave exports from Western Africa therefore responded to local conditions as well as to Atlantic pressures. This chapter analyses the interplay
of these factors and their effects on societies in Western Africa, marshal-
ling a wide array of archival sources never before used to analyse the
rise of the trans-Atlantic trade. These sources show why different groups
were targeted by the trade in Upper Guinea and how these experiences
shaped their responses, analysing in detail and for the first time the effect
of early trans-Atlantic slavery on individual societies in Western Africa
and its connection to creolisation.

THE BIRTH OF A PAN-ATLANTIC SPACE DEPENDENT ON SLAVING IN THE EARLY SIXTEENTH CENTURY

In May 1510 João Jorge, the procurator of Santiago, Cabo Verde, underlined the importance of Santiago in a letter to the king of Portugal. It was
vital that the island should not be abandoned, because it was "one of the
main helps of India and Guinea ... and the islanders serve Your Highness
with great love and diligence, because if they had not given 70 blacks to
the fleet of Afonso d'Albuquerque to help him man his pumps with the
strength of their arms and take him back to Lisbon the fleet would have
been lost [Albuquerque arrived in Lisbon from Calicut in January 1504] ...
and in the same way they aid all the ailing ships of Your Majesty which
arrive there".[9]

As Jorge's letter shows, Cabo Verde was pivotal to the Portuguese voyages to the East Indies and Brazil. Most voyagers to distant lands had
called in there, and Columbus too had spent long periods in Western
Africa prior to the 1492 voyage. It is false to pretend that historians have
been unaware of this prior African experience of Columbus, but certainly
the way in which it may have shaped his decisions in the New World has
not been analysed in any depth.[10] Yet just as Fernão de Loronha had been
active in West Africa before his commercial interests developed in Brazil
(cf. Chapter 4), the same was true of the most famous mariner in history.

---

[9] MMAII: Vol. 2, 38–9 – "*hũa das principaes escapullas da India e Guinee, hé a dicta
Ilha. E serven a vosalteza cõ muito amor, e deligençia, porque se nom deram á armada
de Afonso d'Albuquerque obra de setenta negros, que a poder de força de braços, dando
aa bomba, a trouxerão a Lisboa, a armada se perdera ... e pello mesmo modo forneçam
todos [os] navios de vossalteza que hi chegão desvaratados*".
[10] Abulafia (2008: 30), Cortesão (1935: Vol. 1, 196), and Thomas (1997: 88) mention
Columbus's sojourns on the African coast before 1492. Wilson (1990: 49) notes that
"the idea that the [Lucayos] islands could be a source of slaves, as the Portuguese viewed
their lands in West Africa, was present from the beginning", but goes no further.

Knowledge of trading practices in Africa and America were connected from the start.

Both Columbus and some of those on his first voyage to the New World had spent time on the West African coast in the 1470s and 1480s. Columbus wrote, "I was in the Castle of the King of Portugal at Mina, which lies below the equinoctial line, and so I am a good witness that it is not inhabitable as some people say".[11] According to Bartolomé de las Casas, "elsewhere in his writings [Columbus] affirms that he had sailed many times from Lisbon to Guinea".[12] That this experience was not just confined to Columbus was shown in his log of the 1492 voyage; on arriving in Cuba, he sent a present to a nearby king "with a sailor who had been on the same sort of mission in Guinea".[13]

Thus there was a significant African component in the experience of Columbus and his crew. The evidence implies that this pre-existing experience shaped how Columbus engaged with his "discoveries". In the first place, his emphasis of this prior experience in West Africa implies that he thought this relevant to his project. Moreover, his selection of people with African experience to carry presents to local rulers shows that he valued such African experience and thought it mattered.

The extent of Columbus's African experience emerges through the use of language.[14] Whilst in Caribbean waters late in 1492, Columbus named a cape "el Cabo Verde" [Cape Verde].[15] Coming from someone who had sailed the African coast, this act of naming was almost certainly related by association to the Cape Verde peninsula. The island of Jamaica was first called by him St. Jago, perhaps bringing to mind something of Santiago, Cabo Verde.[16] Later on in Cuba, on December 6, 1492, he named another headland "Cabo del Elefante" [Cape of the Elephant].[17] Possibly the promontory reminded Columbus of the shape

[11] Las Casas (1966b: Vol. 62, 49) – "*yo estuve en el castillo de la Mina del Rey de Portugal que está debajo de la equinoccial, y ansí soy buen testigo que no es inhabitable como dicen*".

[12] Ibid. – "*En otras partes de sus escritos afirma haber muchas veces navegado de Lisbona á Guinea*". A strong argument for Las Casas's value as a historical source is in Wilson (1990: 8–10). Penny (1990) discusses Las Casas's use of language in his annotating of Columbus's log to adduce support for its accuracy. Though there are unquestionably elements of rhetoric and exaggeration, the value of Las Casas as a historical source is immense.

[13] Lardicci (1999: 336–7) – "*un marinero que avía andado en Guinea en lo mismo*".

[14] See Penny (1990) for a strong argument that Las Casas was quoting Columbus's language verbatim in his abridgement of his log.

[15] Lardicci (1999: 333).

[16] Atkins (1970: 233).

[17] Lardicci (1999: 362).

of an elephant, or alternatively, it may have been called after a similarly
shaped piece of land that Portuguese mariners had named in Africa. The
importance of African categories in Columbus's mind emerges nowhere
more clearly than in his repeated use of the word "almadía"; this was the
word which the Portuguese had adopted in Africa to describe the canoes
which African peoples used on the rivers.[18]

Elsewhere in his log and letters, Columbus showed a detailed knowledge of Senegambia and Upper Guinea. In describing the languages of
the Caribbean islands, Columbus wrote that language "is all one in these
islands of India, and everyone understands each other and travels about in
their canoes, which is not the case in Guinea, where there are a thousand
different types of language and those who speak one don't understand
those who speak another". Thus he clearly had at least some knowledge
of the different languages of Western Africa.[19] Meanwhile, arriving on
the South American mainland in 1498, Columbus compared the trade in
textiles there to that of the cloths "that are brought from Guinea, from
the rivers to Sierra Leone".[20]

Although he still thought of the Caribbean as "India", therefore,
Columbus was on stronger ground when it came to patterns of trade
and culture in Senegambia and Upper Guinea. This becomes clear both
from the naming of "Cabo Verde" – referring to Senegambia – and also
in the detail on the cloth trade from the rivers of Guinea (present-day
Casamance and Guinea-Bissau region) to Sierra Leone. In his journal he
conceptualised both the useful and the numinous through his African
knowledge, comparing edible roots on Hispaniola with others he had seen
in Guinea, and later comparing mermaids in the Caribbean islands with
others he had "seen" on the Malaguetta coast (present-day Liberia).[21]

This material matters a great deal not only in verifying the importance
of African experiences in the settlement and initial conceptualisation of the
New World, but also in telling us about trade in Africa at this time. If, as
shown here, Columbus's language and ideas in the New World were drawn
in part from his African experience, it may also be that the way in which
he and other early European adventurers engaged with peoples in the New
World can tell us much about the pre-existing patterns in Africa.

---

[18] For example, ibid., 324.
[19] Ibid., 345 – "*es toda una en todas estas islas de Yndia, y todos se entienden y todas las
andan en sus almadías, lo que no han en Guinea, adonde es mill maneras de lenguas que
la una no entiende la otra*".
[20] Las Casas (1966b: Vol. 63, 240) – "*como los llevan de Guinea, de los ríos á la Sierra
Leona*".
[21] Lardicci (1999: 372, 400).

It matters, therefore, that Columbus thought a great deal about slaving. One of his first recorded thoughts was that the people of the first island he visited, in the Bahamas, "would be good servants".[22] Later, on Hispaniola, he suggested that "they are great cowards, and 1,000 [of them] would not resist three [of us], and so they are very good to be controlled and made to work, sew crops and do everything else which might be necessary".[23] Capturing and enslaving the Taíno of the Caribbean islands would be easy, Columbus wrote to Ferdinand and Isabela of Aragón and Castile after his first voyage: "Your Highnesses, whenever you decide to order it, can take all [the Indians] to Castile or keep them enslaved on the island, because 50 men could control them all".[24]

Thus some of Columbus's first thoughts on arriving in the New World related to how quickly the new lands could be turned into slaving colonies. After a vicious war waged with dogs against the Cacique Guatiguana of Hispaniola in late 1494, Columbus sent more than five hundred slaves back to Castile on February 24, 1495.[25] Very rapidly, he had "determined to load the ships which came from Castile with slaves, and send them to sell in the islands of the Canaries, the Azores and Cabo Verde".[26] In 1498, he sent a further five ships back to Spain with eight hundred slaves.[27] He also borrowed from his experience in Africa by sending seven Taíno back to Spain after his first voyage to train as interpreters, which was exactly what the Portuguese had sought to do previously among peoples of the coasts of Senegambia and Upper Guinea.[28]

This evidence is suggestive as to how the opening to Atlantic trade might have affected societies in Senegambia and Upper Guinea in the late fifteenth century. Here we have the account of someone who we know traded often in these regions in the 1470s and 1480s, and although clearly the enslavement of the doomed Guanche people of the Canary islands in these years may have affected his ideas, surely events in Western Africa were also important. His first thought in the Americas was how

---

[22] Ibid., 321 – *"Ellos deven ser buenos servidores"*.

[23] Ibid., 373 – *"muy cobardes, que mill no aguardarían tres, y así son buenos para les mandar y les hazer trabajar, sembrar y hazer todo lo otro que fuere menester"*.

[24] Las Casas (1966b: Vol. 62, 303) – *"Vuestras Altezas, cuando mandaren, puédenlos todos llevar á Castilla ó tenerlos en la misma isla captivos, porque 50 hombres los ternan todos sojuzgados"*.

[25] Ibid., Vol. 63, 84–5.

[26] Ibid., Vol. 63, 177 – *"tenia determinado de cargar los navíos que viniesen de Castilla de esclavos, y enviarlos á vender á las islas de Canarias y de los Azores, y á las de Cabo Verde"*.

[27] Ibid., Vol. 63, 340.

[28] Metcalf (2005: 50). Later Vespucci and Francisco Pizarro did the same (ibid., 5–6, 50).

to obtain slaves and turn a profit, which suggests that similar patterns also held in Western Africa. Moreover, this picture also emerges from the famous letters of Amérigo Vespucci. Although Vespucci's accounts have been heavily criticised for their stereotypes, one suspects that his portrait of the psychologies of his crew was accurate when he described how, on the first of his four voyages, they demanded to return to Castile after a year at sea and "for that reason we resolved to capture slaves, load the vessels with them, and head toward Spain".[29] Like Columbus, Vespucci had African as well as American experience, writing that "I ... have been in many parts of Africa and Ethiopia ... to Zanaga [Senegal], to Cape Verde [i.e., the Cape Verde peninsula], to Río Grande, to Sierra Leone".[30] Two of his four voyages to America called at the African coast, once at Cape Verde and once at Sierra Leone.

Similar patterns also emerge from Brazil, as Metcalf has shown. She suggests that during the first landfall in Brazil in April 1500, made by a fleet captained by Pedro Alvares Cabral, "everything Cabral did in Brazil was informed by what the Portuguese had learned from their experience in Africa".[31] Subsequently, Metcalf suggests, the first contracts for the brazilwood trade, issued by the Portuguese crown in 1504, were modelled on similar commercial contracts for the West African coast, whereas the development of a trade in internal slavery on the Brazilian coast was also modelled on the Portuguese experience in West Africa.[32]

In all these cases, therefore, we have evidence suggesting that the development of American slave economies were mediated through experiences first developed in Africa. Both Columbus and Vespucci reveal how the trade in slaves was the most immediate commercial possibility. This is indeed confirmed by Las Casas, who wrote that taking slaves was what the "Spanish, here in this island [of Hispaniola] and later in all of the Indies, sought to achieve, and this was what their thoughts, desires, efforts, words and good deeds were always directed at".[33] That this was the first thought of sailors in the Caribbean suggests strongly that this was also how African trade was perceived by Portuguese sailors in the late fifteenth century.

---

[29] Formisano (1992: 15).

[30] Ibid., 39.

[31] Metcalf (2005: 17–8).

[32] Ibid., 57–8, 159–60.

[33] Las Casas (1966b: Vol. 64, 47) – "*es lo que principalmente los españoles, aquí en esta isla, y después en todas las Indias, pretendieron, y á esto enderezaron siempre sus pensamientos, sus deseos, sus industrias, sus palabras y sus buenos hechos*".

This analysis confirms the picture of Chapter 2, which showed how, whatever the Portuguese crown's macro-economic motivations may have been, slaving – not gold – was the principal commercial aim of those participating in the voyages on the African coast. Yet it also reveals how, from the very beginning, it was understood that the development of a pan-Atlantic space would depend on the use of slaves. This would be of immense economic and social importance to Western Africa, because the overwhelming majority of slaves taken to the Americas in this early period came from this region. As we have seen, because the development of the Creole culture in Cabo Verde had also been fundamentally linked to the needs of a new colonial economy based on slavery, as well as to the increasing exchanges between Africans and Europeans on the mainland which this required, the development of a pan-Atlantic space in which such features were also connected would soon bring wider global pressures to bear on the phenomenon of creolisation in Western Africa.

THE AMERICAN GENOCIDE AND THE NEED FOR DIRECT TRANS-ATLANTIC TRADE

As the work of Las Casas attests, slavery was fundamental to early Spanish undertakings in the New World. As Columbus described the situation to Ferdinand and Isabela, a shortage of Native American slaves there was not. Thus in order for events in Senegambia and Upper Guinea to develop a pan-Atlantic significance, one further condition was necessary: the genocide of the Taíno people who lived in the Caribbean.

The Taíno population of Hispaniola in 1492 is generally reckoned not to have been less than 300,000. According to Las Casas, who had original documents which no longer exist, the Dominican friar Bernardo de Santo Domingo wrote in 1515 that when the Spanish first arrived in the Caribbean they had found 1.1 million Taíno on Hispaniola, but that at the time that he was writing there were only 10,000 left.[34] Even though these estimates are unreliable, a 1508 census suggested an original population of around 400,000.[35] This is in line with current estimates of the population of Hispaniola in 1492, which range from 300,000 to 500,000, and certainly there is no question that all these people died during the process of Spanish colonisation.[36]

[34] Ibid., Vol. 65, 338.
[35] Moya Pons (1998: 34).
[36] Davis (2006: 98). Indeed, there were only 500 Taíno left by 1519 (Moya Pons 1998: 37).

Such devastation spread around the Caribbean. When hardly any Taíno were left in Hispaniola, the neighbouring Lucayo islands (Bahamas) were raided, so that within a few years perhaps 40–50,000 slaves had been brought to Hispaniola.[37] In around 1512 a Spaniard sent a ship to find the last remaining peoples from the Lucayos, and after three years of searching only eleven souls were found.[38] By the time Las Casas wrote his *Brevíssima Relación de la Destruycion de las Indias* in 1542, there were, according to him, no native peoples at all left in the Lucayos, Jamaica, Cuba and Puerto Rico.[39] Las Casas was not the only writer to describe this human desolation. El Inca Garcilaso also described how the people of Cuba had all hung themselves in order to escape the labour regime imposed by the Spanish and that "with this atrocious plague the inhabitants of this island were entirely consumed so that today [1605, when his book *La Florida* was published] there are hardly any left".[40]

In general, disease is seen as the cause of the demise of the Native American population; as Eltis puts it, "plague in the Americas … helped ensure plantation slavery for Africans".[41] Certainly, some historians will cavil at the use of the word "genocide". An illustrious historian of the Mediterranean recently disputed that the word genocide is appropriate here because this word requires murders to be planned.[42] Yet genocide is appropriate. One need only look to a slaving voyage made to Florida in 1511 for evidence of this. These ships went first to the Bahamas, but such was the population collapse that no people were found there.[43] They continued to Florida, where they tricked people on board and sailed off with them as slaves. The Spanish sailors had already seen the effect of slave hunting on the Bahamas and that moreover these slaves had not lived long on Hispaniola. They must therefore have known that the death of most or all of these Floridians would result from their capture.[44]

---

[37] Las Casas (1966b: Vol. 64, 222–6).

[38] Ibid., Vol. 64, 232.

[39] Las Casas (1966a: 10–11). Population decline was such that people in Puerto Rico were desperate to import African slave labour in the 1540s, and they frequently sent their own ships directly to Cabo Verde – see AGI, Justicia 996, No. 2, Ramo 2

[40] El Inca Garcilaso (1988: 134). This quote can be seen to suggest that Las Casas exaggerated the desolation; and indeed there are documents which do suggest a Native American population in Cuba in the late sixteenth century (personal communication from David Wheat, San Francisco, November 19, 2010). Nevertheless, the general devastation of the populations is not in doubt.

[41] Eltis (2000: 7).

[42] Abulafia (2008: 4).

[43] For more on the Lucayos, see Wilson (1990: 47).

[44] El Inca Garcilaso (1988: 109–10); Las Casas (1966b: Vol. 64, 458–9).

The importance of the American genocide raises serious implications for African history. In general, moral issues surrounding the African presence in the Americas have been looked at through the lens of the slave trade. The fact that this trans-Atlantic trade itself began only after the genocide of the Taíno peoples of the Caribbean has been under-discussed.[45] Yet the American atrocity was fundamentally connected to the way in which people perceived and justified the importance of the trans-Atlantic slave trade. From the very start, therefore, such questions took on a pan-oceanic, international quality emblematic of this early Atlantic world, a world in which the institutionalised violence which facilitated creolisation in places such as Cabo Verde became the norm. A fundamental characteristic of this new pan-Atlantic space was thus that the violence which accompanied both the American genocide and the processes of creolisation and enslavement in Western Africa were connected, because conquest and the economic development of the European empires of the Atlantic world through the requisitioning of surplus labour and production could occur in neither place without it.

The connection between the genocide in the Caribbean and the trans-Atlantic slave trade from Western Africa was direct. It was Las Casas himself who, having travelled to Spain in 1517, managed to persuade Charles V to grant a licence in 1518 so that slaves could be taken directly to the Caribbean from Africa.[46] The licence was granted to Laurent de Gouvenot, the governor of Bresse, who sub-contracted it to Genoese merchants. Four thousand slaves were to be transported directly from Africa to Hispaniola to relieve the labour shortage there.[47] The contract had a direct effect. In December 1517, Alonso Suazo, the judge of the *Audiencia* of Santo Domingo, was asking for ships to travel from Hispaniola to Seville to buy trade goods with which to purchase slaves in Cabo Verde.[48] Then, in 1518, the three Jeronymite monks governing Hispaniola requested that ships from Hispaniola be allowed to go straight to Cabo Verde and bring slaves.[49] Las Casas later wrote that what moved him to make this petition was the desire to relieve the Native Americans of their appalling suffering. Thus had there been no genocide, Las Casas would never have made such a request.

---

[45] Although Newson (2006: 157) discusses the connection of the demographic collapse of the Native Americans to imports of African slaves.

[46] Las Casas (1966b: Vol. 65, 380–1).

[47] Ibid., Vol. 65, 381; E. Lopes (1944: 4).

[48] Toletino Dipp (1974: 155); cit Torrão (2006: 1).

[49] AGI, Patronato 174, Ramo 6.

Yet such moral considerations had already been foreshadowed by the spectre of economics. The financial catastrophe brought on by the genocide had concentrated minds. There was a need to provide a reliable labour supply in the New World. A system of licences to import Black slaves to the Caribbean via Iberia began in 1513.[50] This was another case of the state catching up with reality: African slaves had been imported to work on Hispaniola as early as 1502.[51] King Fernando of Spain had even sent one hundred African slaves directly to Hispaniola in 1505 to work for him in the mines.[52] In 1510, he had ordered fifty more slaves to be used in the royal mines.[53] Such was the quantity of African slaves in Hispaniola that in 1511 he wrote to a representative there: "I do not understand how so many blacks have died: look after them carefully".[54] By 1520, the volume of African slaves on the island was such that there was widespread fear of their revolt.[55] There is a way, therefore, in which the royal licences issued in the 1510s did not precipitate a situation but rather codified it. Moreover, the royal permission of 1518 was also just catching up with reality, as slaves probably were being dispatched directly from Cabo Verde to the Caribbean since 1514.[56] The way in which the trade was taking off by 1520 is emphasised by the contract given on December sixteenth 1519 to Afonso Lopes de Ávila to found a *feitoria* on Cabo Verde, a depot for the organising of slave exports.[57]

We can therefore pinpoint this era as the time when the trans-Atlantic slave trading era really began: the Atlantic was pan-Atlantic by the late 1510s at the latest.[58] Western Africa had more than sixty years of experience in the procurement of African slaves. Its economic space was fully integrated, with the provision of slaves for Caboverdean and Iberian markets the cornerstone of its Atlantic economy. It was much nearer

[50] Ventura (1999: 23).
[51] Davis (2006: 80); Palmer (1976: 7–8). This followed official instructions given in 1501 by Ferdinand King of Aragón (Deive 1980: Vol. 1, 19).
[52] Palmer (1976: 8); Moya Pons (1973: 70).
[53] AGI, Contratación 5089, Legajo 1, fol. 38r.
[54] Saco (1879: Vol. 1, 67).
[55] I. Wright (1916: 772). Most of these, of course, had come straight from Europe.
[56] T. Hall (1992: Vol. 2, 439–40). Mendes (2007: 29–33; 2008: 66) suggests that only in the 1530s did more ships go directly from West Africa to the Americas; however, this may underestimate both the 1518 decree permitting a direct trade from Africa to America and this evidence of trade by 1514, illustrating the need which the 1518 decree sought to meet.
[57] E. Lopes (1944: 22).
[58] Torrão (2006: 1; idem., 2010: 2) concurs that direct slaving between Cabo Verde and the New World had begun by the end of the 1510s.

to the Caribbean islands than Benin and Kongo. It turned out that the administration and institutionalisation of violence on the archipelago itself were not the only factors encouraging creolisation; this reality was supplemented by the violence of the New World, which accelerated the processes that had already begun to occur there.

THE EXPANSION OF THE PAN-ATLANTIC SLAVING ECONOMY
AND THE GROWTH OF CABO VERDE

By the 1520s and 1530s, the Iberian empire of the pan-Atlantic was growing inexorably. Tenochtitlan fell in 1521; Cuzco, thirteen years later. As the Spanish advanced in America, African slaves became commonplace. Most were initially sent first to Iberia and then to the New World.[59] One of the four men to survive the 1528–36 journey from Florida to what today is northwestern Mexico made famous by Cabeza de Vaca's *Naufragios* was a Black slave born in Morocco.[60] Smallpox was said to have been brought to New Spain by a Black slave on Nárvaez's expedition in 1520[61]; as disease and violence triggered demographic collapse, the *parvenu* slavemasters of the New World sought scapegoats.

African slaves typically participated in Spanish military campaigns in America. They were in Pizarro's army during his conquest of the Incas in the early 1530s; one of them, Juan de Valiente, became a military commander.[62] Following Cuzco's fall in 1534, 150 Blacks went with Almagro from Cuzco to Chile in 1535, and between 1529 and 1537 at least 363

---

[59] There was, however, a dislike of slaves who had become too acculturated to Iberia and had spent longer than a year there, and decrees barring these *ladino* slaves from entering the New World were passed in 1526, 1531 and 1543 – Encinas (1945–6: Vol. 4, 383–4). Early inventories regularly mention *ladino* slaves; for instance, Estevan de Baziniana's on Cuba in 1532 cited four slaves, all *ladinos* (AGI, Justicia 11, No. 3; although the same file details a charge against Baziniana for failing to provide accounts for some slaves that he received in Cabo Verde and took to Cuba, showing that by the early 1530s both direct trans-Atlantic trade and the trade via Iberia were in operation). Although the direct Cabo Verde to America trade gradually took precedence, the custom of sending slaves via Iberia continued throughout the sixteenth century, though these slaves rarely stayed long on the Iberian peninsula. In 1557 the slave importers of Mexico City wrote that "un-acculturated slaves [*negros boçales*] have been and are brought from the kingdom of Portugal after the blacks who are constantly being sent from the islands of Cabo Verde have been gathered together" ("*los negros bocales se an traydo y trae del rreyno de portugal despues de tener recogidos los negros que continuamente se trae de las yslas de cabo verde*") – AGI, Justicia 204, No. 3, Ramo 1.

[60] Cabeza de Vaca (1989: 222).

[61] See, e.g., Aguirre Beltrán (1989: 19).

[62] Thomas (1997: 102).

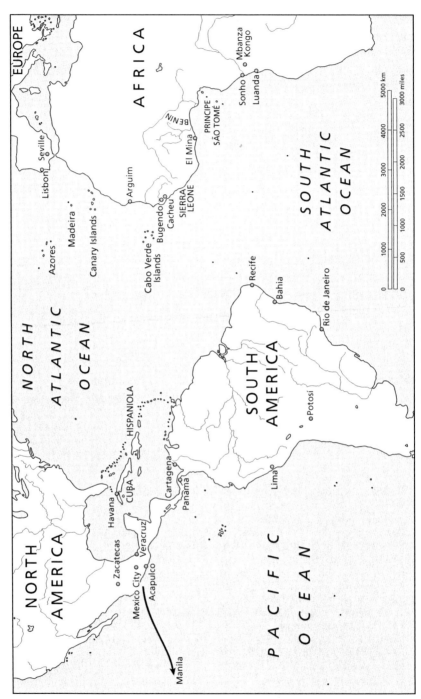

MAP 4. Atlantic World Circa 1550.

Black slaves were licensed to go to Peru alone simply to help with building the new colonial infrastructure.[63] By the 1540s, Black soldiers were used by both sides in the vicious civil conflicts which overran the Peruvian colony, and in the 1546 battle of Añaquito, Gonzalo Pizarro's army may have had as many as 600 Black auxiliaries.[64]

That Western Africa was the epicentre of the trans-Atlantic slave trade in this era is not in doubt. The picture we have just seen for the 1510s was consolidated in the second quarter of the sixteenth century. The route from Cabo Verde to the Indies was fully established by the mid-1520s, with licences initially given to various residents of Hispaniola to bring slaves under the general licence granted to Gouvenot in 1518.[65] Several documents have been discovered by María Manuel Ferraz Torrão which confirm merchants in Seville sending ships to Santo Domingo via Cabo Verde from 1525 at the latest.[66] From 1528 to 1532 the Germans Heinrich Ehinger and Hieronymus Seiler were given a general licence to purvey four thousand slaves to the Indies, and thereafter individual merchants bought licences at the Casa de la Contratación in Seville until 1595 and the reinstitution of larger contracts (*asientos*).

However, widespread illegal trade meant that the actual numbers of slaves imported to America in these early years was higher than the number of licences granted. An official wrote to Charles V from Hispaniola in 1526 suggesting that six hundred contraband slaves had been introduced to that island in that year alone.[67] Indeed, contraband had been recognised as a problem in the slave trade in Western Africa since 1514 at least, when one of the royal decrees issued by Manoel noted a problem with the traders and ship crew at Cantor/Kantora on the River Gambia, who did not "tell the truth about the trade for the merchandise that they take there".[68] The possibilities for this contraband are also demonstrated by the fact that by 1535, the numbers of slaves loaded on individual ships in Kongo for transport to São Tomé and between São Tomé and Elmina

---

[63] Bowser (1974: 5–6).

[64] Ibid., 9, and ff. for a general picture of Africans in the early Peruvian colony. See O'Toole (2007) for a more recent transnational perspective.

[65] Torrão (1991: 308, 332).

[66] Torrão (2010: 6).

[67] Deive (1980: Vol. 1, 159).

[68] MMAI : Vol. 4, 74: "*por quanto muchas vezes mandamos fazer armações pera Cantor: & pera outras partes : onde os capitães levam poder por si resgatar as ditas armações: declaramos que os ditos nossos capitães : & bem assi os de nossos tratadores: ou piloto : ou mestre: como outra qualquer pessoa que poder levar pera fazer os ditos resgates : nom fazer verdade no resgate das mercadorias que levam*".

regularly reached anywhere between 375 and 662.[69] Although these were much shorter journeys than the trans-Atlantic voyages, this certainly suggests that the carrying capacity of early sixteenth-century ships was large and that the numbers loaded for the crossing to the New World were routinely higher than the numbers of licences to ship slaves sold to captains by the _Casa de la Contratación_ in Seville, which was generally between 100 and 200 per voyage.

From Hispaniola, many of the slaves were taken with the Spanish to their conquests on the American mainland.[70] However, from the mid-1520s residents in New Spain contracted directly to obtain slaves in Cabo Verde.[71] Slaves were being imported directly from Cabo Verde to Nombre de Dios in Panamá by 1534 at the latest.[72] Escaped slaves, known as _cimarrones_, were widespread in Panamá by 1535, and in Cuba by 1536. They roamed the roads with weapons, assaulting people on the roads and attacking the farms of Spanish colonists.[73] Indeed, there were so many African slaves in Mexico City by 1537 that when a feared slave uprising was put down, several dozen Africans were hung, drawn and quartered.[74]

Key to this trade were Sevillano merchants, most of whom were New Christians.[75] In the early 1530s they operated as agents of Ehinger and Seiler, but after the lapsing of this contract in 1532 they contracted directly to ship slaves at the _Casa de la Contratación_.[76] These traders used contraband techniques to expand their commercial potential in Western Africa, loading goods illegally in Seville to be taken to Cabo Verde under the pretence that they were destined for the Indies.[77] One well-known trader was Juan de la Barrera – himself an Old Christian – who was

---

[69] Ibid., Vol. 15, 101–2 (375 slaves on the ship _Santo Espírito_); ibid., Vol. 15, 115–6 (662 slaves on the ship _Urbano_); ibid., Vol. 15, 125 (512 slaves on the ship _Conceição_).

[70] Aguirre Beltrán (1989: 20).

[71] Thomas (1997: 101). See also Aguirre Beltrán (1989: 20) on the contract with Ehringer and Seiler. The earliest such case of direct traffic from Cabo Verde I have found is from 1526, detailed in AGI, Justicia 9 No. 7; but cf. also above on the request from the Jeronymite monks governing Hispaniola in 1518 for a direct traffic, and the evidence of illegal contraband trade in 1514, which suggests it may have taken place much earlier.

[72] AGI, Panamá 234, Libro 5, fols. 182v-183r (a case from 1534) and 197v (a case from 1535).

[73] AGI, Panamá 235, Libro 6, fols. 24v-25r; Santo Domingo 1121, Libro 1, fols. 173v-174r.

[74] Aguirre Beltrán (1989: 22–3).

[75] Gil (2001: Vol. 3, 149–51).

[76] AGI, Indiferente 1092, no. 42 – January 13th 1533; AGI, Indiferente 1092, no. 104 – July 7, 1535.

[77] AGI, Indiferente 1092, no. 45 – June 10th 1533.

regularly making the Seville–Cabo Verde–Veracruz run by the 1530s.[78] Between 1532 and 1534 the number of Africans in Cuba doubled, and by 1536 the Audiencia of Hispaniola had written to the crown stating that the price of slaves had more than doubled in Cabo Verde, which almost certainly represents a corresponding spike in demand.[79] Indeed, during the 1530s, letters permitting the transfer of slaves from Africa to the New World tended to refer exclusively to the Western African region (known then as Cabo Verde and Guiné), and in Mexico Cortés himself contracted in 1542 to bring five hundred slaves from Cabo Verde.[80] By the 1540s, the price of African slaves was shooting up in the Indies as the demand for labour increased.[81] In 1543, a contract was signed to bring three hundred African slaves to Guatemala.[82] By the end of the 1540s *cimarrones* were widespread around Cartagena de las Indias (hereafter, Cartagena) and Panamá.[83] It was clear that the importation of Africans to the new colonies was a process which would not be reversed.

The proportion of American slaves derived from Western Africa was certainly significant. Curtin suggests that between 1526 and 1550 they constituted 80 percent of the slaves making for the New World, and Hugh Thomas claims that in the period to 1550 three-fourths of the slaves in Lima and Arequipa came from the "Guinea of Cape Verde".[84] The picture may have been even more pronounced than these figures suggest, because 247 of the 252 ships legally plying for slaves to Africa from Portugal between 1544 and 1550 went to Cabo Verde.[85] A royal decree of 1549 concerning taxes derived from slaves transported to the Indies only mentioned Cabo Verde as a source.[86] In 1557 a petition from

---

[78] Pike (1972: 119). Barrera's daughter, Maria, married an English sailor, Robert Tomson – see Conway (1927: 14).

[79] Scelle (1906: Vol. 1, 202 and 202 n.2).

[80] See the instructions to Don Pedro de Mendoza for his voyage to the Río de la Plata in 1534: "*vos daremos licéncia … para que destos Nuestros Regnos o del reyno de Portugal o Islas de Cabo Verde y Guinea, vos o quien nuestro poder hubieres podais llevar y lleveis a las tierras…. 200 esclavos negros …*" – H. and P. Chaunu (1955: Vol. 2, 245); Aguirre Beltrán (1989: 22).

[81] AGI, Indiferente 737, no. 49 – December 12, 1540.

[82] AGI, Guatemala 49, no. 26 – March 12, 1543.

[83] Navarrete (2003: 27).

[84] Curtin (1975: 13); Thomas (1997: 117). Both these figures derive from Lockhart (1968: 173).

[85] For the statistics of these ships, including their names and destinations, see Ventura (1999: 121–33).

[86] AGI, Indiferente 1964, fol. 366v: "*sobre lo que toca al pago de los derechos de almoxarifazgo de los esclavos que se cargaren pa' las yndias en cavo verde*".

Mexico City noted that all the factories of Lisbon slave merchants were in Cabo Verde; it would be impossible to differentiate slaves brought from Cabo Verde from those from São Tomé and [Upper] Guinea, it said, because slaves did not come directly from either São Tomé or [Upper] Guinea to New Spain.[87] Indeed, as Gonzalo Aguirre Beltrán, the path-finding historian of African slavery in Mexico wrote, up to the 1560s "the islands of Cabo Verde and the rivers of Guinea were the only noted [places from which slaves were registered as arriving in Mexico]".[88] This conclusive data warns us to beware of the arguments of Heywood and Thornton as to the predominant role of West-Central Africans in shaping "Atlantic Creole" identity in the late sixteenth and early seventeenth centuries.[89]

Quantification is not a prime purpose of this book, but certainly the volume of slaves exported from Western Africa in these years was large. Writing circa 1560, Las Casas estimated that in the years since the direct export of slaves began in 1518, 30,000 had been brought direct to Hispaniola and over 100,000 to the Indies as a whole.[90] Bowser suggests that this figure was exaggerated, and it must be noted that Las Casas exhibited a tendency to inflate numbers.[91] Yet Las Casas felt ashamed at having promoted the export of African slaves and may not have been as inclined to exaggerate with this statistic as he was with others.[92]

Las Casas's figures may have been broadly accurate. By the middle of the sixteenth century, two thousand African slaves per year were entering Hispaniola, before being transported to other parts of the Americas.[93] Each sugar plantation, or *ingenio*, on that island alone often employed between 150 and 200 slaves.[94] A judge from the Audiencia of the island who resided there between 1557 and 1564 wrote that there was one *ingenio* with 900 slaves and that there were 20,000 Black slaves on the

[87] AGI, Justicia 204, No. 3, Ramo 1 – Question 9 of the *interrogatorio* of merchants from Mexico City relating to the slave trade; also, fol. 7v: "*de guinea y santo tome no vienen negros derechamente aesta nueva españa*". That is, slaves from Upper Guinea were taken first to Cabo Verde and transported thence to the Indies.

[88] Aguirre Beltrán (1989: 29).

[89] Heywood/Thornton (2007). For a further critique of the "Angolan wave" hypothesis founded on new data from Cartagena, see Wheat (2009: 103).

[90] Las Casas (1966b: Vol. 66, 30).

[91] Bowser (1974: 11).

[92] On Las Casas's remorse over this issue, see Mellafe (1975: 15).

[93] Deive (1989: 55). Torrão (2010: 8) also sees an annual average of approximately 2000 slaves as a reasonable estimate for exports of slaves from Cabo Verde during this period.

[94] Ratekin (1954: 14).

island in total – a figure which makes Las Casas' estimate of 30,000 slaves imported to the island between 1518 and 1560 look reasonable.[95]

It was easy for the actual number of slaves in the Indies to surpass those for whom licences had been granted in Spain. Because no register of slaves was kept on ships departing Cabo Verde and such registers were taken only on arrival in Hispaniola, contraband was easy, and slaves could be offloaded in secret before arrival for their official registry at the port of Santo Domingo.[96] As we saw previously, contraband to Hispaniola was widespread by 1526 at the latest, and by 1541 there was contraband to Puerto Rico, with 241 slaves alleged to have been sailed there without licence; in his letter describing this, Licenciado Villalobos noted the danger of a general fraud in the slave trade through "the fraud which … it would be possible to carry out, using the said licence to bring many more slaves than those permitted in the actual licence".[97] Contraband is impossible to estimate for these years; although it is known to have been widespread by the early seventeenth century, this evidence suggests it began considerably earlier.[98] This meant that the actual number of slaves imported was probably much greater than official figures would allow, and using these figures for the sixteenth century is likely to lead to serious errors.[99]

Taken in the round, this data suggests that an estimate of a total annual average of roughly 2,500 slaves exported from Western Africa to the Spanish Indies in the second quarter of the sixteenth century is not unreasonable. This figure is probably rather conservative if we recall the estimates we saw in Chapter 2 of Duarte Pacheco Pereira of roughly 3,500 exported annually from Upper Guinea circa 1505, especially if we remember than an additional annual quantity of slaves would have been

[95] Echagoian (1941: 446).
[96] AGI, Justicia 883, no. 3: the ship captain Gregorio de Espinosa asked of his witness whether it is not true that "*quando se an de cargar esclavos para yndias en las yslas de cabo verde no se asse ni faze ninguna Registro de los dichos esclavos que se cargan mas de el que se haze en esta ciudad [de Santo Domingo]*" – "when slaves are loaded for the Indies in the islands of Cabo Verde no register is made of the said slaves except for that which is made in this city [of Santo Domingo]".
[97] AGI, Justicia 991, No. 1, Ramo 4, fol. 1v: "*los fraudes q … se podria hazer q con color de la dha licencia se podría llevar mucho mas numero de esclavos de los tenidos en la dha. licencia*".
[98] On the importance of contraband in this period, see Mellafe (1975: 72). On contraband in the seventeenth-century trade to Cartagena, see Newson/Minchin (2007: 65–6) and Green (2007b: Part 3).
[99] For a new perspective on the volume of the slave trade between 1570 and 1640, see Wheat (2009: 77–120).

destined for Portugal and for Cabo Verde. These need to be added to
the figure quoted by Las Casas to give an idea of the total trade here.
Moreover, we should bear in mind that Las Casas's figure does not take
into account slaves bound for Brazil, though there was a trickle of these
by the 1540s.[100] Certainly, this sort of volume is credible for the export
trade from Western Africa when we consider that the slave trade from
Kongo to São Tomé and Elmina was regularly estimated at between four
and five thousand annually in the 1530s and 1540s.[101]

This figure is, however, far higher than most historians will allow. Even
Bühnen, whose work acts as a corrective to previous extremely low estimates, only suggests the possibility of a minimum annual export figure
of one thousand slaves in the years 1500–1550.[102] The problem is that
the historiography of slave export figures in these years has been petrified
ever since the mid-1950s by the work of the Chaunus.[103] However, as
Bühnen noted, reliance on Spanish shipping licences in the period 1551–
1595 (their preferred method) would lead to an annual average of slaves
exported of only 421.[104] Although the new Trans-Atlantic Slave Trade
Database suggests higher figures, these are still insufficient to take into
account the contraband and voyages for which we have no record (cf.
Introduction).

For these lower figures are incompatible with both contemporary slave
export figures as noted in first-hand accounts and also with the need for
labour in the Americas following the genocide there. When we consider
the collapse of the Taíno population, the idea of an import of roughly
1,000 African slaves per annum to supply labour needs to Hispaniola
alone seems reasonable, and certainly much more plausible than the far
lower figure which relying on the export licences produces. As we saw
earlier, Puerto Rico was another locale where the Native American population had vanished, and thus again there is evidence of contraband from
1541 and of unlicensed ships sent directly to Cabo Verde to procure slaves
in 1553.[105] By 1560 petitions in Lima were describing the purchase of a
"very large number of slaves" and stating that "there is such a large number of slaves" in the viceroyalty.[106] The chronicler of the Spanish conquest

---

[100] By the 1540s the volume of general trade with Brazil was quite considerable, much more
than allowed by previous historians according to Coelho Filho (2000: 65–6).
[101] MMAI: Vol. 2, 58; ibid., Vol. 2, 200.
[102] Bühnen (1993: 84–6).
[103] H. and P. Chaunu (1955).
[104] Bühnen (1993: 83).
[105] AGI, Justicia 996, No. 2, Ramo 2.
[106] AGI, Justicia 432, No. 1, Ramo 2, fols. 1r ("*muy gran suma de negros*") and 8r ("*como
ay tanta copia de esclavos*").

of Mexico, Bernal Díaz, described the Mexica who ruled Tenochtitlán under Cuáhtemoc and Moctezuma as bringing "as many slaves to be sold in the market [of Tlatelolco] as the Portuguese bring blacks from Guinea".[107] These phrases would have had little resonance if only a few hundred slaves were annually entering New Spain and Peru.

Thus we would certainly do well, as Bühnen suggests, to take the reports of eyewitnesses as giving an "impression of the order of magnitude"; though perhaps exaggerated at times, they are corroborated and broadly borne out by different eyewitness accounts and also by pan-Atlantic factors.[108] An egregious problem with the quantitative approach to the early trans-Atlantic trade therefore is that it has made many historians obsessed with numbers and encouraged them to forget the social, cultural and political implications in Africa of the trans-Atlantic slave trade – it is also that, having encouraged them to focus on numbers, it has encouraged them to focus on the wrong ones.

In Cabo Verde, the trade had important effects. As the most important slaving factory at this time, the development of new markets in the Americas stimulated commercial activity.[109] By 1550 an anonymous pilot would recount how ships were "continually arriving with goods from many countries, and provinces, principally the Spanish Indies".[110] The arrival of these goods allowed both trade and the urban apparatus to grow. Ribeira Grande, said the pilot, was a city of 500 hearths.[111] The extent of the growth in the preceding generation is emphasised by the census of 1513, which gave the city a population of seventy-four residents [*vyzinhos*], fifty-six temporary residents [*estantes*], sixteen Blacks [*negros*], twelve clerics and three friars.[112] Although these figures exclude slaves and the consonance between residents and hearths is inexact, considerable growth is clearly represented. Indeed, in a 1572 census the average number of residents per registered hearth was 9.8.[113] This would indicate a population of circa 4,900 in 1550, as opposed to the 159 residents recorded in 1513; even assuming a ratio of slaves to free men of 10:1, this would not give a population much more than 1,600, or less than one-third of that thirty-five years later.[114]

---

[107] Díaz (1963: 222).
[108] Bühnen (1993: 86).
[109] Vila Vilar (1977: 145); Torrão (1991: 309).
[110] Anonymous (1551/2: 89).
[111] Ibid., 85.
[112] HGCV: CD, Vol. 1, 221.
[113] MMAII: Vol. 3, 28–53.
[114] This was the ratio in a 1582 census of Francisco de Andrade – see ibid., Vol. 3, 99, 102.

The accelerating commercial interest in Cabo Verde was revealed also by the sheer numbers of traders coming to the islands. In the inquisitorial trial of Branca Dias examined in Chapter 4, large numbers of witnesses were consulted in Lisbon in 1543, all of whom gave evidence gleaned from trading visits to Santiago and Fogo. Some of these witnesses were Caboverdeans trading in Lisbon, others were Portuguese who had been in Cabo Verde recently.[115] One of the witness statements taken in Ribeira Grande for this trial came from a Madeiran trader who had most likely come to buy slaves.[116] Similarly, in an earlier case examined on Hispaniola in 1528 concerning a slave who claimed he had been freed by his master in Cabo Verde and illegally sold, many witnesses had recently arrived from Cabo Verde.[117]

Thus international trading patterns confirm the commercial importance of Cabo Verde in the emergent Atlantic world of the sixteenth century. Moreover, this evidence shows also that the early trans-Atlantic slave trade coincided with the rapid growth of the urban economy and apparatus of Cabo Verde. Ribeira Grande's city status was confirmed by the creation of the see there in 1533, indicating its importance.[118] The consolidation of urban space is also revealed by the growing attraction of the islands to other European powers, notably France. By 1536 there were reports of French ships in Cabo Verde.[119] By 1540 the attacks of pirate French ships in the African Atlantic were sufficient to make the brother of the king of Kongo fearful of the voyage to Lisbon.[120] Further reports of French attacks in Cabo Verde came in 1542 and 1544.[121] Yet none of this was enough to deter the Portuguese traders, and by 1544 the city was important enough that commercial families in Lisbon sent relatives there to act as their agents.[122]

---

[115] IAN/TT, Inquisição de Lisboa, Processo 5729, fols. 26v, 27v.

[116] Ibid., fol. 20v.

[117] AGI, Justicia 11, No. 4.

[118] MMAII: Vol. 2, 235–6; this came with the bull *Pro Excellenti*.

[119] Ford (1931: 274): a letter of João III which states that "*encomendovos muito que trabalhais pera aver verdadeira enformaçam dos navios de França, que dizeis que foram achados na Ilha de Cabo Verde*".

[120] AG, Vol. 5, 160.

[121] MMAII: Vol. 2, 345, 370; Barcellos (1899: 120).

[122] AGI, Indiferente 416, Libro 2, 54v-55r: a document dated September 4, 1544, on the Armada of Francisco de Orellana going to Nueva Andalucía: "*en lo que dis que un hombre rrico portugués q vive en Portugal prometió al adelantado quando allí estubo de darle cinquenta vacas en la ysla de Santiago de Cabo Verde y que un hijo suyo questa en esa ciudad…*"

French attacks were a product of Ribeira Grande's perceived success and illustrated how the urban growth of Ribeira Grande was directly connected to the boom in Atlantic slaving, which was a concrete reality, on this evidence, by the end of the 1530s. It was Cabo Verde's position at the heart of the web of connections linking Europe with Africa and America that saw its rapid expansion in this period. Without the appropriation of surplus labour from Africa and the insertion of the people who provided it in America, there could be no growth either in Ribeira Grande or in the Atlantic as a whole. The Atlantic boom at its heart required the appropriation of a new labour supply; further, it needed the requisitioning of the products of that supply for the boosting of the economic markets of Europe, not the African locales from which the people who provided that labour had come. Thus the creation of an urban economy in Ribeira Grande was the product of the violence that went with the growth of the slave trade and of the American genocide. It was no accident that, as we saw in the last chapter, as this pattern of trans-Atlantic violence and slaving accelerated, so did the pattern of creolisation across the Western African region; for thus was the institutional violence of Atlantic slavery connected to the accommodations and mixtures inherent in creolisation of language and cultures from the beginning.

THE IMPACT OF TRANS-ATLANTIC SLAVING ON CYCLES OF VIOLENT DISORDER AND CREOLISATION, TO CIRCA 1550

As we have seen in this chapter, the pivotal role of Cabo Verde as a slaving hub in the early trans-Atlantic trade had many implications for the Western African region. It reinforced the institutionalisation of violence and thus of creolisation on Cabo Verde. It did so, moreover, within an economic paradigm which encouraged the growth of the Caboverdean economy as a whole, particularly of the metropolitan economy associated with Ribeira Grande. It also encouraged the increasing frequency of the exchanges between the islands and the coast, because slaves for the Atlantic market had to go through Cabo Verde; thus the growing demand necessitated an increase in links between the islands and the coast. As Caboverdeans traded for slaves, the labour demands from the wider Atlantic region beyond Cabo Verde became connected to the growth of creolisation across Western Africa.

This connection of the trans-Atlantic demand for labour to African-European exchanges on the mainland was extremely important. We saw in the last chapter how the pattern of creolisation among Kassanké elites was connected to benefits which different lineages accrued from connection to *lançados*. Here, through the connection to trans-Atlantic slaving, we see in more detail than ever before how and why this pattern developed. For the connections of *lançados* to African lineage heads was impossible to separate from the *lançado* trade in slaves. Connections to *lançados* meant connection to the violence of the pan-Atlantic economy, and this was something that inevitably brought about changes in the fortunes of both individual lineages and of the relationships between one lineage and another. Very soon, trans-Atlantic slaving became impossible to separate from the political and social changes that had begun to transform the region. It had become clear that the role of the demand side of the Atlantic economy was having a strong influence in intra-lineage struggles and the growing cycle of violent disorder affecting Western Africa.

We can begin to look at the evidence for this through the inquisitorial case we looked at in the last chapter involving António Fernandes and Manoel Garcia. In the petition of the elders of Cacheu to Fernandes, it was claimed that Garcia had seized "*negros*" from the region, tied them up and sold them as slaves, and that he "took slaves tied up which he seized by force in the said River".[123] This suggests that the Brames who lived in the Cacheu region were suffering from raids linked to the expansion in the slave trade. This supposition is supported by the evidence on slave identities from America. Here, the Brame are one of the most represented groups for this period (see Table I.1).

It is useful here to recall that, elsewhere in the trial, Fernandes accused Garcia of being "*lançado*" with the "King of Cassamanssa" and had supplied him with firearms. This evidence, when put together with the petition from Cacheu, therefore suggests that Garcia may have been acting as something like an agent for the Kassanké lineage head, seizing slaves from the southern Cacheu region which was the extremity of his zone of control and taking them to Bugendo for sale into the Atlantic market. This would suggest not only that the Kassanké remained the most powerful force in the region, but also that the demands for labour in America were aggravating the tensions between groups in Upper Guinea and leading to predatory attacks by powerful groups on others. Indeed, the large number of Brame slaves in the Americas at this time is evidence for this pattern and implies that they were seized through a combination of

---

[123] IAN/TT, Inquisição de Lisboa, Proceso 801, fols. 62v, 63r: "*levava negros amarrados q tomava por força no dito Rio*".

Kassanké and *lançado* rapacity (see Table I.1). It may have been precisely this pattern which precipitated both the violent resistance to *lançado* and Caboverdean traders in Casamance in the 1550s (cf. Chapter 5) and the willingness of smaller decentralised groups such as the Balanta and Floup to enter into the slave trade by securing captives through village raids, as is suggested by the data of slave origins (see Table I.2 for the 1560s). As Hawthorne has shown, such strategies were vital for these groups to secure the quantities of iron and other goods which were necessary for self-defence.[124] Taken in the round, this material would suggest that it was from the mid- to late 1540s that such strategies began to be developed in Upper Guinea.

Thus the alliance between *lançados* and Kassanké and its connection to trans-Atlantic trade led both to violent raids of more powerful groups on others in Upper Guinea and to new strategies among decentralised groups. This hypothesis tallies with other material. Almada documented attacks by the Mandinka of the Gambia on the Arriata people who lived along the coast between the Gambia and Casamance estuaries, describing how "[the Mandinka] prepared very beautiful battle canoes, and travelled along the River Gambia out to sea, following the coast south of the Cabo de Santa Maria, until they met with Arriatas and Floups who live there. And when this conquest and war began, they captured many people".[125] These attacks clearly dated from some time before Almada was writing in the late sixteenth century, probably from around the period of this dispute between Fernandes and Garcia: Almada noted that the Arriatas, though initially not knowing how to defend themselves, had improved and had learnt to "fight and defend themselves and kill and capture their enemies".[126]

This heavy depredation of Mandinka slavers is suggestive of the growing power of the Kaabu federation in these years. A noteworthy aspect of the evidence from the Americas on slave identities in the 1540s and 1550s is that the Biafada were the most represented group (see Table I.1). The Biafada were, as we saw in Chapter 2, located at the southern boundary of Mandinka-influenced Upper Guinea. The large numbers of Biafada traded to the Americas in these years suggests that their independent

[124] Hawthorne (2003).

[125] MMAII: Vol. 3, 288: "*armando almadias de guerra mui formosas, e botando pelo Rio de Gâmbia fora, correndo a costa do Cabo de Santa Maria para baixo, e dão nos Arriatas e Falupos, que vivem ao longo dessa costa. E quando começaram esta conquista e guerra, cativavam muita gente*".

[126] Ibid.: "*pelejam e se defendem e matam e cativam aos inimigos*".

status was being eroded by their proximity to the Kaabu Mandinka. Thus as in Casamance, weaker groups such as the Biafada were squeezed by the alliance of powerful local polities and the emissaries of the new Atlantic trade.[127] As the trans-Atlantic trade expanded, so did existing tensions between lineages, as alliances and strategies for dealing with long-distance maritime trade were developed to try to overcome the new patterns of violence.

However, as well as preying on the weaker groups of Upper Guinea, these new Atlantic traders also supplied the wherewithal for self-defence. Indeed, both the violence of the slave trade and the opportunity for defence were connected. Societies sought to procure iron to defend themselves from slavers and enhance their agricultural potential and therefore their populations, in what Hawthorne has called the "iron-slave cycle".[128] At least some of this iron was smelted in Sierra Leone and then exchanged in Casamance ports for slaves, as evidenced by the 1526 expedition of the ship Santiago.[129] The role of *lançados* as middlemen in this trade and conduits for new sources of iron from the Atlantic meant that new avenues opened up which these societies would not be slow to explore in shoring up their positions in this Atlantic world. Crucially from the Upper Guinean perspective, these new avenues were connected to a realignment of ritual as well as political power, because the opportunity for finding new sources of iron eroded the influence of the smiths and left the door open for alternative spirit shrines believed to mediate with the supernatural to emerge.[130] Thus the new patterns of violence and war related to Atlantic slaving helped to bring about changes in ritual and belief systems which had enduring effects on the peoples of the region.[131]

However, these new and transformative patterns of belief and exchange were overlaid with patterns of intra-lineage violence, as illustrated by these charges against Garcia and by Almada's account of Mandinka raids on the Arriatas, so that many of the slaves sold in Casamance had been seized rather than bartered. The "iron-slave" cycle could not be separated from the "slave-gold" and "slave-sugar" cycles which had sprung up in

---

[127] The Biafada were subject to vicious slaving attacks from the Bijagó in the late sixteenth and early seventeenth centuries (cf. Chapter 8), but these were not the cause of their presence in the slave registers of the 1540s and 1550s; following an attack by Caboverdeans on the island of Canhabaque in 1538, Bijagó shunned the Atlantic trade for many years (Brooks 1993b: 263).

[128] Hawthorne (2003: 92–3).

[129] T. Hall (1992: Vol. 1, 122–32).

[130] Baum (1999).

[131] Ibid.; Shaw (2002).

the Americas, whereby gold and sugar were returned to Europe in the very ships which had brought slaves from Western Africa, in a foretaste of Britain's well-known triangular trade of the eighteenth century.[132] Thus the cultural exchanges which went with extensive *lançado* presence in Casamance and facilitated the evolution of a mixed culture, as well as the expansion of Atlantic creolisation from Cabo Verde, were the flip-side of the violence which went with the procurement of slaves in the first place.

This interconnection of trans-Atlantic slavery to intra-lineage relations is confirmed by events in Senegambia. As we have seen, the early focus for the procurement of slaves among the Jolof had needed to change as the Jolof became more hostile to Atlantic trade (cf. Chapter 2). From then on, although Jolof slaves did go to the Americas, their numbers were much lower than in the trade with the Iberian peninsula of the late fifteenth and early sixteenth centuries (cf. Table I.1). For the Jolof, relationships of supply and demand shifted. In 1529, three years before the decree prohibiting the import of Jolof slaves to America, the Damel of Cajor wrote to the Portuguese crown asking for masons and carpenters to be sent to help build a fort. In an interesting aside, the Damel noted that he sent the same request with a gift of fifteen slaves eight years previously. Evidently nothing had happened. The hostility directed towards Portuguese traders by some Jolof in the early 1500s had affected how Atlantic traders saw their trade with the Jolof. The Jolof may have been major trading partners in the recent past, but the Portuguese were inclined to leave them alone to sort out internal struggles which they had in part precipitated.[133]

Moreover, religious questions were coming to be of increasing importance in the relationships between Cajor and the Atlantic world. Almada noted the importance which Cajor had once held in the trade with the Caboverdean islands and also how that importance had declined:

> In the past, the islanders of Santiago had their greatest trade with this land of [Cajor], when there was a king called Nhogor who was a great friend of our people. In that time there was a great famine on that coast, caused by locusts, and slaves were sold for half an *alqueire* of millet or beans [about six and a half litres]; and mothers cast out their children from them and sold them in exchange for provisions, saying that

---

[132] On the existence of this slave-gold cycle, see AGI, Indiferente 1092, no. 242 – April 1537; and AGI, Indiferente 1962, Libro 5, fols. 1–2–1536. On the slave-sugar cycle, see AGI, Indiferente 1092, no. 118 – November 17, 1535; and AGI, Indiferente 1962, Libro 4, fols. 13r-v – also 1535.

[133] For this letter, see MMAII: Vol. 2, 215. As things transpired, the Damel emerged as the most powerful of the Jolof kings, according to Almada (ibid.,Vol. 3, 241).

it was better for them to live, even as captives, than to die because of the famine.... Ships sailed every year from Santiago laden with horses and other goods for this trade. Then a new king succeeded to the throne called Budumel, a *bixirim* [Moslem scholar], who did not drink wine or eat pork; he lived permanently at his court in Lambaia, a long way from the sea, and paid our people badly ... and this was why the people of Santiago left this trade.[134]

This passage illuminates how regional patterns changed. The trade of Nhogor with the Caboverdeans, praised by Almada, was essentially that of a comparatively weak ruler who suffered difficulties because of the environmental stresses of famine and who also wanted to achieve independence from the centre of the Jolof empire. By contrast, the latter king's attitude is one of greater strength and is shaped substantially, at least on Almada's hostile account, by cultural patterns and a strong adherence to Islam. From the evidence we have seen, this strength was itself the product of earlier Atlantic trade by rulers of Cajor.

The upshot was that the Portuguese began to look elsewhere for a reliable slave supply to meet the growing American demand. In particular, they turned to the Jolof's immediate southern neighbours, the Sereer. We should recall here that the growing strength of the Sereer may date to around 1500 and that they themselves had been forged as a hybrid group from Kaabunké, Sereer-Cosaan and Jolof components (cf. Chapters 1–2). This was therefore a new lineage which needed allies to bolster its strength, and this made the ability of the Portuguese to forge an alliance with them much easier to understand.

This was an instance of a complete cycle within the African-Atlantic paradigm, for the strengthened Sereer polity was as we have seen itself triggered in part by the growing weakness of the Jolof empire that followed the Atlantic opening. Thus the ability of Atlantic traders to liaise with the Sereer in the first half of the sixteenth century was a direct

---

[134] Ibid., Vol. 3, 250–1: "*Antigamente o maior trato que tinham os moradores da Ilha de Santiago era para esta terra do Budomel, no tempo que nela reinava um rei chamado Nhogor, muito amigo dos nossos, no tempo do qual houve tamanha fome naquela costa, causada dos gafanhotos, que se vendiam os escravos por meio alqueire de milho ou feijão; e tiravam as mães os filhos de si, e os vendiam a troco de mantimento, dizendo que mais valia viverem, ainda que cativo, que não morrerem à pura fome...da Ilha de Cabo Verde iam todos os annos carregados de cavallos e outras mercadorias a este resgate. Sucedeu neste Reino o Rei chamado Budomel, bixirim, o qual não bebia vinho nem comia carne de porco; este residia contínuo na sua côrte de Lambaia, longe do mar, e fazia maus pagamentos aos nossos ... E por essa causa deixaram os moradores desta Ilha este resgate*".

consequence of the new Atlantic world. In this case Atlantic factors not only helped to precipitate Sereer autonomy, but also helped to consolidate it through the opportunities which they offered for alliances and the trade of horses for slaves, which strengthened the Sereer cavalry.

Fundamental to the new Sereer-Portuguese relationship was the pre-Atlantic history of the Sereer. They and their forerunners had long been preyed on for slaves by the Jolof for the trans-Saharan trade. The advent of the Atlantic trade meant that Sereer leaders saw an opportunity to increase their own relative power vis-à-vis the Jolof. Thus, over the middle third of the sixteenth century, the Sereer became one of the main partners of Atlantic traders in the region.[135] Shortly after describing the relationship of Caboverdeans with Cajor, Almada described how the islanders had had a long and fruitful trade with the Sereer, with "many shipments ... with horses"; the Caboverdeans also clearly used their contacts farther south in Upper Guinea; they brought "wax and ivory" as well as cloths woven in their islands to trade among the Sereer.[136]

It is clear from the documents that have survived that the Sereer's entrance to the Atlantic world expanded their power. According to Almada, by the 1570s they often fought with the Jolof and defeated them, reversing previous patterns.[137] That this strength derived from an especially intense engagement in Atlantic trade is shown by an event in early 1542, when French ships seized a trading vessel from Cabo Verde, which had been sailing in the company of "six or seven other ships belonging to the residents [of Santiago] which were trading, and which were forced by gunfire to take shelter in the Barbacin river [kingdom of the Sereers]. And they stayed behind the bar for fifteen days before they could leave".[138] Clearly, the Sereer were allies of the Caboverdeans or these ships could not have sheltered there; moreover, the large number of ships hints at a vital trade. Thus it can be surmised that the early Atlantic trade with the Jolof had been displaced to the lands of the Sereer.

The evidence becomes even clearer when we consider the proportions of Jolof and Sereer slaves in the Americas by the late 1540s and 1550s (see Table I.1). The Jolof were the third largest group in the Americas

---

[135] On the Sereer as major trading partners of Caboverdeans at this time, see T. Hall (1992: Vol. 1, 143–6).
[136] MMAII: Vol. 3, 257, 257 n.3 – the Porto manuscript of Almada's treatise refers to the trade in horses; the Lisbon one to the trade in cloths, wax and ivory.
[137] Ibid., Vol. 3, 256.
[138] Ibid., Vol. 2, 344: "*E correram [atrás de] seys ou sete navyos outros dos moradores que estavam em resgate, e com zabras de remos artilhados os foram meter no Rio das Barbaçys. E esteveram na boqua da barra xb dias aguardãdo que saysem*".

then, with perhaps twice the numerical strength of that of the Sereer. The likelihood is that many of these slaves were sold to the Caboverdean and Portuguese traders by the Sereer, and that this was a pattern which had developed by the late 1530s and 1540s, when most of the slaves whose origins are recorded for this period would have been procured.

From the evidence we saw earlier from Almada, the Sereer alliance with the Caboverdeans stood them in good stead, so that in the 1570s they were still frequently defeating their Jolof neighbours in battle. The requirements of labour supply from the Americas had thus not only helped to catalyse the shift in the locale of African-European relations in Senegambia from Jolof lands to the Sereer; it had also contributed to a shift in Senegambian power relations, as the evidence of slave populations in the Americas and this evidence from Almada confirm. Whereas pre-existing cultural factors in the region had shaped how African-European exchanges first began, by the middle third of the sixteenth century the way in which those exchanges evolved could no longer be separated from wider Atlantic factors.

Nevertheless, the internal structures of African societies and continuity with pre-existing patterns of trade continued to be of fundamental importance in shaping African-European exchanges. As we saw in the first half of this book, external trade demands were not simply imposed on African societies. The importance of continuities emerges, for instance, in the commercial networks which *lançados* helped to develop in the Casamance during this era around the procurement of slaves. For these were overlaid on existing trade patterns, such as the networks linking Bainunk in the north and Biafada and Sape in the south of the Upper Guinea region, and which hitherto had dealt largely with the exchange of kola nuts, salt, dried fish and other agricultural goods (cf. below, Chapter 8).[139]

The importance of pre-existing structures for the patterns of African-European relations emerges most clearly in settlement patterns of Europeans living in Africa and connected to the trans-Atlantic trade. To the north of the Gambia River, societies were structured along patrilinear kinship lines, which meant that power was wielded and inherited through the male line; thus the children of incoming Europeans could not be accommodated by marrying local women.[140] Although the Caboverdeans therefore had some success among both the Jolof and the Sereer, by the

[139] Hawthorne (2003: 56–7, 92); Brooks (1980: 6) and Brooks (1993b).
[140] Barry (1998: 28).

time that Almada was writing he noted ruefully that the Caboverdean trade with the Sereer was increasingly weak and that the English and the French had taken over.[141]

The inability to have a settled population acting as brokers was probably decisive here, because Caboverdean trading success depended on having members of their mercantile diaspora settled in Africa. As cultural structures north of the Gambia made this difficult, Caboverdeans turned to the south of the Gambia. As we have seen, it was there in the matrilinear "rivers of Guinea" that the *lançados* achieved the most success. The societies there allowed them to integrate and form a new caste, because children inherited their (African) mother's lineage ties. This area was, moreover, the growing focus of the slave trade, as is shown by Almada's reference to the English and French trade among the Sereer; the English and French did not trade slaves to America at this time, and thus their trade with the Sereer must have been for other goods such as ivory, wax and hides.[142]

The structure of African societies had thus not only affected the settlement patterns of Caboverdeans. It had also helped to determine which areas were most affected by the trans-Atlantic slave trade itself. For it was the Caboverdeans, hailing from one of the original slave societies of the Atlantic world and deeply involved with the shipment of slaves to America, who were key to the functioning of that trade. Thus as the sixteenth century developed, it was to Upper Guinea that the Caboverdeans increasingly turned in their quest to procure slaves. As the contraband trade exploded after 1550, Senegambia's importance to the trans-Atlantic slave trade became increasingly marginal, and processes of cultural and political transformation related to slavery were concentrated south of the Gambia. With the structure of societies there helping *lançados* to integrate, they would also find other local factors which made this region the epicentre for the procurement of slaves for transport to America in the second half of the sixteenth century.

---

[141] MMAII: Vol. 3, 259.

[142] For instance, as a letter of the friar Diogo de Encarnação noted in September 1584, regarding events farther south along the African coast, the French on the Malaguetta coast (modern Liberia) went specifically to trade pepper and ivory – MMAI: Vol. 3, 276 – "*falavão algũas palavras em Francès, & hé porque todo seu trato tem com Francezes, que vão resgatar com elles Malagueta & Marfim*".

7

Trading Ideas and Trading People

The Boom in Contraband Trade from Western Africa, circa 1550–1580

The period between 1550 and 1580 saw a rapid expansion in the trade in slaves from Africa to the Americas. The conquest of the two major imperial powers in the Americas, the Incas and the Mexica, had seen similar demographic realities to those which had already devastated the Caribbean islands. However, the vast territorial expanse and the riches offered by the silver and gold mines of Mexico and Peru meant that the expense of buying African slaves could be offset by the wealth of the colonies. As new mines were discovered in the Nuevo Reino de Granada in the 1580s, the demand for slaves continued to grow. The Spanish imperial economy became characterised by the mines of the mainland; the prosperous sugar plantations of Hispaniola and Puerto Rico fell into decline in the late sixteenth century as these islands were displaced from official trading routes and the *carrerra de Índias* took shape via Havana, Cuba.[1]

Throughout this period, Western Africa remained the dominant source of American-bound slaves. There was a steady trickle of slaves from Angola and Kongo to the New World, but the clear majority still came from the region that traded via Cabo Verde to America, and only with the Portuguese conquest of Luanda in 1575 did this begin to change. The expanding cycle of demand in the Americas therefore initially had most impact among the peoples of Upper Guinea, as new strategies were developed both to procure slaves in this region and for defence against predatory attacks by slave raiders.

These realities, however, took time to filter through to the Iberian crowns. As we have seen at previous points in this book, Iberian

[1] Fuente (2008: 138).

institutions of state often passed decrees which merely caught up with reality. For all the professions of divine and imperial grandeur, the Iberian monarchies of the early sixteenth century did not have the institutional power to shape the reality of trade in the new Atlantic world as much as they would have liked. This trade was shaped just as much by the actors on the ground: in Africa, by Upper Guinean elites and members of the New Christian trading diasporas; and in the Americas, by the colonists whose needs changed much more quickly than the Spanish crown's bureaucracy could accommodate. Such institutional frailties meant that throughout the sixteenth century, the numbers of licenses sold by the Spanish crown to import African slaves to the Americas were far less than what was required.

Thus a vast contraband trade grew up to secure the labour supply of the New World, a trade which tapped the new systems of slave procurement of Western Africa. This chapter's major focus is to analyse in great detail and for the first time these contraband networks and the likely numbers involved. A variety of sources originating in Iberia and Latin America are consulted to show that the official figures for slave exports in these years are gross underestimates, and thus that constructing estimates based on these figures is a flawed enterprise. This quantitative conclusion has far-reaching consequences when it comes to considering the impact of the sixteenth-century trans-Atlantic slave trade on the societies of Western Africa; this aspect of the question is touched on here, but is analysed in far greater depth in the chapter which follows.

The second major theme of this chapter is to expand our understanding of the contours of what I have called pan-Atlantic space in the sixteenth century. A consequence of the Atlantic contraband trade was the growth in direct interconnections between Africa and the Americas, meaning that the commercial and social changes on both continents were linked. Fundamental to these links were the New Christians we followed in Chapters 4 and 5, whose trading connections in the Americas facilitated both the contraband trade and the connections between one continent and the other. By seeing how these New Christian networks operated on both sides of the Atlantic, we learn about both their role in contraband and the importance of diasporic links that worked alongside the imperial infrastructure in building the trade of the Atlantic. This picture supports new perspectives which have emphasised the role of diasporas in building the early Atlantic system.[2] The expansion of the trans-Atlantic slave

---

[2] Israel (2002); Studnicki-Gizbert (2007); Ebert (2008).

trade in the second half of the sixteenth century therefore depended on the successful role of this diaspora and, in continuity with previous commercial relationships, its interactions with host communities in Western Africa, a process which was examined in the first half of the book.

I concentrate here on the trans-Atlantic dimension of the trade from Western Africa to continue the argument of the previous chapter as to the global pressures that were increasingly coming to bear on societies there. Understanding how and why Creole society expanded in Western Africa in this era, and how and why the lineages there adapted to the pressures of Atlantic trade, requires a grasp of the broader global forces shaping the intensification of creolisation and slavery in the second half of the sixteenth century. For this was the era in which the contours of the Iberian Atlantic began to be defined, with the establishment of the *carrera de Índias* in the 1560s.[3] As the demands and opportunities of the new American economies developed, the direction of political and social changes became irreversible. Some concrete examples emerge in this chapter through examination of new patterns of production and supply that affected Western Africa in these decades.

The Atlantic perspective also allows us to see a further corollary of New Christian involvement in these processes. For this was the era in which the discrimination against New Christians based on *limpeza*, and the growing strength of the discourse of race on both sides of the Atlantic, began to produce increasingly transnational ideas of identity predicated on categories of caste; these ideas acted as a sort of shared ideology which helped to bind the trading networks of the Atlantic together.[4] As the lynchpin joining the regional trades within Western Africa to the global trades of the Atlantic, Cabo Verde was a place in which these new ideas intersected and were thus shaped by both local African and broader global influences.

Thus the chapter concludes by examining changes in Creole identity in Cabo Verde in detail, and by showing how these were connected to the global forces which helped to shape events in the islands with the expansion of trans-Atlantic trade. New Christian involvement in Western Africa and the growing importance of ideas of race influenced aspects of Creole identity in Cabo Verde, especially among the elite Creole traders whose connections opened them to ideas elsewhere in the Atlantic world.

---

[3] H. and P. Chaunu (1955: Vol. 3, 144).

[4] Thus here I follow Bayly's view that a "transnational history of ideas" is a key element in understanding histories of transnationalism – Bayly et al. (2006).

This was an important factor in the construction of a shared ideological bond for the networks which expanded slavery in the second half of the sixteenth century, in continuity of the shared ideologies which for centuries had bound long-distance trading networks in West Africa since the days of the trans-Saharan trade.

THE DEMOGRAPHIC COLLAPSE IN THE AMERICAS AND THE ROLE OF CONTRABAND IN THE TRANS-ATLANTIC SLAVE TRADE FROM UPPER GUINEA

In the Americas, the demographic impact of the Spanish conquest was almost as bad as it had been in the Caribbean islands. Though the Inca, Mapuche, Mexica, Purépecha and other Native American peoples did not share the fate of the Taíno in disappearing completely, their populations were decimated. Estimates as to the demographic impacts vary, but many scholars agree that a total population loss of 90 percent of the original is not an unreasonable estimate.[5] Epidemics weakened the Native Americans and made them more prone to military defeat. Research suggests that key to the Spanish conquest of the Incas in the 1530s was the fact that smallpox had already devastated the Inca empire even before the Spanish arrived there, leading to weakness and internal divisions which the Spanish readily exploited.[6]

To take another example, the demographic impact in New Spain was no different. The first smallpox epidemic struck in 1520, and thereafter there were repeated catastrophes. The epidemic of 1545 was especially severe. In Tlaxcala, the city-state that had been a vital ally of Hernando Cortés's in the defeat of the Mexica, 150,000 people died; in nearby Cholula, 100,000.[7] To the north of Mexico City, in Michoacán, an estimated nine-tenths of the population passed away.[8] A further smallpox epidemic followed in Michoacán in 1563 and another epidemic in 1576. By 1580, in smaller towns of the sierra of Michoacán such as Xiquilpa, there was just one-twelfth of the original population.[9] Down by the Pacific coast, the population of Epatlan had dropped from five hundred to ten, and in Cuxquaquautla, from four hundred to five.[10]

---

[5] A good discussion of these debates is in Mann (2005: Part 1).
[6] Ibid., 87–90.
[7] Mendieta (1870: 515).
[8] López Sarrelangue (1965: 72).
[9] Ochoa/Sánchez (1985: 73).
[10] Ibid., 89.

Such were the demographic realities that characterised the Americas in the sixteenth century. Already by 1550, as these examples show, the situation was severe. The Native American population was simply too broken by the conquest and too weakened by a lack of epidemiological resistance to Old World diseases to offer the labour which the Spanish required. But with the Spanish crown slow to assimilate this reality and the prices of slave licenses still high in the *Casa de la Contratación* in Seville, legally importing the requisite number of slaves was costly. Although licenses for the import of 23,000 slaves were sold in Seville in 1557, this was still not enough to meet the demand.[11] Thus it was that the contraband trade in slaves from Western Africa, which had already begun in the 1520s, exploded in the years after 1550. This trade was soon key in the transport of peoples from Upper Guinea to America, and indeed, in the consolidation of the new American and European economies.

The new contraband trade operated through the Canary Islands. The register of goods on ships involved in the slave trade from Western Africa was taken on Gran Canaria.[12] Ships heading from Seville to Cabo Verde and Upper Guinea usually therefore called in at the Canaries to have the registers taken and to load wine, which was in high demand on Santiago, Cabo Verde.[13] This gave Canariote islanders a privileged position in developing links with Western Africa, and from at least the 1550s onwards, a heavy contraband trade developed, with the Canary Islands as a focal point. By January 1559 Portuguese men living in the Canaries were accused of preparing ships to go and trade slaves or seize them from the coast of West Africa, and this accusation was described as highly likely to be accurate "because of the custom of the Canariotes of going to Guiné … to trade and seize [slaves]".[14] Indeed, the writer of the letter in which these accusations were made, Martim Correia e Silva, said that he had received witness statements "that were taken in the Canaries in which the guilt of all these who go to Guiné and trade regularly there are very clear".[15]

---

[11] On the sale of these licenses, see AGI, Panamá 236, Libro 9, fol. 213v.

[12] AGI, Mexico, Legajo 22, no. 82, Ramo 1: "*en Gran Canaria, donde se suelen tomar registro.*"

[13] For examples of ships stopping at the Canaries see AGI, Escribanía 36A; AGI, Escribanía 165A, No. 1; AGI, Escribanía 947A, no. 2; AGN, NE, Cundinamarca, SC43, Legajo 8, fol. 690v.

[14] MMAI: Vol. 4, 219 – "*pelo custume em que estavão os das Canareas hirē a Guiné e ás outras terras de sua demarquação a resgatar e fazer saltos…*".

[15] Ibid., Vol. 4, 220: "*que se tirarão nas Canarias per que se constava muito claras as cullpas destes todos que vão a Guiné e tratão ordinariamente lá*".

The Portuguese authorities were well aware of this, and by 1564 their ambassador at the Spanish court, Francisco Pereira, had obtained precise details of this trade. He described how one Pedro Rodriguez of Tenerife had traded illegally for slaves in Guinea, buying one hundred fifty slaves and despatching them to Puerto Rico. This had been going on for ten years, said Pereira, and involved not only Rodriguez, but twenty-two other Canariotes, who had each sent ships on several occasions to get slaves from Western Africa and send them on to America. In a letter of March 1563, Philip II cited twenty-six Canariotes all involved in this trade. Rodriguez did not deny this but argued that it was not illegal; he admitted that the residents of Gran Canaria were heavily involved in the trade on the "coast of Guinea".[16] Other documents exist from Portuguese archives showing a concern about contraband trade in slaves from the Canaries.[17] This fits a wider pattern in which the Canaries were well-known as a focal point for Atlantic contraband in the sixteenth century.[18] The contraband slave trade affecting peoples of West Africa was thus heavily interconnected to that plying to Iberian settlements of the New World.

In America, too, officials lamented the growth of contraband. Havana was one favoured site, with ships accused of illegal slaving there from the 1560s onwards.[19] However, the main site for the illegal trade was Hispaniola. In August 1562 royal officials described how unlicensed slaves came to the Americas through ships docking at the port of Ocoa on Hispaniola, seventeen leagues from the city of Santo Domingo (approximately fifty miles/eighty-five kilometres). There was no colonial authority in Ocoa, and slaves were taken to a sugar mill a league from the port and smuggled elsewhere from there, both within Hispaniola and also on to New Spain.[20] Ships arrived directly from Upper Guinea with slaves who vanished out of sight of colonial officials. On April 21, 1562, for instance, a ship arrived at Ocoa filled with contraband slaves directly from the Magarabomba River in Sierra Leone, captained by a man named Garrucho.[21] It was well known that this was the usual stratagem, and just two years later a royal official in Veracruz urged the king to prohibit ships from stopping at Ocoa because this was where unregistered slaves

[16] AGI, Justicia 1167, no. 4 for this whole complaint.
[17] BA, Códice 49-X-2, fol. 289r.
[18] Fuente (2008: 24–5).
[19] Ibid., 40.
[20] AGI, Santo Domingo 899, Libro 1, fol. 265v.
[21] AGI, Patronato 173, No. 1, Ramo 5.

were unloaded.[22] But Ocoa retained its role in the smuggling trade, and cases emerged again in the 1570s where it was claimed that hundreds of slaves coming from Western Africa had been smuggled into Hispaniola through Ocoa.[23] So rife was this trade that it prompted disputes among royal officials as to who should take the register of newly arrived ships – the implication being that the disputes arose because of the potential to receive bribes in return for covering up the contraband trade.[24]

The connection between the trans-Atlantic slave trade and contraband ran deep in the sixteenth century. Alejandro de la Fuente has argued that the high price of slaves made them the perfect merchandise for illegal trade, and certainly this may have been a factor.[25] Yet also important was that the high price of slaves made it difficult legally to import the requisite labour force to build the new colonies of America: perceived practical necessity as well as a desire for short-term profits may have underwritten the way in which the contraband trade from Western Africa developed in these decades.

Who was bringing these unlicensed slaves to the Americas? Often this was done by traders who had initially bought some slave licenses and smuggled many more aboard their ships than that permitted by their licenses, as emerges from countless denunciations made to the *Casa de la Contratación* in Seville. However, in addition to these individuals, many of these contraband traders were people who had bought no slave licenses at all and whose entire cargo was contraband and unregistered by the Spanish authorities, as with the case of Garrucho mentioned previously. This was also the case of the Canariote traders and some traders from Lisbon; three ships were accused of having gone unlicensed from that port to the coast of Upper Guinea and thence with slaves to America in 1565 alone.[26]

It is worth pausing to think through the implications of this contraband trade both for its effects in Africa and for its role in supplying labourers to the New World in the sixteenth century. In his denunciation of the Canariote trade in the 1560s, the Portuguese ambassador cited one trader as taking 150 slaves to Puerto Rico and named twenty-six traders as regularly involved in this trade. Even supposing both these figures to be

---

[22] AGI, Mexico, Legajo 19, No, 39, Ramo 1.

[23] AGI, Escribanía, 36A: a case from 1574. See also AGI, Santo Domingo 868, Libro 3, fol. 47v: the crown refers to the smuggling of slaves through Hispaniola in 1575.

[24] AGI, Santo Domingo 868, Libro 3, fol. 47v, March 30, 1575 – "*y que quando llegan los navíos a los dhos puertos ay diferencia entre vosotros sobre qual ha de yr a visitarlos*".

[25] Fuente (2008: 40).

[26] AGI, Indiferente 427, Libro 30, fol. 173v.

exaggerated by a factor of 50 per cent, that would still leave an additional eighteen traders taking perhaps one hundred slaves per year outside the official licenses to the Americas. To this would need to be added the three Lisbon ships cited earlier, which would add roughly 2,000 individuals per year to the official slave export figures recorded in Spanish archives.

These figures need to be combined with the current Trans-Atlantic Slave Trade Database, which suggests that 93,104 African slaves were embarked from Senegambia and Upper Guinea between 1550 and 1600, or roughly 1,862 per year.[27] Combining both figures would produce an annual export from this region of at least 3,850 a year. Moreover, this figure does not take account of the contraband of those traders who had themselves purchased licenses in Seville but imported more slaves than permitted by their license. The numerous cases taken against official contractors for smuggling suggests that this was very frequent, and thus an average of 5,000 slaves exported annually to the Americas from the Upper Guinea region does not seem unreasonable for the second half of the sixteenth century.[28] It is worth recalling that this was the same average proposed by Rodney in his *History of the Upper Guinea Coast*.[29]

The evidence considered in this book as to the realignments of societies in Upper Guinea following the opportunities and constraints offered by Atlantic trade supports this figure. If less than two thousand slaves were exported annually from the entire Upper Guinea coast, why had the political and social changes that have been observed in Casamance and the rivers of Guinea begun as early as the 1540s? And why, as mentioned previously, did authors refer to the large number of African slaves in the American colonies? A touching faith in the reliability of surviving official documentation in forging quantitative data and the data themselves have blinded historians to the considerable evidence which show this data to be extremely incomplete.[30]

[27] www.slavevoyages.org, data accessed May 11, 2011.
[28] For such cases see AGI, Patronato 259, Ramo 52; AGI, Justicia 878, No. 2; AGI, Escribanía 36A; AGI, Justicia 1002, No. 1, Ramo 1; AGI, Escribanía 1A, No. 2; and many other places. The estimate mooted here is similar to that of Manoel Alvares in the early seventeenth century, who said that at the trade's zenith 1,800 slaves per year went from Bugendo to America and a further 1,800 from Bugendo to Cabo Verde (many of whom would have been sold on to ships going to the Indies). Because this figure does not include those who sailed from Guinala, my total estimate here is if anything probably on the conservative side. See SG, *Étiopia Menor*, fols. 18r-v.
[29] For the Rodney estimate, see Rodney (1970: 98). His estimate is of an average of five thousand slaves per year between 1562 and 1640.
[30] This confirms G. Hall's (2010) view on the substantial problems regarding the use of quantitative data in analysing the histories of Africans in the Atlantic world.

An example from Western Africa itself can help to make this point. As we shall see in the next chapter, the Sierra Leone region was disrupted by violent wars in the 1550s and the 1560s. Records of slave "ethnicities" from the Americas reveal many Sape slaves as a result of these conflicts (cf. Tables I.1 and I.2). Yet official figures as collated by the Trans-Atlantic Slave Trade Database suggest that only 700 slaves were landed from Sierra Leone in the Americas between 1561 and 1565, and only 468 between 1566 and 1570.[31] Thus it is only by recognising the role and the importance of the contraband trade that a more accurate quantification can be assessed. Time and again traders caught attempting to slip the net claimed that they had been blown off course and ended up in America "by accident" with their cargo of slaves from Upper Guinea.[32] America was a vast continent with many ports and a tiny number of royal officials; for all those caught, many more must have gone unseen.

The records which these slavers have left are remarkable for one thing: their extremely narrow economic focus. Those documents reveal a mind-set uninterested in the world beyond the narrow perimeters of profit and survival. The legal cases brought by the Spanish crown, records of sale, inventories of ship contents and slave "ethnicities" all point to the same conclusion. Violence may, as William Vollmann suggests, be an inescapable quality of human societies, but a particular mindset marks out more violent outlooks from less violent ones.[33] In this case, it is as José Faur has put it: that "blindness, willful or natural, is the key for success in a persecuting society".[34] There may well have been reasons to seek profit through slaving even when such profit, as this book has shown, contributed to the weakening of African economic and political structures; yet it is still no wonder that slave traders found it ever harder to look beyond the abstractions of their books of paper accounting.

TRADE NETWORKS AND THE RECIPROCAL INFLUENCES OF ATLANTIC SLAVING IN AFRICA AND THE AMERICAS

The arrival of large numbers of slaves from Upper Guinea in America was facilitated by this contraband trade. However, it also required commercial networks which could operate within the parameters of the new Iberian Atlantic. These networks were provided by New Christians who, as we

[31] www.slavevoyages.org, data accessed May 11, 2011.
[32] AGI, Justicia 996, No. 2, Ramo 3, fols. 1r-3v; AGI, Escribana 2A, fol. 462r.
[33] Vollmann (2005).
[34] Faur (1992: 69).

have seen earlier in this book, were by the 1550s the key diaspora traders linking the commercial spaces of the African mainland to Cabo Verde.

Although the evidence for the Canaries is not clear on this point, the evidence on the ground in Africa suggests that many of these contraband traders were New Christians. Although we should not forget that this contraband had undoubted commercial and practical impulses deriving from the New World and may also have been designed to make the slave trade commercially viable, there were other motivations behind this New Christian involvement.[35] For the repressive legislation directed at the New Christians in Portugal in the sixteenth century often made it very hard for them to export their wealth from a country in which the Inquisition could confiscate it all. This being the case, it was hardly surprising that New Christians sought other means to safeguard their goods. The combination of this circumstance and the New Christian networks in Africa and America, where the Inquisition in these decades was not nearly as strong as it was in Europe, meant that the contraband slave trade was an ideal opportunity to move their property out of reach of the Inquisition.

Important evidence for this comes from the activities of Duarte de Leão, whose networks we examined in Chapter 5. Even after the Mestre Dioguo affair of 1562, Leão retained active commercial interests in Western Africa throughout the 1560s and into the 1570s. A judicial case relating to events of Christmas 1574 in Upper Guinea, taken in Hispaniola against Cristobal Cayado, derived from a ship which had belonged to Duarte de Leão.[36] Because many *lançados* sailed on this ship and it sailed directly from Bugendo in 1574, this confirms the deep connections of New Christians such as Leão to *lançado* communities up to the 1570s.[37] Moreover, the fact that the ship left Bugendo on Christmas Eve, one of the holiest days in the Catholic calendar, certainly does not suggest that these *lançados* had any great attachment to the Catholic faith.

Another of Duarte de Leão's associates was Blas Ferreira [Blas Herrera in Spanish documents]. In 1565 Ferreira was tried by the Spanish authorities for trading slaves to Cartagena without a license. The sites for introducing slaves to America were changing. In the period up to the 1550s, many slaves had been sent directly to Hispaniola and trans-shipped thence to America.[38] However, as Hispaniola's decline began in the 1560s,

---

[35] On the issue of the profitability of the slave trade, see Newson/Minchin (2007: 69–70).

[36] AGI, Escribanía 2A, fol. 27r. Indeed, the case taken by the new *contratadores* was taken against the widow of Leão, Graçia Correa, and their daughter Isavel (ibid.).

[37] On the Bugendo aspect and the date of departure, see ibid., fol. 25r.

[38] In 1556 people from Santafé de Bogotá in present-day Colombia were still being sent to Hispaniola to get slaves, and not to Cartagena (AGN, NPB, Vols. 1–3, fol. 71r).

Cartagena was becoming increasingly important, as was Veracruz in New Spain.[39] In this case, Ferreira described how he had been sent by Leão and his fellow contractor Antonio Gonçalves de Gusmão to the River São Domingos in 1563 to procure slaves. There they spent the rainy season and procured provisions before proceeding to the Sierra Leone region, where they obtained 180 slaves. This was all according to the "mode, use and custom of the contractors [Leão and Gonçalves]".[40]

Ferreira's evidence is important. It implies that Leão operated a contraband trade and that Cartagena was already a site of contraband trading in slaves.[41] The importance of Cartagena in the trade grew throughout the 1560s and 1570s, coming into its full flowering in the 1580s with the opening of new mines of Zaragoza, in the Antioquia region of the Nuevo Reino de Granada [present-day Colombia].[42] On this evidence, Leão and his associates were among the first to use a port which grew to be the most important in the whole of South America – a port where contraband trade in slaves was vast by the early seventeenth century.[43]

The connection of Leão's New Christian network to the contraband slave trade is confirmed by evidence surrounding the unravelling of Leão's finances in the 1570s. Then, the Portuguese crown complained that not only did Leão and his fellow contractor Gusmão owe the crown large sums after the end of their contract in 1570, but that "they were not left with enough property in this Kingdom to pay what was owing".[44] In fact, the Portuguese crown only began to investigate Leão's overseas holdings as the money was needed "for payment of what [Leão and Gusmão] owe for the said trade [in Cabo Verde] ... for which up till now they have not given any account nor paid that which they were obliged to".[45] Moreover,

---

[39] For examples of direct shipping from Cabo Verde to Hispaniola in the 1560s, see AGI, Patronato 173, No. 1, Ramo 15 (1562) and AGN, Negocios Exteriores, Legajo 4, fols. 350–384 (1568). For other cases from Cabo Verde to Cartagena, see AGN, Contrabandos, Vol. 3, fols. 546–970 (1562), AGI, Patronato 259, Ramo 52 (1574), and AGN, NE, Bolivar SC43/Legajo 13, fols. 1019–1061 (1576). See also Torrão (2010).

[40] AGI, Justicia 878, no. 2.

[41] On this role of Cartagena in the seventeenth century, see Newson/Minchin (2007: 144–7).

[42] For another case involving the trade in slaves to Cartagena, see AGI, Patronato 259, Ramo 52 (1574). Governors' letters from Santa Fe in the 1570s make it clear that there were more slaves in the city than previously (AGI, Santa Fé 37, Ramo 5, no. 23). On the mining boom and associated demand for slaves in the 1580s, see Mathieu (1982: 39–40). On Cartagena and the slave trade between 1570 and 1640, see Wheat (2009: 79–120).

[43] Cf., e.g., Green (2007b: Part 3).

[44] BA, Códice 49-X-4, 223r: "*lhes não fiquou fazenda neste Reyno q baste para paguamento do q devem...*"

[45] BA, Códice 49-X-2, fol. 243r: "*he pa pagamento do que eles devem do ditto trato...de que ate guora não tem dado conta nem paguo tudo o que vão obrigados*".

this money proceeded from "slaves which were taken without registers or licenses".[46] Numerous cases were taken out against Leão and Gusmão in the years that followed for taking slaves without registers, and a letter circa 1580 emphasised the large debts which Leão still owed to the crown from the Caboverdean contract.[47] Smuggling this wealth out of Iberia through the contraband slave trade helped New Christians such as Leão to launch their Atlantic diaspora which became so important to trade in the late sixteenth century and the first third of the seventeenth century.[48]

The evidence on this network does not only show how New Christian networks in Western Africa were connected to the contraband trade analysed in the preceding section. It also reveals just how much pan-Atlantic forces were beginning to influence the pressures leading to increased slave supply in Upper Guinea in these decades. For Leão's entire commercial operation ran in a pan-Atlantic dimension, with his trade in Western Africa just a part of a highly complex network of operations. During the 1570s, the Portuguese crown investigated Leão's holdings in Cartagena, Hispaniola and Flanders.[49] As we have seen, Bras Ferreira, Leão's factor in Upper Guinea, was prosecuted by the bailiff of Cartagena for illegal trading there.[50] Leão himself was well travelled in America: his great-nephew had been told an anecdote by his father where Leão had been near Mexico City.[51] That Leão's network in Cabo Verde was constructed in an Atlantic dimension is emphasised by the fact that his nephew, Carvajal *viejo*, married Guiomar de Ribera, daughter of Miguel Núñez, factor of slaves in Hispaniola, shortly after his return to Spain from Cabo Verde. This followed contacts developed through the slave trade between Cabo Verde and Hispaniola: Carvajal *viejo* also had connections with Manuel Caldeira, one of the most powerful New Christian slave traders of this period, who had sent slaves to Cartagena through Cabo Verde since at least 1557, when Carvajal *viejo*, according to his own evidence, was still operating as the royal treasurer there (cf. Chapter 5).[52]

---

[46] Ibid.: "*escravos q se levarão sem registros, nem licenças*".

[47] In addition to the aforementioned case from Cartagena, see also AGI, Patronato 291, 145r: a case about slaves taken to Cartagena without being registered; BA, Códice 49-X-4, fol. 223r.

[48] On the Atlantic diaspora of New Christians, see Israel (2002), Green (2007b) and Wachtel (2001).

[49] BA, Códice 49-X-2, fols. 243r-245r.

[50] AGI, Justicia 518, no.1 – "*Bras Ferreira feitor dos dittos Contratadores…*".

[51] González Obregón (1935: 364).

[52] On the 1557 date, see AGI, Justicia 853, No. 3 (this case has no fol. numbers). On a 1562 case, see AGN, Contrabandos, Vol. 3, fols. 31r-v. For more information on Caldeira, see Ventura (1999).

This required a connection between Carvajal and Núñez, because the latter was Caldeira's factor on Hispaniola.[53]

This evidence on the complex pan-Atlantic nature of trading networks such as Leão's is important. These networks were key in the supply of labour to the New World in the 1560s and 1570s and thus oiled the wheels of the expanding Spanish empire. As we have seen, they channelled the labour demands of the New World into the procurement of slaves in West Africa. Yet as we also saw in Chapter 5, members of this network were heavily involved in the processes of cultural exchange which characterised the Atlantic trading settlements of Upper Guinea in these years. The growing slave trade indeed required intensification of these exchanges, and thus there was a need for more *lançados* to inhabit Africa and procure the slaves on which the new Atlantic economy depended. Thus networks such as Leão's acted as bridges between the different requirements of the Atlantic, matching the labour demands of America to the supply side in Africa. Making this happen required settlement by New Christians in Africa, and thus trans-Atlantic influences shaped the intensification of creolisation which we have already observed in these decades. This was how global patterns and Atlantic slavery helped to shape new modes of cultural exchange in Western Africa.

Moreover, this pattern went beyond processes of cultural exchange in Africa. These macro-Atlantic factors were also important in influencing patterns of agricultural production among Upper Guinean societies. A key aspect of Blas Ferreira's evidence from Cartagena, cited earlier, is his account of the provisioning of his slaving expedition in Bugendo in 1565. We saw in Chapter 3 how agricultural products from Upper Guinea supplied communities in Cabo Verde and slave ships from São Tomé, and that this may already have affected the social organisation of agricultural labour in Upper Guinea by 1500. Ferreira's evidence demonstrates that by the 1560s at the latest – and almost certainly considerably before – slaves were also supplied with food for the Atlantic crossing from the Bugendo region. His information is corroborated by other sources. A year later, in 1566, the ship captain Baltasar Barbosa was instructed to buy food for the slaves in Upper Guinea "so that they are well treated".[54] Twenty-two years later, in 1588, Juan de Narria loaded a ship in Upper Guinea with provisions including eight barrels of rice.[55] Thus the rapid growth of the

[53] AGI, Justicia 35, Pieza 3, fols. 1r, 48r-v.
[54] AGI, Justicia 996, No. 2, Ramo 3, fols. 12v-13r.
[55] AGI, Escribanía 2B, no. 3 – this case has no fol. numbers.

Atlantic trade meant that the surplus produce initially extracted to feed the small colony of Cabo Verde had to grow. This surplus had to be hived off for the provisioning of slave ships, in addition to that which was already supplying the trans-Saharan caravans.[56] This required an increase in agricultural productivity, something which was a characteristic of the birth of the Atlantic era in Upper Guinea, as the work of Judith Carney, Fields-Black and Hawthorne on rice production has shown.[57] Yet it also meant, as we have seen, that this enhanced productivity could not go back into assisting the growth of the local economy.

The fact that this produce came from Bugendo in these years suggests that it was in Casamance that increased productivity began to be most marked. Some of this would have been possible through increased availability of iron-edged tools. However, some of it may only have been possible through developing new means of social production, by solidifying the use of age grades in agricultural labour for instance, as occurred with the Balanta.[58] This may explain some of the political tensions which had developed in Casamance by this time (cf. Chapter 5). That agricultural production in Upper Guinea was much more intensive than, for instance, in Angola, has been shown recently by Linda Newson and Susie Minchin, who have used data on hernias for slaves arriving in Cartagena in the early seventeenth century to argue that this derived from the greater intensity of agricultural labour in Upper Guinea.[59]

Yet the pattern of influence in the pan-Atlantic was by no means one way. The investment of New Christian networks such as Duarte de Leão's in both Africa and America meant that just as American demands influenced Africa, so experiences in Africa influenced events elsewhere in the Atlantic. For the practices connected to slaving and the development of mixed cultural practices which were developed by the *lançados* were in turn connected to the wider Atlantic through the activities of these networks.

This becomes apparent, for instance, in the trajectory of Carvajal *viejo* (cf. Chapter 5). When one considers how very young he was when he

---

[56] On the volume of provisions required by slave ships, see Newson/Minchin (2007: chapters 3 and 4).

[57] Hawthorne (2003); Fields-Black (2009). This documentary evidence confirms Carney's (2001: 69) link of Atlantic slavery with surplus agricultural production in Upper Guinea.

[58] Hawthorne (2003: 161–3).

[59] Newson/Minchin (2007: 130–1). Twenty-three percent of slaves arriving from Upper Guinea had hernias, as opposed to only 7 percent from Angola.

reached Western Africa – just eight years old – it becomes obvious that his experiences there must have decisively helped to shape his outlook. The evidence on Leão is that he was heavily involved in the contraband trade in slaves. Surely this was also Carvajal *viejo*'s business as a young man in Western Africa. Later, when he became the first governor of Nuevo León in New Spain, he was said to have hunted Native Americans "like hares", to have enslaved them and sent them on in chains to Mexico City.[60] As with the early Spanish narratives of the New World, it may be that this evidence offers a hint of previous activities in Africa.

This conclusion about the role of African experiences in the early Atlantic world tallies with other evidence that we have on Duarte de Leão. In his evidence to the inquisitors of Évora, in 1544, Alvaro Leão referred to his brother Duarte as a "single man and that he has gone travelling with goods, although [Alvaro Leão] does not know if to Guiné or elsewhere".[61] Surely, this journey of Duarte de Leão's was to the region to which he subsequently despatched his brother Francisco and nephew Luis. Thus the presence of Francisco Jorge and his network depended on Duarte's prior experience there.[62] Moreover, experience also was important in economic activity; this evidence might suggest that the Portuguese crown often received bids for contracts in the *ultramar* from people with personal experience of a region.

This second conclusion tallies with Duarte de Leão's predecessors. The holder of the first (1469) contract for Guiné, Fernão Gomes, had in 1456 previously been made receiver of all slaves and other goods to come from the Guiné trade.[63] Subsequently, Fernam de Loronha had taken part in the first expedition after his consortium was awarded the Brazilian contract in 1503, one year before Loronha bid for the contract for Cabo Verde.[64] Moreover, this expedition would almost certainly have stopped in Cabo Verde, given the early administrative and commercial ties between the two regions which we examined in Chapter 4. Thus during the first half of the sixteenth century, it was personal experience of African trade which helped people to become successful contractors there; moreover, this often led to subsequent activities

---

[60] Huerga (1984: 955); Toro (1944: Vol. 1, 128–30).
[61] IAN/TT, Inquisição de Évora, Proceso 8779, fol. 66v: "*e ome solteiro e que ha ido com mercadaria não sabe se pa guine ou as partes dalem*".
[62] Francisco himself had merely studied in Salamanca: ibid.: "*e que a outro irmão q se chamã Francisco e estuda ẽ Salamanca*".
[63] Vogt (1973: 2).
[64] Wiznitzer (1960: 6–7).

in America, creating a pan-Atlantic sphere of activity. The process of mental abstraction required for the modernisation of thought and the viewing of reality in terms of space and number was ongoing.[65] The development of the abstract scientific mentality which led to new technological innovations had yet to bring with it, perhaps, complete trust in abstract concepts such as "Western African" or "Atlantic" space.[66] That space still had to be made real, and in this process of "making real," personal, empirical experience was fundamental – and often, as these case studies show, experience in Africa came first.

Thus as men such as Carvajal and Leão learnt first hand to assimilate the strategies of violence and accommodation which had long characterised the mixed cultural framework of Upper Guinea and which now characterised the trading environment in which the *lançados* operated, they could bring this experience to bear in their activities in the wider Atlantic world. As the trans-Atlantic slave trade expanded after 1550, the reciprocal influences which Africa and the Americas had on one another could grow through networks like the one which they operated. The complex relationship between trading diasporas and host communities which had long been fundamental to the cultural, economic and political environment of Upper Guinea began to spread, along with the people of Upper Guinea, who themselves were transported, chained and bound in the ships in which both new diasporas travelled across the Atlantic Ocean.

CREOLE SOCIETY IN TRANS-ATLANTIC PERSPECTIVE: THE CREATION OF SHARED IDENTITIES AND NEW IDEOLOGIES IN CABO VERDE

Mercantile diasporas in West Africa had traditionally been united by shared religious or lineage bonds. As we saw in Chapter 1, there was a way in which Islam had long been a religion of trade in the region. Bonds of trust were easier to create in an environment where people belonged to the same religion, practised the same rituals and believed in the same divine powers. The difficulties inherent in long-distance trade before the industrial age meant that some such unifying feature was often an important aspect of the success of diaspora traders.[67]

---

[65] Jeannin (1972: 108–12) shows how this process had drawn some dividends by 1506.
[66] On new technological innovations, see Albuquerque (1983).
[67] Greif (1993).

Research has shown that similar considerations affected the New Christian diaspora of the Atlantic world in the sixteenth and seventeenth centuries. So important was the creation of shared ritual bonds among members of the New Christian diaspora that some Old Christians even adopted aspects of crypto-Judaism in order to be accepted into the trading networks.[68] New Christian identity was a "faith in memory" – the memory of ancestral practices that were in reality ever more remote – and also a way of securing confidence in highly precarious trading systems.[69]

As we have seen in this book, the structural similarity of the New Christian condition in Western Africa to that of the North African and *dyula* traders who had preceded them facilitated their success there. This is not to say, of course, that there were not important differences between the two, especially in the religious sphere; as we have already seen, New Christians had a very variegated attitude to their religion (cf. Chapters 4–5), and even for those who were real crypto-Jews, their religion acted as a sort of secret grouping, not an officially codified religion, and thus we should recognise these differences. Yet nevertheless, whatever its official structures, for Upper Guineans the faith of New Christians was an outsider one, and the combination of this and their status as a trading caste was very familiar. In this way, outsiders helped to broker the incursion of the new economic and political realities of the Atlantic onto Upper Guinean societies, just as they had previously with the trans-Saharan trade through the *dyula*.

The *lançado* ability to do this related partly to their connections to Cabo Verde, where, as we have seen, an Atlantic Creole society had first emerged before being transplanted to the African coast. The flexibility which such a society required made it easier for *lançados* to adapt as necessary in West Africa. Thus central to the development of shared bonds of identity for the diaspora in these years was Cabo Verde. Most licensed ships taking slaves to the Americas in the years 1571–5 still went to Cabo Verde.[70] When Francisco Nuñez de Padilla came from the Canaries to load slaves in May 1574, for instance, he obtained sixty-six slaves that had just arrived from the River São Domingos on the ship Santa Cruz.[71] There

---

[68] Green (2007b: 195–201).

[69] Wachtel (2001).

[70] Thomas (1997: 138).

[71] AGI, Escribanía 119A, 15r-17v. There was very little organizational structure to this supply, and occasionally the system broke down: See for instance, AGI, Justicia 864, No. 7, July 10, 1563–April 11, 1564 – where Luis de Mercado from Seville claimed he

was a constant trade in these years of wine, cloth, cotton and horses from Cabo Verde for slaves from the coast, according to André Donelha.[72] As in the foundational period of the colony, slavery was the lynchpin of the entire economy (cf. Chapter 3). For instance, the *barafulas* woven in Cabo Verde and used as a form of currency on the Upper Guinea coast were called "*panos de resgate*" ["trading cloths"] in the archipelago and were perceived as being woven solely to trade for slaves: "*resgate*" itself was perceived as the trade of goods from Portugal or Cabo Verde on the Upper Guinea coast in return specifically for slaves.[73]

Cabo Verde's importance to the development of shared identities lay partly in this commercial importance in the Atlantic slave trade and its consequent importance for *lançados*. However, it also derived from the fact that it offered an intersection of two diaspora trades, one linking the islands to the rest of the Atlantic world and another linking the various parts of Western Africa. Thus the Creole society which emerged there was strongly influenced by both African and Atlantic factors which had been brought together by the expansion of trans-Atlantic trade in these years. Understanding the expansion of Atlantic slaving from this region at this time, therefore, requires some understanding of changing boundaries of Creole identity at this time, as it solidified at precisely the same moment as the trans-Atlantic influences became most intense.

As we have seen in previous chapters, the vernacularisation of the Kriolu language had probably been completed by the 1560s in Cabo Verde, and thus to talk of a Creole identity by this time is not unfounded. This identity was of course bound deeply to both the institution of slavery and the trade in slaves, but of growing importance to it were also changes in ideology which developments in the Atlantic world had precipitated – changes which related to a proto-racial awareness which had grown out of the increasing connection of slavery to skin colour.

---

was unable to take thirty slaves to the Indies as they weren't to be had in Cabo Verde. In the case dealt with here, Padilla obtained a further 119 from elsewhere on the island of Santiago, some of whom may have been Caboverdean Creoles rather than recent arrivals, as Caboverdean Creoles were found as slaves in the Americas – see for instance AGN, NE, Cundinamarca, SC 43, Legajo 8, fol. 708r ; AGN, ANS/NP, Rollo 1507294, fols. 129r-v ; AGN, NT, Rollo 4, Legajo 11, fol. 235v ; AGN, NT, Rollo 7, Legajo 23, fols. 161r and 271r.

[72] MMAII: Vol. 5, 139.

[73] AGI, Escribanía 2A, fol. 461r: "*Si saben que los paños de algodon que llaman paños de resgate que llevan a los Rios de guinea para Resgatar esclavos...*"; ibid., fol. 368r-v, the *contratadores*' definition of *resgate* was "*todas y qlesquiera m|ane|ras que ordinariamente se suelen llebar del reyno de Portugal o de cabo verde a los rrios de guinea para con ellos conprar e resgatar esclavos en los dhos rios*".

Cabo Verde's multiple connections to all parts of the Western hemisphere through the Atlantic slave trade ensured that ideas developing elsewhere came to matter on the islands too, and so as the Atlantic slave trade expanded in the late sixteenth century, so also did the influence of broader Atlantic trends on Creole society there. Though Western Africa had offered one of the first locales for an Atlantic Creole society, creolisation there came to depend also on influences brought from elsewhere by the trans-Atlantic trade.

In the sixteenth century Atlantic world, the evolving discourse on race was extremely complex and depended greatly on local factors. Ideas were by no means universal, though there certainly were some general tendencies towards negative connotations associated with a darker skin colour. In fifteenth-century Valencia, where slaves were not only from sub-Saharan Africa but also came from Circassia, Iberia itself, and North Africa, this association of darker skin colour with slavery did exist, but it was not a universal rule of thumb.[74] However, in late sixteenth-century Havana, Cuba, Black and mixed-race residents were barred from the "better" quarters of the city and confined to more squalid areas such as Campede.[75] By this time, Iberians were familiar with African slavery as a social practice, and as Fuente argues, there was a particular need to delineate contours of social inclusion and exclusion in new colonial centres such as Havana because of the bewildering speed of changes which threatened to loosen the structures of what was seen as an ordered society.[76] Where the changes were the most acute, ideas and boundaries hardened. Such factors were of course also at work in the minds of the new Caboverdean Creoles, for in Cabo Verde there were many of the same insecurities as there were in Havana. As in Havana, there was the threat of foreign invasions by the English or French, and as in Havana the entire social edifice was only maintained through the institutional violence of the system of slavery. In this situation, it is not surprising that colour distinctions and judgements about them were prominent in the minds of some Caboverdeans in the late sixteenth century.

This is illustrated by the accounts of Almada. Almada used colour as a descriptor, noting how the Pullo (or Fulos, as he called them) were of "a mixed colour" and "not black", whereas the Gambia River

---

[74] Blumenthal (2009).
[75] Fuente (2008: 116).
[76] Ibid., 178.

was peopled by "Mandinka blacks on both sides".[77] This distinction between the colour of the Pullo and the Mandinka in Almada's mind is noteworthy, for he himself was a Caboverdean of mixed race, and his observation of the colour of African peoples reflect preoccupations which mixed-race Caboverdeans themselves had developed by the time that he was writing.

Why was it that colour was of such importance in the mind of a Caboverdean like Almada? As we saw in the early chapters of this book, Cabo Verde was the first Atlantic locale where slavery adopted an exclusively racial quality, with slaves being all from sub-Saharan Africa. On Cabo Verde, a Black skin colour was equated with slavery, and therefore, the lighter the skin colour, the further up the hierarchy of the islands' society a person was. There was, in other words, a clear link between skin colour and slavery which events in Western Africa had been instrumental in developing. In subsequent centuries, of course, such analogies would become commonplace in the slave-based plantation economies of the Caribbean islands and the southern United States. For the wealthy mixed-race trading class, for people such as Almada in fact, such proto-racial gradations allowed the creation of a hierarchy which shored up their own social position and offered a modicum of protection in an insecure world.

The international trading connections of this mobile class of Caboverdeans meant that they could quickly assimilate these ideas as they developed elsewhere, for these ideas came to Western Africa from the outside. Such ideas do not appear to have characterised the early Creole colony in its infancy in the early sixteenth century, when, as we have seen, the rights of free Blacks were staunchly defended and free or slave status, not colour, defined social position (cf. Chapter 3). Black sailors worked as ship captains plying between Cabo Verde and the African coast until 1516.[78] Furthermore, in Cabo Verde the graves of the earliest church mixed the bodies of Africans and Europeans, whereas in Portugal dead African slaves were simply thrown outside the city walls until 1515.[79]

Thus the negative association of skin colour and status was something that Caboverdeans learnt from their contact with the wider Iberian world. It was one which in all likelihood was assimilated particularly

---

[77] MMAII: Vol. 3, 244 ("*a cor amulatada*"); 246 (*não serem negros*); 271 (*negros Mandinkas, de uma banda e outra*").

[78] Saunders (1982a: 11); Barcellos (1899: 85).

[79] On the graves of the first church in Ribeira Grande, see Evans/Sorensen/Richter (forthcoming). On burial practices in Lisbon, Vogt (1973a: 12).

by elite traders such as Almada, who stood to benefit from it and who may have felt most at threat from the atmosphere of permanent threat to the social order which characterised Atlantic slave economies. Perhaps this need to import the proto-racism of the sixteenth century to Cabo Verde from outside should not surprise us, because, as suggested in the Introduction, the discourses of creolisation and race are in a deep tension with one another, with one pointing towards a blending of practices and the other towards essentialism.

If it was the insecurity and danger of the new economy and society founded on trans-Atlantic slavery which encouraged some Caboverdean Creoles to assimilate ideas of race, it should not be a surprise that race was not the sole prejudicial discourse at work in Almada. Other discourses could help to combat such insecurities. Writing about the griots of Senegambia, like Fernandes at the start of the sixteenth century (cf. Chapter 4), Almada described them as "Jews". In a telling gloss on Fernandes, however, Almada added that the Jews/griots had "large noses" [*são abastados de narizes*].[80] This passage clearly shows how ideas about Jews continued to affect ideas about Africans, even among Caboverdeans like Almada, for though there is little evidence that the griots of Western Africa were renowned for the size of their noses, this was not the case in Portugal where the perception of the Jews was concerned.[81]

These passages from Almada illuminate the elite Creole Caboverdean worldview at the endpoint of the "boom" in the trans-Atlantic slave trade from Western Africa. They reveal that colour and slavery were interconnected in that mindset, and that ideas about Jews had influenced how Africans were perceived, both in terms of structural similarities as with the griots and in terms of the concept of race as developing from the idea of *limpeza*, which had evolved in late fifteenth-century Iberia. This intermingling of ideas about race and religion gave the discourse a powerful flexibility, and also of course connected Caboverdean "masters" to their peers in other parts of the Atlantic where similar ideas were at work. Here was a shared identity which could cross local borders and be a potential vehicle of discrimination which could be religious, racial or a

---

[80] MMAII: Vol. 3, 263.

[81] See for instance IAN/TT, Inquisição de Évora, Livro 91, fols. 174 r-v: a case from 1594 where a student from Faro, Francisco Nunes, denounced an old man he had met the previous day as a crypto-Jew. Nunes described him in what were clearly preconceived ideas of what such a person might look like: "*hū home velho có barba quasi toda branca pequeno de corpo e tem o naariz grande*" (tr.: "an old, short man with a beard almost entirely white and a large nose").

combination of the two, depending on the particular local circumstances. This was a transnational ideology whose manifold nature would make it peculiarly useful in acting as a moral support for the otherwise unacceptable demands and consequences of the plantation system of agriculture in the New World.[82]

In fact, as these passages from Almada indicate, the legacy of the Iberian anti-Semitism of the fifteenth century pervaded Caboverdean society in the sixteenth century. The cases of both Miçia Dias and Joana Coelha's great-grandmother, discussed in Chapter 5, suggest that by the 1550s and 1560s there was a distinct caste consciousness evolving in Caboverdean society not only along racial lines, but also along religious lines. New Christians were made to live apart from the Old Christians in the Calhau, just as the Jews had lived apart in fifteenth-century Iberia in their *judiarias*. The importance and success of the New Christian trading networks we have looked at in this chapter must have contributed to the divisions which grew up between the two groups in the colony. Thus the presence of the New Christians helped to cement the Old Christian caste consciousness and their perception of the importance of caste in Cabo Verde. The large New Christian community helped to reconstitute familiar categories in a new environment and became a prop in helping to maintain those old categories and transfer them to Africans in a new form of caste identity related to race.

It turns out, therefore, that there were extremely complex connections linking the expansion of the slave trade through contraband to both New Christian diaspora networks and changes in Creole identity in Western Africa. The widespread presence of New Christians in Western Africa at this time influenced how discourses hardened into a flexible religio-racial ideology in the late sixteenth century among those Caboverdean communities connected to the regional and international trades. Shared bonds of identity were formed among elite Creoles which borrowed from analogous ideologies elsewhere in the Atlantic world, assisting in the construction of a sort of mobile ideology to suit the new mobile Atlantic and showing how the growth of the slave trade brought wider global factors to bear on the emergent Creole identity which we analysed in Part 1. The massive contraband, meanwhile, facilitated the boom in the slave trade

---

[82] Other instances from the New World illustrate the segue between ideas of race and ideas of religion. Bennett (2003: 38–41) has argued that in Mexico Iberian practices of stripping Jews and Moslems of a culturally sanctioned juridical status was applied to the treatment of African slaves in the New World.

which American economies required. All these factors had serious effects
on the societies of Upper Guinea, as we shall see in the following chapter, and they all derived from the way in which global forces had come
to influence events in Western Africa in the second half of the sixteenth
century, and from the expansion of the slave trade which these forces
had required.

8

Cycles of War and Trade in the African Atlantic, circa 1550–1580

A masquerade associated today with the circumcision ritual in the Casamance is called the *kankuran*. The night before the ceremony people gather in compounds and make percussive rhythms in fear of the morrow. In the morning, the *kankuran* prowls through the streets dressed in a fearsome mask and wielding a machete. People flee from him in terror. Whilst in Casamance, I was often told that the *kankuran* was a Mandinka phenomenon.[1]

Some anthropologists with symbolist leanings have attempted to analyse various performative dances, masking traditions and magical rituals in West African contexts as memorialisations of the trans-Atlantic slave trade. In Sierra Leone, Rosalind Shaw argues that the magical discourse related to beliefs in invisibility and witchcraft stem from the very invisibility accorded to people who disappeared through that trade.[2] In the grassfields of Cameroon, Nicolas Argenti sees echoes of forced marches of captives and of slave raids in dances associated with masking traditions.[3] For the *kankuran* in Casamance, one could attempt something similar and ask whether the flight from the Mandinka *kankuran* may not represent a memorialisation of the flight from Mandinka slave raiders of the Gambia River states and Kaabu in the Atlantic era.

Whilst the trajectory of the Kaabu federation between the sixteenth and the early nineteenth centuries remains sketchy, scholars generally agree with what we shall see in this chapter: Kaabunké power was a

[1] Green (2001: 264, 271). See also de Jong (2008: Chapter 6).
[2] Shaw (2002).
[3] Argenti (2007).

major beneficiary of the Atlantic trading system, and Kaabu consolidated its role in Upper Guinea in part through participation in the slave trade.[4] The settlement of *lançados* in Mandinguised areas which we observed in Chapter 6 may also be significant in this context given their connection to the Atlantic slave trading networks. Thus the importance of the Mandinka to the raiding culture of Upper Guinea is unquestionable, and it could be that this is related to fearful reactions to the *kankuran* in Casamance today. Of course, such speculative hypotheses – though intriguing – are hugely problematic. Elsewhere, they have been widely lauded.[5] Often, however, they fail to acknowledge the real controversy which surrounds the projection of an externalised meaning to West African cultural practices.[6] This is an overly reductionist interpretation, and probably the meaning of the *kankuran* masquerade incorporates both past and present histories, where perhaps aspects of Kaabu's power in pre-colonial times are meshed with the current political and cultural situation in the Casamance, as Ferdinand De Jong suggests, or with more recent memories of nineteenth-century raids among the Diola of the Casamance.[7]

Nevertheless, taking a symbolist view of the *kankuran* may not be entirely fanciful. This view is supported by the fact that supernatural discourses and memories of historical oppression most certainly are connected in some areas of West Africa. In Ziguinchor, Casamance, I was told by an individual of the escape of his Sarahollé grandfather from French colonial forces in Mauritania; according to my informant, his grandfather had been on the point of being shot by the French army before flying mystically to the Casamance and escaping.[8] Thus we should not dismiss such symbolist interpretations, but rather we must recognise their limitations. Perhaps their real value does lie not in seeing them as ends in themselves, but in helping to show the multi-dimensional nature of memories and identities relating to the trans-Atlantic slave trade today. These interpretations demonstrate the constant need to reach beyond usual sources and ideas in trying to understand that trade. Most particularly, they show the importance of grasping cultural contexts. Ethnographic approaches

---

[4] See for example Havik (2004b: 21).

[5] Thus Shaw's book bears an encomium from Ralph Austen; Argenti's from Jean Comaroff, Peter Geschiere and Filip de Boeck.

[6] I am grateful for this point to discussions with Karin Barber, Reg Cline-Cole and Keith Shear. See also Pratten (2007: 12).

[7] De Jong (2008); on the hypothesis of the nineteenth-century raids, I am grateful to a personal communication by Peter Mark, and see also aspects of Baum (1999).

[8] Interview with El Hadji Mamadou Kabir Ndiaye, Ziguinchor, January 2000.

to this subject may require a solid historical component, but the historical approach cannot do without the ethnographic.

These considerations matter greatly when it comes to the discussion of this chapter, the aim of which is to show how the pan-Atlantic cycles revealed in the foregoing two chapters affected the peoples of Senegambia and Upper Guinea by 1580. They highlight the importance of African responses to Atlantic trade and of understanding how African responses can tell us much about the nature of that trade: its extent, the fears it produced, and its perceived meaning. By looking at cycles of war and trade on mainland Africa and their connections to the cycles of Atlantic trade, we see in detail and for the first time how the expansion of the trans-Atlantic slave trade in Western Africa in the sixteenth century influenced cultural, productive and social trends in the region. The extensive evidence of the changes which developed and of their connection to the Atlantic trade in effect bolsters the evidence of Chapter 7 as to the volume of the trade in this era, for only a substantial trade could have helped to precipitate the effects analysed here. Thus one of the important contributions of this chapter is to supply socio-historical evidence from the African perspective to support the evidence in this book as to the extent of the trans-Atlantic slave trade from Western Africa in the sixteenth century.

The analysis of these changes is built using extensive archival sources originating in Latin America. The data put forward supporting these historiographical conclusions comes initially from the Sierra Leone region and clarifies the importance of wars between groups known to contemporary Atlantic chroniclers as the Manes and the Sapes in reshaping patterns of trade in Upper Guinea as a whole. However, the wars there affected not only the peoples of Sierra Leone and present-day Guinea-Conakry, but also their trading partners to the north. The decline of the Biafada, the rise of the Mandinka of Kaabu and the consolidation of the Luso-African trading castes of the region were all connected as the Atlantic world took off, and the histories of the peoples of Western Africa were reshaped by forces which even today can induce terror. When we recall the figure of the *kankuran*, the Mandinka masquerade from whom everyone flees prior to the symbolic act of sexual violence implicit in circumcision, the sudden expansion of cycles of violent disorder in the sixteenth century takes on a more tangible and frightening form; in that distant time, it was Mandinguised power that expanded in Upper Guinea through the Kassanké king Masatamba, the Manes of Sierra Leone, and the federation of Kaabu.

This connects to the political analysis offered here for changes in West African societies in the late sixteenth century. We see how Mande power grew throughout the region, consolidated in part through the trading alliances which Mandinka and Mandinguised groups were able to make with Atlantic traders in continuity with their previous histories. The fundamental historiographical aim of this chapter, therefore, is to integrate the two major themes of this book in showing how the expansion of the Atlantic slave trade in the late sixteenth century expanded the influence and cultural mixing of creolised communities in mainland West Africa. By 1580 these creolised communities had developed a significance which went beyond trade to their role as go-betweens for important aspects of ritual practice in Africa. Thus trade and cultural practice became fundamentally connected, just as they had been for centuries in the trans-Saharan trade, and the *lançado* caste connected to both Atlantic and African trades was able to cement its social position and expand the influence of its Atlantic Creole culture on the African mainland. Their ability to do this depended on the influences of Atlantic trade in Western Africa, and thus the expansion of Atlantic Creole society from Cabo Verde to the African mainland was fundamentally an Atlantic phenomenon connected to the growth of trans-Atlantic slavery.

ATTACK, DEFENCE AND PRODUCTION: THE EFFECTS OF THE MANE INVASIONS IN SIERRA LEONE

As with the region to the north of the River Grande, the peoples inhabiting the coastlines of present-day Guinea-Conakry and Sierra Leone had a long history of cultural sharing prior to the arrival of Atlantic traders.[9] This was apparent to early Atlantic mariners. Fernandes's informants in the early 1500s described to him how the people known collectively by them as Sapes were "mixed in with many other peoples".[10] The alliances of different lineages had promoted a general mixture of customs; Fernandes noted how the peoples of the Nunes River and Cape Verga "border on Sierra Leone and for this reason have the same customs and provisions and rituals".[11] This was also a zone of much linguistic sharing, with the languages of the Sape lineages of Sierra Leone and the Bagas

---

[9] Fields-Black (2009) expands on this in great detail.
[10] MMAII: Vol. 1, 722: *"mesturados de muytas outras gerações"*.
[11] Ibid., Vol. 1, 723: *"comarcã cõ Serra de Lyoa, por ysso tê seus custumes e mãtimentos e assy adorã"*.

and Cocolís of the Nunes River area said by Almada to be as alike as Portuguese was to Spanish.[12] Bagas, Cocolís and Nalus, the peoples whose lands were closest to those of the Biafada on the Grande River, all understood one another.[13] The area of Sape trade networks operated along similar cultural-historical lines to that of the Mandinka-influenced zone to the north. Both Almada and Donelha described how the Sape kingdom south of Cape Verga to Sierra Leone incorporated many different groups, including Tagunchos, Bagas, Sapes, Volons, Temnes, Limbas and Jalonkés, and that all these groups understood one another.[14] Moreover, as with the history of Kaabu and the region of present-day Guinea-Bissau, some of these groups were probably migrants who had been pushed out of the Fouta Djalon highlands to the east following the formation of Kaabu in the thirteenth and fourteenth centuries, and more recently following the Pullo migrations under Koli Tenguella in the late fifteenth and early sixteenth centuries (cf. Chapter 2).[15]

There were two important trades in the region of present-day Guinea-Conakry. One was of salt from the coast to the interior.[16] The other was operated by the Sape lineages and supplied kola from the forests of the whole coast to Biafada middlemen who traded this on to Mandinka and Mandinka-influenced groups farther north. The area itself was fertile and rich in provisions; its peoples were said to be less warlike than those farther north.[17] Probably, it had not been affected so badly by the dry period from 1100 to 1500, which had encouraged the migration of Mandinka and exacerbated inter-group tensions north of the Grande River. The area was productive, and in return for its goods the Sape trade networks brought back desired goods from the north. The importance of salt allowed Caboverdean traders to integrate quickly into this trading picture, because salt was easily found in their arid Atlantic islands.[18]

---

[12] Ibid., Vol. 3, 341. Fields-Black (2009) shows that there were two major groups in coastal regions here, some descended from highland speakers who had migrated to the coast and others established for longer periods by the Atlantic.

[13] MMAII: Vol. 3, 341.

[14] Ibid., Vol. 3, 353 (Almada); Vol. 5, 104 (Donelha).

[15] For oral histories of the driving out of Jalonke lineages from Kaabu, see NCAC/OHAD, Transcribed Cassette 539A, pages 1 and 52–3. Also embedded in this source appears to be a memory of the role of the Pullo migrations in this process, with the informant also describing how "Futa also came from Maasina/They found the Jalunkas there/and drove them away" (ibid., 53); a clearer recollection of the Futa's forcing the Jalonke into migration is found at NCAC/OHAD, Transcribed Cassette 490A, pages 5–6.

[16] Fields-Black (2009: 65–6).

[17] MMAII: Vol. 3, 356.

[18] On the importance of salt, ibid., and Fields-Black (2009).

Caboverdean traders soon demanded slaves, and thus networks of slave supply began to operate in a region which probably had been little affected by the trans-Saharan trade in slaves before the fifteenth century.[19]

This picture changed abruptly in the mid-sixteenth century. In the period between the 1540s and the 1560s, the invasion of a group of Mande warriors known as the Manes represented an important political shift. From the 1550s through to the 1570s, the major group attacked by the Manes, the Sapes who hitherto had operated the riverine trade system between Sierra Leone and Biafada territory on the Rio Grande, came to constitute one of the largest groups despatched by slavers to the Americas (see Tables I.1 and I.2).[20] However, by the 1620s the Manes had settled in relative peace and indeed adopted many Sape customs, just as the Imbangala raiders eventually adopted many Mbundu customs following decades of war and pillage in West-Central Africa in the first half of the seventeenth century.[21]

The Mane appear to have begun arriving in the 1540s. Donelha stated that the wars began in around 1545 and that the Manes had subjugated Sape territories by 1560.[22] However, Donelha was writing eighty years after the events he described, and data on the arrival of Sape slaves in the Americas suggests that these dates require revision. Ships arrived to obtain slaves on this coast throughout the 1560s, and the numbers of Sapes arriving in the Americas were much greater in the 1560s and early 1570s than they were in the 1550s (see Tables I.1 and I.2). Donelha elsewhere states that the wars were still continuing in 1560, so perhaps it was not until the mid-1560s that the Manes held sway.[23] That is, it was in precisely the period when the contraband trade to the Americas was exploding that these wars were concluded.

Almada described the Manes as a cannibal army. Their soldiers, the so-called Sumbas, were taken by the Manes from among the groups

[19] Almada noted that the Caboverdean trade here was for slaves, wax and ivory – MMAII: Vol. 3, 356. The lack of trans-Saharan slave trading can be deduced from the lack of diaspora Mandinka merchants here. This supports Rodney's (1965) view that prior to the fifteenth century slavery as such did not exist in this region.

[20] On the Sape-Biafada links before the onset of Atlantic trade, see Brooks (1993b). On the way in which "Sape" was an external ethnonym simplifying a more complex reality of lineage, see Fields-Black (2009: 81).

[21] Thus by 1627, the Manes were known to the Spanish in the New World as "Manes Sapes" – Sandoval (1627: 62); on this aspect of the Imbangala in West-Central Africa, see especially Miller (1976a: 224–64).

[22] MMAII: Vol. 5, 109.

[23] Ibid., Vol. 5, 110; Donelha's father visited Sierra Leone in 1560 and bought three Manes captured in the wars.

whom they vanquished as they progressed northwards from the Gold Coast region. According to Rodney, by the time they reached Sierra Leone many were Bulloms and Temnes from that very region.[24] The Sumbas were trained as soldiers and forced, said Almada, to eat human flesh. The Sapes begged the Caboverdean and *lançado* traders to take them as slaves rather than leave them with the Manes.[25]

These tales of cannibalism are wild exaggerations. We should recall that other peoples in West Africa were tarred with the brush of cannibals by European authors in these years, such as the Imbangala of Angola (cf. Chapter 2).[26] It should be recognised that in the case of the Imbangala the truth-value of these accusations may have had more substance than is the case with the Manes, but even then these accusations were clearly exaggerated and their prime function within travel accounts composed for a European audience was to satisfy preconceptions regarding others.[27] These tales primarily reflect the oral cultures of Western and West-Central Africa, in which the metaphor of cannibalism was often vested in groups such as witches and others perceived as wielding destructive powers; indeed, this legacy is evident today in Western Africa, where people of Gambia and Senegal frequently use the term "eat/manger" from their respective languages of colonization to describe the destructive corruption of ruling elites in their countries.[28] In the sixteenth century, such ritual power was likely associated with the success of the Manes by the Sapes, particularly as the Manes brought with them important new secret societies. This was probably the origin of the story of cannibalism purveyed by Almada and also by Fenton.[29]

Who, then, were the Manes? Certainly, they were a Mande group. Donelha stated that the Manes left the court of Mandimansa under a princess, Macarico. They reached the sea and then passed the Portuguese fortress at Elmina on the Gold Coast. As they went, the Manes picked up more followers, but Macarico died of grief when her son was killed more than forty years after leaving the court.[30] Almada also thought that the

---

[24] Rodney (1970: 56).

[25] MMAII: Vol. 3, 364: "*rogando e pedindo, por amor de Deus, os comprassem*".

[26] Rodney (1970: 43–44) thought the stories of the Imbangala and Sumba related.

[27] The key interpretation of the evidence on the role of these accounts for satisfying European preconceptions is Miller (1973); see idem. (1982: 26–7) for a brilliant interpretation of the cannibalism of the Imbangala deriving from drought and famine in late-sixteenth-century West-Central Africa.

[28] On cannibalism and witchcraft, see for example Hawthorne (2010b: Ch. 6); Argenti (2007).

[29] Taylor (1959: 105).

[30] MMAII: Vol. 5, 110.

Manes came from Mali, "because they speak the same language ... and use the same clothes and weapons as the people of Mali, there being no difference whatever between them".[31]

Such stories of imperial origins in Mali should not be taken at face value. It was of course to the advantage of the newcomers to claim this origin for themselves, in the assertion of royal legitimacy.[32] Yet research by Brooks and Yves Person has shown that this is extremely unlikely, because both the Mande language introduced by the Manes and the secret societies that they developed came from the southwest and not from among the northern Mande associated with Mali.[33] On Person's account, the Mane leaders came from a blacksmith clan in the Konyan highlands, the Camara.[34]

Yet although the Manes probably never have left this court as they claimed, it may have been around forty years since their migration had begun, as Donelha suggested. Elsewhere he notes that of those who had originally departed, only eight old men accompanied the Manes when they reached Sierra Leone in 1545.[35] Thus if the Mane wars began around 1545, we can date the departure of the Manes to around 1500. And although the connection to Mali's court is tenuous, this allows us to suggest that Mali's decline and the Mane migrations may be linked, which is important when we come to assess how Atlantic exchanges were influencing reactions and realignments in African societies by the middle of the sixteenth century.

If the Mane departure came circa 1500, it occurred at precisely the same time that, as we saw in Chapter 2, the empire of Mali was losing its influence on the Upper Guinea coast following fifty years of Atlantic trade. This process had begun in the 1430s with the stirrings of Songhay's independence, which culminated in 1489. This event precipitated disorder in the 1490s and political realignments followed, including the new independence of Kaabu. Brooks suggests that the Camara clan may have fled advancing Mande horse warriors who were themselves fleeing the break-up of the court at Mali, an event that on this timeline could well have occurred in the late 1490s – which fits with the date of the departure

---

[31] Ibid., Vol. 3, 360: "*porque falam a mesma língua ... trazem as mesmas armas e vestidos como estes trazem, sem haver diferença nenhuma*". On the probability of this hypothesis, see Rodney (1970: 40–5).

[32] Brooks (1993b: 289).

[33] Ibid.

[34] Person (1971: 675).

[35] MMAII: Vol. 5, 110.

of the Camara clan mooted here.[36] The arrival of the Manes was of course not a product alone of these Atlantic influences, but it may have been related to them through the loss of Mali's influence among the far-flung viceroyalties of the Jolof empire on the Atlantic coast and the contemporaneous transfer of power to the east. Here, then, could be a confirmation of the pattern which we saw in Chapters 2 and 3, which shows the relationship of the beginnings of Atlantic demand with new cycles of violent disorder in Western Africa.

Indeed, the Mane invasions led to violent social changes among the peoples of present-day Guinea-Conakry and Sierra Leone. There was a particularly severe effect on gender relations, because slave ships in the 1560s sailing from Sierra Leone routinely carried many more women and children than men. In 1564 a ship sailing with a large majority of Sape and Susu slaves to Cartagena carried thirty-four Sape women and children, nineteen Susu women and children, and just thirteen Sape men and nine Susu men, a ratio of approximately two women and children for each man.[37] In 1566, when the ship *Santiago* arrived in Puerto Rico from Sierra Leone, it carried seventy-seven women and children and just fifteen men, a 5:1 ratio.[38] This is noteworthy because the typical slave contractor in Seville in this period requested their ship captains to procure slaves in a ratio of two men for each woman.[39] These figures are thus in such stark contrast to the usual demands of American and Iberian slavers for male slaves that they must suggest a devastating effect of these wars on Sape men, a mortality relating both to death in war and the incorporation of captured males into the Sumba infantry. This fact supports the idea that Sape lineages faced sudden pressures in this era which saw their political structures largely collapse; for, as Herbert Klein has suggested, the importance of female agricultural labour in West African societies might suggest that "an indication of the viability of a given African region or state in the epoch of the Atlantic slave trade was its ability to retain women and keep them from the trans-Atlantic trade. The shipping of

---

[36] Brooks (1993b: 289).

[37] AGI, Justicia 518, No. 1, fols. 36v-44v.

[38] AGI, Justicia 996, No. 2, Ramo 3, fols. 74r–76r.

[39] This itself was a new departure because during the late-fifteenth- and early sixteenth-century trade from Senegambia and Arguim to Iberia, the highest demand had been for female and child slaves – see Mendes (2007: 87); and Mendes, presentation at the conference *Brokers of Change: Atlantic Commerce and Cultures in Pre-Colonial "Guinea of Cape Verde"*, June 11–13, 2009, at the University of Birmingham. Gender balances of African slaves in Seville between 1471 and 1525 exhibit relative equality between the sexes – see Franco Silva (1979: 177–8).

more women than normal might indicate a fundamental breakdown in the economic or social viability of the state".[40] Thus this data is supportive of the sixteenth-century sources describing the sudden and transformative effects of the Mane invasions.[41]

Large numbers of Sapes were exported to the Americas in these years (see Table I.2). In Panamá, members of Sape lineages and groups neighbouring the Sapes represented a significant proportion of the *cimarrón* communities by the 1570s.[42] Slave ships carried members of neighbouring groups to the Sapes such as the Susu, Limba and Volon.[43] The entire coast between Cape Verga and Sierra Leone was changed by this violence, and groups who had escaped offshore to the Los islands (off the site of present-day Conakry) were well aware, as with the Jolof near the Cape Verde peninsula in the early sixteenth century, that Atlantic slave ships exacerbated violence even if they were not alone a sufficient cause of it. Crew members of the ship *Santiago* were attacked here when they tried to stock up with water in 1566, and one of them was killed.[44]

Architectural styles in the region changed markedly also. In 1586 the Englishman John Saracoll reached Sierra Leone, and recounted the following scene:

> wee went on shore to a towne of the Negros ... which were found to be but lately built: it was of about two hundreth houses, and walled about with mightie great trees, and stakes so thicke, that a rat could hardly get in or out. But as it chanced, wee came directly upon a port which was not shut up, where wee entred with such fiercenesse, that the people fled all out of the towne, which we found to bee built after their fashion, and the streetes of it so intricate, that it was difficult to finde the way out, that we came in at.[45]

Here is a first-hand account of the sort of fortified settlement, or *tabanka*, which became common farther north among the Balanta and Floup in the seventeenth century.[46] Indeed, the very word *tabanka* derived from the Mane fortifications in the Sierra Leone region.[47] It is not clear that

---

[40] H. Klein (1997: 36).
[41] It could also be seen to require a re-shaping of revisionist ideas of some important historians of West Africa suggesting that the Mane migration was more gradual – see, for example, Jones (1981: 175–6); Mark (2007: 197–8).
[42] AGI, Patronato 231, Ramo 6, fol. 212v: "*los demas negros de puerto velo y particularmte donde son los zapes y longas y otras naciones comarcanas a los dichos zapes*".
[43] See AGI, Justicia 518, No. 1, fols. 36v-44v for evidence of this.
[44] AGI, Justicia 996, No. 2, Ramo 3, fols. 18v, 20r.
[45] Hakluyt (1904: Vol. 11, 206).
[46] Baum (1999: 121); Hawthorne (2003: 12, 121–3).
[47] According to Almada: MMAII: Vol. 3, 367 – see also Hawthorne (2003: 122).

Saracoll's account refers to a Mane village, and it may refer to a village built up by Sapes to deter predatory slaving raids. In this latter case, this evidence demonstrates how communities, the need for self-defence, and predatory militaristic raids linked to Atlantic slaving had all coalesced in Upper Guinea by the late 1580s.

What was it about the Sapes that made them comparatively soft targets for the Manes and their Sumba troops? If Almada is to be believed that there were fewer wars here than farther north, it may be that their previous lack of warfare experience did not help them. Yet a further clue may lie in the iron trade. As we have seen, the iron of most of the coast of present-day Guinea-Conakry was of an inferior quality, and such good iron as there was in Sierra Leone was made inland by the Susu, a Mande group (cf. Chapter 1).[48] It may be that the lack of a secure supply of good-quality iron in these years hindered the Sape ability to erect strong defences and their ability to expand their cycles of agricultural production in response to the new Atlantic trade. This would support the hypothesis of Hawthorne that it was access to iron which determined many societies' success in this new interconnected and violent world; moreover, it is supported by events among the Biafada.[49]

For here, to the north, agricultural activity had fallen off rapidly by the end of the sixteenth century, even though in the fifteenth century Biafada had cultivated rice and millet.[50] The Biafada's iron had previously been traded from Sierra Leone (cf. Chapter 1), but the Mane wars had cut access to this supply. As we shall now see, just as among the Sapes, the impact of Atlantic trade was severe for the Biafada. Thus, like the Sapes, it would be the lack of this commodity of such ritual and actual power in Upper Guinea which helped to shape the problems they faced as the sixteenth century progressed, and more and more Biafada, like the Sapes, were exported in the dungeon holds of slave ships to America (see Tables I.1 and I.2).

LANÇADO TRADE AMONG THE BIAFADA AND THE GROWTH OF MANE POWER IN UPPER GUINEA

Hitherto, historians of Mali have tended to see the transfer of the seat of empire to Songhay as part of a long process of imperial decline which

---

[48] Fields-Black (2009: 144–54).

[49] Cf. Hawthorne (2003).

[50] MMAII: Vol. 1, 648: Pacheco Pereira said that the Biafada cultivated rice and millet by the River Grande; but Almada stated that they "sew very little in the way of provisions ... even though the land is very fertile" (ibid., Vol. 3, 324–5: "*semeiam muito pouco mantimento ... sendo a terra aparelhada para dar muito*").

reached a critical point with the Moroccan invasion of 1591. However, although this process went with an attenuation of Mande power in the large, flat and dry spaces of the Sahel, in Upper Guinea things were different. Here, the period of the sixteenth and seventeenth centuries offered consolidation of Mande hegemony. The victory of the Manes in Sierra Leone was one manifestation of this, and another was the rise to power of the Kaabu federation. Among groups such as the Biafada, squeezed between these two groups, the effects were very serious. As Kaabu rose to power and their trading routes were disrupted by the Manes, Biafada were forced to turn to alliances with other groups such as *lançados* for some sort of protection. In this picture pre-existing social patterns were disrupted, and with this came the falloff in agricultural production we saw at the end of the previous section.

The rise of Mandinka power in the sixteenth century and the associated rise of Kaabu can be gleaned from various sources. We have already seen how by the 1550s Mandinka war canoes were raiding for slaves along the coast south of the Gambia estuary and the important evidence on Biafada slave numbers in early America (cf. Chapter 6). The high numbers of Biafada among slaves being sold to America continued in the 1560s and 1570s (see Table I.2). Writers such as Almada noted the way in which Biafada people sold each other into slavery:

> In the [Rio Grande] there are large canoes operated by thieves known as gampisas in the local language. They are like bandits, and they always go about in the same way; they steal slaves, which they bring to sell to the ships, killing them if no one buys them so as not to be discovered. And these blacks, like all blacks who sell stolen slaves, have the custom of giving the slaves something to eat or drink when they sell them, paid for by the very black who is selling them. And they give them this food and drink, because they say it helps them to clear their consciences, because the person who has been sold has helped to use up their money. And they are so cunning that if they see some person newly arrived from the hinterland, they pretend that they want to welcome them, and invite them into their homes, and then after a few days mention that they have some friends in the sea and that they want to introduce them to [their new friend]; and going to the ships they sell them.[51]

[51] MMAII: Vol. 3, 337–8: "*Neste Rio andam almadias grandes, em que andam muitos negros ladrões, que pela língua da terra chamam gampisas. São como bandoleiros, continuadamente andam neste ofício; furtam escravos, que trazem a vender aos navios e se os não compram matam-nos, por não serem descobertos. E têm costume estes negros e todos os mais que vendem negros furtados, quando os vende |m| dão-lhe |s| a beber vinho ou comer alguma cousa, que lhes dão à conta do mesmo negro que vendem. E dão-lhe o comer ou beber, porque dizem que ficam descarregados da consciencia, porque o mesmo*

Such accounts may be evidence of a society in the throes of social upheaval and collapse, under great pressure from both Kaabunké expansion and proximity to Atlantic traders. The growth of Kaabu's power may also be glimpsed in other phenomena, particularly relating to the Gambia River. Extremely telling is a curious passage in Almada, where he talks of a "squadron" of monkeys in the Upper Gambia whose leader rode on horseback and was able to speak intelligibly. Though Almada claimed to have seen this himself, this can only be hyperbole, and his willingness to believe this is indicative of the incipient racialized ideas discussed in the previous chapter. More likely is that he was repeating oral accounts of others, who were referring to the Kaabunké *nyancho* soldiers known as Sulas, who according to modern oral sources were given the nickname of "monkeys".[52] One informant recounts it thus: "These nyancoos. Why did they call them Nyanchos? The woman I mentioned to you, who settled at Durubali, the woman's name is Faama.... She begot these nyanchos. This nyanchoyaa, is like monkeys. There are certain types of monkeys. These are the ones called Sula nyancoos."[53]

That these troops were active by the late sixteenth century and called by the name which they were subsequently known by suggests strongly that Kaabu was already formed and powerful by this time, and had been for some time. Related to this expanding Kaabunké power is the fact that by the 1570s the major Atlantic trade of the Gambia River was in slaves, many of whom according to Almada had been stolen in raids by the Mandinka of the South bank, that is, in areas of the Casamance where Kaabunké power was growing.[54] So heavy was the trade in slaves on the Gambia in the 1580s that Donelha saw seven ships trading at the port of Casão on one visit, and nine on another occasion.[55] That these were probably *lançado* vessels brought from elsewhere is suggested by the fact that in a different passage Donelha described how he had sailed down the Gambia in 1585 with "four tangomão [*lançado*] ships, which had already carried out their trade and were making for the Rio Grande".[56]

---

vendido ajudou a comer o seu dinheiro. E são tão sagazes que se vêem algum bisonho do sertão, fingem que os querem agasalhar, e os recolhem em suas casas, e tendo-os nelas alguns dias lhe [s] metem em cabeça que tem no mar amigos e os querem levar lá para que sejam conhecidos deles e para folgarem; e indo aos navios os vendem".

[52] For the passage in Almada, see MMAII: Vol. 3, 282.
[53] NCAC/OHAD, Transcribed Cassette 491B, pages 12–3
[54] MMAII, Vol. 3, 273–5.
[55] Ibid., Vol. 5, 130.
[56] Ibid., Vol. 5, 135: *"com quatro naviyos de tangomaos, que ya tinhão feito ho resgate, he hião pero ho riyo Grãde".*

The growth of power of Mandinka or Mandinguised groups emerges also from the Kassanké monarch Masatamba, whose activities were discussed in Chapter 5. Masatamba was heavily involved in supplying slaves. Donelha described how in the 1570s he had sold ten to fifteen slaves for one good horse, in an echo of the high prices in Senegambia a century previously.[57] Almada described how many Europeans and Caboverdeans lived in Bugendo "because of the high volume of trade", adding that "in this river of São Domingos there is a higher slave trade than in all the other [rivers] of Guinea".[58] The volume of Masatamba's slave trade is illustrated by the English captain Edward Fenton, who described how in 1582 a Portuguese *lançado* had told him that Masatamba possessed five thousand horses.[59]

Even if these horses were not all procured in exchange for slaves, they indicate a heavy trade.[60] The growing power of Masatamba was likely related to an increased slave supply, suggestive of changes in Kassanké society in these years. The increased slave supply went with an increasingly autocratic style of governance. Almada described how whole families were sent into slavery if found guilty of certain crimes, and Donelha described how Masatamba had sent a woman and her husband into slavery for a false accusation of rape.[61] Such evidence of capricious enslavement coupled with that we have seen in the increasing agricultural productivity of the zone suggests a new and more coercive social environment accompanying the consolidation of Mandinka hegemony.

That Masatamba's authority derived substantially from his participation in the Atlantic trade was revealed by the Jesuit Manoel Alvares, who, writing in the first decade of the seventeenth century, noted that Masatamba had been the king to "win" the title of emperor, and that "this Masatamba was the best friend that the Portuguese Nation has had here ... he prided himself greatly at being called 'Brother in Arms of the King of Portugal'".[62] This shows that Masatamba had increased the power of Kassanké kingship and how that change accompanied close alliance with the Portuguese and their trade, which, as Almada and Donelha

---

[57] Ibid., Vol. 5, 141.
[58] Ibid., Vol. 3, 303–4, 307: "*muitos dos nossos, por causa do muito trato*"; "*Neste Rio de São Domingos ha mais escravos que em todos os outros de Guiné*".
[59] Taylor (1959: 106). See also Nafafé (2007: 80).
[60] The reliability of this figure is questioned by Brooks (1993b: 233).
[61] MMAII: Vol. 3, 293–4 and Vol. 5, 140–1.
[62] SG, *Etiopia Menor*, fol. 13r: "*Este Imperador ganhou hum Rey, que se chamava Masatamba ... foi este Masatamba o maior amigo, que cá teve a Nação Portugueza...se prezava muito de lhe chamarem Irmão em Armas dElRey de Portugal*".

showed, was heavily accented towards the procurement of slaves. Thus as Atlantic traders settled among Mandinka or Mandinguised groups, the new opportunities offered by this trade only expanded Mandinka power in Upper Guinea, which meant that whereas the sixteenth century was a time of crisis for Mande power in the Sahel, by the Atlantic coast things were rather different.

For groups such as the Biafada, the outlook was bleak. In Sierra Leone, wars were still widespread in 1582 according to Edward Fenton, with the Sapes still the main victims. But these wars did not produce slaves as they had done before; the Manes apparently preferred to incorporate the Sapes into the new communities which they were building.[63] Slave imports to the Americas in the 1570s and 1580s confirm this evidence (see Table I.2). Moreover, it was probably also in this period that the Bijagó began their slaving raids, launched in their war canoes, among the Biafada villages: Biafada numbers were severely depleted by these raids according to the Jesuit missionary Manoel Alvares, who described how the Bijagó had torched entire Biafada villages and forced people into the interior.[64] With the accent on slave supply swinging away from Sierra Leone and back to the north and the region of present-day Guinea-Bissau, the Biafada had an urgent need to protect themselves, and so they turned to the *lançados*.

As with the Kassanké before them, the Biafada willingness to do this followed from continuities with existing practices. By the time that Almada was writing, they were subject to the king, or *farim*, of Kaabu; large numbers of Mandinka were settled among them, especially the Islamic scholars known to Almada as *bixirins*.[65] Because these scholars were the diaspora traders *par excellence* in Upper Guinea, it is clear that diaspora Mandinka traders whose caste identity was defined in part through their outsider religion were an accepted part of Biafada society.[66] This conditioned the Biafada to be welcoming to other diaspora traders, the *lançados*, who began to settle in greater numbers at the Biafada port of Guinala.

Biafada lineage heads must have hoped that the *lançados* could act as a buffer against both the Kaabunké and any possibility that the

[63] Taylor (1959: 103, 105).
[64] SG, *Étiopia Menor*, fol. 43v: "*pondo Aldêas inteiras a fogo, e a sangue; e por esta causa vive o Gentio em suas cabanas pelo sertão*".
[65] MMAII: Vol. 3, 327.
[66] On the *bixirins* as the pre-eminent Mandinka merchants in Upper Guinea, see Donelha – ibid., Vol. 5, 137.

Manes might seek to expand the gains they had made in Sierra Leone. Meanwhile, the collapse of the Sapes and the consequent encroachment of the *lançados* on the kola trade had deprived the Biafada of their main trading advantage. The multiple pressures meant that they could not vie with the *lançados* for this trade. Rather than struggle against them, some lineage heads invited them into their communities, and a fortification was built in the Guinala area, probably in the 1580s.[67]

A zone of heavy inter-cultural exchange between the Biafada and the Portuguese emerged in the Grande River area, which by the 1570s and 1580s had begun to rival that of the Kassanké zone farther north. Almada noted many Portuguese speakers on the Rio Grande at Guinala, evidence of the heavy Portuguese presence. These *ladinos* and *ladinas*, the *grumetes* and *tangomas*, accompanied the Portuguese from river to river and even to Cabo Verde, and became an important segment of the acculturated Kriston population of the Guinea-Bissau region in the seventeenth century. They wore Portuguese clothing and made these alliances with the Caboverdeans and Portuguese with the approval of their parents and elders.[68]

However, as among the Kassanké, there were serious differences among the Biafada lineages concerning this approach to the *lançados*. Just as in Casamance, where Masatamba's strategy had produced rebellions from different lineages and attacks on the *lançados* in Bugendo (cf. Chapter 5), so with the Biafada many lineages were hostile. Almada described how in the 1580s *lançados* who ventured out of their villages were likely to be attacked, with Biafada saying that they had imposed themselves onto their territory by force.[69] It may have been that these discontented lineages were those who had suffered most attacks from slavers feeding the Atlantic trade. Either way, as with the Kassanké, the decision of some lineages to welcome the *lançados* in order to shore up their own position was a source of discord, which may further have undermined the strength of the Biafada as a whole.

Nevertheless, the way in which some Biafada lineages acculturated in these years reflects the growing forces of creolisation in this era on the coast of Upper Guinea. Biafada allies of the *lançados*, their wives (*tangomas*) and commercial agents (*grumetes*), spanned both the creeks and swamps of the coast and the islands and had formed new kinship

[67] Newson/Minchin (2007: 36).
[68] All the material from Almada in this paragraph is from MMAII: Vol. 3, 325–6.
[69] Ibid., Vol. 3, 330.

alliances with Caboverdean and Portuguese men. This was testament to how the emergent Atlantic Creole society of Western Africa spanned both the archipelago and the coast. The region lay on the threshold of a new type of identity which the exchanges that had occurred here had helped to form. It was to be a pan-regional Creole identity characterised by the fusion of violence and flexibility, and in which a common language – the Kriolu imported from Cabo Verde – would help to create a shared identity among groups such as the Kriston descendants of Biafada who had been squeezed by the pressures which Atlantic slaving had brought to bear in Upper Guinea.

For among the Biafada, as among other creolising groups of the Atlantic world, the role of slavery cannot be ignored. As we have seen, Almada described the Biafada as great thieves of people whom they sold as slaves.[70] Donelha said that in this period close to three thousand slaves a year had been exported from the Grande River at one time.[71] The large numbers of Biafada who found their way to the Americas in the sixteenth century reflect this reality, as well as that of a people facing great and irreconcilable pressures from different quarters (cf. Table I.2). The forces of violence and flexibility which wrought the Creole world coalesced as slaves were sold to traders in Africa, America and Europe branded on the neck, some with the stomach or face red with smallpox, others with open sores, others without teeth and others with swollen limbs.[72]

The willingness of some Biafada lineages to accept this violence and its Atlantic agents, in the shape of the *lançados*, resulted from the pressures they faced. Yet at the same time, the earlier heavy presence of *dyula* traders representing the Mandinka trading diaspora predisposed Biafada accommodation to this pattern. This was not true of some of their neighbours. Whereas the Biafada accepted *lançado* activity, the Nalu – the Biafada's immediate neighbours to the south – rejected it. The Nalu did, however, trade for Atlantic products via the Biafada, but not directly.[73] The Biafada position as intermediaries between two productive and cultural zones allowed them to act as go-betweens. They could open themselves to the *lançados* as groups such as the Nalu did not. Their strategy of accommodation as a means of self-defence was one which the Kassanké had

[70] Ibid., Vol. 3, 324.
[71] Ibid., Vol. 5, 145.
[72] Instances of this can be found in registers of slaves arriving in the Americas. See AGI, Escribanía 2A, fols. 495r-498v and AGI, Justicia 518, No. 1, fols. 36v-38r.
[73] MMAII: Vol. 3, 340–1 for this information and that contained in the preceding sentence.

already tried. However, in the long run, and as with the Kassanké, it was a strategy that failed, for by the end of the era of Atlantic slavery both these groups had declined significantly from their position of importance in the Upper Guinea of the sixteenth century.

LANÇADO PATTERNS OF SETTLEMENT AND THE KOLA TRADE IN THE ERA OF MANDE EXPANSION

The Biafada decision to accept *lançado* settlement among their communities was connected to multiple aspects of the growth of Mande power in Upper Guinea. Not only did it connect to the expansion of Kaabu in these decades and to the predatory power of the Mandinguised king Masatamba, but also to the way in which the Mane wars in Sierra Leone had disrupted their networks of trade linking the Rio Grande and Sierra Leone. For hitherto, the Sape lineages had been the major trading partner of the Biafadas in this area, purveying kola north.

Understanding the picture of Atlantic trade and its influences among the various peoples in Upper Guinea is thus very important, for it allows us to see how Atlantic pressures helped to reshape the trading routes which linked the entire region. With Sape links to the Biafada disrupted by the Mane wars, *lançado* middlemen stepped in, supplanting the Sapes in their kola trade between the rivers of present-day Guinea-Conakry and Sierra Leone and the trading posts of the Biafada on the Rio Grande. This was not a new trade for the *lançados*, for as the Luso-African ivories from Sierra Leone show, there had been long-standing links between *lançados* and this part of Upper Guinea since the late fifteenth century.[74] However, it was certainly in these years that *lançado* domination of this trade was cemented, which consolidated their commercial and social position in Upper Guinea.

As we have seen, during the Mane wars and their aftermath, the main focus of *lançado* settlement was around the Casamance and São Domingos rivers. Yet whilst they were settled principally here, *lançados* in these decades operated in small craft in the rivers south to Sierra Leone. In a famous passage, Almada described how the Sapes fled to lançado boats, begging to be taken by them. Almada described how "our people" (*os nossos*) lurked with small caravels and other craft beside the rivers

---

[74] See Mark (2007) and Mark/Horta (2011: Chapter 5) for analyses of these ivories, which have been dated back to 1490, and were traded into the Atlantic market through to the seventeenth century.

and estuaries, wherever the Mane army was nearby, waiting for people to come fleeing from the wars so that they could capture them and take them to the larger slave-trading vessels.[75] Almada's use of "*os nossos*" is ambiguous. As he was a Caboverdean, it implies Caboverdean involvement; but as he also had many connections to the *lançados*, it also implies heavy *lançado* involvement. These *lançados* had probably come from the larger rivers such as the Grande and the São Domingos because Almada describes the boats returning from Sierra Leone to "the mother of the Rivers" (*à madre dos Rios*) to offload their human cargoes.[76] Certainly there was a connection to *lançados* from the Cacheu area, because it was they who brought Sape lineage heads from Sierra Leone to the São Domingos region, where they built a village for themselves at Cacheu separated from those of the other peoples of the area, as were the villages of the *lançados*.[77]

This incorporation of Sape elders within the framework of the Brame, Floup and Kassanké settlements of the Cacheu area is important for various reasons. In the first place, it emphasises a key argument of this book, which has been that this was an area whose pre-Atlantic history meant that outsider castes could be incorporated within existing structures. However, what this evidence also reveals is that these Sape elders had themselves developed a relationship of clientship with the *lançados*. Almada mentions that the lineage head of the Sape village at Cacheu was a Christian named Ventura de Sequeira who had been raised on Santiago Island in Cabo Verde, which confirms this relationship between *lançados*, Caboverdeans, and Sapes.[78] This was very important to the *lançados*, because it placed the previous operators of the kola trade from Sierra Leone in a subordinate position to them. This was therefore a key moment in the cementing of the *lançado* position in the commercial network that supplied kola to the peoples of the northern part of Upper Guinea and Senegambia, which indicates how *lançado* engagement moved to a new level in these decades.[79]

Lançado interest in the kola trade was not new. Almada described how for many years the *lançados* had traded salt for kola and other

[75] MMAII: Vol. 3, 363
[76] Ibid.
[77] Ibid., Vol. 5, 110–1. This is according to Donelha. Almada also mentions this settlement (ibid., Vol. 3, 302–3).
[78] Ibid., Vol. 3, 302.
[79] Francisco de Andrade described the importance of the kola trade in 1582. It was the main trade good used on the Gambia to buy slaves and other commodities, and all the kola was brought by ships from Sierra Leone. Ibid., Vol. 3, 106.

provisions there.[80] However, the Mane wars had led to serious interruptions in the kola trade and a possibility of the *lançados* decisively capturing the lion's share of it from Sape-Biafada networks. By 1573 at the latest, *lançados* were living in the Nunes River area, and were trading so far inland that they could not be reached by messengers sent by a Caboverdean official vessel.[81] Indeed, to judge by a series of questions relating to 1574 asked by the experienced Upper Guinea trader Cristobal Cayado in a legal case heard on Hispaniola, the Nunes was one of the main areas of settlement for *lançados* then.[82] The extent of settlement and communications implied here suggests that *lançado* settlement probably dated at least back to the 1560s, and thus can be connected temporally to the disruption of Sape trading networks following the Mane invasions.

The importance of the kola trade provides an important nuance in our understanding of how and why *lançado* communities were able to operate successfully in Upper Guinea in these years. Moreover, it also encourages us to differentiate between African and Atlantic perspectives on Atlantic trade, and to see how they differed and how they were connected. Documents from the Americas suggest that, in the context of the Iberian empires, the activities of *lançados* were assessed purely in relation to the slave trade. The taxes which the *lançados* paid if they ceased to live in Upper Guinea were known as "taxes of slaves" [*derechos desclavos*].[83] Elsewhere, witnesses referred to the "*tangos maos* [*lançados*] and everyone else who trades for slaves in Guinea".[84] There were many advantages for *lançado* slave traders over Caboverdeans and Iberians, for the cost of slaves on the Upper Guinea coast was half that of slaves on Cabo Verde.[85] Not surprisingly therefore, registries of slaves brought to the Americas show that the richest slavers were all *lançados*. Where many

[80] Ibid., Vol. 3, 356.

[81] AGI, Escribanía 2A, fols. 145v–146r.

[82] Ibid., fol. 283r: "*si saben q a los dos ni tres ni quatro dias del mes de diciembre del ano de setenta y quatro passado en los rios de guinea nombrados de nuno y sant domingos no abia factores ni rrecebidores ni escrivanos nuevos de los nuevos contratadores ...*". Cayado clearly had strong connections in the Nunes River area because on leaving Santiago in 1574 he had gone first to the Nunes before going north to Bugendo (ibid., fols. 461v–462r).

[83] Ibid., fol. 135r.

[84] Ibid., fol. 134v: "*los dhos tangos maos y los demas q traten en los Resgates de negros en guyne*".

[85] Ibid., fol. 461r: the *contratadores* Bejar and Algarve asked their witnesses "*si saben que los esclavos negros en la costa y rrios de guinea valen mucho mas barato y asi la mitad menos que en la ysla de cabo verde*".

Caboverdeans just had one or two slaves laden on the ship, *lançados* often had nine, ten or twelve.[86]

Certainly, as the trans-Atlantic slave trade from Western Africa expanded in the second half of the sixteenth century, *lançado* slaving activities increased. Yet whereas from the Caboverdean and European perspective *lançados* were purely slave traders, from the African perspective things seemed different. The expanding slave trade may have mediated *lançado* presence and allowed them to take over preceding trading patterns such as the kola trade once operated by the Sapes, but the role of the kola trade itself testified to the importance of the African perspective on this process. For across Upper Guinea, the exchange of kola had both a commercial and a ritual function. Kola nuts were offered by visitors and at important ceremonies such as weddings and betrothals. Kola nuts were grown in present-day Sierra Leone and Guinea-Conakry and traded north to present-day Guinea-Bissau, as indeed they still are.[87]

This position in the ritual exchanges of a region where ritual and power associations linked to magical prowess were so important cemented the *lançado* position in Upper Guinea. From their facilitation of Atlantic trade, the *lançados* developed a position intimately connected to the wider beliefs and practices of the region and became a discrete caste in their own right. From the African perspective, it was their role in the kola trade which really helped to enhance their status, given the role of kola in ritual and exchange. *Lançado* dominance of the kola trade, emerging in these years along with their role in the contraband slave trade, created ritual as well as lineage bonds for them in Upper Guinea. It was thus their ability to articulate their activities within a framework that offered continuities from preceding patterns which cemented *lançados* as a new caste in the region.

This relationship was important not only in the Casamance region, as we saw in the preceding chapters, but also among the Biafada. By stepping into the shoes of Sape traders, *lançados* began to integrate more fully into the Biafada communities which hitherto had represented the main trading partners of the Sapes in this kola trade.[88] It was surely this which allowed them to expand their position and to develop large mixed communities on the Grande River in the 1570s and the 1580s as access through the Casamance River to the Kassanké monarch at Bugendo

---

[86] Ibid., fols. 295r–296v.
[87] Observation derived from interviews at Bula market, Guinea-Bissau, April 2011.
[88] Brooks (1993b).

became more difficult (cf. Chapter 5). By the late 1570s, when the Mane position in Sierra Leone was established and the number of Sape war captives lessened (cf. Table I.2), the *lançados* were in the right position to expand their trade in Biafada territory on the Rio Grande. Thus a complex combination of the expanding power of different Mande groups in Upper Guinea affected the Biafada willingness to accept *lançado* communities; as a consequence, the expansion of the Atlantic Creole society in Upper Guinea was facilitated as Biafada women intermarried with *lançados* and forged the Luso-African Kriston.

The importance of ritual in Western African societies and its long-standing relationship to patterns of trade through kola and the role of Mandinka smiths thus all helped to create a situation in which Kriston communities speaking the Kriolu language emerged in Upper Guinea in the later seventeenth and eighteenth centuries. Significantly, many of these Kriston were descended from Biafada women, the *tangomas*, who as we have seen, joined the Atlantic trading communities in this era and often married *lançados*.[89] Biafada inability to retain their women follows the same pattern we have observed here for the Sape lineages. As we have seen, Biafada society fragmented in this era, and Biafada agricultural production connected to female labour collapsed. As Atlantic trade accelerated and new patterns of trade developed across the region, the peoples of Upper Guinea could no longer ignore the effects of pressures from beyond Africa's shores in shaping new opportunities and potentially lethal challenges.

THE ROLE OF CONTINUITIES IN SHAPING PATTERNS OF CREOLISATION AND POLITICAL TRANSFORMATIONS DURING THE ERA OF THE BOOM IN TRANS-ATLANTIC SLAVING

When we consider the large expansion of the trans-Atlantic slave trade from Western Africa in the late sixteenth century, therefore, it emerges that, as with the early trans-Atlantic trade, continuities with preceding patterns of trade and settlement of outsider trading castes are extremely important. In the very early era of African-European relations, in the 1440s and 1450s, the Portuguese had tried to disrupt patterns and to seize slaves rather than trade for them; but this had failed, and thereafter the Atlantic trade expanded through the interconnection of global trans-Atlantic pressures with existing patterns in Senegambia and Upper

---

[89] This origin is well known by Biafada even today – see Seibert (forthcoming, 2012).

Guinea.[90] Through this interconnection African trading practices could influence Atlantic patterns and, increasingly, African societies could themselves be influenced by the demands of the Atlantic.

The settlement pattern of *lançados* is a key marker of these continuities. As we saw in earlier chapters of this book, their zones of contact in Casamance were made possible by the pre-existing relationship of Upper Guinean lineage heads with analogous outsider trading castes. Such patterns influenced political changes in Senegambia, and indeed continued in the era of the Mande expansion of power in the sixteenth century and the Mane wars. For in addition to their activities in Casamance, *lançados* were also settled in Sierra Leone in the 1560s, acting as intermediaries between the Manes and Atlantic traders.

Evidence for this comes from the ship *Santiago*, captained by Baltasar Barbosa and attacked on the Los islands in 1566: after the attack, it was then able to stock up with water in Sierra Leone, where it had bought slaves earlier.[91] Barbosa noted that he had bought slaves from "Gaspar Lopez and Gaspar Ribero and Francisco Lopez and Gonçalo Nunez and Gaspar Alvarez and Luis de Espindola and from other resident Portuguese".[92] Barbosa procured 106 Sape slaves from these *lançados*.[93] This must have been in Sierra Leone, because it was here that Barbosa had taken on water before the first attempt to cross the Atlantic. Thus in Sierra Leone, as hitherto in Casamance and on the Grande River, Caboverdeans and *lançados* sought alliances with Mande or Mandinguised groups.

In return for the sale of these slaves to Barbosa, meanwhile, the *lançados* bought "wine and cloth and raisins and figs and jerkins and shirts and hats and socks and oil" from the sailors on the ship.[94] Thus they sought goods which maintained the appearance of the European side of their identity, both in terms of clothing and food, whilst residing in Sierra Leone and procuring slaves through strategies which required accommodation to their African locale (cf. Chapter 5). This evidence makes it clear that, as in Casamance, the ability to operate plural identities was a real and practical element of the daily interactions of *lançados*, and helped them to bridge the gap between Atlantic and African trades and

---

[90] On the initial attempts to seize slaves, see Thornton (1995).

[91] AGI, Justicia 996, No. 2, Ramo 3, fol. 20v.

[92] Ibid., fols. 55r-55v: "*gaspar lopez e de gaspar rribero e de franc[is]o lopez e de gonçalo nunez e de gaspar alvarez e de luis de espindola e de otros hombres Portugueses residentes*".

[93] Ibid., fols. 20v, 29r, 38r-v, 55r-v.

[94] Ibid., fol. 38v: "*bino e rruan e pasa e higo e jubones e camisas e sombreros e calzado e azeyte*".

worldviews. On the one hand they were able to integrate and accommodate to African practices (cf. Chapters 4–5), and yet on the other – as we
shall see below – they retained a firm sense of European identity. This
pluralism was itself a testament to the African locale in which they were
situated, where such pluralism had long been a feature of the region (cf.
Introduction, Chapter 1).

Moreover, this pluralism occurred in a situation where peoples of Sierra
Leone were engaged in a similar process. According to Mark, the Luso-
African ivories from Sierra Leone, though exhibiting clear West African
sculptural styles, also show that "the artists were clearly responding to a
hybrid Luso-African cultural presence".[95] That is, as in Casamance, the
development of a mixed African-Atlantic cultural outlook emblematic of
creolisation was a requirement for both Africans and *lançados* in Sierra
Leone. Indeed, this process was fundamental in the provision of slaves
for the Atlantic trade as demand increased in this era. Once again, we
see how the reciprocal incorporation of cultural practices and material
aspects of one another's culture by Africans and Europeans was essential to the success of genuinely cross-cultural trade in sixteenth-century
Western Africa. The key to this was the ability to adopt plural identities
discussed in the foregoing paragraph; the preservation of strong cultural
differentiation may have been important to some cross-cultural networks
studied by historians in the eighteenth century, but this evidence shows
that here such strong cultural differentiation was balanced by, and co-
existed with, cultural reciprocity, a mixture in keeping with the pluralism
inherent in Western Africa.[96] What this may indicate is that the determining feature for the success of long-distance trade diasporas in the early
modern period was the ability of their members to adapt strongly to the
requirements of their host locale, and whether this required cultural differentiation, pluralism, or rather integration.

There were two cycles of Atlantic trade here: one of European goods
traded by crews of European ships for the slaves that would help to expand
the cycle of European consumption, through the mining of metals and the
produce of goods such as sugar in the Americas, and another of produce
from Western Africa, which saw salt and woven cloths from Cabo Verde
exchanged for kola from Upper Guinea. In order to be successful in both
these cycles, *lançados* had to understand the worldviews and operations
of both systems. Thus did the *lançados* act as the bridge between both

---

[95] Mark (2007: 190).
[96] Trivellato (2009).

African and African-Atlantic trading patterns. This was how they became go-betweens inter-linking Western Africa and the Atlantic world.[97]

Evidence on how they served as go-betweens is rich for the 1570s, principally because of a legal case taken by the contractors of the trade in Upper Guinea and Cabo Verde, Francisco Nuñez de Bejar and Antonio Nuñez de Algarve, against Cristobal Cayado and his associates, all of whom were said to be *lançados*. The case related to events in 1574 and 1575 and reveals much new material on the status of *lançados* in this crucial period.[98]

One of the key things to emerge is the importance for *lançados* of maintaining the trappings of their European identity. We have just seen how *lançados* in Sierra Leone were keen to procure European clothing and foods. In the case between the *contratadores* of Cabo Verde and Guinea and Cayado, much of the evidence hinged on what constituted a *lançado* and on the taxes which *lançados* were obliged to pay. All witnesses agreed that a *lançado* – from the Iberian perspective, of course – was someone who had lived for over a year in Upper Guinea.[99] Yet even beyond this period they remained subject to Iberian laws if desiring to leave Africa, and there were taxes to be paid if they did so. *Lançados* returning to Cabo Verde or elsewhere in the Portuguese-controlled territories had to pay half of their property to the crown.[100] Numerous witnesses confirmed this, and the relevant excerpt of the royal decree from the main administrative centre in Lisbon dealing with the African trade, the Casa da Mina, was cited, suggesting that this was far from uncommon and that people who had spent long periods in Upper Guinea did return to the Iberian world. That is, many of them retained commercial links with this world, and, judging from the produce which the *lançados* in Sierra Leone bought from Barbosa in 1565, they also retained cultural links and sought to re-create aspects of that world.

We have seen that this maintenance of a sense of differentiation occurred within a framework of pluralism where *lançados* also adopted aspect of their host cultures. What is striking, however, is that from the African perspective the balancing of this *lançado* acculturation with the maintenance of cultural difference by the *lançados* was in fact encouraged

---

[97] For the idea of the go-between in this context, see Metcalf (2005).

[98] The one-thousand-plus folios of the case are a key new source for the history of sixteenth-century Western Africa. They are located at AGI, Escribanía 2A.

[99] Ibid., fols. 135r, 255v, 364r, and many other places. This was put as spending "*año y dia*" in Upper Guinea.

[100] Ibid., fols. 265v, 364r.

by host communities, just as earlier it had been among Moslem diaspora traders from North Africa in the Sahel.[101] While the ability to adapt and take on some aspects of the host culture was of course essential, the significance to West Africa of diasporas retaining elements of their distinctiveness to secure trading advantages has been well documented by Greif and Paul Lovejoy.[102] Western Africa was no different, and in the São Domingos area, *lançado* settlements were built in quarters separated from those of the other peoples there.[103] And because the *lançados* met by Barbosa in 1565 had settled among a Mande group, the Manes, this desire to accentuate difference was also a recognised strategy for them, for surely they had long engaged with *dyula* traders before their migration. Thus whereas from the perspective of Atlantic traders the *lançado* maintenance of European traits made them acceptable business partners, from the African perspective this maintenance of distinctive traits followed a pre-existing pattern where distinctiveness of diaspora traders coexisted with their adoption of some local practices and rituals.[104] It was this accommodation which enabled the *lançados* to play a pivotal role in the expansion of Atlantic slavery in Western Africa in these decades; and this perspective therefore reinforces the importance of one of the key arguments of this book, that is, the necessity of understanding the cultural role of African trading diasporas in the emergence of the Atlantic world, and the importance of analysing the cultural forms taken by long-distance economic networks in the early modern era.

Yet although such patterns were key to the expansion of both Atlantic slavery and the Atlantic Creole culture in Africa, outside of the Mande and Mandinguised communities of Upper Guinea, this pattern of receptivity towards Atlantic traders was by no means universal. Indeed, decentralised societies and other groups exhibited different patterns of connections to the Atlantic world in which creolisation was not a factor. An extremely important correlation of this was that in this era, these communities were precisely those in which the trans-Atlantic slave trade became less significant as a factor.

To the north of the Gambia River, this is clear among the Sereer. We saw in Chapter 6 the importance of the Sereer as suppliers of slaves in

---

[101] Farias (2003: Chapter 3, Section 3.1, Numbered paragraph 265).

[102] Lovejoy (1973: 636, 651); Greif (1993: 537).

[103] MMAII: Vol. 5, 111 – Donelha's account.

[104] On *lançados* as acceptable business partners, see Barbosa's defence in the 1566 case that on reaching Upper Guinea he bought slaves only from *lançados* and not from any African lineage head or trader: AGI, Justicia 996, No. 2, Ramo 3, fol. 38v.

the mid-sixteenth century. However, by the later sixteenth century this pattern had changed, and Almada described how the Portuguese traders among the Sereer sold goods to the English and French, "acquiring the goods from river to river, and many leagues into the interior. And every year the English and French procure a large number of cowhides and hides of buffaloes and gazelles ... and also much ivory, wax, rubber, ambergris, skins, gold, and other things".[105] This passage is notable for the absence of a mention of the trade in slaves. Following their initial desire to trade as much as possible for horses and to sell slaves in exchange, the Sereer had developed strategies to avoid the sale of slaves and yet to persist in Atlantic trade. Not only were slaves not sold by the Sereer, but the goods which they did exchange with the English and French were exchanged principally for iron.[106] Evidence from the Americas shows a notable falling off in the numbers of both Jolof and Sereer slaves from the 1560s onwards (see Table I.2), which suggests a much smaller trade in slaves here than before because the trade at Arguim had also declined by then.[107] In these circumstances the English and French, who did not trade for slaves at this time, were more willing to trade for other products than the Caboverdeans and the Portuguese. Thus patterns of *lançado* settlement were affected, and with them the concomitant patterns of creolisation.

Similar patterns of resistance to the slave trade existed elsewhere. We saw in Chapter 5 how resistance to the slaving raids of Masatamba created increasing insecurity in Casamance and placed Kassanké power in the balance. The resistance of Floup and Jabundo-Bainunk and their attacks on Atlantic traders forced the whole political configuration of the Casamance region into the balance by the 1570s. In these circumstances the Portuguese were forced to access the Kassanké court via the São Domingos River up to Cacheu and the creek at Guinguin.[108] The area around Cacheu was heavily populated by Brames, and whereas in the late 1540s New Christians like Manoel Garcia seized slaves there (cf. Chapter 6), thirty years later conditions were different. Alliances needed to be formed with the Brames to ensure that this passage up to the Casamance could be used without trouble, and lineage heads in Cacheu

---

[105] MMAII: Vol. 3, 251: "*adquirindo-lhes os despachos de rio em rio, e muitas léguas pelo sertão. E todos os annos tiram os Ingleses e franceses muita soma de couros vacuns e de búfaros e gazelões ...e assim muito marfim, cera, goma, ambar, algália e ouro*".

[106] Ibid.: "*tratando com ferro e outras mercadorias que trazem de Inglaterra e França*".

[107] Mendes (2008: 65).

[108] Bocandé (1849: 284–5).

accompanied Portuguese officials on expeditions by the mid-1570s.[109] These changes, and the resistance by many Kassanké to the slaving policies of Masatamba, signalled the demise of Kassanké power, because by the early seventeenth century they had become increasingly subordinate to the Mandinka kingdom of Braço (or Bidassou), which itself was subordinate to Kaabu; Bidassou was located in the Upper Casamance around the present-day towns of Kolda and Sédhiou.[110]

This evidence reveals the importance of the reaction of Upper Guinean peoples to the new slave trade in constraining its activities. The rebellion by Jabundo-Bainunk, Floup and some Kassanké in Bugendo limited Portuguese trade in Casamance and encouraged them to look elsewhere, to Cacheu and to Guinala. Cacheu, as we have seen, was a region which hitherto had been subject to the Kassanké ruler. The Brame of Cacheu were not as heavily Mandinguised as the Kassanké, but as we saw in Chapter 1 they possessed areas of cultural similarities with the Bainunk-Kassanké and they were touched by the Mandinka expansion through their connection to the Kassanké monarch. Probably, like the Sereer and the Jolof of Cajor before them, they saw trade with the Portuguese as a way to shore up their position against hitherto more powerful neighbouring groups. They seized the opportunities of Atlantic trade to forge greater independence from the Kassanké, drawing on the continuities with what had gone before.

Thus a similar pattern developed in Casamance in the mid-sixteenth century to that which we observed in Senegambia for the late fifteenth century, where the Atlantic trade destabilised existing power structures and ultimately undermined the more powerful groups nearest to the coast at the time of their arrival. The pressures of the Atlantic world re-oriented political balances throughout Senegambia and Upper Guinea and tended towards political fragmentation. It was only inland among the Kaabunké and farther south among the Mane that it encouraged consolidation. On the coast, smaller political units asserted independence and used the Atlantic as an opportunity, just as did the ruler of the Kongo province of Sonho in the seventeenth century. However, they were unable to operate along the lines of the "multi-cultural" Casamance kingdom of the pre-Atlantic era (cf. Chapter 1). Thus political fragmentation brought about by the Atlantic trade also, in time, would lead to what we can term,

---

[109] AGI, Escribanía 2A, fol. 145v.
[110] Mota (1981: 155–8); a remnant of historical memory remains, as for instance in the name of the village Simbandi-Bidassou, located between Samin and Tanaf in Upper Casamance.

for want of a better word, "ethnic" fragmentation, or the fragmentation of kinship lines and alliances into smaller political groups. In the coastal regions of Upper Guinea, there was a way in which the Atlantic opening encouraged the consolidation of decentralised societies rather than of larger-scale states.[111] Thus the resistance of peoples to the physical and social violence of the slave trade, coupled with their skilful appropriation of the opportunities of Atlantic trade, had effects which went far beyond the immediate realignments of the sixteenth century.

Taken in the round, this evidence reinforces something which historians of Africa have long known: that exchanges related to the Atlantic trade were two way and that Atlantic traders had to respond to local patterns of culture, economics and politics in order to meet their commercial needs. As the pattern of the settlement of Atlantic diaspora traders shows, where they brought useful goods and trading opportunities, the pre-existing disposition to accept diaspora traders ensured their welcome – as linguistic evidence attests.[112] According to the practices of Upper Guinea, marriage alliances were made and new lineages such as the Kriston developed. Farther south, however, in Sierra Leone, where this history of trans-Saharan diasporic connections was less entrenched, *lançados* did settle, but more permanent creolised Atlantic communities did not develop. Where weaker lineages of groups such as the Biafada and the Kassanké or decentralised societies saw themselves as preyed upon by the trade, they responded by violent attacks on traders and by reshaping the institutions of their societies.

Thus the Atlantic Creole society which had originated in Cabo Verde and become solidified in a Kriolu language and mixed cultural framework did come to influence West Africa itself, but the nature of this influence depended on other factors. Where worlds of cultural exchange and creolisation opened up, they were predicated on the expansion of trans-Atlantic slavery and dependent on the cultural and social frameworks of African societies, the labour demands of America and the consumer demands of Europe. Over the next two centuries, it was to be this world which would come to characterise the Atlantic as a whole.

---

[111] On the importance of acephalous societies in the Atlantic slave trade, in contrast to the views of earlier historians, see Hawthorne (2001) and M. Klein (2001).

[112] See Bradshaw (1965) on the incorporation of Portuguese loan words into the languages of Sierra Leone and also into Mandinka. Most loan words were related to trade goods brought by the Portuguese, which is suggestive of how the utility of Portuguese diaspora traders was seen here (34–5).

9

Creole Societies and the Pan-Atlantic in Late-Sixteenth-Century Western Africa and America

The end of the sixteenth century saw important changes both within Western Africa and in the region's Atlantic trade. Starting in 1580, a series of devastating droughts afflicted Cabo Verde. The droughts precipitated famines. Many Caboverdeans relocated to the coast of Upper Guinea. This accentuated the cultural and economic ties binding islands and coast and brought changes in the relationships between Upper Guineans and their Caboverdean and Iberian guests. In 1589 the *lançados* built a fortification at Cacheu in Brame territory. Here was an attempt to shift the landlord-stranger relationship onto a different footing.[1]

This process produced major changes in the emerging creolised community in Western Africa. The arrival of many Caboverdeans swelled this community on the African mainland. Moreover, the fact that there had long been connections between Cabo Verde, the Caribbean islands and America meant that the pan-Atlantic nature of these communities on the African mainland was accentuated. As we have seen, the Kriolu language and mixed Atlantic cultural practices predated these events by some decades, and yet it was in these last years of the sixteenth century that the idea of a Creole community developed. The idea originated in the Americas, which itself stands as testament to the way in which global forces had come to influence local identities and responses in Western Africa by this time.

One of the main aims of this chapter is to show in detail and for the first time how this process unfolded. Key new documentary finds illustrate

---

[1] See Brooks (1993b) on landlords and strangers. Rodney (1970: 90) saw the fort as symbolising a new relationship between hosts and guests in Upper Guinea.

that the idea of the "Creole" that emerged in the sixteenth century was a proto-transnational ideology which emerged as an explanatory paradigm of this uncertain new and modernising world. This makes this idea analogous to the conceptual lexicon of caste-based, proto-racial identities discussed in Chapter 7. These analogies for ideas with such different contents are surprising, but the similarity lies in the context of the mass mobility which underpinned the transnational nature of both ideologies, and which, as we saw in Chapter 4, was a key aspect of the modernising processes of the sixteenth century.[2] Both the new class dependent on the security of colonial hierarchies and those who had been born of the violence and accommodations which those hierarchies required needed new ideas to make sense of relationships which were very new. Here were ideas applicable throughout the Atlantic world which informed the mixed social context in which the new Kriolu language and identities had already emerged.

At the same time, events thousands of miles to the south also became relevant to Western Africa. In West-Central Africa, the 1560s saw a shift from what Miller has described as the "relatively peaceful transfer of dependents which had characterised the early intra-African slave trade" to more outright slave raiding.[3] This situation was exacerbated by the Portuguese wars in Angola from 1575 onwards and the founding of the settlement of São Paulo de Loanda. The result was a sharp rise in the number of slaves from West-Central Africa making for the Americas by the mid-1580s.[4] Although Western Africa remained important as a source of slaves in the first third of the seventeenth century, West-Central Africa came to have a dominant role.[5] However, although this was important from a macro-economic point of view, and of course also to the peoples of West-Central Africa, in Western Africa the consequences of this were slight, at least at first, as the volume of slave exports did not diminish.

Indeed, in the short term the changes of the 1580s heralded a period of intense slaving in Upper Guinea. As we shall see in this concluding chapter, large numbers of Upper Guinean slaves continued to be exported to America. A further goal of this chapter is to detail new evidence for this picture and argue for a connection of this process to the Kriolu-speaking

---

[2] Gruzinski (2005).
[3] Miller (1976b: 83).
[4] Heywood/Thornton (2007); Mendes (2008); Alencastro (2000).
[5] Heywood/Thornton (2007); on the continued importance of Western Africa, see Green (2007b: Part III) and Newson/Minchin (2007: 66). Wheat (2009) shows how the region predominated in slave exports to Cartagena until circa 1620.

communities of Cacheu and its hinterland. Whereas new slaving ports
such as Havana saw a sharp rise in slave imports from West-Central Africa
in these years, all but two of the slave ships whose cargoes were registered
in Cartagena between 1573 and 1592 came from Western Africa.[6] Thus
the emergence of Creole communities which spoke Kriolu as a vernacular
on the African mainland and engaged in Atlantic trade coincided with the
intensification of the trans-Atlantic slave trade, indicating again the links
of creolisation and slavery in the Atlantic world.

The agency of Upper Guinean societies which we have observed in
this book was thereby overlaid on a pattern of worsening violent disorder instigated by Atlantic pressures. We must recognise, therefore, the
limits of this agency and the pressurising situations in which it had to
be exercised. However, this did not mean that societies could not take
the initiative in responding to the forces of creolisation and slavery; they
were able to reshape their communities and build institutions and histories of which today's Upper Guineans are the proud inheritors. In its
final section, this chapter shows how the attempts to reshape institutions
following Atlantic slavery in Western Africa went with enslaved Upper
Guineans to the Americas and helped to transfer to the Americas some
of the processes and ideas which had developed with creolisation in
the specific locale of Western Africa. Thus the expansion of slavery and
creolisation at the end of the sixteenth century became genuinely pan-
Atlantic phenomena, which emphasises the need to place the events we
have analysed in this book in a broad global perspective.

THE ECOLOGICAL CRISIS OF THE 1580S ON CABO VERDE
AND ITS EFFECTS IN WESTERN AFRICA

In 1572 Martín de Centinera visited Cabo Verde en route to the
Americas. He wrote a letter on December 22 describing how the mariners of his ship had purchased meat, wood and water there. Thirty
cows had been bought together with maize and other provisions.[7] Yet
ten years later when Diego Flores de Valdés wrote from the islands on
January 24, 1582, he described a sterile land and a complete lack of
provisions.[8] Both men wrote just after the end of the rainy season. The

---

[6] On Cartagena, see Wheat (2009: 111). 40 per cent of the slaves reaching Havana came
from Congo and Angola, and 57 per cent from Western Africa (Fuente 2008: 41).
[7] AGI, Patronato 29, Ramo 26.
[8] AGI, Patronato 33, No. 3, Ramo 19.

difference in what they found relates to the onset of the ecological crisis which shaped Cabo Verde's relationship with the Atlantic world in the seventeenth century.

In the 1570s, Cabo Verde was well settled and apparently thriving. There were many parishes on Santiago, with large settlements in Santa Catarina and São Domingos as well as at Ribeira Grande.[9] There were two sizeable parishes in Fogo.[10] Visiting Maio in 1578, the English pirate-hero Francis Drake found vineyards producing good quality grapes tended by people living in low cottages nearby; meanwhile, the Portuguese on Fogo lived "very commodiously … as in the other islands thereabouts".[11] The dominant role which the Cabo Verde islands had in the trans-Atlantic slave trade created this situation. It was still normal for ships to collect slaves in Cabo Verde rather than to go directly to Upper Guinea.[12] This stimulated the economy both through the sale of slaves and the supply of provisions, as Centinera's letter attests. It also fostered cosmopolitanism, with many people in Ribeira Grande having commercial contacts in the Americas and experience of travelling to and fro on the slave ships.[13] Some of these people returned from America to Seville before plying again to Santiago, which shows just how deeply involved many traders on Cabo Verde were with pan-Atlantic networks.[14] People in the Americas, meanwhile, had frequently spent periods in Cabo Verde.[15] This of course continued the pattern for the 1540s and 1550s, when witnesses for inquisitorial cases relating to Western Africa were frequently interrogated in Lisbon (cf. Chapter 6). Cabo Verde remained located in a pan-Atlantic economy and worldview, and it was of course this which had facilitated the development of Atlantic ideas of caste and proto-racial identity there, as we saw in Chapter 7.

[9] MMAII: Vol. 3, 28–53: a census of the parishes of Cabo Verde taken in 1572–3.
[10] Ibid., Vol. 3, 44, 53.
[11] Upcott (1936: 124, 127).
[12] See e.g. AGI, Justicia 864, No. 7 (1564); AGI, Justicia 883, No. 3 (1566); AGI, Contaduría 1174, No. 6 (1572); AGI, Escribanía 119A, fol. 15r (1574); AGI, Escribanía 36A (1574); AGI, Santa Fe 37, Ramo 5, No. 42 (1580) – and many others.
[13] Thus during the Cayado case of the 1570s, Cayado was imprisoned in Hispaniola and there asked many witnesses detailed questions about commercial operations and norms related to *lançados*, revealing very close connections between Cabo Verde and Hispaniola. See Escribanía 2A, fol. 270vff.
[14] AGI, Escribanía 1069A, No. 5. A case from 1583 in which two residents of Cabo Verde, Gaspar Dias and Pedro de Bega, were arrested in a ship returning with the fleet from New Spain to Seville.
[15] In addition to the Cayado case, see AGI, Justicia 204, No. 3, Ramo 1, fols. 8r and 9v for this.

The islands' commercial orientation naturally affected society. Like the New Christian diaspora, Caboverdean traders were themselves early exemplars of transnationals, which made the islands a centre for exchanging ideas and goods.[16] Meanwhile, the concentration on slaving meant that there was a large population of escaped slaves in the interior of Santiago. They had taken the island's best and most fertile land, and the people in Ribeira Grande feared them.[17] It was these *vadios*, or vagrants, who would shape Caboverdean society after the crises of the late sixteenth and early seventeenth centuries; they were the ancestors of the *Badius*, the name for people from Santiago in Cabo Verde today.

This picture changed radically after 1580, with the simultaneous onset of political and ecological crises. The political crisis followed the union of the crowns of Portugal and Spain in 1580.[18] This resulted in the accession of Filipe I (Felipe II of Spain) to the Portuguese crown and a sixty-year dual monarchy. Some have seen the Caboverdean archipelago's decline in the period 1580–1640 as stemming, at least in part, from this union.[19] The dominance of the Spanish crown in the Portuguese *ultramar* – even though the colonies of the two nations were administered separately – meant that Santiago was usually bypassed by ships from Seville.[20] Portuguese slaving vessels became fair game for English pirates, and by the late 1580s attacks on them were commonplace.[21] However, the view that this decline stemmed from the Filippine period of Portuguese government takes an overly metropolitan view of history. Imperial power and wealth are significant players in the historical process, but as this book has shown, they cannot entirely override environmental and local forces.

In Cabo Verde, 1580 also saw the onset of a series of famines that caused widespread devastation. The three major episodes occurred in 1580–3, 1590–4, and 1609–11.[22] The one that began in the 1580s was so bad that the news reached Europe and alms were sent in the form of flour and grain.[23] The principal cause of the environmental collapse of

[16] On New Christians as "transnationals", see Patricia Seed in Bayly et al. (2006). Yovel (2009) also sees New Christians as prototypes of modernity, to which transnationalism usually refers.
[17] Upcott (1936: 125).
[18] For a good account of this crisis, see Diffie/Winius (1977: 423–30).
[19] See for example C. Ferreira (1964: 74).
[20] Scelle (1906: Vol. 1, 463); M. Silva (1970: Vol. 25, no. 98, 218).
[21] Heywood/Thornton (2007: 15) make this point. See also Hakluyt (1904: Vol. 10, 184–91) for two examples of this.
[22] Carreira (1972: 191).
[23] ASV, Secretaria di Stato di Portogallo, Vol. 1, fol. 408v. See also AHU, Cabo Verde, Caixa 1, Doc. 23, where the governor of Cabo Verde, Francisco Ruiz de Sequeira, mentions that millet was sent to the islands during the 1583 famine.

the islands was agricultural improvidence.²⁴ Widespread overgrazing is implied by the documentary evidence of feral cattle on Santiago as early as the 1480s.²⁵ Goats were wild on all the islands by the early sixteenth century.²⁶ The effects of overgrazing were aggravated by tree felling to provide wood for passing ships (mentioned in Centinera's letter), leading to soil erosion and the reduced reliability of springs.²⁷ As Jared Diamond has shown, in this process of failed environmental brinkmanship, Cabo Verde was merely one of many societies which have overreached without heeding signs of their own imminent collapse.²⁸

However, it was not immediately clear that the drought of 1580–3 heralded a decisive shift in the islands' ecology and geopolitical importance. When Francis Drake sacked Ribeira Grande in 1585, his men found that there was still running water in the stream, and up the valley there were "gardens and orchards well replenished with divers sorts of fruites, herbes and trees, as lymons, oranges, sugar canes, [coconuts], plantans, potato-rootes, cucumbers, small and round onions, garlicke".²⁹ Just as it may not have seemed that there had been a permanent shift in the Caboverdean ecology, the same went for the islands' role in the Atlantic trade. The fact that Drake still thought Ribeira Grande worth attacking demonstrates that the shift in Western Africa's Atlantic trading hub to the coast was not yet complete.³⁰ According to one witness in Cartagena, Drake's fleet had consisted of twenty ships.³¹ Ribeira Grande was still thought of as a prize, and two years before, in 1583, it had also been attacked, leading to the capture there of a ship from Elmina.³² Yet soon it became clear that a deeper process was under way, and by 1588 there was rampant inflation on the islands, confirming the extent of the crisis.³³

The combined effect of Iberian political rivalries, piracy and environmental collapse created a situation from which Cabo Verde's international trade never entirely recovered. The extractive cycle of the islands had reached its limits. A shift developed in Western Africa. Absence from

²⁴ This view is shared by T. Hall (1992: Vol. 1, 5).
²⁵ HGCV: CD, Vol. 1, 53 .
²⁶ Costa (1939: 48–51).
²⁷ This point is made tellingly by Brooks (1993b: 148).
²⁸ Diamond (2005).
²⁹ Hakluyt (1904: Vol. 10, 105, 106). Admittedly this visit in November came just after the rains, but nevertheless it shows that Santiago had recovered somewhat since 1583.
³⁰ ASV, Secretaria di Stato di Portogallo, Vol. 1A, fol. 77r – provides a good account of the sacking of Ribeira Grande. See also Upcott (1936: 270).
³¹ AGI, Santa Fe 37, Ramo 6, No, 72, fol. 1v.
³² ASV, Secretaria di Stato di Portogallo, Vol. 1, fol. 388v.
³³ AHU, Cabo Verde, Caixa 1, Doc. 13, No. 12, fol. 2r.

Cabo Verde became endemic from the 1580s onwards, with people both settling in Upper Guinea and refusing to go to the region at all. The bishop of Cabo Verde between 1585 and 1607, Frei Pedro Brandão, was absent for more than ten years in the latter part of his episcopate.[34] From having been a lynchpin in the trans-Atlantic slave trade, Cabo Verde began its long decline.

REORIENTATIONS IN WESTERN AFRICA AND THE NEW SETTLEMENTS AT CACHEU AND GUINALA

The movement of people from Cabo Verde to settle in Upper Guinea of course followed pre-existing patterns. As we have seen in this book, by 1580 this was becoming a unified cultural and political space. When Martín de Centinera referred to the provisions he procured at the islands in 1572, he was probably referring to millet and rice brought from Africa rather than to crops grown on the islands. In Cristobal Cayado's 1574 journey, the ship captain Christoval Fernandez described how they had sailed from Santiago to the Nunes River and thence to the São Domingos before trying to return to Santiago.[35] The ship manifest of the free Blacks on this voyage included people identifying themselves as Jolof, Pepel and Sape, but also several people from the island of Santiago.[36] Caboverdeans and peoples of Senegambia and Upper Guinea frequently mixed, and thus it was logical that it was to the African coast that Caboverdeans turned when the droughts struck.

As we have seen, the *lançado* communities on the coast were already large. In 1582, Andrade described how there were about fifty *casas de brancos* [white households] at both the Grande and São Domingos Rivers. At the São Domingos the trade was for slaves, wax and ivory, and at the Grande it was for slaves, gold and ivory.[37] A sudden influx of Caboverdeans accentuated the numbers of traders and contributed to an expansion in the slave trade. It disrupted the equilibrium which had developed between *lançados* and Upper Guineans, and led to an attempt to shift the relationship between Africans and Europeans towards that which Caboverdeans had known on the archipelago. This tells us much about the effects of Atlantic slavery in Western Africa in the sixteenth

---

[34] Cerrone (1983: 25): in 1604, Filipe II wrote to Brandão, urging him to go to the see since he had not been there for 10 years.

[35] AGI, Escribanía 2A, fols. 461v–462r.

[36] Ibid., fols. 499v–501v.

[37] MMAII: Vol. 3, 105.

century, and, given the way in which Cabo Verde was interconnected to all corners of the Atlantic world, about how this process affected the emergence of new ideas in the sixteenth century Atlantic.

For some time, the accent of *lançado* contacts with Kassanké and Brame peoples had been shifting away from Bugendo and towards Cacheu. The construction of the fort at Cacheu in 1589 was the culmination both of this process and of the migration from Santiago. Indeed, it is noteworthy that according to Almada the fort was instigated by Manuel Lopes Cardoso, a resident of Santiago.[38] The Brames around Cacheu tried to rebel in 1590, but they could not destroy the new fortified settlement.[39] By 1591 Cacheu was a focal point for the exchange of slaves for iron brought from the Gambia and the Petite Côte between the Cape Verde peninsula and the Saluum delta.[40] Within a few years, the fort at Cacheu was increasingly accepted by the Brames, and relations became more amicable.[41]

The fort at Cacheu symbolised, as Rodney saw, a new era in the relationship between hosts and guests.[42] For some time Caboverdeans and *lançados* had been forging alliances with the Brames of the Cacheu region. In 1573 the lineage head of Cacheu had accompanied Caboverdean officials on a punitive expedition against *lançados*.[43] At this time the number of *lançados* there was low, but the migration from Cabo Verde and the shift in *lançado* attention from Bugendo to Cacheu in the 1580s changed this situation and led to tensions. Almada describes how the *lançados* living there were increasingly afflicted by robberies and physical attacks, just as they were among the Biafada in the Grande River and among the Kassanké at Bugendo (see Chapters 5 and 8).[44] The *lançado* impact on the Cacheu region soon became ever greater, with the proportion of Brame slaves exported to the Americas growing in the 1580s and 1590s (see Table I.2). Moreover, the Brames were under pressure from the Floup in this period, whose numbers had expanded according to Almada, and who had moved into the area of the São Domingos River.[45]

[38] Ibid., Vol. 3, 300.
[39] Ibid.
[40] The account of Richard Rainolds, published in NGC, Vol. 1, Book 2, 245.
[41] MMAII: Vol. 3, 300.
[42] Rodney (1970: 90).
[43] AGI, Escribanía 2A, fol. 145v.
[44] MMAII: Vol. 3, 299.
[45] Ibid., Vol. 3, 290.

The physical assaults which the *lançados* suffered may reflect some of these tensions with the Floup and the raids led by Masatamba from Casamance; they also illustrate the discord among Brame lineages as to the wisdom of the trade with Caboverdeans and *lançados*. This confirms the picture we have seen for both the Biafada and Kassanké. The peoples of Upper Guinea had widely different views as to the best way of dealing with Atlantic pressures, and whereas some lineages thought they would benefit from alliances, other lineages resisted. This indeed emphasises how it is important to try to understand changes in Atlantic Africa through the concept of lineage rather than that of some "ethnicised" identity.

Thus the construction of the fortifications at Cacheu and at Guinala reflected this growing insecurity which *lançado* traders faced. Yet these developments may also have reflected Caboverdean priorities and indeed confirm just how much the spaces of Western Africa were connected by the end of the sixteenth century. The decision to build the Fortaleza de São Filipe at Ribeira Grande was taken after the attack by Drake in 1585, just four years before the construction of the fort at Cacheu. It is quite probable that the two projects were connected. Moreover, Caboverdeans were accustomed to being masters of their territory and of their Upper Guinean slaves. They were not accustomed to living among Upper Guineans in a complex host-guest relationship. It may therefore be that part of the reason for the assaults on *lançados* at Cacheu was that the Caboverdeans imported a different, arrogant way of behaving which previous *lançados* had learnt to attenuate. We know, for instance, that the arrogance of new arrivals in Cacheu caused problems in African-European relations in the seventeenth century, as the case of Gonçalo Gamboa de Ayala attested in the 1640s.[46] Certainly, Caboverdeans such as Manuel Lopes Cardoso were well accustomed to segregating themselves from others, as they did with the construction of this fortification. These Caboverdeans imported a ghetto mentality from Ribeira Grande, where, as we have seen, those of New Christian blood were confined to the *Rua do Calhau* (cf. Chapter 7).

Thus the construction of the forts at Cacheu and Guinala illuminates the difference between the worldviews of Caboverdeans who traded for slaves and did not live among Africans and the *lançados* who did. By the end of the sixteenth century, mobile Caboverdean traders had developed a system of racial hierarchy which encouraged them to separate

---

[46] Green (2007b: 317) describes the problems Ayala faced in Cacheu as governor, problems his rivals said were due to his *hauteur* when relating to the Pepels of the settlement.

themselves from those they perceived as impure, but *lançados* had a different approach. The birth of the trans-Atlantic slave trade accompanied the birth of racial hierarchies among those who depended on slaves for their economic livelihoods but did not live among the peoples from whom these slaves came. Such racism was at bottom a form of moral instrumentalism designed to make more palatable the new economic and social realities upon which the hierarchies which now ruled society depended.

It is worth remembering that the ratio of whites to slaves in Cabo Verde in the 1580s was similar to that on Caribbean islands such as Jamaica in the eighteenth century, by which time a system of racial differentiation had emerged which had derived from the *sistema de castas* developed in the Americas in the sixteenth and seventeenth centuries, and which categorised people according to the proportion of African and Amerindian ancestry.[47] Thus similar racial demographics in the eighteenth-century English Caribbean to sixteenth-century Cabo Verde produced analogous ideological contours there to those which had developed in the Iberian Atlantic in the sixteenth and seventeenth centuries. The interconnection of Cabo Verde to the Atlantic world at this early period, and Cabo Verde's focal place in the early trans-Atlantic slave trade, meant that the subsequent ideological condition of the Caribbean had been influenced by these ideologies which were to have such long-lasting effects on the Atlantic world.

Thus the fortification of Cacheu helps us to understand how ideas had changed during the sixteenth century. The droughts of the early 1580s and the migration of Caboverdeans to the coast meant that some of these changes came to exert new pressure in Upper Guinea. The increased *lançado* population of the 1580s meant that there were more traders actively seeking to procure slaves for the Atlantic trade.[48] It is therefore perhaps to this movement from Cabo Verde that we should look for an explanation as to the growth in Upper Guinea of the trans-Atlantic slave trade in the 1580s and 1590s. This was linked to the additional demand for labour which emerged with new mines at Zaragoza in the Nuevo Reino

---

[47] In 1582 the ratio of white Europeans to slaves was roughly 1:10 on Santiago (MMAII: Vol. 3, 99). This was similar to the ratio on Jamaica in the eighteenth century (Jordan 1974: 72). See Fredrickson (2002: 40) on the *sistema de castas*. This unravelled by the eighteenth century, but its legacy in the English Caribbean was the same system, with quatroons and mustees replacing the original Spanish labels.

[48] The increased *lançado* population is revealed by the crown's increased desire to deal with them. In 1591 the governor Brás Soares wrote to Filipe II on the urgency of dealing with the *lançados*, and in 1595 Filipe confirmed the legislation relating to them. See M. Silva (1970: Vol. 25, no. 98, 218).

de Granada and the consolidation of the mines at Potosí.[49] The direct
trade linking Cabo Verde and Bugendo to Cartagena had begun to grow
in the 1560s and 1570s (cf. Chapter 7), and by the 1580s it was well
established.[50] Hitherto historians have emphasised the new system for
the awarding of slave contracts following the union of Portuguese and
Spanish crowns when explaining this expansion of the trade after the
1580s, but African and American factors were equally as important, if
not more so.[51]

Certainly, the increased presence of Caboverdeans led to an increase in
slave exports from Upper Guinea in the 1580s. A royal official based in
Veracruz wrote in 1592 that there were at that time thirteen ships trading for slaves in Upper Guinea.[52] As slave ships in these years regularly
carried between 250 and 300 slaves, this would be equivalent to between
3,250 and 3,900 slaves exported at this moment alone.[53] To these need
to be added an estimated 1,500 per year exported from Upper Guinea to
Brazil in the 1570s and 1580s.[54] An indication of the order of magnitude
was given by Andrade for 1582, when he wrote that the Grande River
was of such importance that twenty to thirty ships could be found there
at any one time trading for slaves.[55] Although Santiago retained a powerful position in the Atlantic networks which supplied these slaves, these
events were harbingers of change in Western Africa, both in terms of the
respective importance of the Cabo Verde islands and the African mainland and in terms of the peoples of Upper Guinea as a whole.[56]

Indeed, these pieces of evidence provide important corroboration
for the general argument of the book as to the importance of the trans-
Atlantic slave trade from Western Africa in the sixteenth century. The fact

---

[49] Mathieu (1982: 39–40).

[50] For examples of this in the 1580s, see AGI, Santa Fe 37, Ramo 5, No. 56 (1584); AGI,
Santa Fe 37, Ramo 6, No. 81 (1588); and also AGI, Santa Fe 37, Ramo 6, 103, a register
of all the ships arriving with slaves in Cartagena between 1585 and 1589.

[51] For this type of explanation, see Palmer (1976: 12).

[52] AGI, Mexico, Legajo 22, No. 82, Ramo 1.

[53] Christopher Newport seized a Portuguese slave ship with a cargo of 300 Africans in 1591
(Hakluyt: Vol. 10, 184); in 1592 William King seized another such ship with 270 slaves
(ibid., Vol. 10, 191).

[54] Godinho (1981: Vol. 4, 172).

[55] MMAII: Vol. 3, 105. These boats included the small vessels plied by *lançados* and
Caboverdeans as well as larger Atlantic sailing ships.

[56] Torrão, for instance, holds that Santiago did not lose its function as an important slaving
post until circa 1610 (Torrão 1995: 35), citing the role of traders from Santiago such as
Diogo Ximenes Vargas in acting as go-betweens for the governors of Cabo Verde in the
coastal trade.

that officials in both Cabo Verde and Veracruz offer similar estimates of the volume of shipping offers confirmation that this was sizeable. And as we have seen, Atlantic trade resulted from a complex interplay of factors related to pre-existing histories, societies facing particular pressures, and economic demands from the Atlantic. It is surely unlikely that this volume of trade could have sprung from nowhere. Instead, this expanding trade built on what had gone before during the sixteenth century as a whole, which was a much larger trade than official estimates have previously countenanced.

THE PAN-ATLANTIC AND THE EMERGENCE OF CREOLE IDENTITIES IN WESTERN AFRICA AND THE NEW WORLD

The importance of detailed localised studies of West African societies in the early modern period was highlighted at the start of this book as a means of examining just how varied the response of African societies was to Atlantic forces. Although this book has only looked at one part of Atlantic Africa in detail, analogous studies could be made for other regions to enhance this picture. As we can now see, these local studies cannot be separated from the interaction of the local with the global. It is in this interaction that something like a "world" history can be identified, together with West Africa's place in that history.

Over the past two decades, revisionist scholars have challenged previous ideas of world history, which were connected to a Eurocentric paradigm in which European actors joined up the world's dots. The work of scholars such as Abu-Lughod led to the idea that prior to the sixteenth century the world consisted of several distinct "world-systems", none of which sought to achieve hegemony across the whole globe as the European empires later did.[57] As Bayart has suggested, these world economic systems necessarily included Africa through the trans-Saharan and Indian Ocean trades.[58]

We have seen in this book that the sixteenth century saw a continuity of this process of global connections through the very early involvement of Western Africa in Atlantic trade. Societies of Western Africa were heavily linked to societies elsewhere in the Atlantic world and influential in the ways in which those societies developed. Just as there were constant exchanges between here and points in the Americas and Europe,

[57] Abu-Lughod (1989).
[58] Bayart (2000: 218).

the same was also true within Africa. As we saw in the preceding section of this chapter, a ship from Elmina was attacked on Santiago in 1583. Such connections were continuities from patterns that had been apparent from much earlier in the sixteenth century. In 1514 ships plying the route between São Tomé and Lisbon were ordered to stop on the Senegambian coast to buy provisions for their slaves (cf. Chapter 3); and as early as the 1520s, there were *grumetes* in Kongo who probably came from the Bugendo area.[59] In the light of these long-standing connections, it should be no surprise that, on a Caboverdean mission in Upper Guinea in 1573, one of the crew, Andres Hernandez, was nicknamed "Angola".[60] Perhaps this was testament to earlier experiences he had had there; perhaps he was always talking about them, a sixteenth-century "travel bore". Influences also ran in the opposite direction; the so-called Jaga cannibals, or Imbangala, roamed throughout much of Kongo and Ndongo in West-Central Africa in the late sixteenth and early seventeenth centuries and were thought by many to be related to the "cannibal Sumba" troops who had devastated Sierra Leone under the Manes (cf. Chapter 8), which indicates that ideas and news travelled frequently from one to another part of the African Atlantic.[61] Certainly, this suggests that Caboverdeans were well acquainted with events and ideas elsewhere in the African Atlantic, just as they were with what was happening in Hispaniola and New Spain.

It was such interconnectivity which facilitated the emergence of transnational ideologies such as racial hierarchies and the idea of the Creole society. In a space of constant mobility, these supra-national ideas created a common sense of identification in an era of such enormous change. Just as common religion was a frequent source of shared identity for members of trading diasporas in West Africa, both among the *dyula* and among the New Christians, so the shared racism of the slaving classes of the Atlantic world and the shared sense of dislocation of the enslaved could

---

[59] MMAI: Vol. 4, 76 for the Sãotomense ships stopping in Senegambia ["*Bezeguiche : & em outros partes dali derredor*"]; Ibid., Vol. 1, 479 for the *grumetes* in Kongo.

[60] AGI, Escribanía 2A, fol. 145v: "*el navio...de que era piloto Andres Hernandez, angola de sobrenombre m[orad]or en la ysla de Santiago*".

[61] Jadin (1975: Vol. 1, 346) – the Dutch representative in Luanda, Pieter Moortamer, stated that "*Les Yakas dont je viens de parler sont, dit-on, des brigands originaires de Sareel Joens [Sierra Leone]*"; meanwhile, the Englishman Andrew Batell, who met the "Jaga" circa 1600, described how "they told us that they were Gagas, or Gindes, that come from Sierra de Lion" (Ravenstein (1901: 19–20) – of course the Imbangala did not come from as far away as Sierra Leone, but most likely were using the circulation of the story of the Manes and the Sumbas for their own ends. For a useful discussion of the linked perception of the Imbangala and the Manes, see Miller (1973: 123).

also create such an identification.[62] This was why these ideas emerged along with the mobility, violence and forced displacement that accompanied the rise of modernity in the sixteenth century. Racism served as a legitimating ideology, whereas the idea of a Creole society allowed those who had been displaced through this process to articulate the new circumstances of their position. This elucidation explains why the category of the "transnational" is relevant, even for such a distant time. It helps to contextualise these new ideas and their conceptual origins, showing how it was precisely through the proto-modern mobility and the needs for badges of shared identities among the new dispersed communities that they emerged.

This can be seen with the trajectory of the idea of the "Creole", which in fact was developed in the Americas and was then transferred to West Africa. Although not found in sixteenth-century documents produced in Western Africa, the term "*criollo*" was frequently used to denote slaves born in America and also those born in Iberia.[63] By the 1560s at the latest this is apparent in the notarial records of slave sales in the Americas, with slaves variously identified as "*criollo de Santo Domingo*", "*criollo de la ysla de Madera*", and "*criollo de la Ysla de San Juan de Puerto Rico*".[64] This represented a change, because in the early 1550s slaves born in Cuba had still sometimes been described without the epithet *criollo*.[65] By 1559, however, slaves were being described as *criollos*, and thus the emergence of this category can probably be placed at some point in the 1550s.[66]

This change was not accidental. Similar processes were at work in the recording of the origins of slaves brought to the Americas. Although in the 1530s, 1540s and 1550s the "ethnic" origins of these slaves were at times recorded, scribes failed to do this rigorously.[67] From the 1550s onwards,

---

[62] On Islam as a badge of shared identity of the *dyula* diaspora see Chapter 2, this volume, and A. Cohen (1971). On crypto-Judaism as a form of shared identity in the seventeenth-century New Christian Atlantic diaspora, see Green (2007b: Part III, Chapter 2).

[63] On Iberian *criollos*, see Schorsch (2008: Vol. 1, 35).

[64] AGN, NT, Rollo 4, Legajo 12, fols. 4v, 221v, 291r (all 1568). Other *criollos* were said to be from the Canaries (ibid., Legajo 13, fol. 194v: 1568), Spain (ibid., Legajo 11, fol. 232r: 1568), and Santa Fe de Antioquia (AGN, NT, Rollo 13, Legajo 44, fol. 212v).

[65] AGN, NT, Rollo 02, Legajo 3, fol. 149r (1552).

[66] AGI, Justicia 35, Pieza 3, fols. 222r-224r.

[67] Among the slaves sold by Estevan Justiniano to Pedro Sarmiento on Hispaniola in 1531, just four out of thirty-two African slaves had their ethnic origins recorded (AGI, Justicia 9, No. 7, fols. 25v-26r). AGN, NT, Rollo 2, Legajos 3–4 contains several examples of slave sales in which the slaves sold were simply recorded as "*un negro*". Records from Mexico City indexed in Millares Carlo/Mantecón (1945) contain no ethnic origins for slaves in the 1520s or 1530s.

such ethnonyms were recorded with increasing frequency, and by the
1560s and 1570s it was very rare to have a document in which they were
not recorded. The reason for this was almost certainly economic. In 1556
the Spanish crown had passed a law stipulating the sale price of slaves
from various regions of West Africa in the Americas, and thus proof of a
slave's origins affected the price for which they were sold. This law created an uproar, with complaints registered from Mexico City in 1557 and
from Lima in 1560, testament to how the law changed the approaches
of slave traders.[68] Thus the institutionalisation of "ethnicity" – which, as
we saw earlier, was usually attributed following projections from both
Mandinka and Portuguese in Western Africa (see Chapter 1) – was related
to the profit motive. This was as true for the *criollos* of the Americas as it
was for the slaves from Upper Guinea.

Given the importance of place of origin for slaves imported to the
Americas, those brought directly from Cabo Verde began to be ascribed
criollo status. This can be discerned from the late 1560s onwards.[69]
Moreover, it was an identification which people from Cabo Verde themselves recognised. A Caboverdean from Santiago, arriving in Hispaniola
in 1575, described himself as a free *criollo* to the scribe taking the ship
register.[70] That this was a distinctive identity of a similar category to the
new ethnicised identities ascribed to peoples of Western Africa is shown
by the fact that other Africans on this ship described themselves according to one of these ethnonyms – as Jolof, Brame, and so on.[71] Thus by the
mid-1570s, at least some Caboverdeans recognised the term *criollo* and
attributed it to themselves. The origins of this identification must have
come through Cabo Verde's position in the trans-Atlantic trade and the
frequent passage of Caboverdeans to Hispaniola, New Spain and other
points in the Americas where the term "*criollo*" was in common usage.
Thus in Western Africa, the idea of the Creole society emerged from the
region's pan-Atlantic connections.

We must recognise however that this term was used here to relate to
hostile bureaucrats making an economic judgement of a potential slave's

[68] See AGI, Justicia 204, No. 3, Ramo 1: a long protest from Mexico City in 1557. See also
AGI, Justicia 432, No. 1, Ramo 2: this contains a long protest from Lima in 1560.
[69] AGN, NT, Rollo 4, Legajo 11, fol. 235v (1568); ibid., Rollo 7, Legajo 23, fol. 161r (1576)
and Legajo 24, fol. 36r (1576). See also Wheat (2009: 72) for a case in Havana from
1579.
[70] AGI, Escribanía 2A, fol. 499v: "*otro negro llamado amador lopez que dixo hera criado
en la ysla de Santiago y era horro y otro llamado atanasio cardoso que dixo era criollo y
horro.*"
[71] Ibid.

worth. We cannot know whether Caboverdeans used this term among themselves even though this individual used it here. Certainly it would not have been a universal term, because slaves in Ribeira Grande were still referred to according to their Upper Guinean origins in the seventeenth century.[72] Most likely *criollos* referred solely to those born in Cabo Verde who spoke the vernacularised Kriolu, which differentiated them from those who had come over to the islands from Upper Guinea. By the late sixteenth century, Caboverdean society had subtler categorisations than "masters" and "slaves". In a world where attributions of caste and "ethnicity" were increasingly connected to hierarchies and the potentiality of slavery, the idea of the Creole made sense to those who were speaking the new vernacular form of Kriolu and needed a marker of identity and belonging with which to differentiate themselves from Upper Guineans.

In this situation, the migration of many Caboverdeans to Cacheu and Guinala in the 1580s becomes a significant factor in the spread of the idea of the Creole society. The fact that the caste of *criollos* was a recognised part of Caboverdean society by the 1570s is a strong reason for supposing that the idea was transferred from here to the African-European relations then being developed in Upper Guinea. As we have seen earlier in this book, Kriolu had vernacularised in Cabo Verde by the 1560s, and the strong connections between the islands and the coast and the coastward migration post-1580 are good arguments for supporting Jacobs's new evidence for the emergence of Kriolu on Santiago and its transference to Upper Guinea as a vernacular prior to the seventeenth century.[73]

Importantly, evidence for the continued consolidation of the Kriolu vernacular in Cabo Verde, which would have facilitated this process, exists for this period. A Caboverdean scribe annotating the manifest of *lançados* in Bugendo in 1573 used the modern Kriolu word for man, "*homi*", to describe the mixed-race Caboverdeans on the list; but when describing other individuals, he referred to them with the Portuguese "*home*".[74] Thus when large numbers of Caboverdeans migrated to the Upper Guinea coast in the 1580s, this language and these ideas went also. We should recognise that this affected only those parts of Upper Guinea connected to Atlantic trading communities, but nonetheless, the

---

[72] IAN/TT, Jesuitas, Cartório, Maço 37, doc. 18: the will of Catarina Fernandes of 1632 includes the freeing of Bijagó and Sape slaves (fol. 2v).

[73] Jacobs (2010); Quint (2000: 19).

[74] AGI, Escribanía 2A, fols. 142v–143r: "*nuno G[onçal]vez homi bajo, morador na Ilha de Santiaguo … Jeronimo de Souza home…*".

development of an Atlantic Creole identity among these communities would have far-reaching effects, helping to consolidate the Kriston community as it emerged in the seventeenth century as the new go-betweens linking Upper Guinea and the Atlantic world.

This exposition of the emergence of the idea of the "Creole" in Western Africa reveals several important things. The spread of this term and its widespread usage followed directly from economic factors, confirming the deep interconnections between the expansion of the trans-Atlantic slave trade, the profit motive, and the emergence of "ethnic" or proto-national identities in the sixteenth century. As we have seen, this was in parallel to the development of racial hierarchies which also accompanied the birth of trans-Atlantic slavery. For the imperialism of the early Atlantic world required classificatory typologies, not mestizo logics, to create hierarchies of both labour and value which left a deep mark on subsequent histories.

What were the attitudes like of those participants in the slave trade whose commercial demands affected these interconnected processes? A clue emerges in the account of Juan de Narria, accused of smuggling contraband slaves into Hispaniola in 1588. Narria said that the ship which he had laden in Cabo Verde, called Santa Maria del Puerto, had had with it a small vessel [*patax*] "as is the custom to bring one, called Nuestra Señora del Rosario, so that slaves who get ill on the voyage can be put there so that their illness does not infect the other slaves".[75] As far as Narria was concerned, the health of the ailing slaves was immaterial; what mattered was that the other healthy slaves did not fall ill too and so endanger the profits of the voyage. This was the mentality which had emerged along with the classificatory typologies of the sixteenth century. This psychology in later centuries would turn its attention to other typologies and would build the detailed classificatory systems of the natural world which remain so important to worldviews today.

Yet although cold economics and hierarchical systems of value and belonging were entrenched by the Atlantic system, there were other more nuanced consequences. As a variety of historians have shown, Upper Guineans who were sold into Atlantic slavery sought to connect to their memories of Africa. As Fuente has shown for Havana, many Upper Guineans tried to marry others from among their own lineages.[76]

---

[75] AGI, Escribanía 2B, No. 3: "*un patax como es costumbre llevarse nonbrado n[uest]ra s[eñor]a del Rosario para meter los esclavos q enfermasen por que no se pegue la enfermedad a los demas esclavos*".

[76] Fuente (2008: 167).

Bennett concurs with this picture, and has shown in great detail how both Angolans and Upper Guineans in New Spain used the Spanish legal system to their advantage in an attempt to assert their rights.[77] Marrying someone from one's own lineage was an important way of trying to reconstruct communities and identities that had been ruptured by the Middle Passage. And whereas some married people of their own group, others lived among them or forged religious confraternities according to these African identities.[78] Other ways of reconstituting Upper Guinean societies could be forged from the types of food consumed and the development of family structures, and these too were important strategies used by Upper Guineans in eighteenth-century Maranhão, Brazil, as Hawthorne has shown.[79]

And as some enslaved Upper Guineans in the Americas sought to reconstitute familiar contours of society through the institutions of the Spanish colonial empire, others escaped, as had done the *vadios* in Cabo Verde and the *cimarrones* in Cuba, Hispaniola and Panama before them. Often, large groups of runaway slaves from the same Upper Guinea background congregated together.[80] These groups sometimes flourished in topographies of marshes and lagoons, which were similar to those that they had known in Upper Guinea.[81] The struggle to maintain elements of the Old World when transplanted so brutally to the New became a key part of African identities in the New World, as the forge of creolisation was transplanted from Africa to America along with the institutional violence and cultural mixtures which Atlantic slavery had always brought with it.

[77] Ibid., 161, 167; Bennett (2003).

[78] This emerges from the description of *criollo* slaves in the Americas as belonging to a particular ethnic group – that is, as having been born in the Americas from two parents of the same group. See AGN, ANS/NP, Rollo 1507294, Legajo 2, 1596, fol. 81r: "*Dominga Criolla de Casta Biafara*" and "*Salvador negro criollo portuguese çape*". Also, some groups of *cimarrones* banded together according to ethnic affiliation. There was a large community of Jolof *cimarrones* near Cartagena in the early 1580s (AGI, Santa Fe 37, Ramo 5, no. 42 (1581) and 43 (1580)). See also Fuente (2008: 167). On the confraternities, see Bowser (1974: 249).

[79] Hawthorne (2010b).

[80] See for example AGI, Patronato 234, Ramo 6, fols. 416v-419v.

[81] Ibid., fol. 214v: the Sape *cimarrones* in Panamá are said to live in an area with great lagoons and marshes – "*de grandes çienegas e lagunas*".

Conclusion

Lineages, Societies and the Slave Trade
in Western Africa to 1589

In a village near the modern town of Gabú, in Guinea-Bissau, a Mandinka descendant of the Kaabunké explained to me why everyone in his village was concerned at the aging of their *marabout*, or *mooro*, Talla Seydi. The reason, he explained, was that a good *marabout* helped a village to keep ahead. When Talla Seydi died, his village would no longer have the advantage that it then had over its neighbours and rivals. All the villagers feared the consequences.[1]

In Guinea-Bissau *marabouts* are held to have strong supernatural powers. They are able to make charms which protect the wearer from knife attacks and gunfire, and other charms enable them to pass unseen through moments of danger.[2] The invocation of magical prowess by my informant seemed to relate a village's ability to be more powerful than its rivals to its access to these significant spiritual gifts. The Mandinka of Kaabu are still revered for the powers of their *marabouts*. Yet within and between different Mandinka villages of the region, the powers of the *marabouts* are also differentiated and are held responsible for a village's success.

The worries of this village in the Gabú region also revealed the rivalries between villages in the zone and the potential dangers that could result. What could these dangers be? Baum and Hawthorne have shown how young men from different villages of Upper Guinea raided one another for captives in the era of the trans-Atlantic slave trade as a rite of passage; this represented a means to secure cattle in the ransoms paid for the

---

[1] From a discussion in March 2000, near Gabú.
[2] See Green (2001).

return of these captives or the acquisition of Atlantic goods through the selling of these captives to middlemen in the slave trade if the ransom was not paid.[3] Neighbouring villages were thus always a potential threat. The spiritual powers and success of intermediaries between this world and the supernatural were held to be decisive in ensuring a village's success in the face of these dangers (and opportunities). Thus as Kaabu became the most powerful political force in the region, Kaabu's *marabouts* became the most respected.

This interpretation may illuminate some of the debates concerning the role of ritual, witchcraft and representations of the supernatural in memorialising the trans-Atlantic slave trade (cf. the discussion in the introduction to Chapter 8). Baum has shown that spirit shrines relating to the Atlantic slave trade emerged among the Floup by the early nineteenth century.[4] This discussion of Talla Seydi's powers may suggest how rituals and the supernatural became hard to separate from the Atlantic trade. Given what we saw in Chapter 1 as to the importance of power associations forged by Mandinka smiths in the pre-Atlantic era, as well as the association of ritual and power in West Africa, and indeed in all societies, the fact that a village or lineage's autonomy depended on successful defence from raiders motivated by the opportunities of Atlantic trade meant that the guardians of ritual power could not be separated from the forces triggered by the Atlantic encounters. This may indeed explain how, as we saw in Chapter 8, the supernatural continues to be connected to stories of external oppression. On this account, the work of symbolist anthropologists such as Argenti and Shaw may not offer a purely externalised form of explanatory paradigm. Although externalised, this type of explanation may also in some way resonate with the violent forces which ritual practices in Western Africa needed to adapt to as the trans-Atlantic slave trade expanded.

The evidence of Tables I.1 and I.2 suggest that some of the triggers of the deep-rooted historical memories which may be contained here had begun to occur by the 1580s and 1590s. Although the initial export of slaves to the Americas concentrated largely on a few major groups, by the end of the sixteenth century many other lineages were involved, including Balanta and Floup. The heavy numbers of Brame exported may also mask raiding between villages. Baum suggests that Floup began selling slaves into the Atlantic trade through Brame intermediaries by the late

---

[3] Baum (1999); Hawthorne (2003).
[4] Baum (1999: 112).

sixteenth century, and the fact that the Floup had moved near the São Domingos by the 1580s (cf. Chapter 9) suggests that such raids could have begun at around this time.[5]

Taken as a whole, the evidence in these tables tells us much about how different lineages responded to the Atlantic trade. As this book has shown, it was always the groups under most pressure who predominated in the export figures. The Sapes were prominent among the exports of the 1560s, ground into political extinction by the Manes. The Brames were otherwise consistently the most preyed-upon group, attacked from the north by the raids of Masatamba, challenged from the south by the migrations of the Floup, and so close to the Atlantic coast that *lançados* and Atlantic shipping were ever present. Nearly equal to the Brames in terms of export were the Biafada, who again were threatened by Kaabunké, Bijagó, and the loss of their dominance of the kola trade with Sierra Leone through the political disintegration of their main trading partners, the Sapes. Both Brames and Biafada lived on the fringes of Mandinka territories and were used to the activities of diaspora *dyula* traders distinguished by their outsider religion. Ruling lineages among both thus welcomed in the *lançados* in the 1580s, hoping that their presence might protect them and offer them new opportunities. Thus as this book has shown so clearly, peoples of Western Africa adapted to the new existential threats of the violent disorder triggered by Atlantic trade, as peoples throughout the world so often have, by falling back onto familiar patterns. In doing so, they did indeed exercise agency, but their actions were nevertheless circumscribed by powerful and often destructive forces.

However, as we have also seen, these strategies of the Biafada and Brame lineage heads were not universally supported. In both areas *lança-dos* were attacked frequently, testament to the disagreements which their presence provoked. Moreover, the same pattern had occurred previously among the Kassanké where there had been disagreements, and again the *lançados* had been subject to attacks. On this evidence, one of the major changes emerging in Senegambia and Upper Guinea as a result of the Atlantic trade was the realignment of lineage alliances. In Sierra Leone, the incorporation of groups such as Bulloms and Temnes into the Sumbas, and of those Sapes who were not killed in wars or sold into slavery, led to the formation of new lineages. In Senegambia, the Sereer asserted their independence as a group from the Jolof with the formation of the kingdom of Saluum. Meanwhile, the construction of *tabankas* for self-defence

---

[5] Ibid., 109.

such as those in Sierra Leone and among the Balanta led to new lineages and disputes between existing ones. It may be that among the products of these disputes were the very raiding parties whose activities produced slaves for sale into the Atlantic market.

This construction of new lineages was accompanied by the fragmentation of the larger political entities which hitherto had governed zones in which multiple lineages had co-existed. The multi-cultural polity of the Kassanké would eventually disappear as the Floup, Bainunk and Kassanké struggled for pre-eminence in the Casamance in the seventeenth and eighteenth centuries. Mali collapsed with the assertion of Songhay's power to the east, following in part the diversion of some of its profits from the Western Saharan trade to the Atlantic. The Jolof empire fragmented as well, as coastal lineages asserted themselves through the access to military power offered by the trade in horses for slaves. This fragmentation was only reversed when Kaabu consolidated its power by harnessing the possibilities of Atlantic trade rather than being undermined by them. Coastal groups, however, remained fragmented. As was the case along the whole West African littoral, this fragmentation forced them to remain open to Atlantic trading in order to defend themselves from their rivals, which enhanced the influence of Atlantic traders in the region and exacerbated the dependency which coastal groups had on these traders for securing the goods and materials which would offer them self-defence. Here lay a foretaste of the African-European relationships of the nineteenth and twentieth centuries.[6]

As throughout history, therefore, the construction of a new economic framework and of new political units was inevitably accompanied by violence. The cycle of violent disorder and the political re-orientations were connected. This violence turned out to be an inherent quality of the process of modernisation which began in the sixteenth century and in which, as this book has shown, Western Africa had a key role. The region was a pivot for the growth in forced and voluntary migration associated with the mobility of modernity. It was perhaps the key locale in the first half of the sixteenth century for the construction of a variant of the Atlantic Creole identity which subsequently became so central to the social systems of the plantation economies of the New World. Experiences here contributed to the growing abstraction of thought and ideology, which contributed to the conceptual revolutions in the worldviews of Iberians in the sixteenth century and to the rise of the scientific mentality. Moreover,

---

[6] A similar pattern can be discerned on the Loango coast – see Martin (1982: 217–8).

as we saw in Chapter 3, it was here that the requisition of economic and productive surpluses for transfer to the economic systems built by Europeans in the Atlantic first took shape, a process which contributed fundamentally to the growing economic disjunction between West Africa and Europe as well as to the political fragmentation which were principal legacies of modernity for the region. These disturbing qualities of the modernising process were only made possible in Western Africa by the expansion of systems of administrative control – or putative control – associated with the power structures of nascent states in Europe, and expressed through new institutions in Cabo Verde and attempts by the Iberian monarchies to regularise the slave traffic to the Americas. One does not need to turn to the twentieth century and the punctiliousness of an Eichmann to trace the long-standing relationship between institutionalised cruelty and bureaucratisation.

Into this picture came a completely new group in Western Africa, that of the *lançados*. In the sixteenth century, when the many social and political changes of Upper Guinea led to multiple lineage changes and confrontations, it was relatively easy for the *lançados* to find a space. There was always one group or lineage which would offer them protection in the hope of enhancing their security. *Lançados* forged marriage alliances, meaning that their settlements had a heavy dominance of Western African women over men, something which led to an important role for women traders in Upper Guinea and to changes in gender relationships.[7] In all cases the *lançados* operated among groups experienced in the incorporation of members of outsider trading diasporas. In a moment when society in Upper Guinea was changing rapidly, it is easy to understand how the *lançados* could also be welcomed as a new group whose status could be determined according to pre-existing customs of the acceptance of foreign traders and to the pre-existing importance of the role of diasporas in the commercial practices of the region.

The trading settlements which *lançados* formed were heavily dependent on the hinterland for supplies. Provisions were supplied to slave ships and sent to Cabo Verde. In this situation, enhanced agricultural production was required, which necessitated more concentrated labour.[8] Given the rapid expansion of the slave trade in the sixteenth century and the demands it placed on Upper Guineans, these are processes which almost certainly developed at this time. As villages became fortified and

---

[7] Cf. Havik (2004b).
[8] Cf. Hawthorne (2003).

agricultural labour intensified, society changed markedly, and communities became more defensive and their labour more coercive. In these circumstances, the *lançado* settlements offered alternatives, and this helps to explain the willingness of Upper Guineans to go there to be *grumetes* and *tangomas*, particularly because many of them came from groups such as the Biafada who were experiencing severe and continuing problems.

As we have seen in this book, the *lançados* were only able to operate with such success because of their cultural predisposition towards flexibility, which was a result of their New Christian origins and the recent history of the New Christians in Portugal. The pre-existing history of violence and nascent modernity in Iberia and the violence and cultural flexibility instigated by Mandinka expansion in Africa met in the creeks and forests of Upper Guinea and helped to create the social accommodation by which slaves were procured and sold into the Atlantic in the sixteenth century. In order to be successful, *lançados* had to be able to be both African and European, just as successful Mande emperors of Mali had had to be able to manifest Islamic and African narratives and rituals. This plural identity was thus an existing facility of communities in Africa which *lançados* adapted to, testament to what Amselle has called the "mestizo logics" of the region. It was a facility which New Christians, forced into being both Christian and Jewish by their experiences in Portugal, were easily able to learn. In their subsequent commercial success, they helped to bring this quality of plural identities and affiliations into the modernisation of Atlantic trade in the sixteenth and seventeeth centuries. Here, at least, successful cross-cultural trade required the assimilation to the predominant cultural attitudes of the region by diaspora traders, not only the maintenance of cultural distinctiveness. By the seventeenth century, such pluralism was a cornerstone of New Christian networks in the Iberian Atlantic world. In this sense, and in others explored in this book, African traits emerged into the formation of the Atlantic world.

Taken as a whole, these issues are all fundamental to rethinking the histories of the sixteenth and seventeenth centuries and the pre-histories of the formation of the modern global industrial system. They remind us to be cautious of what can anachronistically be portrayed as an inevitable imperial teleology. As this book has shown, far away from the seats of power in Amsterdam, Lisbon, London, Madrid and Paris, activities of individuals were structured through the formation of local and transnational patterns of diaspora trade which did not necessarily fit with the stated philosophies of the new European empires. In the formation of these patterns, both the existing cultural and political worlds of African societies and the effects which Atlantic trade had on them have been significantly underestimated. Understanding the consequences of this interplay in the formative Atlantic era has been the task of this book. However, grasping the full extent of these patterns requires us to look at the broader trajectories of both Western and West-Central Africa in the seventeenth century, during the run-up to what historians call "the long eighteenth century" that foreshadowed industrialisation; and this will be the subject of the projected second volume of this study.

Already, however, this book has shown how much may be derived from this type of analysis. This conclusion has recapitulated how in Western Africa changes in lineage patterns, political structures, labour organisation, gender relationships and the manifestation of ritual power all accompanied the birth of Atlantic slavery, and how these changes all emerged in response to the maritime vector of international trade which gradually overtook the role of the trans-Saharan trade in shaping the region's place in the broader world system. Diasporas had been crucial in this earlier trade, and they were so again in shaping the Atlantic trade. New Christian traders extended the boundaries of their earlier Mediterranean and trans-Saharan diasporas into the Atlantic, and Caboverdeans did so too as their archipelago became one of the key zones in the Atlantic world, with direct and regular contacts with places as far apart as Hispaniola, New Spain, Cartagena and Iberia.

Thus began the long history of the Caboverdean diaspora which remains to this day; its current zones of influence reach to Boston, Lisbon and Rotterdam. Trading diasporas have never lost their importance in West Africa, as the Mauritanian and Chinese shopkeepers of today attest. This transnational sphere emerged following the role of the trans-Saharan diasporas and was another instance of the role of West Africa's pre-Atlantic history shaping early exchanges and dynamics in the Atlantic. Moreover, the internationalisation which was made possible by these diasporas had effects far beyond Africa. The wealth which developed in the Atlantic empires assisted in the expansion of European power on a global level and led ultimately to European powers supplanting the empires of Asia.[9]

The early Atlantic trade in slaves was a segue between the preceding Mediterranean slave trade and the later industrial level of the trade in the long eighteenth century. Although on one level more similar to and

---

[9] Cf. Frank (1998); Darwin (2007). On the role of Africans in England's industrial revolution, see Inikori (2002).

a continuity from the earlier trade, it was the step which made both the later trade and the ideas which accompanied it possible. It was thus a prime example of a continuity from a previous pattern which in fact also represented the start of something new.[10] Commerce and the operations of merchants were thus an essential part of both the cultural history of Western Africa in the Atlantic era and the way in which the region related to the Atlantic world. However, that is a very different thing from stating that the effects of Atlantic slavery can only be understood through that prism. To concentrate only on the economic effects of the trade is to re-enact the blindness of those traders who, as the case of Juan de Narria showed us in the previous chapter, thought only of money. As we have seen, the effects in Africa were every bit as much political, ritual and social as they were economic, while in the Atlantic the effects were deep-rooted in the psychology of Atlantic slavers and their descendants; as we have seen, the ideology of racism emerged as a justification of the profits derived from violence. Societies and allegiances changed as the consumer economies of early modern Europe emerged along with new concepts of politeness and wage labour.

Yet to cast judgement on those times – to proclaim incomprehension of the acts of slave traders and of consumers of the produce of slave labour in the new coffee shops of the metropole – would be a failure of imagination and a declaration of bad faith. We have to recognise that human beings are capable of ghastly acts. One of the cruel paradoxes of existence is that those very acts often accompany beautiful artistry and thought. The appropriation of surplus produce from Africa and the Americas lowered the cost of staples in Europe, freeing up people's time and capital for other endeavours and thus beginning the subsequent symbiotic relationship of Western capital and culture. At the very same time that the Iberian powers were engaged in the trans-Atlantic slave trade of the sixteenth century, Spain was experiencing its Golden Age of artistic and literary endeavour, the flowering of Cervantes and El Greco. As Chapter 4 showed decisively, the scientific changes which followed in the early modern period were also catalysed by the new worldview opened up by the experiences of the Atlantic voyages of discovery. As Meillassoux noted, "the surge of philosophical or political thought in ancient Greece or Rome is partly attributed to the leisure time slavery made available to the ruling classes".[11]

---

[10] Mendes (2007: 29) suggests that this early trade has more in common with previous European slave trades than it does with later Atlantic slavery.

[11] Meillassoux (1991: 332).

As Iberian societies flourished in this "Golden Age," in Upper Guinea the institutions and badges of identity were created which are the very ones which the peoples of present-day Cabo Verde, Senegal, Gambia, Guinea-Bissau, Guinea-Conakry and Sierra Leone identify with. Violence was an inevitable part of enslavement, as becomes clear in the descriptions of slaves arriving in the Americas and in the history of intra-lineage raids in Upper Guinea. Yet with that violence came a cultural accommodation, exemplified by linguistic changes, which became known as Creole and which emerged as a defining characteristic of Atlantic slave societies. The Kriolu language and mixed communities which emerged in Cabo Verde at the end of the fifteenth century soon influenced Atlantic trading communities in West Africa. Gradually, a Creole identity inseparable from slavery and its complexities emerged in a variegated way across the Atlantic world.

Instead of wringing hands at this violence, which accompanied this as all other moments of radical change, I prefer to end by thinking of the inheritors of this history today. I remember the old Manjaku in Simbandi-Balante who welcomed me into the shade of his mango tree in January 2000 and fed me fish from the nearby creek; the king of Canogo in the Bijagó who invited me to stay for a few days in December 1996 and plied me with palm wine as I offered tobacco leaves and aguardente in return; and the young Caboverdeans shouting "*fixe!*" ("Cool!") in October 2003 as they tended plantations of maize and cassava in the ruins of the old city of Ribeira Grande, where once their enslaved ancestors had worked. These people were the inheritors of a multi-layered history of violence and exchange, of coercion, self-defence and autonomy, and of the shaping of Creole societies through slavery at an unusually early moment in the history of the world. That history had stood as a marker for what happened later in the Atlantic. Like their ancestors, they made the best of the situation they had been born into, and it was able to bring them joy as well as sadness.

Bibliography

Manuscript Sources

Archivio Segreto Vaticano (ASV), Rome
Secretaria di Stato di Portogallo

Vols: 1, 1A, 9.

Archivo General de la Nación (AGN), Bogotá
Archivo Histórico de Boyacá, Notaría Primera de Tunja

Legajos 1–69, Rollos 1–20

Archivo Notarial de Santander, Notaría Primera de Pamplona

Rollo: 1507294, 1577–1590

Contrabandos

Legajo 3, fols. 546–970

Fondo Enrique Ortega Ricaurte

Caja 182, Carpeta 669: *Negros y Esclavos*

Negocios Exteriores

Legajo 4, fols. 714–784

Negros y Esclavos

Antioquia: SC43/Legajo 1, fols. 997–1018; SC43/Legajo 4, fols. 625–657; SC43/ Legajo 4, fols. 731–745; SC43/Legajo 5, fols. 280–443; SC43/Legajo 6, fols. 352–411
Bolívar: SC43/Legajo 4, fols. 289–383; SC43/Legajo 13, fols. 1019–1061; SC43/ Legajo 14, fols. 704–727
Boyacá: SC43/Legajo 2, fols. 133–167
Cauca: SC43/Legajo 3, fols. 133–167
Cundinamarca: SC43/Legajo 3, fols. 991–1112; SC43/Legajo 5, fols. 1–242; SC43/Legajo 6, fols. 1036–1045; SC43/Legajo 8, fols. 132–138; SC43/ Legajo 8, fols. 792–820; SC43/Legajo 8, fols. 686–924;
Santander: SC43/Legajo 2, fols. 981–1103
Tolima: SC43/Legajo 2, fols. 185–230; SC43/Legajo 2, fols. 958–996; SC43/ Legajo 4, fols. 714–784

Notaría Primera de Bogotá

Vols. 1 – 5B, 9–11A, 13

Archivo General de las Indias (AGI), Seville
Contaduría

Legajo 1174, No. 6

Contratación

Legajos 145, No. 18; 1075, No. 3, Ramo 1; 5282, No. 83; 5539, Legajo 5

Escribanía

Legajos 1A, Nos. 1 and 2; 2A; 2B, No. 3; ; 119A, No. 2; 165A, No. 1; 947A, No. 2; 1012A

Guatemala

Legajo 49, No. 26

Indiferente

Legajos 416, Libro 2; 423, Libro 21; 425; 427, Libro 30; 737, Nos. 49, 50; 740, No. 202; 741, No. 243; 1092, Nos. 42, 45, 104, 118, 242; 1962, Libros 4–5; 1963, Libro 9; 1964, Libros 10–11; 1966, Libro 15; 2061, No. 23; 2085, No. 91; 2093, No. 186; 2096, No. 17; 2105, No, 55

Justicia

Legajos 9, No. 7; 11, Nos. 3 and 4; 16, No. 1, Ramo 4; 35, No. 3; 204, No. 3, Ramo 1; 432, No. 1, Ramo 2; 518, No. 1; 853, No. 3; 864, No. 7; 878, No. 2; 991, No. 1, Ramo 4; 996, No. 2, Ramos 2–3; 1002, No. 1, Ramo 1; 1025, No. 3, Ramo 1; 1167, Nos. 4 and 5, Ramo 2; 1182, No. 1, Ramo 2

México

Legajos 19, Nos. 39, Ramo 1 and 74; 22, No. 82, Ramo 1

Panamá

Legajos 33, No. 83; 234, Libro 5; 235, Libros 6, 8; 236, Libro 9; 237, Libro 12

Pasajeros

Legajos 3, E. 4258; 4, Es. 3352, 4551; 5, E. 1546.

Patronato

Legajos 29, Ramo 26; 33, No. 3, Ramo 19; 173, No. 1, Ramo 15; 234, Ramos 1, 6; 259, Ramo 52; 291

Santa Fe

Legajos 37, Ramo 4, No. 14; 37, Ramo 5, Nos., 23, 40, 42, 43, 56; 37, Ramo 6, Nos. 69, 72, 76, 81, 96, 103

Santo Domingo

Legajos 868, Libro 3; 899, Libro 1; 1121, Libro 1

Arquivo Histórico Nacional (AHNCV), Praia
Colecção Cidade Velha

No. 01945: "Operação Cidade Velha: Nota Histórica Sobre Cidade Velha"
No. 01946: "Preservação do Património Cultural e Arquitectural de Cabo Verde"

Arquivo Histórico Ultramarino, Lisbon

Cabo Verde: Caixas, 1 – 6A.

Biblioteca da Ajuda (BA), Lisbon

Códices: 44-XIV-4, 44-XIV-6, 49-X-1, 49-X-2,, 49-X-4, 50-V-37, 51-VIII-7, 51-VIII-25, 51-IX-7, 56-VI-54

Instituto dos Arquivos Nacionais da Torre do Tombo (IAN/TT), Lisbon
Cartório Notarial

No. 2, Caixa 12, Livro 57
No. 2, Caixa 13, Livro 63
No. 2, Caixa 14, Livro 66
No. 2, Caixa 14, Livro 68

Chancelaria D. João III

Livros 9, 16, 19, 26, 38, 44–45, 60, 65–66, 68

Chancelaria D. Sebastião e Dom Henrique

Livro 1

Conselho Geral do Santo Ofício (CGSO)

Livros 90–92, 96, 98–100, 118, 129–130, 159, 184–185, 314, 365, 367–369, 433–435

Corpo Cronológico

Part 1, Maços 2, 4, 7, 9, 15, 17–18, 23, 25, 30, 36–37, 42, 44–45, 49, 51, 53, 56–57, 67, 73, 76, 82–83
Part 2, Maço 8

Inquisição de Évora

Livros 84–85, 89–92
Procesos 5035, 11267

Inquisição de Lisbon

Livros 6–8, 38, 52–60
Procesos 801, 2075, Maço 25 no. 233, 3199, 5729, 5754, 6580, 7312, 11041, 13107, 16034

Jesuitas

Cartório: Maço 37, doc. 18

National Council for Arts and Culture, Oral History and Antiquities Division, Fajara, The Gambia (NCAC/OHAD)
Transcribed Cassettes : 020, 434, 466, 491, 539, 550, 553, 554, 566

Sociedade de Geografia (SG), Lisbon

"Etiópia Menor: Descripção Geographica da Provincia da Serra Leoa" by Manuel Alvarez.

The Trans-Atlantic Slave Trade Database

Viewed online at www.slavevoyages.org

Primary Sources (Published Material)

A Collection of Voyages (1729): London: James & Knapton; 4 vols.

A New General Collection of Voyages and Travels: Consisting of The Most Esteemed Relations, Which Have Hitherto Been Published in any Language: Comprehending Every Thing Remarkable in its Kind, in Europe, Asia, Africa, and America (1745: Abbreviated as NGC). London: Thomas Astley; 4 vols.

Africanus, Leo (1600): *A Geographical Historie of Africa*. London: George Bishop.

Albuquerque, Luís de and Santos, Maria Emília Madeira (eds.) (1988–1990): *História Geral de Cabo Verde: Corpo Documental* (Abbreviated as HGCV: CD). Lisbon: Instituto de Investigação Científica Tropical; 2 vols.

(1993–2000): *Portugaliae Monumenta Africana*. Lisbon: Imprensa Nacional – Casa da Moeda; 3 vols.

Almeida, M. Lopes de (ed.) (1977): *Crónicas de Rui de Pina*. Porto: Lello & Irmão – Editores; abbreviated as CRP.

Anguiano, Mateo de (1950): *Misiones Capuchinas en Africa: Vol. I, la Misión del Congo*. Madrid: Consejo Superior de Investigaciones Científicas.

Anonymous (1551/2?): "Navegação de Lisbon á Ilha de S.Thome, escrita por hum Piloto Portugues", in *Colecção de Noticias...*(1812), Vol. II, no. II.

(1585): "Relaçao da gente que vive desde o Cabo dos Mastos té Magrabomba na costa de Guiné", in André Donelha (1977), 344–57.

(1985): *Noticia Corográfica e Cronológica do Bispado de Cabo Verde Desde o Seu Princípio Até o Estado Presente, Com um Catalogo dos Exmos Bispos, Governadores e Ouvidores, e os Sucessos Mais Memoráveis e Verídicos, Tirados de Livros e Papéis Antigos. E Assim Alguma Insinuações dos Meios Mais Conducentes Para o Restabelecimento Dele, por se achar na Última Decadência*. Lisbon: Edição do Instituto Caboverdeano do Livro; ed. Carreira, António.

Atkins, John (1970): *A Voyage to Guinea, Brazil & The West Indies in His Majesty's Ships, The Swallow and Weymouth*. London: Frank Cass & Co.

Axelson, Eric (ed.) (1998): *Vasco da Gama: The Diary of His Travels Through African Waters, 1497–1499*. Somerset West: Stephen Phillips (Pty) Ltd.

Bernáldez, Andres (1962): *Memorias del Reinado de los Reyes Católicos*. Madrid: Real Academia de la Historia.

Blake, J.W. (ed. and trans.) (1942): *Europeans in West Africa: 1450–1560: Documents to Illustrate the Nature and Scope of the Portuguese Enterprise in West Africa, the Abortive Attempt of Castillians to Create an Empire There, and the Early English Voyages to Barbary and Guinea*. London: Hakluyt Society; 2 vols.

Brásio, António (ed.) (1953–1988): *Monumenta Misionaria Africana: África Ocidental* (Abbreviated as MMAI). Lisbon: Agência Geral do Ultramar; 15 vols.

(1958–2004): *Monumenta Misionaria Africana: África Ocidental: Segunda Série* (Abbreviated as MMAII). Lisbon: Agência Geral do Ultramar; 7 vols.

Cabeza de Vaca, Álvar Núñez (1989): *Naufragios*. Madrid: Ediciones Catédra S.A.

Carletti, Francesco (1965): *My Voyage Around the World*. London: Methuen & Co.

Carreira, Antonio (1983): *Documentos para a história das Ilhas de Cabo Verde e "Rios de Guiné": séculos XVII e XVIII*. Lisbon: Privately Printed.

Castanheda, Fernão Lopes de (1979): *História do Descobrimento e Conquista da Índia Pelos Portugueses*. Porto: Lello & Irmão Editores; 2 vols.

Coelho, José Ramos (ed.) (1892): *Alguns Documentos do Archivo Nacional da Torre do Tombo Ácerca das Navigações e Conquistas Portuguezas*. Lisbon: Imprensa Nacional.

Cohen, Martin A. (ed. and trans.) (1971b; first published 1935): "The Autobiography of Luis de Carvajal, the Younger", in Cohen, Martin A. (ed.) (1971), Vol. I, 201–42.

Colecção de Noticias para a Historia e Geografia das Nações Ultramarinas, que Vivem nos Dominios Portuguezes, ou lhes são Visinhas (1812: Abbreviated as CN). Lisbon: Typografia da Academia Real das Sciencias; 7 vols.

Conway, G.R.G. (ed.) (1927): *An Englishman and the Mexican Inquisition 1556–1560 – Being an Account of the Voyage of Robert Tomson to New Spain, His Trial for Heresy in the City of Mexico and Other Contemporary Historical Documents*. Mexico City: Privately Printed.

Costa, A. Fontoura de (1939): *Cartas das Ilhas de Cabo Verde de Valentim Fernandes (1506–1508)*. Lisbon: Divisão de Publicações e Biblioteca Agência Geral das Colónias.

Díaz, Bernal (1963): *The Conquest of New Spain*. Harmondsworth: Penguin; tr. Cohen, J.M.

Donelha, André (1977): *Descriçao da Serra Leoa e dos Rios de Guiné do Cabo Verde*. Lisbon: Junta de Investigaçôes Científicas do Ultramar; ed. Teixeira da Mota, Avelino (with an English translation by P.E.H. Hair).

Donnan, Elizabeth (ed.) (1930): *Documents Illustrative of the History of the Slave Trade to America*. Washington: Carnegie Institute of Washington; 4 vols.

Echagoian, Lic. (1941): "Relación de la Isla Española", in *Boletín del Archivo General de la Nación (Santo Domingo)* (4/19), 441–63.

Encinas, Diego de (1945–6): *Cedulario Indiano*. Madrid: Ediciones Cultura Hispánica; 4 vols

Ford, J.D.M. (ed. and trans.) (1931): *Letters of John III, King of Portugal*. Cambridge, Mass.: Harvard University Press.

Formisano, Luciano (ed.) (1992): *Letters From a New World: Amerigo Vespucci's Discovery of America*. New York: Marsilio.

Formisano, Luciano and Symcox, Geoffrey (eds.) (2002): *Italian Reports on America, 1493–1522: Accounts by Contemporary Observers*. Turnhout: Brepols.

Freire, Anselmo Braancamp et al. (eds.) (1903–1918): *Archivo Histórico Portuguez* (Abbreviated as AHP). Lisbon: Of. Tip.; 11 vols.

García Mercadal, J. (ed.) (1999): *Viajes de Extranjeros por España y Portugal*. Salamanca: Junta de Castilla y León; 5 vols.

Garcilaso, El Inca (1988): *La Florida*. Madrid: Alianza Editorial S.A.

Geraldini, Alessandro (1977): *Itinerario por las Regiones Subequinocciales*. Santo Domingo, República Dominicana: Editora del Caribe.

Giesing, Cornelia and Vydrine, Valentin (eds.) (2007): *Ta : rikh Mandinka de Bijini (Guinée-Bissau)*. Leiden and Boston: Brill.

Godinho Magalhães, Vitorino (ed.), (1945): *Documentos Sôbre a Expansão Portuguesa*. Lisbon: Editorial Gleba; 3 vols.

Góis, Damião de (1949): *Crónica do Felicíssimo Rei D. Manuel*. Coimbra: Por Ordem da Universidade; 2 vols.

   (1977): *Crónica do Príncipe D. João*. Lisbon: Universidade Nova de Lisbon.

González Obregón, Luis (ed.) (1935): *Procesos de Luis de Carvajal (El Mozo)*. Mexico City: Talleres Gráficos de la Nación.

Hakluyt, Richard (1904): *The Principal Voyages, Traffiques & Discoveries of the English Nation*. Glasgow: James MacLehose & Sons; 12 vols.

Ife, B.W. (ed.) (1990): *Journal of the First Voyage of Christopher Columbus*. Warminster: Aris & Phillips.

Inchaustegui, J. Marino (ed.) (1958): *Reales Cedulas y Correspondencia de Gobernadores de Santo Domingo*. Madrid: Colección Histórico Documental Trujilloniana; 5 vols.

Innes, Gordon (1976): *Kaabu and Fuladu: Historical Narratives of the Gambian Mandinka*. London: School of Oriental and African Studies.

Jadin, Louis (1975): *L'Ancien Congo et l'Angola 1649–1655, D'Après Les Archives Romaines, Portugaises, Néerlandaises et Espagnoles*. Brussels and Rome: Institute Historique Belge de Rome; 3 vols.

Julien, Ch.-A., Herval, Beauchesne, Th. (eds.) (1946): *Les Français en Amérique Pendant la Première Moitié du XVIe Siècle*. Paris: Presses Universitaire de France.

Lardicci, Franceca (ed.) (1999): *A Synoptic Edition of the Log of Columbus's First Voyage*. Brepols: Turnhout.

Las Casas, Bartolomé de (1966a): *Brevíssima Relación de la Destruyción de las Indias*, in *Colección de Documentos Inéditos para la Historia de España* (Vaduz: Kraus Reprint Ltd., 1966; 2nd edition), Vol. 71, 1–72.

   (1966b): *Historia de las Indias*, in *Colección de Documentos Inéditos para la Historia de España* (Vaduz: Kraus Reprint Ltd., 1966; 2nd edition), Vols. 62–66.

Levtzion, N. and Hopkins, J.F.P. (2000): *Corpus of Early Arabic Sources for West African History* (abbreviated as CEA). Princeton: Markus Wiener Publications.

Mauny, R. , Monod, Th. and Teixeira da Mota, A. (eds.) (1951): *Description de la Côte Occidentale d'Afrique (Sénégal au Cap de Monte, Archipels) par Valentim Fernandes (1506–1510)*. Bissau: Centro de Estudos da Guiné Portuguesa.

Mendieta, Gerónimo de (1870): *Historia Ecclesiástica Indiana*. Mexico City: Antigua Librería.

Mercado, Thomas de (1587): *Summa de Tratos y Contratos*. Seville: Fernando Diaz Impressor; 2nd edition.

Millares Carlo, A. and Mantecón, J.I. (eds.) (1945): *Índice y Extractos de los Protocolos del Archivo de Notarías de México, D.F.*. Mexico City: El Colegio de México.

Ochoa, Álvaro and Sánchez, Gerardo (eds.) (1985): *Relaciones y Memorias de la Provincia de Michoacán, 1579–1581*. Morelia: Universidad Michoacana de San Nicolás Hidalgo.

Osorio, Jerónimo (1944): *Da Vida e Feitos de el-Rei D. Manuel*. Porto: Livraria Civilização Editôra; 2 vols.

Pereira, Isaías da Rosa (ed.) (1987): *Documentos para a História da Inquisição em Portugal (Século XVI)*. Lisbon: n.p.

Peres, Damião (ed.) (1952): *Os Mais Antigos Roteiros da Guiné*. Lisbon: Academia Portuguesa da História.

(1953): *Duas Descrições Seiscentistas da Guiné*. Lisbon: Academia Portuguesa da História.

Raccolta di Documenti e Studi Publiccati Dalla R. Commissione Colombiana del Quarto Centenario della Scoperta dell'America (1892–96) (Abbreviated as RD). Rome: Reale Commissione Colombiana; 6 vols.

Ravenstein, E.C. (ed.) (1901): *The Strange Adventures of Andrew Batell of Leigh, in Angola and the Adjoining Regions*. London: Hakluyt Society.

Rego, A. Da Silva (ed.) (1960–1975): *As Gavetas da Torre do Tombo* (Abbreviated as AG). Lisbon: Centro de Estudos Históricos Ultramarinos da Junta de Investigações Científicas do Ultramar; 11 vols.

Sandoval, Alonso de (1627): *Naturaleza, Policia, Sagrada, Profana, Costumbres, Ritos, Disciplina, Catechismo Evangélico de Todos Etiopes*. Seville: Francisco de Lira Impressor.

Splendiani, Anna María (1997): *Cincuenta Años de Inquisición en el Tribunal de Cartagena de las Indias, 1610–60*. Santafé de Bogotá: Centro Editorial Javeriano CEJA; 4 vols.

Taylor, E.G.R. (ed.) (1959): *The Troublesome Voyage of Captain Edward Fenton, 1582–1583*. Cambridge: The Hakluyt Society.

Toro, Alfonso (ed.) (1932): *Los Judíos de la Nueva España: Selección de Documentos del Siglo XVI, Correspondientes al Ramo de la Inquisición*. Mexico City: Talleres Gráficos de la Nación.

Upcott, J.D. (ed.) (1936): *Three Voyages of Drake*. London: Gunn and Company.

Urueta, José P. (ed.) (1887): *Documentos Para la Historia de Cartagena*. Cartagena: Tipografía de Antonio Araújo L., Á Cargo de O'Byrne.

Wiznitzer, Arnold (ed.) (1955): *O Livro de Atas das Congregações Judaicas: Zur Israel em Recife e Magen Abraham em Mauricia, Brasil, 1648–1653*. Rio de Janeiro: Biblioteca Nacional.

Wolf, Lucien (ed. and trans.) (1926): *Jews in the Canary Islands, Being a Calendar of Jewish Cases Extracted From the Records of the Canariote Inquisition of the Marquess of Bute*. London: The Jewish Historical Society of England.

Reference

Anonymous (1930): *Catálogo de los Fondos Americanos del Archivo de Protocolos de Sevilla: Siglo XVI*. Madrid: Compañía Ibero-Americana de Publicaciones S.A.

Carson, Patricia (1962): *Materials for West African History in the Archives of Belgium and Holland*. London: The Athlone Press.

Farinha, Maria do Carmo Jasmins Dias (1990): *Os Arquivos da Inquisição*. Lisbon: Arquivo Nacional da Torre do Tombo.

Gray, Richard and Chambers, David (1965): *Materials for West African History in Italian Archives*. London: The Athlone Press.

Guerra, Luiz de Bivar (1972): *Inventário dos Processos da Inquisição de Coimbra (1541–1820)*. Paris: Fundação Calouste Gulbenkian; 2 vols.

McCarthy, Joseph M. (1977): *Guinea-Bissau and Cape Verde Islands: A Comprehensive Bibliography*. New York: Garland Publishing, Inc.

Morel-Fatio, Alfred (1892): *Catalogue des Manuscrits Espagnols et des Manuscrits Portugais*. Paris: Imprimerie Nationale.

Pina, Isabel Castro and Santos, Maria Leonor Ferraz de Oliveira Silva (2000): *Guia de Fontes Portuguesas Para a Historia de Africa*. Lisbon: Imprensa Nacional.

Ryder, A.F.C. (1965): *Materials for West African History in Portuguese Archives*. London: The Athlone Press.

Tovar, Conde do (1932): *Catálogo dos Manuscritos Portugueses Existentes no Museu Britânico*. Lisbon: Academia das Ciências.

General

Abitbol, Michel (ed.) (1982): *Communautés Juives des Marges Sahariennes du Maghreb*. Jerusalem: Institut Ben-Zvi.

Abu-Lughod, Janet L. (1989): *Before European Hegemony: The World System A.D. 1250–1350*. New York and Oxford: Oxford University Press.

Abulafia, David (2008): *The Discovery of Mankind: Atlantic Encounters in the Age of Columbus*. New Haven and London: Yale University Press.

Aguirre Beltrán, Gonzalo (1989; 3rd edition): *La Población Negra de México: Estudio Etnohistórico*. Mexico City: Fondo de Cultura Económica.

Albuquerque, Luís de (1983): *Ciência e Experiência nos Descobrimentos Portugueses*. Lisbon: Instituto de Cultura e Língua Portuguesa.

Albuquerque, Luís de and Santos, María Emilia Madeira (eds.) (1991): *História Geral de Cabo Verde, Vol. I*. Coimbra: Imprensa de Coimbra.

Alencastro, Luis Felipe de (1996): "The Apprenticeship of Colonization", in Manning, Patrick (1996), 83–108.

(2000): *O Trato dos Viventes: Formação do Brasil no Atlântico Sul, Séculos XVI e XVII*. São Paulo: Editora Schwarcz Ltda.

(2007): "The Economic Networks of Portugal's Atlantic Worlds", in Bethencourt, Francisco and Curto, Diogo Ramada (2007a), 109–137.

Almeida, Fortunato de (1967): *A História da Igreja em Portugal*. Porto: Portucalense Editora.

Almeida, José Maria (ed.) (1998): *Descoberta das Ilhas de Cabo Verde*. Praia: Arquivo Histórico Nacional.

Amador de los Ríos, José (1960; first published 1875): *Historia Social Política y Religiosa de los Judíos de España y Portugal*. Madrid: Aguilar S.A. de Ediciones.

Amaral, Ilídio do (1964): *Santiago de Cabo Verde: A Terra e os Homens*. Lisbon: Memórias da Junta de Investigações do Ultramar.

(1996): *O Reino do Congo, os Mbundu (Ambundos), O Reino dos "Ngola" (Angola) e a Presença Portuguesa, de Finais do Século XV a Meados do Século XVI*. Lisbon: Instituto de Investigação Científica Tropical.

Ameal, José (1966): "Perspectiva Histórica Sobre o Guiné e Cabo Verde", in Brito, Raquel Soeiro de et al. (1966), 87–108.

Amselle, Jean-Loup (1998): *Mestizo Logics: Anthropology of Identity in Africa and Elsewhere*. Stanford: Stanford University Press.

Anderson, Benedict (1991, revised edition; first published 1983): *Imagined Communities: Reflections on the Origin and Spread of Nationalism*. London: Verso.

Anderson, Perry (1976): "The Antinomies of Antonio Gramsci", *New Left Review* (100) Nov. 1976 – Jan. 1977, 5–78.

Andrade, Elisa Silva (1989): "La Formation des Villes au Cap-Vert", in Cahen, Michel (ed.), 23–41.

(1996): *Les Îles du Cap-Vert, de la "Découverte" à l'Indépendance Nationale (1460–1975)*. Paris: Éditions de l'Harmattan.

Antunes, Cátia and Ribeiro da Silva, Filipa (2011): "Cross-Cultural Entrepreneurship in the Atlantic: Africans, Dutch and Sephardic Jews in Western Africa, 1580–1674," *Itinerario* (35), 49–76.

Appadurai, Arjun (1990): "Disjunction and Difference in the Global Cultural Economy", *Public Culture* (2/1), 1–24.

Arbell, Mordechai (2002): *The Jewish Nation of the Caribbean: The Spanish-Portuguese Jewish Settlement in the Caribbean and the Guianas*. Jerusalem: Gegen Publishing House.

Arends, Jacques (ed.) (1995): *The Early Stages of Creolization*. Amsterdam and Philadelphia: John Benjamins Publishing Company.

(2001): "Social Stratification and Network Relations in the Formation of Sranan", in Smith, Norval and Veenstra, Tonjes (2001), 291–308.

Argenti, Nicolas (2007): *The Intestines of the State: Youth, Violence and Belated Histories in the Cameroon Grassfields*. Chicago and London: Chicago University Press.

Armitage, David (2002): "Three Concepts of Atlantic History", in Armitage, David and Braddick, Michael (eds.), 11–27.

Armitage, David and Braddick, Michael (eds.) (2002): *The British Atlantic World, 1500–1800*. Basingstoke: Palgrave Macmillan.

Augeron, Mickaël and Vidal, Laurent (2007): "Creating Colonial Brazil: The First Donatary Captaincies, or the System of Private Exclusivity (1534–1549)", in Roper, L.H. and Van Ruymbeke, B. (eds.), 21–53.

Austen, Ralph A. (ed.) (1999): *In Search of Sunjata: The Mande Oral Epic as History, Literature, and Performance*. Bloomington and Indianapolis: Indiana University Press.

(2001): "The Slave Trade as History and Memory", *William and Mary Quarterly* (58/1), 229–44.

Austen, Ralph A. and Smith, Woodruff D. (1992): "Private Tooth Decay as Public Virtue: The Slave-Sugar Triangle, Consumerism, and European Industrialization", in Inikori, Joseph E. And Engerman, Stanley L. (eds.), 183–203.

Azevedo, João Lucio d' (1922): *Historia dos Christãos Novos Portugueses*. Lisbon: Livraria Clássica Editora.

(1929): *Épocas de Portugal Económico: Esboços da História*. Lisbon: Livraria Clássica Editora.

Ba, Oumar (1981): "Royaume du Kabou: Enquêtes Lexicales," *Éthiopiques* (28), 22–32.

Baechler, Jean (1975): *The Origins of Capitalism*. Oxford: Basil Blackwell; tr. Cooper, Barry.

Baer, Yitzhak (1966): *A History of the Jews in Christian Spain*. Philadelphia: The Jewish Publication Society of America; 2 vols.; tr. Schoffman, Louis.

Baião, António (1921): *A Inquisição em Portugal e no Brazil: Subsídios para a sua História*. Lisbon: Of. Tip.

Baião, António et al. (eds.) (1937): *História da Espansão Portuguesa no Mundo*. Lisbon: Editorial Ática; 3 vols.

Bailyn, Bernard (2002): "Preface", in Armitage, David and Braddick, Michael (eds.), xiv–xx.

(2005): *Atlantic History: Concepts and Contours*. Cambridge, Mass.: Harvard University Press.

Baleno, Ilídio Cabral (1991): "Povoamento e Formação da Sociedade", in Albuquerque, Luís de and Santos, Maria Emília Madeira (1991), 125–77.

Ballong-wen-Menuda, J. Bato'ora (1993): *São Jorge da Mina, 1482–1637: La Vie d'Un Comptoir Portugais en Afrique Occidentale*. Paris and Lisbon: Fundação Calouste Gulbenkian; 2 vols.

Balutansky, Kathleen M. and Sourieau, Marie-Agnès (eds.) (1998): *Caribbean Creolization: Reflections on the Cultural Dynamics of Language, Literature, and Identity*. Gainesville: University Press of Florida.

Banks, Marcus (1996): *Ethnicity: Anthropological Constructions*. London and New York: Routledge.

Barata, Oscar (1966): "O Povoamento de Cabo Verde, Guiné, e São Tomé", in Brito, Raquel Soeiro de et al. (1966), 923–58.

Barcellos, Christiano José de Senna (1899): *Subsídios para a História de Cabo Verde e Guiné, Vol. I*. Lisbon: Por Ordem e na Typographia da Academia Real das Sciencias.

Barnett, R.D. (ed.) (1971): *The Sephardi Heritage: Essays on the History and Cultural Contribution of the Jews of Spain and Portugal*. London: Valentine, Mitchell & Co.; 2 vols.

Barreto, Luís Filipe (1982): *Descobrimentos e Renascimento: Formas de Ser e Pensar nos Séculos XV e XVI*. Lisbon: Imprensa Nacional – Casa da Moeda.

Barreto, João (1938): *História da Guiné 1418–1918*. Lisbon: Ediçao do Autor.

Barros, Simão (c.1939): *Orígens da Colónia de Cabo Verde*. Lisbon: Edições Cosmos.

Barry, Bouabacar (1998): *Senegambia and the Atlantic Slave Trade*. Cambridge and New York: Cambridge University Press; tr. Armah, A. Kwei.

Baum, Robert M. (1999): *Shrines of the Slave Trade: Diola Religion and Society in Precolonial Senegambia*. New York and Oxford: Oxford University Press.

Baxter Wolf, Kenneth (1994): "The 'Moors' of West Africa and the Beginnings of the Portuguese Slave Trade", *Journal of Medieval and Renaissance Studies* (24/3), 449–69.

Bayart, Jean-François (2000): "Africa in the World: A History of Extraversion", *African Affairs* (99/1), 217–67.

Bayly, C.A. et al. (2006): "AHR Conversation: On Transnational History", *American Historical Review* (111/5), 1441–64.

Beinart, Haim (1981): *Conversos on Trial: The Inquisition in Ciudad Real.* Jerusalem: The Magnes Press; tr. Guiladi, Yael.

Benito Ruano, Eloy (2001): *Los Orígenes del Problema Converso.* Madrid: Real Academia de la Historia.

Benítez-Rojo, Antonio (1998): "Three Words Towards Creolization", in Balutansky, Kathleen M. and Sourieau, Marie-Agnès (eds.), 53–61.

Bennett, Herman (2003): *Africans in Colonial Mexico: Absolutism, Christianity and Afro-Creole Consciousness, 1570–1640.* Bloomington and Indianapolis: Indiana University Press.

Berlin, Ira (1996): "From Creole to African: Atlantic Creoles and the Origins of African-American Society in Mainland North America", *William and Mary Quarterly, 3rd Series, (53),* 251–88.

(2000): *Many Thousands Gone: The First Two Centuries of Slavery in North America.* Cambridge, Mass.: Harvard University Press; 2nd edition.

Bernal, Martin (1991): *Black Athena: The Afroasiatic Roots of Classical Civilization, Volume 1.* London: Vintage; 2nd edition.

Bernardini, Paolo and Fiering, Norman (eds.) (2001): *The Jews and the Expansion of Europe to the West, 1450–1800.* New York: Berghahn Books.

Bethencourt, Francisco (1994): *História das Inquisições: Portugal, Espanha e Itália.* Lisbon: Circulo de Leitores.

(1998): "O Contacto Entre Povos e Civilizações", in Bethencourt, Francisco and Chaudhuri, Kirti (eds.), 88–110.

(2009): *The Inquisition: A Global History, 1479–1834.* Cambridge and New York: Cambridge University Press.

Bethencourt, Francisco and Chaudhuri, Kirti (eds.) (1998a). *História da Expansão Portuguesa: Vol. 1, A Formação do Império (1415–1570).* Navarra: Temas e Debates e Autores.

(1998b): *Historia da Expansão Portuguesa, Vol. 2: Do Índico ao Atlântico (1570–1697).* Lisbon: Círculo de Leitores.

Bethencourt, Francisco and Havik, Philip (2004): "A África e a Inquisição Portuguesa: Novas Perspectivas", *Revista Lusófona de Ciência das Religiões,* Ano III, 2004, no.5/6, 21–27.

Bethencourt, Francisco and Curto, Diogo Ramada (eds.) (2007a): *Portuguese Oceanic Expansion, 1400–1800.* Cambridge: Cambridge University Press.

(2007b): "Introduction", in Bethencourt, Francisco and Curto, Diogo Ramada (eds.), 1–19.

Bhabha, Homi K. (1985): "Signs Taken for Wonders: Questions of Ambivalence and Authority Under a Tree Outside Delhi, May 1817", *Critical Inquiry* (12/1), 144–65.

(1994): *The Location of Culture.* London and New York: Routledge.

Birmingham, David (1966): *Trade and Conflict in Angola: The Mbundu and their Neighbours Under the Influence of the Portuguese, 1483–1790*. Oxford: Clarendon Press.

Blackburn, Robin (1997): *The Making of New World Slavery: From the Baroque to the Modern, 1492–1800*. London: Verso.

Blake, John W. (1977; first published 1937): *West Africa: Quest for God and Gold 1454–1578*. London: Curzon Press.

Blazquez Miguel, Juan (1989): *Toledot: Historia del Toledo Judío*. Toledo: Editorial Arcano.

Blumenthal, Debra (2009): *Enemies and Familiars: Slavery and Mastery in Fifteenth-Century Valencia*. Ithaca and London: Cornell University Press.

Bocandé, Bertrand (1849): "Notes sur la Guinée Portugaise ou Sénégambie Méridionale", *Bulletin de la Société de Géographie, 3rd Series, (11 and 12), May/June 1849*, 11: 265–350 and 12: 57–93.

Bodian, Miriam (1997): *Hebrews of the Portuguese Nation: Conversos and Community in Early Modern Amsterdam*. Bloomington and Indianapolis: Indiana University Press.

(2007): *Dying in the Law of Moses: Crypto-Jewish Martyrdom in the Iberian World*. Bloomington and Indianapolis: Indiana University Press.

Bovill, E.W. (1958): *The Golden Trade of the Moors*. London: Oxford University Press.

Böhm, Günter (1948): "Los Judíos en Chile Durante la Colonia", *Boletín de la Academia Chilena de la Historia, no. 38*, 21–100.

(1963): *Nuevos Antecedentes para una Historia de los Judíos en Chile Colonial*. Santiago de Chile: Editorial Universitaria.

Borrero Fernandez, Mercedes (1983): *El Mundo Rural Sevillano en el Siglo XV: Alfaraje y Ribera*. Seville: Publicaciones de la Excma. Diputación Provincial de Sevilla Bajo la Dirección de Antonia Heredia Herrera.

Boulègue, Jean (1972): *Les Luso-Africains de la Sénégambie: XVIe-XIXe Siècle*. Dakar: Université de Dakar.

(1980): "L'Ancien Royaume du Kasa (Casamance)", *Bulletin de l'I.F.A.N. (42/ Series B/3)*, 475–86.

(1987a): *Le Grand Jolof (XIIIe – XVIe Siècle)*. Blois: Éditions Façades.

(1987b): *Les Anciens Royamues Wolofs*. Blois: Editions Façades.

(ed.) (1987c): *Contributions à l'Histoire du Sénégal*. Paris: Éditions Karthala.

Bowser, Frederick P. (1974): *The African Slave in Colonial Peru, 1524–1650*. Stanford: Stanford University Press.

Boxer, C.R. (1963): *Race Relations in the Portuguese Colonial Empire 1415–1825*. Oxford: Clarendon Press.

(1965): *Portuguese Society in the Tropics: The Municipal Councils of Goa, Macao, Bahia and Luanda, 1510–1800*. Madison and Milwaukee: The University of Wisconsin Press.

(1969): *The Portuguese Seaborne Empire 1415–1825*. London: Hutchinson.

(1975): *Mary and Misogyny: Women in Iberian Expansion Overseas 1415–1815*. London: Duckworth.

Bradshaw, A. T. Von S. (1965): "Vestiges of Portuguese in the Languages of Sierra Leone", *Sierra Leone Language Review* (4), 5–37.

Brásio, António (1944): *Os Pretos em Portugal*. Lisbon: Agência Geral das Colónias.

(1958): *A Acção Missionária no Período Henriquino*. Lisbon: Comissao Executiva das Comemoraçoes do Quinto Centenário da Morte do Infante D. Henrique.

(1962): "Descobrimento/Povoamento/Evangelização do Arquipélago de Cabo Verde", *Studia, no. 10, July 1962, 49–97*.

Brathwaite, Edward (1971): *The Development of Creole Society in Jamaica, 1770–1820*. Oxford: Clarendon Press.

Braudel, Fernand (1966; first published 1949): *La Méditérranée et le Monde Méditérranéen à l'Époque de Philippe II*. Paris: Librairie Armand Colin; 2 vols.

Brito, Raquel Soeiro de (1966): "Guiné, Cabo Verde, São Tomé e Príncipe: Alguns Aspectos da Terra e Dos Homens", in Brito, Raquel Soeiro de et al. (eds.), 15–46.

et al. (1966): *Cabo Verde, Guiné, São Tomé e Príncipe: Curso de Extensão Universitária Ano Lectivo de 1965–1966*. Lisbon: Instituto Superior de Ciências Sociais e Política Ultramarina.

Brooks, George E. (1980): *Luso-African Commerce and Settlement in the Gambia and Guinea-Bissau Region*. Boston: Working Papers No. 24, African Studies Center, Boston University.

(1993a): "Historical Perspectives on the Guinea-Bissau Region, Fifteenth to Nineteenth Centuries", in Lopes, Carlos (ed.), 25–54.

(1993b): *Landlords and Strangers: Ecology, Society and Trade in Western Africa, 1000–1630*. Boulder: Westview Press.

(2003): *Eurafricans in Western Africa: Commerce, Social Status, Gender, and Religious Observance from the Sixteenth to the Eighteenth Century*. Oxford: James Currey.

Burnard, Trevor (2004): *Mastery, Tyranny and Desire: Thomas Thistlewood and His Slaves in the Anglo-Jamaican World*. Chapel Hill and London: University of North Carolina Press.

Bühnen, Stephan (1993): "Ethnic Origins of Peruvian Slaves (1548–1650): Figures for Upper Guinea", *Paideuma* (39), 57–110.

Buis, Pierre (1990): *Essai Sur la Langue Manjako de la Zone de Basserel*. Bissau: Instituto Nacional de Estudos e Pesquisa.

Bulmer-Thomas, Victor, et al. (eds.) (2006): *The Cambridge Economic History of Latin America, Volume 1: The Colonial Era and the Short Nineteenth Century*. Cambridge and New York: Cambridge University Press.

Cabral, Iva (1995): "Ribeira Grande: Vida Urbana, Gente, Mercancia, Estagnação", in Santos, Maria Emília Madeira (ed.), 225–73.

Cahen, Michel (ed.) (1989): *"Vilas" et "Cidades": Bourgs et Villes en Afrique Lusophone*. Paris: Éditions de l'Harmattan.

Canny, Nicholas P. and Pagden, Anthony (eds.) (1987): *Colonial Identity in the Atlantic World, 1500–1800*. Princeton: Princeton University Press.

Carmona Ruiz, Maria Antonia (1995): *Usurpaciones de Tierras y Derechos Comunales en Sevilla y su "Tierra" Durante el Siglo XV*. Madrid: Ministerio de Agricultura, Pesca y Alimentación, Centro de Publicaciones.

Carneiro, Maria Luiza Tucci (1983): *Preconceito Racial no Brasil Colonial: Os Cristãos Novos*. São Paulo: Editora Brasiliense, S.A.

Carney, Judith A. (2001): *Black Rice: The African Origins of Rice Cultivation in the Americas*. Cambridge, Mass.: Harvard University Press.

Caroço, Jorge Vellez (1948): *Monjur, o Gabú e a sua História*. Bissau: Centro de Estudos da Guiné Portuguesa.

Carreira, António (1947): "Mandingas da Guiné Portuguesa", *Centro de Estudos da Guiné Portuguesa (4)*.

(1961): "Organização Social e Económica dos Povos da Guiné Portuguesa", *Boletim Cultural da Guiné Portuguesa* (16/64), 641–736.

(1964): "A Etnonímia dos Povos de Entre o Gâmbia e o Estuário do Geba", *Boletim Cultural da Guiné Portuguesa* (19/75), 233–76.

(1972): *Cabo Verde: Formaçao e Extinçao de Uma Sociedade Escravocrata (1460–1878)*. Porto: Centro de Estudos da Guiné Portuguesa.

(1984): *Os Portuguêses nos Rios de Guiné, 1500–1900*. Lisbon: Litografia Tejo.

Carroll, Patrick J. (2001; 2nd edition): *Blacks in Colonial Veracruz: Race, Ethnicity, and Regional Development*. Austin: University of Texas Press.

Carvalho, Inácio dos Santos (1998): "Introdução à História das Ilhas de Cabo Verde", in Almeida, José Maria (ed.), 15–26.

Carvalho, Joaquim Barradas de (1981): *Portugal e as Origens do Pensamento Moderno*. Lisbon: Livros Horizonte.

Castro, Américo (1954): *La Realidad Histórica de España*. Mexico City: Editorial Porrua.

Cerrone, Frederico (1983): *Historia da Igreja de Cabo Verde (Subsídios)*. Mindelo: Gráfica do Mindelo Ltda..

Chaplin, Joyce E. (2002): "Race", in Armitage, David and Braddick, Michael (eds.), 154–72.

Chaunu, Huguette and Pierre (1955–1956): *Séville et l'Atlantique (1504–1650)*. Paris: Librairie Armand; vols. 2–5 of 8.

Chelmicki, José Conrado Carlos de (1841): *Corografia Cabo-Verdiana, ou Descripção Geographico-Historica da Provincia das Ilhas de Cabo-Verde e Guiné*. Lisbon: Typ de L.C. Da Cunha.

Cissoko, Sékéné-Mody and Sambou, Kaoussou (1974): *Recueil des Traditions Orales des Mandingues de Gambie et de Casamance*. Niamey: Centre Régional de Documentation Pour la Tradition Orale.

Clifford, James (1994): "Diasporas", *Cultural Anthropology* (9/3), 302–38.

Coates, Timothy J. (2001): *Convicts and Orphans: Forced and State-Sponsored Colonizers in the Portuguese Empire, 1550–1755*. Stanford, Calif.: Stanford University Press.

Coelho, António Borges (1987): *Inquisição de Évora*. Lisbon: Editorial Caminho.

Coelho Filho, Luiz Walter (2000): *A Capitania de São Jorge e a Década do Açúcar (1541–1550)*. Salvador: Editora Vila Velha.

Cohen, Abner (1969): *Custom and Politics in Urban Africa*. London: Routledge and Kegan Paul.

(1971): "Cultural Strategies in the Organization of Trading Diasporas", in Meillassoux, Claude (ed.), 266–81.

Cohen, Martin A. (ed.) (1971a): *The Jewish Experience in Latin America.* Waltham, Ma.: American Jewish Historical Association; 2 vols.

(1971b): "The Letters and Last Will and Testament of Luis de Carvajal, the Younger", in Cohen, Martin A. (ed.), 243–312.

(2001; first published 1973): *Martyr: Luis de Carvajal, a Secret Jew in Sixteenth-Century Mexico.* Albuquerque: University of New Mexico Press.

Cohen, Robin and Toninato, Paola (2010a): "Introduction", in Cohen, Robin and Toninato, Paola (eds.), 1–21.

(2010b): *The Creolization Reader: Studies in Mixed Identities and Cultures.* Abingdon: Routledge.

Cohen, Zelinda (1992): "O Provimento dos Oficiais da Justiça e da Fazenda Para as Ilhas de Cabo Verde", *Studia, no.* 51, 145–76.

(1994): "Subsídios Para a História Geral de Cabo Verde: Os Contratos de Arrendamento Para a Cobrança das Rendas e Direitos Reais das Ilhas de Cabo Verde (1501–1560)", *Studia, Lisbon,* no.53, 317–64.

(2002): "A Administração das Ilhas de Cabo Verde Pós-União Ibérica: Continuidades e Rupturas", in Santos, Maria Emília Madeira (ed.), 67–156.

(2007): *Os Filhos da Folha (Cabo Verde – Séculos XV – XVII).* Praia: Spleen Edições.

Comas, Juan (1951): *Racial Myths.* Paris: UNESCO.

Correia, Claudia (1998): *A Presença dos Judeus em Cabo Verde.* Praia: Arquivo Histórico Nacional.

Correia e Silva, António Leão (1991): "A Tributação nos Primórdios da História de Cabo Verde (1460–1516)", in Albuquerque, Luís de and Santos, Maria Emília Madeira (eds.), 347–70.

(1995): "Cabo Verde e a Geopolítica do Atlântico", in Santos, Maria Emília Madeira (ed.), 1–16.

(1996): *Histórias de um Sahel Insular.* Praia: Spleen-Edições.

Correia e Silva, António Leão de Aguiar Cardoso (1990): *A Influência do Atlântico na Formação de Portos em Cabo Verde.* Lisbon: Instituto de Investigação Científica Tropical.

Cortes, Vicenta (1964): *La Esclavitud en Valencia Durante el Reinado de los Reyes Católicos (1479–1516).* Valencia: Publicaciones del Archivo Municipal de Valencia.

Cortesão, Armando (1935): *Cartografia e Cartógrafos Portugueses dos Séculos XV e XVI.* Lisbon: Edição da "Serra Nova"; 2 vols.

Costa, General Gomes da (1927): *Descobrimentos e Conquistas.* Lisbon: Serviços Gráficos do Exército.

Couto, Jorge (1995): *A Construcção do Brasil: Ameríndios, Portugueses e Africanos, do Início do Povoamento a Finais de Quinhentos.* Lisbon: Edições Cosmos.

Crosby, Alfred W. (1986): *Ecological Imperialism: The Biological Expansion of Europe, 900–1900.* Cambridge and New York: Cambridge University Press.

Crowley, Eve L. (2000): "Institutions, Identities and the Incorporation of Immigrants Within Local Frontiers of the Upper Guinea Coast", in Gaillard, Gérard (ed.), 113–37.

Curtin, Philip D. (1969): *The Atlantic Slave Trade: A Census*. Madison and London: University of Wisconsin Press.

(1975): *Economic Change in Precolonial Africa: Senegambia in the Era of the Slave Trade*. Madison: University of Wisconsin Press.

(1984): *Cross-Cultural Trade in World History*. Cambridge and New York: Cambridge University Press.

(1998; first published 1990): *The Rise and Fall of the Plantation Complex: Essays in Atlantic History*. Cambridge and New York: Cambridge University Press.

Curto, Diogo Ramada (1998): "Cultura Escrita e Práticas de Identidade", in Bethencourt, Francisco and Chaudhuri, Kirti (eds.), 458–531.

Daaku, K.Y. (1970): *Trade and Politics on the Gold Coast, 1600–1720: A Study of African Reaction to European Trade*. Oxford: Clarendon Press.

Darwin, John (2007): *After Tamerlane: The Global History of Empire*. London: Allen, Lane.

Davis, David Brion (1984): *Slavery and Human Progress*. Oxford and New York: Oxford University Press.

(1994): "The Slave Trade and the Jews", *New York Review of Books*, (41/21), 14–6.

(1999): "Jews and Blacks in America", *New York Review of Books* (46/19), 57–63.

(2006): *Inhuman Bondage: The Rise and Fall of Slavery in the New World*. Oxford and New York: Oxford University Press.

Deive, Carlos Esteban (1980): *La Esclavitud del Negro en Santo Domingo (1492–1844)*. Santo Domingo: Museo del Hombre Dominicano; 2 vols.

(1989): *Los Guerrilleros Negros: Esclavos Fugitivos y Cimarrones en Santo Domingo*. Santo Domingo: Fundación Cultural Dominicana.

Delafosse, Maurice (1972; first published 1912): *Haut-Sénégal-Niger*. Paris: G.-P. Maisonneuve et Larose.

Delumeau, Jean (1978): *La Peur en Occident (XIVe-XVIIIe Siècles): Une Cité Assiégée*. Paris: Fayard.

Denucé, Jean (1937): *L'Afrique et le Commerce Anversois au XVIe Siècle*. Antwerp: De Sikkel.

Diamond, Jared (2005): *Collapse: How Societies Choose to Fail or Survive*. London: Allen Lane.

Dias, Manuel Nunes (1963–4): *O Capitalismo Monárquico Português: Contribuição para o Estudo das Orignes do Capitalismo Moderno*. Coimbra: Faculdade de Létras da Universidade de Coimbra, Instituto de Estudos Históricos Dr. António de Vasconcelos; 2 vols..

Diène, Doudou (ed.) (2001): *From Chains to Bonds: The Slave Trade Revisited*. Paris: UNESCO.

Diffie, Bailey W. and Winius, George D. (1977): *Foundations of the Portuguese Empire 1415–1580*. Minneapolis: University of Minnesota Press.

Diop, Cheikh Anta (1987): *Precolonial Black Africa*. New York: Lawrence Hill Books.

Domingues, Angela (1991): "Administração e Instituições: Transplante, Adaptação, Funcionamento", in Albuquerque, Luís de and Santos, Maria Emília Madeira (eds.), 41–123.

Domingues, Francisco Contente (2007): "Science and Technology in Portuguese Navigation: The Idea of Experience in the Sixteenth Century", in Bethencourt, Francisco and Curto, Diogo Ramada (eds.), 460–79.

Douglas, Mary (1989; first published 1966): *Purity and Danger: An Analysis of the Concepts of Pollution and Taboo*. London and New York: Routledge.

Drescher, Seymour (2001): "Jews and New Christians in the Atlantic Slave Trade", in Bernardini, Paolo and Fiering, Norman (eds.), 439–70.

Duncan, T. Bentley (1972): *Atlantic Islands: Madeira, the Azores and the Cape Verdes in Seventeenth Century Commerce and Navigation*. Chicago: University of Chicago Press.

Dunn, Richard S. (1973): *Sugar and Slaves: The Rise of the Planter Class in the English West Indies, 1624–1713*. London: Jonathan Cape.

Earle, T.F. and Parkinson, Stephen (eds.) (1992): *Studies in the Portuguese Discoveries: Proceedings of the First Colloquium of the Centre for the Study of the Portuguese Discoveries*. Warminster: Aris & Phillips Ltd.

Earle, T.F. and Lowe, K.J.P. (2005): *Black Africans in Renaissance Europe*. Cambridge and New York: Cambridge University Press.

Ebert, Christopher (2008): *Between Empires: Brazilian Sugar in the Early Atlantic Economy, 1550–1630*. Leiden and Boston: Brill.

Edwards, Jeremy and Ogilvie, Sheilagh (2008): "Contract Enforcement, Institutions and Social Capital: The Maghribi Traders Reappraised", *Cambridge Centre for Economic Studies and IFO Working Paper Series No. 2254*.

Elbl, Ivana (1997): "The Volume of the Early Atlantic Slave Trade, 1450–1521", *Journal of African History* (38/1), 31–75.

Elliott, J. H. (2006): *Empires of the Atlantic World: Britain and Spain in America, 1497–1830*. New Haven and London: Yale University Press.

Eltis, David (2000): *The Rise of African Slavery in the Americas*. Cambridge and New York: Cambridge University Press.

(2001): "The Volume and Structure of the Transatlantic Slave Trade: A Reassessment", *William and Mary Quarterly* (58/1), 17–46.

Eltis, David and Richardson, David (2008a): *Extending the Frontiers: Essays on the New Transatlantic Slave Trade Database*. New Haven and London: Yale University Press.

(2008b): "Introduction", in Eltis, David and Richardson, David (eds.), 1–60.

Estevão, João (1989): "Peuplement et Phénomènes d'Urbanisation au Cap-Vert Pendant la Période Coloniale, 1462–1940", in Cahen, Michel (ed.), 42–59.

Evans, Christopher, Stig Sorensen, Marie-Louise and Richter, Konstantin (forthcoming, 2012): "Excavation of one of the Earliest Christian Churches in the Tropics: N.ª S.ª da Conceição, Cidade Velha, Cape Verde" in Green, Toby and Nafafé, José Lingna (eds.), (forthcoming, 2012).

Everts, Natalie (forthcoming, 2012): "A Motley Company: Differing Identities Among Euro-Africans in Eighteenth Century Elmina", in Green, Toby and Nafafe, José Lingna (eds.) (forthcoming, 2012).

Faber, Eli (1998): *Jews, Slaves and the Slave Trade: Setting the Record Straight*. New York and London: New York University Press.

Fage, J.D. (1969a; first published 1955): *A History of West Africa: An Introductory Survey*. Cambridge and New York: Cambridge University Press.

(1969b): "Slavery and the Slave Trade in the Context of West African History", *Journal of African History* (10/3), 393–404.

(1980): "Slaves and Society in Western Africa, c. 1445-c.1700", *Journal of African History* (21/3), 289–310.

Fage, J.D. with Tordoff, William (2002): *A History of Africa*, 4th edition.London and New York: Routledge.

Farias, P.F. de Moraes (1967): "The Almoravids: Some Questions Concerning the Character of the Movement During its Periods of Closest Contact with the Sudan", *Bulletin de l'I.F.A.N., Series B*, (29), 794–878.

(1974): "Silent Trade: Myth and Historical Evidence", *History in Africa* (1) 1974, 9–24.

(1985): "Models of the World and Categorial Models: The 'Enslavable Barbarian' as a Mobile Classificatory Label", in Willis, John (ed.), Vol. 1, 27–46.

(1996): "Borgu in the Cultural Map of the Muslim Diasporas of West Africa", in Hunwick, John and Lawler, Nancy (eds.), 259–86.

(1999): "The Gesere of Borgu: A Neglected Type of Manding Diaspora", in Austen, Ralph A. (ed.), 141–69.

(2003): *Arabic Medieval Inscriptions From the Republic of Mali: Epigraphy, Chronicles and Songhay-Tuāreg History*. Oxford: Oxford University Press.

(2007): "Au-delà de l'opposition coloniale entre l'authenticité africaine et l'identité musulmane. L'oeuvre de Waa Kamisòkò, barde moderne et critique du Mali.", in Villasante de Cervelloa, Mariella and Beuvais, Christophe de (eds)., *Colonisations et héritages actuels au Sahara et au Sahel : Problèmes conceptuels, état des lieux et nouvelles perspectives de recherche (XVIIIe-XXe siècles)* (Paris: Editions L'harmattan, 2007; 2 vols.), Vol. 2, 271–306.

Faur, José (1992): *In the Shadow of Modernity: Jews and Conversos at the Dawn of Modernity*. Albany: State University of New York Press.

Fernández-Armesto, Felipe (1995): "Medieval Atlantic Exploration: The Evidence of Maps", in Winius, George D. (ed.), 41–70.

Ferreira, Clarisse Virginia Cardona (1964): *A História do Arquipélago de Cabo Verde Durante o Período Filipino*. Lisbon: Universidade de Lisboa – unpublished MA thesis.

Ferro, Maria Haydée Ferreira (1997): *Subsídios para a História da Ilha de Santo Antão de Cabo Verde*. São Vicente: Geográfica do Mindelo.

Ferronha, António Luis (ed.) (1991): *O Confronto do Olhar: O Encontro dos Povos na Época das Navegações Portuguesas, Séculos XV e XVI*. Lisbon: Editorial Caminho.

Fields-Black, Edda L. (2009): *Deep Roots: Rice Farmers in West Africa and the African Diaspora*. Bloomington and Indianapolis: Indiana University Press.

Fonseca, Domingos (1997): *Os Mancanha*. Bissau: Ku Si Mon Editora.

Fonseca, Jorge (2002): *Escravos no Sul de Portugal: Séculos XVI-XVII*. Lisbon: Editora Vulgata.

(2005): "Black Africans in Portugal During Cleynaert's Visit (1533–1538)", in Earle T.F. and Lowe, K.J.P. (eds.), 113–21.

Fonseca, Luis Adão da (1995): "The Discovery of Atlantic Space", in Winius, George D. (ed.), 5–18.

Franco Silva, Alfonso (1979): *La Esclavitud en Sevilla y su Tierra a Fines de la Edad Media*. Seville: Publicaciones de la Excma. Diputación Provincial de Sevilla.

Frank, André Gunder (1998) : *ReOrient: Global Economy in the Asian Age*. Berkeley and London: University of California Press.

Fredrickson, George M. (2002): *Racism: A Short History*. Princeton: Princeton University Press.

Friedman, John B. (1994): "Cultural Conflicts in Medieval World Maps", in Schwartz, Stuart B. (ed.), 64–95.

Fuente, Alejandro de la, with the collaboration of César García del Pino and Bernardo Iglesias Delgado (2008): *Havana and the Atlantic in the Sixteenth Century*. Chapel Hill and London: University of North Carolina Press.

Gaillard, Gérard (2000a): "Introduction", in Gaillard, Gérard (ed.), 7–38.

Gaillard, Gérard (ed.): (2000b): *Migrations Anciennes et Peuplement Actuel des Côtes Guinéennes*. Paris: Éditions L'Harmattan.

Games, Alison (2002): "Migration", in Armitage, David and Braddick, Michael (eds.), 31–50.

García de Cortázar, José Angel (1976): *La Época Medieval*. Madrid: Alianza Editorial.

  (1988): *La Sociedad Rural en la España Medieval*. Madrid: Siglo XXI de España Editores, S.A.

Gemery, Henry A. and Hogendorn, Jan S. (eds.) (1979): *The Uncommon Market: Essays in the Economic History of the Atlantic Slave Trade*. New York: Academic Press Inc.

Germano Lima, António (1997): *Boavista: Ilha de Capitães: Historia e Sociedade*. Praia: Spleen Edições.

Gil, Juan (2000–2001): *Los Conversos y la Inquisición Sevillana*. Seville: Universidad de Sevilla – Fundación El Monte; 5 vols.

Gilman, Stephen (1972): *The Spain of Fernando de Rojas: The Intellectual and Social Landscape of La Celestina*. Princeton: Princeton University Press.

Gilroy, Paul (1993): *The Black Atlantic: Modernity and Double Consciousness*. London: Verso.

Girard, Jean (1992): *L'Or du Bambouk: Du Royaume de Gabou à la Casamance*. Geneva: Georg Editeur.

Gitlitz, David M. (1996): *Secrecy and Deceit: The Religion of the Crypto-Jews*. Philadelphia and Jerusalem: The Jewish Publication Society.

Godinho, Vitorino Magalhães (1962): *A Economia dos Descobrimentos Henriquinos*. Lisbon: Livraria Sá da Costa Editora.

  (1969): *L'Économie de l'Empire Portugais aux XVe et XVIe Siècles*. Paris: S.E.V.P.E.N.

  (1980; first published 1971): *Estrutura da Antiga Sociedade Portuguesa*. Lisbon: Editora Arcádia.

  (1981): *Os Descobrimentos e a Economia Mundial*. Lisbon: Editorial Presença; 4 vols.

Gonçalves, Nuno da Silva (1996): *Os Jesuítas e a Missão de Cabo Verde (1604–1642)*. Lisbon: Brotería.

Graizbord, David L. (2004): *Souls in Dispute: Converso Identities in Iberia and the Jewish Diaspora, 1580–1700*. Philadelphia: University of Pennsylvania Press.

Grant, Anthony P. (2001): "Language Intertwining: Its Depiction in Recent Literature and its Implications for Theories of Creolization", in Smith, Norval and Veenstra, Tonjes (eds.), 81–112.

Gravrand, Henri (1981): "Le Gabou Dans les Traditions Orales Sereer et Guélwar", *Éthiopiques* (28), 40–59.

(1983): *La Civilisation Sereer: Cosaan, Les Origines*. Dakar: Nouvelles Éditions Africaines.

Green, Toby (2001): *Meeting the Invisible Man: Secrets and Magic in West Africa*. London: Weidenfeld & Nicolson.

(2005): "Further Considerations on the Sephardim of the Petite Côte", *History in Africa* 32, 165–183.

(2006): "Fear and Atlantic History: Some Observations Derived From the Cape Verde Islands and the African Atlantic", *Journal of Atlantic Studies* (3/1), 25–43.

(2007a): *Inquisition: The Reign of Fear*. London: Macmillan.

(2007b): *Masters of Difference: Creolization and the Jewish Presence in Cabo Verde, 1497–1672*. University of Birmingham – Unpublished PhD thesis.

(2008a): "Amsterdam and the African Atlantic: The Role of Sephardim from Amsterdam in Senegal in the 17th Century", in *Proceedings of the Fourteenth British Conference on Judaeo-Spanish Studies*, eds. Hilary Pomeroy, Christopher J. Pountain and Elena Romero (London: Queen Mary and Westfield College, 2008), 85–94.

(2008b): "Equal Partners? Proselytising by Africans and Jews in the 17th Century Atlantic Diaspora", *Melilah*, (12/1), 1–12.

(2009): "Building Creole Identity in the African Atlantic: Boundaries of Race and Religion in 17th-Century Cabo Verde", *History in Africa* 36 (2009), 103–25.

Green, Toby and Nafafé, José Lingna (forthcoming, 2012): *Brokers of Change: Atlantic Commerce and Cultures in Pre-Colonial "Guinea of Cape Verde"*.

Greif, Avner (1993): "Contract Enforceability and Economic Institutions in Early Trade: The Maghribi Traders' Coalition", *American Economic Review* (83/3), 525–48.

(2008): "Contract Enforcement and Institutions Among the Maghribi Traders: Refuting Edwards and Ogilvie", *Cambridge Centre for Economic Studies and IFO Working Paper Series No. 2350*.

Gruzinski, Serge (2002): *The Mestizo Mind: The Intellectual Dynamics of Colonization and Globalization*. New York and London: Routledge.

(2005): "Passeurs y Elites "Católicas" en las Cuatras Partes del Mundo: Los Inicios Ibéricos de la Mundialización (1580–1640)", in O'Phelan Godoy/ Salazar-Soler (eds.), 13–29.

Guibovich Pérez, Pedro (1998): *En Defensa de Dios: Estudios y Documentos Sobre la Inquisición en el Perú*. Lima: Ediciones del Congreso del Perú.

Hair, P. E. H. (1966): "The Use of African Languages in Afro-European Contacts in Guinea, 1440–1560", *Sierra Leone Language Review* (5), 5–27.

(1967): "Ethnolinguistic Continuity on the Guinea Coast", *Journal of African History* (8/2), 247–68.

(1976): "Some Minor Sources for Guinea, 1519–59: Enciso and Alfonce/ Fonteneau", *History in Africa* (3), 19–46.

(1980): "Black African Slaves at Valencia, 1482–1516: An Onomastic Inquiry", *History in Africa* (7), 119–39.

Haïdara, Ismaël Diadié (1997): *L'Espagne Musulmane et l'Afrique Subsaharienne.* Bamako: Editions Donniya.

  (1999): *Les Juifs à Tombouctou: Recueil des Sources Écrites Relatives au Commerce Juif à Tombouctou au XIXe Siècle.* Bamako: Editions Donniya.

Hale, Thomas A. (1998): *Griots and Griottes: Masters of Words and Music.* Bloomington and Indianapolis: Indiana University Press.

Hall, Bruce (2005): "The Question of 'Race' in the Precolonial Southern Sahara," *The Journal of North African Studies* (10), 339–367.

Hall, Gwendolyn Midlo (1992): *Africans in Colonial Louisiana: The Development of Afro-Creole Culture in the Eighteenth Century.* Baton Rouge: Louisiana State University Press.

  (2005): *Slavery and African Ethnicities in the Americas: Restoring the Links.* Chapel Hill and London: University of North Carolina Press.

  (2010): "Africa and Africans in the African Diaspora: The Uses of Relational Databases", *American Historical Review* (115/1), 136–50.

Hall, Stuart (2010): "Créolité and the Process of Creolization", in Cohen, Robin and Toninato, Paola (eds.), 26–38.

Hall, Trevor P. (1992): *The Role of Cape Verde Islanders in Organizing and Operating Maritime Trade Between West Africa and Iberian Territories, 1441–1616.* Baltimore: Johns Hopkins University; 2 vols. (unpublished PhD thesis).

Hannerz, Ulf (1996): *Transnational Connections: Culture, People, Places.* London and New York: Routledge.

Havik, Philip J. (2004a): "La Sorcellerie, L'Acculturation et le Genre: La Persécution Religieuese de l'Inquisition Portugaise Contre les Femmes Africaines Converties en Haut Guinée (XVIIe Siècle)", *Revista Lusófona de Ciência das Religiões, III /5–6,* 99–116 – also published at http://cienciareli-gioes.ulusofona.pt

  (2004b): *Silences and Soundbytes: The Gendered Dynamics of Trade and Brokerage in the Pre-Colonial Guinea Bissau Region.* Muenster/New York: Lit Verlag/Transaction Publishers.

  (2007): "Kriol Without Creoles: Rethinking Guinea's Afro-Atlantic Connections (Sixteenth to Twntieth Centuries)", in Naro, Nancy Priscilla, Sansi-Roca, Roger and Treece, David H. (eds.), 41–73.

Havik, Philip J. and Newitt, Malyn (eds.) (2007): *Creole Societies in the Portuguese Colonial Empire.* Bristol: Bristol University Press.

Hawthorne, Walter (1999): "The Production of Slaves Where There Was No State: The Guinea-Bissau Region, 1450–1815", *Slavery and Abolition* (20/2), 97–124.

  (2001): "Nourishing a Stateless Society During the Slave Trade: The Rise of Balanta Paddy-Rice Production in Guinea-Bissau", *Journal of African History* (42/1), 1–24.

  (2003): *Planting Rice and Harvesting Slaves: Transformations Along the Guinea-Bissau Coast, 1400–1900.* Portsmouth, NH: Heinemann.

  (2010a): "From 'Black Rice' to 'Brown': Rethinking the History of Risiculture in the Seventeenth- and Eighteenth-Century Atlantic", *American Historical Review* (115/1), 151–63.

(2010b): *From Africa to Brazil: Identity, Culture and a Slave Trade From West Africa to Brazil, 1621–1830.* Cambridge and New York: Cambridge University Press.

Henriques, Isabel Castro (2000): *São Tomé e Príncipe: A Invenção de Uma Sociedade.* Lisbon: Vega Editora.

Henry, Christine (1994): *Les Îles Où Dansent Les Enfants Défunts: Âge, Sexe et Pouvoir Chez les Bijago de Guinée-Bissau.* Paris: CNRS Éditions.

Herculano, A (1854): *Da Origem e Estabelecimento da Inquisição em Portugal: Tentativas Históricas.* Lisbon: Imprensa Nacional; 3 vols..

Herzog, Tamar (2003): *Defining Nations: Immigrants and Citizens in Early Modern Spain and Spanish America.* New Haven and London: Yale University Press.

Heywood, Linda M. and Thornton, John K. (2007): *Central Africans, Atlantic Creoles and the Foundation of the Americas, 1585–1660.* Cambridge and New York: Cambridge University Press.

Hilton, Anne (1985): *The Kingdom of Kongo.* Oxford: Clarendon Press.

Hoare, Quentin and Nowell Smith, Geoffrey (eds. and tr.) (1971): *Selections from the Prison Notebooks of Antonio Gramsci.* London: Lawrence & Wishart.

Hofheinz, Albrecht (2004): "Goths in the Land of the Blacks: A Preliminary Survey of the Ka 'ti Library in Timbuktu", in Reese, Scott S. (ed.), 154–83.

Holm, John (1988): *Pidgins and Creoles.* Cambridge and New York: Cambridge University Press; 2 vols.

Holm, John , et al. (eds.) (2006). *Cabo Verde: Origens da Sua Sociedade e do Seu Crioulo.* Tübingen: Gunter Narr.

Hooykass, R. (1979): *Humanism and the Voyages of Discovery in 16th Century Portuguese Science and Letters.* Amsterdam: North-Holland Publishing Company.

Hopkins, A.G. (1973): *An Economic History of West Africa.* London: Longman.

Horta, José da Silva (1991a): "A Imagem do Africano pelos Portugueses antes dos Contactos", in Ferronha, António Luis (ed.), 41–72.

(1991b): "Primeiros Olhares Sobre o Africano do Sara Occidental à Serra Leoa (meados do século XV – inícios do século XVI)", in Ferronha, António Luis (ed.), 73–126.

(1996): "La Perception du Mande et l'Identité Mandingue dans les Textes Européens, 1453–1508", *History in Africa* (23), 75–86.

(2000): "Evidence for a Luso-African Identity in "Portuguese" Accounts on "Guinea of Cape Verde" (Sixteenth-Seventeenth Centuries)", *History in Africa* (27), 99–130.

Horta, José da Silva and Dias, Eduardo Costa (2005): "História da Guiné-Bissau", in *Diccionário Temático da Lusofonia*, 472–83. Lisbon: Texto Editores.

Huerga, Álvaro (1978–1988): *Historia de Los Alumbrados (1570–1630).* Madrid: Fundación Universitaria Española; 4 vols.

Hulme, Peter (1995): "Old Worlds for New", *Bulletin of Latin American Research* (14/1), 63–70.

Hunwick, J.O. (1971): "Songhay, Bornu and Hausaland in the Sixteenth Century", in J.F.A. Ajayi, J.F.A. and Crowder, Michael (eds.), Vol. 1, 202–39.

Hunwick, John and Lawler, Nancy (eds.) (1996): *The Cloth of Many-Colored Silks: Papers on History and Society Ghanaian and Islamic in Honor of Ivor Wilks*. Evanston: Northwestern University Press.

Iffono, Aly Gilbert (2000): "Migrations Mandingues Dans la Zone Littorale Guinéenne du XVème au XIXème Siècle", in Gaillard, Gérard (ed.), 77–80.

Iliffe, John (1995): *Africans: The History of a Continent*. Cambridge and New York: Cambridge University Press.

Inikori, J.E. (ed.) (1982a): *Forced Migration: The Impact of the Export Slave Trade on African Societies*. London: Hutchinson.

(1982b): "Introduction", in Inikori, J.E. (ed.).

(2002): *Africans and the Industrial Revolution in England: A Study in International Trade and Economic Development*. Cambridge and New York: Cambridge University Press.

Inikori, Joseph E. And Engerman, Stanley L. (eds.) (1992): *The Atlantic Slave Trade: Effects on Economies, Societies, and Peoples in Africa, the Americas and Europe*. Durham and London: Duke University Press.

Isaac, Benjamin (2004): *The Invention of Racism in Classical Antiquity*. Princeton: Princeton University Press.

Israel, Jonathan I. (1998; 3rd edition): *European Jewry in the Age of Mercantilism, 1550–1750*. London and Portland, Oregon: The Littman Library of Jewish Civilisation.

(2002): *Diasporas Within a Diaspora: Jews, Crypto-Jews and the World Maritime Empires (1540–1740)*. Leiden and Boston: Brill.

Jacobs, Bart (2008): *Los Fundamentos Afro Portugueses del Papiamento: Una Comparación Lingüística entre el Papiamento y el Criollo Caboverdiano de Santiago*. Amsterdam: University of Amsterdam – unpublished MA dissertation.

(2009): "The Upper Guinea Origins of Papiamentu: Linguistic and Historical Evidence", *Diachronica* (26/3), 319–79.

(2010): "Upper Guinea Creole: Evidence in Favor of a Santiago Birth", *Journal of Pidgin and Creole Languages (26/3)*.

Jeannin, Pierre (1972): *Merchants of the Sixteenth Century*. New York: Harper & Row; tr. Fittingoff, Paul.

Johnson, John William (1999): "The Dichotomy of Power and Authority in Mande Society and in the Epic of Sunjata", in Austen, Ralph A. (ed.), 9–23.

Johnson, Walter (2003): "On Agency", *Journal of Social History* (37/1), 113–24.

Jones, Adam (1981): "Who were the Vai?", *Journal of African History* (22/2), 159–78.

Jong, Ferdinand de (2008): *Masquerades of Modernity: Power and Secrecy in Casamance, Senegal*. Bloomington: Indiana University Press.

Jordan, Winthrop D. (1974): *The White Man's Burden: The Historical Origins of Racism in the United States*. New York and Oxford: Oxford University Press.

Kagan, Richard L. and Morgan, Philip D. (eds.) (2009): *Atlantic Diasporas: Jews, Conversos and Crypto-Jews in the Age of Mercantilism, 1500–1800*. Baltimore: The Johns Hopkins University Press.

Kalra, Virinder S., Kaur, Raminder and Hutyak, John (2005): *Diaspora and Hybridity*. London: Sage Publications.

Kaplan, Yosef (ed.) (1985): *Jews and Conversos: Studies in Society and the Inquisition.* Jerusalem: The Magnes Press.

Kea, Ray A. (1982): *Settlements, Trade, and Polities in the Seventeenth-Century Gold Coast.* Baltimore and London: The Johns Hopkins University Press.

Kilson, Martin L. and Rotberg, Robert I. (eds.) (1976): *The African Diaspora: Interpretetive Essays.* Cambridge, Mass. and London: Harvard University Press.

Klein, Herbert S. (1986): *African Slavery in Latin America and the Caribbean.* New York and Oxford: Oxford University Press.

   (1997): "African Women in the Atlantic Slave Trade", in Klein, Martin A. and Robertson, Claire C. (eds.), 29–38.

Klein, Martin A. (1990): The Impact of the Atlantic Slave Trade on the Societies of the Western Sudan", *Social Science History* (14/2), 231–53.

   (2001): "The Slave Trade and Decentralized Societies", *Journal of African History (42/1),* 49–65.

Klein, Martin A. and Lovejoy, Paul E. (1979): "Slavery in West Africa", in Gemery, Henry A. and Hogendorn, Jan S. (eds.), 181–212.

Klein, Martin A. and Robertson, Claire C. (eds.) (1997): *Women and Slavery in Africa.* Portsmouth, NH: Heinemann; 2nd edition.

Knörr, Jacqueline (2010): "Creolization and Nation-Building in Indonesia", in Cohen, Robin and Toninato, Paola (eds.), 353–63.

Kriger, Colleen (1999): *Pride of Men: Ironworking in 19th-Century West Central Africa.* Portsmouth, NH: Heinemann.

Ladham, J (2003): *The Formation of the Portuguese Plantation Creoles.* London: University of Westminster (unpublished PhD thesis).

Lahon, Didier (2005): "Black African Slaves and Freedmen in Portugal During the Renaissance: Creating a New Problem of Reality", in Earle, T.F. and Lowe, K.J.P. (eds.), 261–79.

Lang, Jürgen (2006): "L'Influence des Wolof et du Wolof sur la Formation du Créole Santiagais", in Holm, John et al. (eds.), 53–61.

Law, Robin (1977): *The Oyo Empire, c. 1600–c.1836: A West African Imperialism in the Era of the Trans-Atlantic Slave Trade.* Oxford: Clarendon Press.

   (1980): *The Horse in West African History: The Role of the Horse in the Societies of Pre-Colonial West Africa.* Oxford: Clarendon Press.

   (1991): *The Slave Coast of West Africa 1550–1750: The Impact of the Atlantic Slave Trade on an African Society.* Oxford: Clarendon Press.

   (2004): *Ouidah: The Social History of a West African Slaving "Port", 1727–1892.* Athens: Ohio University Press.

Law, Robin and Mann, Kristin (1999): "West Africa in the Atlantic Community: The Case of the Slave Coast", *William and Mary Quarterly, 3rd Series,* (56/2), 307–34.

Lawrance, Jeremy (2005): "Black Africans in Renaissance Spanish Literature", in Earle, T.F. and Lowe, Kate (eds.), 70–93.

Lawrence, Vera and Nettleford, Rex (eds.) (1995): *Race, Discourse, and the Origin of the Americas: A New World View.* Washington: Smithsonian Institution Press.

Lefkowitz, Mary (2008): *History Lesson: A Race Odyssey*. New Haven and London: Yale University Press.

Lereno, Álvaro (1942): *Subsídios Para a História da Moeda em Cabo Verde (1460–1940)*. Lisbon: Agência Geral das Colónias.

Lespinay, Charles de (1987): "La Disparition de la Langue Baynunk", in Boulègue, Jean (ed.), 23–9.

   (2000): "Un Lexique Bagnon-Floupe de la Fin du XVIIe Siècle: Apport à l'Histoire du Peuplement de la Casamance", in Gaillard, Gérard (ed.), 193–213.

Levtzion, Nehemia (1980; first published 1969): *Ancient Ghana and Mali*. New York: Africana Publishing Company.

   (2000): "Islam in the Bilad al-Sudan to 1800", in Levtzion, Nehemia and Powels, Randall L. (eds.), 63–92.

Levtzion, Nehemia and Powells, Randall L. (eds.) (2000): *The History of Islam in Africa*. Athens: Ohio University Press.

Lewin, Boleslao (1960): *Los Judíos Bajo la Inquisición en Hispanoamérica*. Buenos Aires: Editorial Dedalo.

Liebman, Seymour B. (1970): *The Jews in New Spain: Faith, Flame and Inquisition*. Coral Gables: University of Miami Press.

Linares, Olga (1987): "Deferring to Trade in Slaves: The Jola of Casamance, Senegal in Historical Perspective", *History in Africa* (14), 113–39.

   (1992): *Power, Prayer and Production: The Jola of Casamance, Senegal*. Cambridge and New York: Cambridge University Press.

Lipiner, Elias (1969): *Os Judaizantes nas Capitanias da Cima (Estudos Sôbre os Cristãos Novos do Brasil nos Séculos XVI e XVII)*. São Paulo: Editôra Brasiliense.

   (1977): *Santa Inquisição: Terror e Linguagem*. Rio de Janeiro: Editora Documentário.

Lobo, António de Sousa Silva Costa (1979; first published 1903): *História da Sociedade en Portugal no Século XV e Outros Estudos Históricos*. Lisbon: Cooperativa Editora.

Lockhart, James (1968): *Spanish Peru, 1532–1560: A Colonial Society*. Madison: University of Wisconsin Press.

Loeb, I (1887): "Le Nombre des Juifs de Castille et d'Espagne", *Revue des Études Juives*, (14), 161–183.

Lopes, Carlos (ed.) (1993): *Mansas, Escravos, Grumetes e Gentio: Cacheu na Encruzilhada de Civilizações*. Bissau: Instituto Nacional de Estudos e Pesquisa.

   (1999): *Kaabunké: Espaço, Poder, Território e Poder na Guiné-Bissau, Gâmbia e Casamance Pre-Coloniais*. Lisbon: Comissão Nacional para as Comemorações dos Descobrimentos Portugueses.

Lopes, Edmundo Correia (1944): *Escravatura: Subsídios para a sua Historia*. Lisbon: Agência Geral do Ultramar.

López Sarrelangue, Delfina Esmeralda (1965): *La Nobleza Indígena de Pátzcuaro en la Época Virreinal*. Mexico City: Universidad Nacional Autónoma de México.

Lovejoy, Paul E. (1973): "The Kambarin Beriberi: The Formation of a Specialized Group of Hausa Kola Traders in the Nineteenth Century", *Journal of African History* (14/4), 633–51.

(1978): "The Role of the Wangara in the Economic Transformation of the Central Sudan in the Fifteenth and Sixteenth Centuries", *Journal of African History* (19/2), 173–93.

(1996): "The Volume of the Atlantic Trade: A Synthesis", in Manning, Patrick (ed.), 37–64.

(2000; first published 1983): *Transformations in Slavery: A History of Slavery in Africa*. Cambridge and New York: Cambridge University Press.

Lowe, Kate (2005): "The Stereotyping of Black Africans in Renaissance Europe", in Earle, T.F. and Lowe, K. J. P. (eds.), 17–47.

Lydon, Ghislaine (2009): *On Trans-Saharan Trails: Islamic Law, Trade Networks and Cross-Cultural Exchange in Nineteenth-Century West Africa*. Cambridge and New York: Cambridge University Press.

MacGaffey, Wyatt (1994): "Dialogues of the Deaf: Europeans in the Atlantic Coast of Africa", in Schwartz, Stuart B. (ed.), 249–67.

Magalhães, Joaquim Romero (1998a): "As Incursões ao Espaço Africano", in Bethencourt, Francisco and Chaudhuri, Kirti (eds.), 65–82.

(1998b): "O Reconhecimento do Brasil", in Bethencourt, Francisco and Chaudhuri, Kirti (eds.), 192–216.

Mané, Mamadou (1978): "Contribution à l'Histoire du Kaabu, des Origines au XIXe Siècle", *Bulletin de l' I.F.A.N.* (40/Series B/1), 87–159.

Mann, Charles C. (2005): *Ancient Americans: Rewriting the History of the New World*. London: Granta.

Manning, Patrick (1990): *Slavery and African Life: Occidental, Oriental and African Slave Trades*. Cambridge and New York: Cambridge University Press

(ed.) (1996): *Slave Trades, 1500–1800: Globalization of Forced Labour*. Aldershot: Variorum.

Mark, Peter (1985): *A Cultural, Economic, and Religious History of the Basse Casamance Since 1500*. Stuttgart: Franz Steiner Verlag Wiesbaden GMBH.

(2002): *Portuguese Style and Luso-African Identity: Precolonial Senegambia, Sixteenth-Nineteenth Centuries*. Bloomington and Indianapolis: Indiana University Press.

(2007): "Towards a Reassessment of the Dating and the Geographical Origins of the Luso-African Ivories, Fifteenth to Seventeenth Centuries", *History in Africa* (34), 189–211.

Mark, Peter and Horta, José da Silva (2004): "Two Early Sephardic Communities on Senegal's Petite Côte", *History in Africa* 31 (2004), 231–56.

(2005): "Judeus e Muçulmanos na Petite Côte Senegalesa do Início do Século XVII: Iconoclástia anti-católica, aproximação religiosa, parceria comercial", *Cadernos de Estudos Sefarditas* (5), 29–51.

(2009): "Catholics, Jews, and Muslims in Early Seventeenth-Century Guiné", in Kagan, Richard L. and Morgan, Philip D. (eds.), 170–94.

(2011): *The Forgotten Diaspora: Jewish Communities in West Africa and the Making of the Atlantic World*. Cambridge and New York: Cambridge University Press.

Marques, A.H. de Oliveira (1972): *History of Portugal*. New York: Columbia University Press ; 2 vols.

Martin, Phyllis (1972): *The External Trade of the Loango Coast, 1576–1870: The Effects of Changing Commecial Relations on the Vili Kingdom of Loango.* Oxford: Clarendon Press.

(1982): "The Trade of Loango in the Seventeenth and Eighteenth Centuries", in Inikori, J.E. (ed.), 202–20.

Martinus, Frank (1999): "The Origins of the Adjectival Participle in Papiamentu", in Zimmerman, Klaus (ed.), 231–50.

Mathieu, Nicolás Castillo del (1982): *Esclavos Negros en Cartagena y sus Aportes Léxicos.* Bogotá: Imprenta Patriótica del Instituto Caro y Cuervo.

Mauny, Raymond (1970): *Les Siècles Obscurs de l'Afrique Noire: Histoire et Archéologie.* Paris: Fayard.

Maya Restrepo, Luz Adriana (2005): *Brujería y Recontrucción de Identitidades Entre Africanos y Sus Descendientes en la Nueva Granada, Siglo XVII.* Bogotá: Ministerio de Cultura.

McIntosh, Roderick James (1998): *The Peoples of the Middle Niger: The Island of Gold.* Oxford and Malden, Mass.: Blackwell.

McLellan, David (ed.) (1971): *Marx's Grundrisse.* London: Macmillan & Co.

McNaughton, P.R. (1988): *The Mande Blacksmiths.* Bloomington: Indiana University Press.

Mea, Elvira Cunha de Azevedo (1997): *A Inquisição de Coimbra no Século XVI: A Instituição, Os Homens e a Sociedade.* Porto: Fundação Eng. António de Almeida.

Medeiros, François de (1985): *L'Occident et l'Afrique (XIIIe – XVe Siècle): Images et Répresentations.* Paris: Karthala.

Meillassoux, Claude (ed.) (1971): *The Development of Indigenous Trade and Markets in West Africa.* London: Oxford University Press.

(1991): *The Anthropology of Slavery.* Chicago: University of Chicago Press; tr. Dasnois, Alide.

Mellafe, Rolando (1964; 2nd edition): *La Introducción de la Esclavitud Negra en Chile: Tráfico y Rutas.* Santiago: Editorial Universitaria.

(1975): *Negro Slavery in Latin America.* Berkeley: University of California Press; tr. Judge, J.W.S.

Mello, José Antônio Gonsalves de (1996; 2nd edition): *Gente da Nação: Cristãos-Novos e Judeus em Pernambuco, 1542–1654.* Recife: Fundação Joaquim Nabuco, Editora Massangana.

Mendes, António de Almeida (2004): "Le Rôle de l'Inquisition en Guinée: Vicissitudes des Présences Juives Sur la Petite Côte (XVe-XVIIe Siècles)", *Revista Lusófona de Ciência das Religiões, Ano III,*(5/6), 137–55.

(2007): *Esclavages et Traites Ibériques Entre Méditerranée et Atlantique (XVe – XVIIe Siècles): Une Histoire Globale.* Paris: École des Hautes Études en Sciences Sociales (unpublished PhD thesis).

(2008): "The Foundations of the System: A Reassessment on the Slave Trade to the Americas in the Sixteenth and Seventeenth Centuries", in Eltis, D. and Richardson D. (eds.), 63–94.

Mesa Bernal, Daniel (1996): *De los Judíos en la Historia de Colombia.* Santa Fe de Bogotá: Planeta Colombiana Editorial.

Metcalf, Alida C. (2005): *Go-Betweens and the Colonization of Brazil, 1500–1600*. Austin: University of Texas Press.

Millar, Carvacho, René (1997): *Inquisición y Sociedad en el Virreinato Peruano: Estudios Sobre el Tribunal de la Inquisición en Lima*. Santiago de Chile: Ediciones Universidad Católica de Chile.

Millares Torres, Agustín (1982; first published 1874): *Historia de la Inquisición en las Islas Canárias*. Santa Cruz de Tenerife: Editorial Benchoma.

Miller, Joseph C. (1973): "Requiem for the 'Jaga'", *Cahiers d'Études Africaines* (13/1), 121–49.

(1976a): *Kings and Kinsmen: Early Mbundu States in Angola*. Oxford: Oxford University Press.

(1976b): "The Slave Trade in Congo and Angola", in Kilson, Martin L. and Rotberg, Robert I. (eds.), 75–113.

(1982): "The Significance of Drought, Disease and Famine in the Agriculturally Marginal Zones of West-Central Africa", *Journal of African History* (23/1), 17–61.

(1988): *Way of Death: Merchant Capitalism and the Angolan Slave Trade, 1730–1830*. Madison: University of Wisconsin Press.

Moore, R.I. (1987): *The Formation of a Persecuting Society: Power and Deviance in Western Europe, 950–1250*. Oxford and Cambridge, Mass.: Blackwell.

Morgan, Edmund S. (1975): *American Slavery, American Freedom: The Ordeal of Colonial Virginia*. New York: W.W. Norton and Company.

Morgan, Philip D. (1998): *Slave Counterpoint: Black Culture in the Eighteenth Century Chesapeake and Lowcountry*. Chapel Hill and London: University of North Carolina Press.

Mota, A. Teixeira da (1954): *Guiné Portuguesa*. Lisbon: Agência Geral do Ultramar, Divisão de Publicações e Biblioteca; 2 vols.

(1969): *Un Document Nouveau Pour l'Historie des Peuls au Sénégal Pendant les XVème et XVIème Siècles*. Lisbon: Junta de Investigações do Ultramar.

(1970): *Fulas e Beafadas no Rio Grande do Século XV: Achegas Para a Etnohistória da África Ocidental*. Lisbon: Junta de Investigações do Ultramar.

(1978): *Some Aspects of Portuguese Colonization and Sea Trade in West Africa in the 15th and 16th Centuries*. Bloomington: Indiana University.

(1981): "Les Relations de l'Ancien Cabou Avec Quelques Etats et Peuples Voisins", *Éthiopiques* (28), 141–67.

Moya Pons, Frank (1973): *La Española en el Siglo XVI (1493–1520): Trabajo, Sociedad e Política en la Economía del Oro*. Santiago, República Dominicana: Universidad Católica Madre y Maestra.

(1998): *The Dominican Republic: A National History*. Princeton: Marcus Wiener Publishers.

Mudimbe, V.Y. (1988): *The Invention of Africa: Gnosis, Philosophy and the Order of Knowledge*. Bloomington and Indianapolis: Indiana University Press.

Nafafé, José Lingna (2007): *Colonial Encounters: Issues of Culture, Hybridity and Creolisation: Portuguese Mercantile Settlers in West Africa*. Frankfurt-am-Main: Peter Lang.

Naro, Nancy Priscilla, Sansi-Roca, Roger and Treece, David H. (eds.) (2007a): *Cultures of the Lusophone Black Atlantic*. Basingstoke: Palgrave Macmillan.

(2007b): "Introduction", in Naro, Nancy Priscilla, Sansi-Roca, Roger and Treece, David H. (eds.), 1–13.

Navarrete, María Cristina (2003): *Cimarrones y Palenques en el Siglo XVII*. Cali: Facultad de Humanidades.

(2005): *Génesis y Desarrollo de la Esclavitud en Colombia, Siglos XVI-XVII*. Cali: Programa Editorial Universidad del Valle.

Netanyahu, B. (1966): *The Marranos of Spain: from the late XIVth to the early XVIth century, according to contemporary Hebrew sources*. New York: American Academy of Jewish Research.

(1995): *The Origins of the Inquisition in Fifteenth Century Spain*. New York: Random House.

Newitt, Malyn (1992): "Mixed Race Groups in the Early History of Portuguese Expansion", in Earle, T.F. and Parkinson, Stephen (eds.), 35–52.

(2005): *A History of Portuguese Overseas Expansion, 1400–1668*. Abingdon: Routledge.

Newson, Linda A. (2006): "The Demographic Impact of Colonization", in Bulmer-Thomas, Victor (ed.), 143–84.

Newson, Linda A. and Minchin, Suzie (2007): *From Capture to Sale: The Portuguese Slave Trade to Spanish South America in the Early Seventeenth Century*. Leiden and Boston: Brill.

Niane, Djibril Tamsir (1989): *Histoire des Mandingues de l'Ouest: Le Royaume du Gabou*. Paris: Éditions Karthala et Arsan.

Nixon, Sam (2009): "Excavating Essouk-Tadmakka (Mali): New Archaeological Investigations of Early Islamic Trans-Saharan Trade", *Azania: Archaeological Research in Africa* (44/2), 217–55.

Novinsky, Anita (1972): *Cristãos Novos na Bahia*. São Paulo: Editôra Perspectiva.

Novinsky, Anita and Carneiro, Maria Luiza Tucci (eds.) (1992): *Inquisição: Ensaios Sobre Mentalidade, Heresias e Arte*. São Paulo: Editora Expressão e Cultura.

O'Phelan Godoy, Scarlett and Salazar-Soler, Carmen (eds.) (2005): *Passeurs, Mediadores Culturales y Agentes de la Primera Globalización en el Mundo Ibérico, Siglos XVI-XIX*. Lima: Pontificia Universidad Católica del Perú.

O'Toole, Rachel (2007): "From the Rivers of Guinea to the Valleys of Peru: Becoming a Bran Diaspora Within Spanish Slavery", *Social Text* 92, 25/3, 19–36.

Oldham, Henry Yule (n/d): *The Discovery of the Cape Verde Islands*. n/p.

Olival, Fernanda (2004): "Rigor e Interesses: Os Estatutos de Limpeza de Sangue em Portugal", *Cadernos de Estudos Sefarditas*, (4), 151–82.

Osório, João de Castro (1937): "Viagens de Penetração e de Exploração no Continente Africano", in Baião, António et al. (eds.), Vol. II, 221–54.

Palacios Preciado, Jorge (1975): *Cartagena de Indias, Gran Factoría de Mano de Obra de Esclavos*. Tunja: Ediciones Pato Marino.

Palmer, Colin A. (1976): *Slaves of the White God: Blacks in Mexico, 1570–1650*. Cambridge, Mass. and London: Harvard University Press.

Parent Jr., Anthony S. (2003): *Foul Means: The Formation of a Slave Society in Virginia, 1660–1740*. Chapel Hill and London: University of North Carolina Press.

Parreira, Adriano (1990): *Economia e Sociedade em Angola na Época da Rainha Jinga (Século XVII)*. Lisbon: Editorial Estampa.

Pavy, David (1967): "The Provenance of Colombian Negroes", *Journal of Negro History* (52/1), 35–58.

Pearsall, Sarah M. S. (2002): "Gender", in Armitage, David and Braddick, Michael (eds.), 113–32.

Penny, R. J. (1990): "The Language of Christopher Columbus", in Ife, B. W. (ed.), xxvii–xl.

Perceval, José María (1997): *Todos Son Uno: Arquetipos, Xenofobia y Racismo. La Imagen del Morisco en la Monarquía Española Durante los Siglos XVI y XVII*. Almería: Instituto de Estudios Almerienses.

Pereda, Francisco (2007): *Las Imágenes de la Discordia: Política y Poética de la Imagen Sagrada en la España del Cuatrocientos*. Madrid: Marcial Pons.

Pereira, Daniel (1986): *Estudos da História de Cabo Verde*. Praia: Instituto Caboverdiano do Livro.

(1985): *Marcos Cronológicos da Cidade Velha*. Lisbon: Instituto Caboverdiano do Livro.

Pereira, Isaías Rosa (1993): *A Inquisição em Portugal: Séculos XVI-XVII – Período Filipino*. Lisbon: Vega Gabinete de Edições.

Peres, Damião (1937): "Génese da Expansão Portuguesa: Antecedentes Históricos. Condições que a Facilitarem. Factores Políticos, Militares, Económicos e Espirituais que a Estimularem", in Baião António et al. (eds.), Vol. I, 121–27.

Person, Yves (1971): "Ethnic Movements and Acculturation in Upper Guinea Since the Fifteenth Century", *International Journal of African Historical Studies* (4/3), 669–89.

(1981): "Problèmes de l'Histoire du Kaabu", *Éthiopiques* (28), 60–72.

Pike, Ruth (1972): *Aristocrats and Traders: Sevillian Society in the Sixteenth Century*. Ithaca and London: Cornell University Press.

Pinto Bull, Benjamin (1989): *O Crioulo da Guiné-Bissau: Filosofia e Sabedoria*. Bissau: Instituto Nacional de Estudos e Pesquisa.

Poliakov, Léon (2003a; first published 1973): *The History of Anti-Semitism, Volume I: From the Time of Christ to the Court Jews*. Philadelphia: University of Pennsylvania Press; tr. Howard, Richard.

(2003b; first published 1973): *The History of Anti-Semitism, Volume II: From Mohammed to the Marranos*. Philadelphia: University of Pennsylvania Press; tr. Gerardi, Natalie.

Porras Tronconis, G. (1954): *Cartagena Hispánica, 1533 a 1810*. Santafé de Bogotá: Editorial Cosmos.

Postma, Johannes Menne (1990): *The Dutch in the Atlantic Slave Trade*. Cambridge and New York: Cambridge University Press.

Pratten, David (2007): *The Man-Leopard Murders: History and Society in Colonial Nigeria*. Edinburgh and Indianapolis: Edinburgh University Press/ Indiana University Press.

Price, Richard and Mintz, Sidney W. (1992): *The Birth of African-American Culture: An Anthropological Perspective*, 2nd edition. Boston: Beacon Press.

Prussin, Labelle (2006): "Judaic Threads in West African Tapestry: No More Forever?", *The Art Bulletin* (88/2), 328–53.

Quenum, Alphonse (1993): *Les Églises Chrétiennes et la Traite Atlantique du XVe au XIXe Siècle*. Paris: Éditions Karthala.

Quinn, Charlotte A. (1972): *Mandingo Kingdoms of the Senegambia: Traditionalism, Islam and European Expansion*. London: Longman.

Quint, Nicolas (2000): *Le Cap-Verdien: Origines et Devenir d'Une Langue Métisse*. Paris: Éditions L'Harmattan.

Randles, W.G.L. (1968): *L'Ancien Royaume du Congo: Des Origines à la Fin du XIXe Siècle*. Paris and The Hague: Mouton & Co.

Ratekin, Mervyn (1954): "The Early Sugar Industry in Española", *Hispanic American Historical Review* (34/1), 1–19.

Reese, Scott S. (ed.) (2004): *The Transmission of Learning in Islamic Africa*. Boston and Leiden and Boston: Brill.

Rego, A. da Silva (1966): "Reflexões Sobre o Primeiro Século da História Cabo-Verdiana (1460–1580)", in Brito, Raquel Soeiro de et al. (eds.), 69–83.

Remedios, J. Mendes dos (1895–1928): *Os Judeus em Portugal*. Coimbra: F. França Amado-Editor; 2 vols.

Renault, François, and Daget, Serge (1985): *Les Traites Négrières en Afrique*. Paris: Éditions Karthala.

Révah, I.S. (1971): "Les Marranes Portugais et l'Inquisition au XVIe Siècle", in Barnett, R.D. (ed.), Vol. I, 479–526.

Ribeiro, Orlando (1954): *A Ilha do Fogo e as Suas Erupções*. Lisbon: Junta de Investigações do Ultramar.

  (1955): *Aspectos e Problemas da Expansão Portuguesa*. Lisbon: Fundação da Casa de Bragança.

Richter, Konstantin Alexander (2009): *The Historic Religious Buildings of Ribeira Grande: Implementation of Christian Models in the Early Colonies, 15th Till 17th Century, On the Example of Cape Verde Islands*. Funchal: University of Madeira; 2 vols. (unpublished PhD thesis).

Riley, Carlos (1998): "Ilhas Atlânticas e Costa Africana", in Bethencourt, Francisco and Chaudhuri, Kirti (eds.), 137–162.

Roche, Christian (1976): *Histoire de la Casamance: Conquête et Résistance: 1850–1920*. Paris: Éditions Karthala.

Rodney, Walter (1965): "Portuguese Attempts at Monopoly on the Upper Guinea Coast, 1580–1650", *Journal of African History* (6/3), 307–22.

  (1966): "African Slavery and Other Forms of Social Oppression on the Upper Guinea Coast in the Context of the Atlantic Slave Trade", *Journal of African History* (7/3), 431–43.

  (1970): *History of the Upper Guinea Coast, 1545–1800*. Oxford: Clarendon Press.

Rodrigues, José Honorio (1964): *Brasil e África: Outro Horizonte*. Rio de Janeiro: Editôra Civilização Brasileira, S.A.; 2 vols.

Roper, L.H. and Van Ruymbeke, B. (eds.) (2007): *Constructing Early Modern Empires: Proprietary Ventures in the Atlantic World, 1500–1750*. Leiden and Boston: Koninklijke Brill.

Roth, Cecil (1959; first published 1932): *A History of the Marranos*. New York: Meridian Books, Inc.

Roth, Norman (2002; 2nd edition): *Conversos, Inquisition, and the Expulsion of the Jews From Spain*. Madison: University of Wisconsin Press.

Rougé, Jean-Louis (1999): "Apontamentos Sobre o Léxico de Origem Africana dos Crioulos da Guiné e Cabo Verde (Santiago)", in Zimmerman, Klaus (ed.), 49–66.

Rumeu de Armas, Antonio (1956): *España en el África Atlántica*. Madrid: Instituto de Estudios Africanos, Consejo Superior de Investigaciones Científicas.

Russell, P.E. (1995): *Portugal, Spain and the African Atlantic, 1343–1490: Chivalry and Crusade from John of Gaunt to Henry the Navigator*. Aldershot: Variorum.

Russell-Wood, A.J.R. (1978): "Iberian Expansion and the Issue of Black Slavery: Changing Portuguese Attitudes, 1440–1770", *American Historical Review* (83/1), 16–42.

    (1995): "Before Columbus: Portugal's African Prelude to the Middle Passage and Contribution to Discourse on Race and Slavery", in Lawrence, Vera and Nettleford, Rex (eds.), 134–68.

    (1998a): "A Sociedade Portuguesa no Ultramar", in Bethencourt, Francisco and Chaudhuri, Kirti (eds.), 266–79.

    (1998b): "Fluxos de Emigração", in Bethencourt, Francisco and Chaudhuri, Kirti (eds.), 224–37.

    (1998c): "Fronteiras de Integração", in Bethencourt, Francisco and Chaudhuri, Kirti (eds.), 238–55.

    (1998d): "Os Portugueses Fora do Império", in Bethencourt, Francisco and Chaudhuri, Kirti (eds.), 256–65.

    (1998e): *The Portuguese Empire, 1415–1808: A World on the Move*. Baltimore: The Johns Hopkins University Press.

Ryder, A.F.C. (1969): *Benin and the Europeans, 1485–1897*. London: Longman.

Sackur, Karen Amanda (1999): *The Development of Creole Society and Culture in Saint-Louis and Gorée, 1719–1817*. London: School of Oriental and African Studies (unpublished PhD thesis).

Saco, José Antonio (1879): *Historia de la Esclavitud de la Raza Africana en el Nuevo Mundo y en Especial en los Países Américo-Hispanos*. Barcelona: Imprenta de Jaime Jepús; 2 vols.

Salvador, José Gonçalves (1969): *Cristãos-Novos, Jesuítas e Inquisição: Aspectos de sua Actuação nas Capitanias do Sul, 1530–1680*. São Paulo: Editôra da Universidade de São Paulo.

    (1976): *Os Cristãos-Novos: Povoamento e Conquista do Solo Brasileiro (1530–1680)*. São Paulo: Livraria Pioneira Editora.

    (1978): *Os Cristãos-Novos e o Comércio no Atlântico Meridional (com enfoque nas Capitanias do Sul 1530–1680)*. São Paulo: Livraria Pioneira Editora.

    (1981): *Os Magnatas do Tráfico Negreiro (Séculos XVI e XVII)*. São Paulo: Livraria Pioneira Editora.

Samb, Amir (1981): "L'Islam et le Ngabou", *Éthiopiques* (28), 116–23.

Samuel, Edgar (2004): *At the End of the Earth: Essays on the History of the Jews in England and Portugal*. London: The Jewish Historical Society of England.

Sanches, Francisco (1998): *"That Nothing Is Known" (Quod Nihil Scitur)*. Cambridge and New York: Cambridge University Press; tr. Thompson, Douglas F.S.

Santos, María Emília Madeira (1978): *Viagens de Exploração Terrestre dos Portugueses em África*. Lisbon: Centro de Estudos de Cartografia Antiga.

(1993): "Lançados na Costa da Guiné: Aventureiros e Comerciantes", in Lopes, Carlos (ed.), 65–78.

Santos, María Emília Madeira (ed.) (1995): *Historia Geral de Cabo Verde (1560–1650), Vol. II*. Lisbon: Instituto de Investigação Científica Tropical.

(2006): *O Domínio da Distância*. Lisbon: Instituto de Investigação Científica Tropical.

Santos, Maria Emília Madeira and Torrão, Maria Manuel (1989): *Subsídios Para a História Geral de Cabo Verde: A Legitimidade da Utilização de Fontes Escritas Portugueses Através da Análise de um Documento do Início do Século XVI (Cabo Verde Ponto de Intercepção de Dois Circuitos Comericiais)*. Lisbon: Instituto de Investigação Científica Tropical.

Santos, Maria Emília Madeira and Soares, Maria João (1995): "Igreja, Missionação e Sociedade", in Santos, Maria Emília Madeira (ed.), 359–504.

Saraiva, António (1985; first published 1969): *Inquisição e Cristãos-Novos*. Lisbon: Editorial Estampa.

Saunders, A.C. de C.M. (1982a): *A Social History of Black Slaves and Freedmen in Portugal, 1441–1555*. Cambridge and New York: Cambridge University Press.

(1982b): "The Depiction of Trade as War as a Reflection of Portuguese Ideology and Diplomatic Strategy in West Africa, 1441–1556", *Canadian Journal of History* (17/2), 219–34.

Scantamburlo, Luigi (1991): *Etnologia dos Bijagós da Ilha de Bubaque*. Lisbon: Instituto de Investigação Científica Tropical: Bissau – Instituto Nacional de Estudos e Pesquisa.

Scelle, Georges (1906): *Histoire Politique de la Traite Négrière aux Indes de Castille: Contrats et Traités d'Assiento*. Paris: Librairie de la Société du Recueil J.-B. Sirey & du Journal du Palais; 2 vols.

Schorsch, Jonathan (2004): *Jews and Blacks in the Early Modern World*. Cambridge and New York: Cambridge University Press.

(2005): "Blacks, Jews and the Racial Imagination in the Writings of the Sephardim in the Long Seventeenth Century", *Jewish History*, (19/1),109–35.

(2008): *Swimming the Christian Atlantic: Judeoconversos, Afroiberians and Amerindians in the Seventeenth Century*. Leiden and Boston: Brill.

Schwartz, Stuart B. (1985): *Sugar Plantations in the Formation of Brazilian Society: Bahía, 1550–1835*. Cambridge and New York: Cambridge University Press.

Schwartz, Stuart B.(1987): "The Formation of a Colonial Identity in Brazil", in Canny, Nicholas and Pagden, Anthony (eds.), 15–50.

Schwartz, Stuart B. (ed.) (1994): *Implicit Understandings: Observing, Reporting, and Reflecting on the Encounters Between Europeans and Other Peoples in the Early Modern Era*. Cambridge and New York: Cambridge University Press.

(2008): *All Can be Saved: Religious Tolerance and Salvation in the Iberian Atlantic World*. New Haven and London: Yale University Press.

Seck, Ibrahima (forthcoming, 2012): "The French in Senegal : Trials and Tribulations of a Laboratory for "Francité" in the French Atlantic World (17th–19th Centuries)", in Green, Toby and Nafafé, José Lingna (eds.) (forthcoming, 2012).

Segerer, Guillaume (2002): *La Langue Bijogo de Bubaque (Guinée-Bissau)*. Louvain and Paris: Peeters.

Seibert, Gerhard (forthcoming, 2012): "Creolization and Creole Communities in the Portuguese Atlantic: São Tomé, Cape Verde and the Rivers of Guinea in comparison", in Green, Toby and Nafafé, José Lingna (eds.) (forthcoming, 2012).

Semedo, José Maria (1998): "Um Arquipélago do Sahel", in Almeida, José Maria (ed.), 27–54.

Shaw, Rosalind (2002): *Memories of the Slave Trade: Ritual and the Historical Imagination in Sierra Leone*. Chicago and London: Chicago University Press.

Sicroff, Albert A. (1985): *Los Estatutos de Limpieza de Sangre: Controversias entre los Siglos XV y XVII*. Madrid: Taurus Ediciones; tr. Armiño, Mauro.

Silva, Filipa Ribeiro da (2002): *A Inquisição na Guiné, nas Ilhas de Cabo Verde e São Tomé e Príncipe (1536–1821): Contributo para o estudo da política do Santo Ofício nos Territórios Africanos*. Lisbon: Universidade Nova de Lisbon; 2 vols.; unpublished MA Diss.

(2004): "A Inquisição na Guiné, nas Ilhas de Cabo Verde e São Tomé e Príncipe", in *Revista Lusofona de Ciência das Religiões, Ano III, 2004, no. 5/6, 157–73* – also published at http://cienciareligioes.ulusofona.pt.

Silva, Maria da Graça Garcia Nolasco da (1970): "Subsídios para o Estudo dos Lançados na Guiné", *Boletim Cultural da Guiné Portuguesa, Vol. XXV, nos. 97–100*.

Simmel, Georg (1990): *The Philosophy of Money*. London and New York: Routledge; tr. Bottomore, Tom and Frisby, David.

Singler, John Victor (1990): "On the Use of Sociohistorical Criteria in the Comparison of Creoles", *Linguistics* (28), 645–59.

(1995): "The Demogaphics of Creole Genesis in the Caribbean: A Comparison of Martinique and Haiti", in Arends, Jacques (ed.), 203–32.

Smith, Michael Peter and Guarnizo, Luis Eduardo (eds.) (1998a): "The Locations of Transnationalism", in Smith, Michael Peter and Guarnizo, Luis Eduardo (eds.), 3–34.

(1998b): *Transnationalism From Below*. New Brunswick and London: Transaction Publishers.

Smith, Norval and Veenstra, Tonjes (eds.) (2001): *Creolization and Contact*. Amsterdam and Philadelphia: John Benjamins Publishing Company.

Soares, Maria João and Torrão, Maria Manuel Ferraz (2007): "The Mande Through and In the Cape Verde Islands (15th-18th Centuries)", *Mande Studies* (9), 135–47.

Soyer, François (2007): *The Persecution of the Jews and Muslims of Portugal: King Manuel I and the End of Religious Tolerance (1496–7)*. Leiden and Boston: Brill.

Studnicki-Gizbert, Daviken (2007): *A Nation Upon the Open Sea: Portugal's Atlantic Diaspora and the Crisis of the Spanish Empire, 1492–1640*. Oxford and New York: Oxford University Press.

Subrahmanyan, Sanjay (1993): *The Portuguese Empire in Asia, 1500–1700*. London and New York: Longman.

(2007): "Holding the World in Balance: The Connected Histories of the Iberian Overseas Empires, 1500–1640", *American Historical Review* (112/5), 1359–85.

Sweet, James H. (1997): "The Iberian Roots of American Racist Thought", *William and Mary Quarterly (54/1)*, 143–66.

(2003): *Recreating Africa: Culture, Kinship, and Religion in the African-Portuguese World, 1441–1770*. Chapel Hill and London: The University of North Carolina Press.

Tardieu, Jean-Pierre (2001): "Origins of Slaves in the Lima Region in Peru (Sixteenth and Seventeenth Centuries)", in Diène, Doudou (ed.), 43–54.

Tavares, Maria José Pimenta Ferro (1982): *Os Judeus em Portugal no Século XV*. Lisbon: Universidade Nova de Lisbon; 2 vols.

(1987): *Judaísmo e Inquisição – Estudos*. Lisbon: Editorial Presença.

Tavim, José Alberto Rodrigues da Silva (1997): *Os Judeus na Expansão Portuguesa em Marrocos Durante o Século XVI: Origens e Actividades duma Comunidade*. Braga: Edições AACDM Distrital de Braga.

Thomas, Hugh (1993): *The Conquest of Mexico*. London: Hutchinson.

(1997): *The Slave Trade: The History of the Atlantic Slave Trade: 1440–1870*. London: Picador.

Thornton, John K. (1995): "Early Portuguese Expansion in West Africa: Its Nature and Consequences", in Winius, George D. (ed.), 121–32.

(1998): *Africa and Africans in the Making of the Atlantic World, 1400–1800*. Cambridge and New York: Cambridge University Press; 2nd revised edition.

(1999): *Warfare in Atlantic Africa*. London: UCL Press.

(2001): "The Origins and Early History of the Kingdom of Kongo, c. 1350–1550", *International Journal of African Historical Studies* (34/1), 89–120.

Tinhorão, José Ramos (1988): *Os Negros em Portugal: Uma Presença Silenciosa*. Lisbon: Editorial Caminho.

Todorov, Tzvetan (1982): *La Conquête de l'Amérique: La Question de l'Autre*. Paris: Éditions du Seuil.

(1989): *Nous et les Autres: La Réflexion Française Sur la Diversité Humaine*. Paris: Éditions du Seuil.

Tolentino Dipp, Hugo (1992; first published 1974): *Raza e Historia en Santo Domingo: Los Orígenes del Prejuicio Racial en América*. Santo Domingo: Fundación Cultural Dominicana.

Toro, Alfonso (1944): *La Familia Carvajal: Estudio Histórico Sobre los Judíos y la Inquisición de la Nueva España en el Siglo XVI, Basado en Documentos Originales y en Su Mayor Parte Inéditos, Que Se Conservan en el Archivo General de la Nación de la Ciudad de México*. Mexico City: Editorial Patria, S.A.; 2 vols.

Torrão, Maria Manuel Ferraz (1991): "Actividade Comercial Externa de Cabo Verde: Organização, Funcionamento, Evolução", in Albuquerque, Luís de and Santos, Maria Emília Madeira (eds.), 237–345.

(1995): "Rotas Comerciais, Agentes Económicos, Meios de Pagamento", in Santos, Maria Emília Madeira (ed.), 19–123.

(2006): "Construção de Redes de Comunicação no Tráfico Negreiro Atlântico", in Santos, Maria Emília Madeira (ed.), 53–7.

(2010): "A Ribeira Grande e o Tráfico Negreiro Quinhentista Para América Espanhola no Século XVI: Rotas, Portos e Quantitativos", Paper presented at the Confernece *Cidade Velha e a Cultura Afro-Mundo, O Futuro do Passado*, Ribeira Grande, Cabo Verde, May 31–June 2, 2010

Trajano Filho, Wilson (2003): "Uma Experiência Singular de Crioulização". Brasilia: Universidade de Brasilia; published at www.unb.br/ics/dan/Serie343empdf.pdf.

Trivellato, Francesca (2009): *The Familiarity of Strangers: The Sephardic Diaspora, Livorno, and Cross-Cultural Trade in the Early Modern Period*. New Haven and London: Yale University Press.

Ullman, Walter (1967; first published 1916): *The Individual and Society in the Middle Ages*. London: Methuen & Co.

Vaughan, Megan (2005): *Creating the Creole Island: Slavery in Eighteenth-Century Mauritius*. Durham and London: Duke University Press.

Veiga, Manuel (2000): *Le Créole du Cap-Vert: Étude Grammaticale Descriptive et Contrastive*. Paris: Éditions Karthala.

Ventura, Maria da Graça Mateus (ed.) (1997): *A União Ibérica e o Mundo Atlântico*. Lisbon: Edições Colibri.

(1999): *Negreiros Portugueses na Rota das Indias de Castela (1541–1555)*. Lisbon: Edições Colibri.

Vertovec, Steven (2009): *Transnationalism*. London and New York: Routledge.

Vieira, Alberto (1992): *Portugal y las Islas del Atlántico*. Madrid: Editorial Mapfre.

Vila Vilar, Enriqueta (1977): *Hispanoamérica y el Comercio de Esclavos*. Seville: Escuela de Estudios Hispano-Americanos.

Vogt, John L. (1973a): "The Lisbon Slave House and African Trade, 1486–1521", *Proceedings of the American Philosophical Society,* (117/1), 1973, 1–16.

(1973b): "The Early São Tomé-Principe Slave Trade with Mina, 1500–1540", *International Journal of African Historical Studies* (6/3), 453–67.

(1979): *Portuguese Rule on the Gold Coast (1469–1682)*. Athens: The University of Georgia Press.

Vollmann, William T. (2005): *Rising Up and Rising Down: Some Thoughts on Violence, Freedom and Urgent Means*. London: Duckworth.

Vries, Jan de (1976) : *The Economy of Europe in an Age of Crisis, 1600–1750*. Cambridge and New York: Cambridge University Press.

Wachtel, Nathan (2001): *La Foi du Souvenir: Labyrinthes Marranes*. Paris: Éditions du Seuil.

Washabaugh, William and Greenfield, Sidney M. (1983): "The Development of Atlantic Creole Languages", in Woolford, Ellen and Washabaugh, William (eds.), 106–19.

West, Robert C. (1972): *La Minería de Aluvión en Colombia Durante el Período Colonial*. Bogotá: Imprenta Nacional; tr. Melo, Jorge Orlando.

Wheat, John David (2009): *The Afro-Portuguese Maritime World and the Foundations of Spanish Caribbean Society, 1570–1640*. Nashville: Vanderbilt University; unpublished PhD thesis.

Wilks, Ivor (1999): "The History of the Sunjata Epic: A Review of the Evidence", in Austen, Ralph A. (ed.), 25–55.

Willis, John (1985): *Slaves and Slavery in Muslim Africa*. London: Frank Cass & co.; 2 vols.

Wilson, Samuel M. (1990): *Hispaniola: Caribbean Chiefdoms in the Age of Columbus*. Tuscaloosa and London: University of Alabama Press.

Winius, George D. (ed.) (1995): *Portugal the Pathfinder: Journeys from the Medieval Toward the Modern World 1300 – ca. 1600*. Madison: Hispanic Seminary of Medieval Studies.

Wiznitzer, Arnold (1960): *Jews in Colonial Brazil*. New York: Columbia University Press.

Wolff, Egon and Freida (1986): *Judaizantes e Judeus no Brasil, 1500–1808: Diccionário Biográfico*. Rio de Janeiro: Cemitério Comunal Israelita.

(1989): *Judeus em Amsterdã: Seu Relacionamento com o Brasil 1600–1620*. Rio de Janeiro: ERCA Editora e Gráfica Ltda.

Woolford, Ellen (1983): "Introduction", in Woolford, Ellen and Washabaugh, William (eds.), 1–10.

Woolford, Ellen and Washabaugh, William (eds.) (1983): *The Social Context of Creolization*. Ann Arbor: Karuma Publishers Inc.

Wright, Donald (1991): "Requiem for the Use of Oral Tradition to Reconstruct the Precolonial History of the Lower Gambia", *History in Africa* 18, 399–408.

Wright, Irene (1916): "The Commencement of the Cane Sugar Industry in America, 1519–1538", *American Historical Review* (21/4), 755–80.

Wyse, Akintola (1989): *The Krio of Sierra Leone: An Interpretative History*. London: C. Hurst & Co.

Young, Robert J. (1990): *White Mythologies: Writing History and the West*. London and New York: Routledge.

(1995): *Colonial Desire: Hybridity in Theory, Culture and Race*. London and New York: Routledge.

Yovel, Yirmiyahu (2009): *The Other Within: The Marrano: Split Identity and Emerging Modernity*. Princeton: Princeton University Press.

Zimmerman, Klaus (ed.) (1999): *Lenguas Criollas de Base Lexical Española y Portuguesa*. Vervuert: Iberoamericana.

Index

Books in this Series